STRUCTURAL CONNECTIONS

Stability and Strength

STABILITY AND STRENGTH

A Series of Books Reviewing Advances in Structural Engineering
Edited by R. Narayanan, The Steel Construction Institute,
Silwood Park, Ascot, Berkshire SL5 7QN, UK

The inspiration for this series comes from the recognition of the significant advances made in our understanding of the behaviour of structures as a result of research during the past decade. These advances have, in turn, set new trends and caused major changes in the design codes in many countries. Even the philosophy of design has seen a major shift from the permissible stress basis to the concepts of limit state.

Much research effort continues to be directed towards a better understanding of the complex behaviour of structures in the post-elastic, post-buckling and ultimate stages. Nevertheless, the ultimate benefit to be derived from the substantially improved knowledge depends on its effective implementation. Much needs to be done to bridge the gap between the results of research and their effective use by practitioners of the art. The purpose of these books is to explain the current theories and to present material which has been (or will be) influential in the generation of design specifications.

Each volume in the series is devoted to a central theme and contains a number of papers of the 'state-of-the-art' type on various topics within the selected theme. The aim is to present articles concerned with current developments along with sufficient introductory material, so that a graduate engineer with some basic analytical background and familiarity with structural stability concepts can follow it without having to undertake any substantial background reading. An effort has been made to limit the treatment to advances of practical significance and avoid lengthy theoretical discussions.

Throughout the series emphasis has been given to the international aspects of structural steel research. In terms of both design codes and safety parameters, the experiences and practices in Europe, North America and Japan are widely referenced. All the authors are well known experts who are internationally recognised for their contributions in the relevant fields.

Titles of published volumes:

(1) Axially Compressed Structures
(2) Plated Structures
(3) Beams and Beam Columns
(4) Shell Structures
(5) Steel Framed Structures
(6) Concrete Framed Structures
(7) Steel–Concrete Composite Structures

STRUCTURAL CONNECTIONS

Stability and Strength

Edited by

R. NARAYANAN

M.Sc.(Eng.), Ph.D., D.I.C., C.Eng., F.I.C.E., F.I.Struct.E., M.A.S.C.E.
Manager (Education and Publications), The Steel Construction Institute, Ascot, United Kingdom

ELSEVIER APPLIED SCIENCE
LONDON and NEW YORK

ELSEVIER SCIENCE PUBLISHERS LTD
Crown House, Linton Road, Barking, Essex IG11 8JU, England

Sole Distributor in the USA and Canada
ELSEVIER SCIENCE PUBLISHING CO., INC.
655 Avenue of the Americas, New York, NY 10010, USA

WITH 24 TABLES AND 269 ILLUSTRATIONS

© 1989 ELSEVIER SCIENCE PUBLISHERS LTD

British Library Cataloguing in Publication Data

Structural connections.
1. Steel structures. Structural connections.
Physical properties and design
I. Narayanan, R.
624.1'821

Library of Congress CIP data applied for

ISBN 1-85166-288-X

Photoset by Interprint Ltd, Malta.
Printed in Great Britain at the University Press, Cambridge.

PREFACE

It gives me great pleasure to write a short preface to the book on Structural Connections, the eighth in the planned series of volumes on *Stability and Strength of Structures*.

Much research and development work have been carried out in recent years on the behaviour of individual structural components, as well as on connections. However, in the analysis and design of complete structures, the joints between the components are generally assumed to follow idealized patterns in order to overcome the computational difficulties posed by the complexities of the problem. Clearly, the actual behaviour of the structure is as much dependent on the connection characteristics as on the individual component elements making up the structure. Ample research evidence exists which establishes that the observed joint behaviour is substantially different from the assumed idealized models.

The solution of problems involving overall frame response to loading has become feasible in recent years, due to the availability of powerful computers (at affordable prices) and sophisticated test equipment and monitoring devices. The book presents the recent advances in the prevailing methods of analysis employed in simple and semi-rigid joints in steel and composite structures. Studies currently in progress which are likely to influence future design standards, are included; thus, recent developments in bolted and welded joints, endplate behaviour, inelastic behaviour of connections, semi-rigid joints, and frame behaviour with flexible joints have all been included for in-depth treatment.

As with other books in the series, the book is aimed at the graduate student and designer; it can be followed by anyone with a basic knowledge of structural analysis. We have continued the practice of inviting internationally recognized experts to contribute state-of-the-art reports on several selected areas.

As Editor, I wish to express my gratitude to all the contributors for the willing co-operation they extended in producing this volume. I do sincerely hope that the readers find the book informative and stimulating.

R. Narayanan

CONTENTS

CONTENTS

LIST OF CONTRIBUTORS

W. F. Chen
Professor, Department of Civil Engineering, Purdue University, West Lafayette, Indiana 47907, USA

E. Cosenza
Researcher, Istituto di Ingegneria Civile, Facoltà di Ingegneria, Università di Salerno, Penta di Fisciano, 84080 Salerno, Italy

J. B. Davison
Lecturer, Department of Civil and Structural Engineering, University of Sheffield, Mappin Street, Sheffield S1 3JD, UK

C. Faella
Professor, Istituto di Ingegneria Civile, Facoltà di Ingegneria, Università di Salerno, Penta di Fisciano, 84080 Salerno, Italy

W. M. Jenkins
Professor, School of Engineering, The Hatfield Polytechnic, PO Box 109, College Lane, Hatfield, Herts AL10 9AB, UK

A. G. Kamtekar
Lecturer, Department of Civil Engineering, University of Birmingham, PO Box 363, Birmingham B15 2TT, UK

A. De Luca
Associate Professor, Istituto di Scienza e Tecnica delle Costruzioni, Facoltà di Ingegneria, Università della Basilicata, Potenza, 85100 Potenza, Italy

D. A. NETHERCOT
  Reader, Department of Civil and Structural Engineering, University of Sheffield, Mappin Street, Sheffield S1 3JD, UK

J. WARDENIER
  Professor, Department of Mechanics and Structural Engineering, Faculty of Civil Engineering, Delft University of Technology, Stevinweg 1, 2628 CN Delft, The Netherlands

R. ZANDONINI
  Associate Professor, Department of Engineering, University of Trento, Via Belezani 12, 38100 Trento, Italy

P. ZOETEMEIJER
  Consulting Engineer, Mannesmann Nederland BV, PO Box 20, 4793 ZG Finjnaart, The Netherlands

Chapter 1

OVERVIEW OF CONNECTION BEHAVIOUR

J. B. Davison & D. A. Nethercot

Department of Civil and Structural Engineering, University of Sheffield, UK

SUMMARY

The role of steelwork connections both in the traditional sense of transferring loads between members and in the more general sense of influencing the way in which a complete structure responds to load is presented and discussed. Attention is given to the individual components used in steelwork connections, and the concept of failure modes and design models for assessing the load-carrying capacity of different types of connection is presented. The ability of connections to provide restraint and to transmit loads is discussed within the context of their influence on the performance of frame structures. It is suggested that the linking of studies on connections with an awareness of the influence of connection behaviour on the response of the structure should feature in all research within the general area of structural connections.

1.1 INTRODUCTION

In the design of steel structures it has been common practice to consider the main members first and to relegate connection design to a secondary role to be sorted out at a later stage, often with rather less attention being given to the task. For building frames a situation in which the designer of the main structure leaves the detailed design of the connections to the fabricator's design staff, supplying only information on the loads for which they need to be designed (moments and shears) and possibly some idea of preferred arrangements, is not uncommon. Such a process fails to recognise the fundamental influence of the connections on the performance of the structure as a whole.

1

Clearly the principal role of any structural connection, whether it is a column base securing the structure to the foundation, a chord to web member joint in a truss or an internal splice in a long box girder, is to transfer forces safely between the various components meeting at that joint. Therefore in the design of joints a clear understanding of load paths, i.e. the exact mechanism by which various components of the joint itself transfer loads through the connection, is essential. Once this is established, the individual bolts, welds, plate elements etc. of the typical connection can be properly arranged and their safety checked. To this end most steelwork design codes contain rules for checking the load-carrying capacity of bolts in shear or tension, for checking the strength of fillet welds and for the spacing of fasteners to avoid local failures in cleats, etc. However, they do not normally contain design models for particular connection types; the designer must therefore consult design guides, textbooks and, when the situation requires, more fundamental research literature. In some cases where unusual arrangements are to be employed and a proper appreciation of actual connection behaviour cannot be obtained from published sources, physical testing of prototypes may be required in support of the design.

The advent of limit states design (LSD) is clearly beneficial for connection design as it directs attention more closely at the various possible failure modes and general aspects of behaviour that ought to be considered. Even for simple connection types it is normally necessary to consider the possibility of more than one type of failure, e.g. a lap splice in tension may fail either by yielding of the gross section or by fracture at the net section; for more complex arrangements the number of possibilities may well run into double figures. Conducting the overall structural design on an LSD basis also, of course, focusses the designer's attention on aspects of overall structural behaviour other than static strength. For example, in offshore structures design of joints will very often be controlled by considerations of fatigue strength (Guy, 1987). Even for nominally statically loaded building frames, considerations of flexibility as it affects both deflections at working load levels and possible unacceptable vibrational behaviour are dealt with more rationally if design is conducted within an LSD framework. This naturally leads to a more complete examination of the role of connections and in particular to the assessment of more than just their static strength.

A particularly fertile area of research in the late 1980s is the consideration of so called 'semi-rigid' joint action on the behaviour of steel frames (Gerstle, 1985; Nethercot, 1986). Such studies require a more comprehensive understanding of connection response, in particular considerations of connection stiffness and deformation capacity. In the case of beam-to-column connections, for which in-plane bending action is the prime semi-rigid consideration, this leads to the concept of the moment-rotation or $M-\phi$ curve. This is simply the relationship between the moment transmitted by the joint and the rotation of the connection; it is most conveniently obtained from physical tests on connections (Jones *et al.*, 1981). Knowledge of the $M-\phi$ characteristic of the connections present in a particular frame enables structural analysis including semi-rigid joint action to be performed (Nethercot, 1985a). Thus the interaction of connection behaviour and frame behaviour can properly be assessed (Anderson *et al.*, 1987). Studies of this type have shown that traditional ideas of pinned or rigid connections can be quite misleading in terms of the deformations and pattern of internal forces actually developed in the structure.

It is the purpose of this opening chapter to provide the reader with a general introduction to the behaviour of connections so that he will better appreciate the more specialist material of the later chapters. A decision has therefore been made to concentrate on principles and general aspects of structural behaviour, illustrated where appropriate with specific reference to particular examples, rather than to try and cover a more limited number of points in greater detail.

1.2 TYPES OF CONNECTION

Structural steel connections may be loosely categorised as those which are required to produce a structural member, those which connect together individual elements and connections between the steelwork and supporting concrete or masonry construction. Examples of the first category are the type of joints used in trusses, latticed structures and compound members, and typical arrangements are shown in Fig. 1.1. The joints may use mechanical fasteners—usually bolts although rivets were extensively used in the past—or they may be welded. In tubular structures, extensive use is made of welding although bolted connections are often used to connect sections of trusses together where transportation or erection of a complete length would be difficult.

In many situations a structural frame is required to resist gravity and lateral loads. Connecting the components of the frame together requires the use of the second category of joint, and some typical beam-to-column connections are shown in Fig. 1.2. The choice of detail may be a function of the fabricator's working practice, reflecting the equipment available or

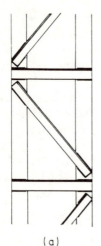

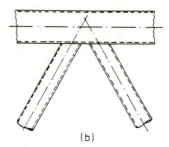

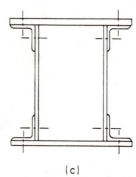

FIG. 1.1.   Connections used to produce a structural member: (a) lattice column; (b) truss; (c) compound member.

simply his particular preference, or it may be dictated by the requirements of the connection. For example, either the extended endplate or the structural T-connection could be used when a moment-resisting connection is necessary. Other examples of this category are column splice, beam splice, roof truss shoe connection and vertical and horizontal wind bracing joints (see Fig. 1.3).

The final category involves connecting steel members to other materials. Within this group, examples of which are shown in Fig. 1.4, are connections to concrete foundations, to masonry walls and the connection of concrete slabs to beams in composite construction.

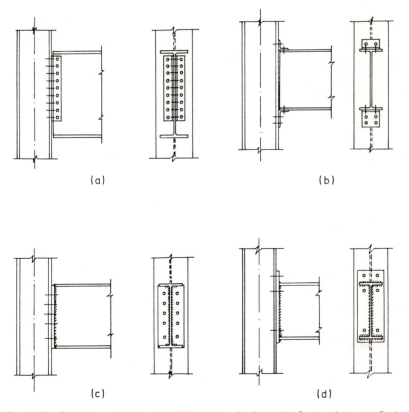

FIG. 1.2. Beam-to-column connections: (a) web cleats; (b) flange cleats; (c) flush endplate; (d) extended endplate.

1.3 DESIGN OF CONNECTIONS

When designing connections to transmit loads safely from one structural member to another, the primary requirement is that the connection has sufficient strength. Further considerations may be the rigidity of the connection, prevention of slip and ductility. Joint design involves the consideration of two distinct aspects: the fasteners which transmit the forces and the resistance of the steel plates and sections in the immediate vicinity of the connection. Failure of a connection can occur in numerous modes; therefore the designer must check each and ensure an adequate margin of safety. In many joints the likely modes of failure are readily identified, for

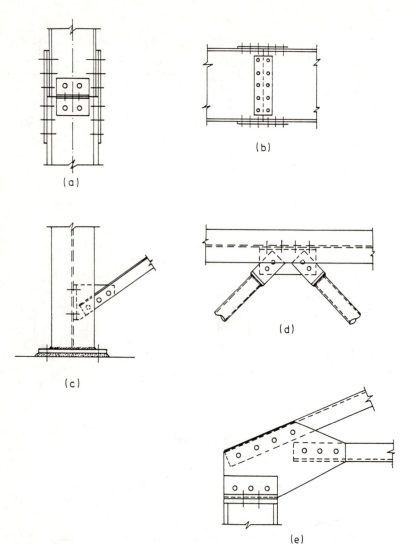

FIG. 1.3. Connecting components together: (a) column splice; (b) beam splice; (c) vertical bracing; (d) horizontal bracing; (e) roof shoe.

example in a simple lap splice (Fig. 1.5), but for others the number of possible modes may be much greater with the result that the complexity of the design calculations is increased proportionately (Fig. 1.6).

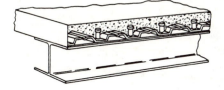

(a)

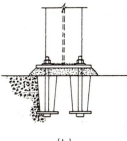

(b)

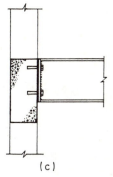

(c)

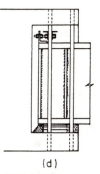

(d)

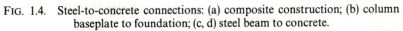

FIG. 1.4. Steel-to-concrete connections: (a) composite construction; (b) column baseplate to foundation; (c, d) steel beam to concrete.

1.3.1 Fasteners

Common fastening components are bolts and welds. Rivets, widely used in the past, are rarely used today, having been replaced by bolting which requires less labour, less skill, is quieter and poses no fire risk. Bolts are

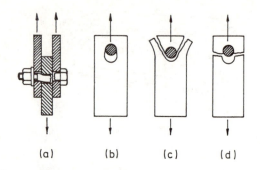

FIG. 1.5.   Failure modes in a simple lap splice: (a) bolt failure; (b) hole elongation;
(c) shear failure of plate; (d) tension failure of plate (Stark *et al.*, 1987).

available in various grades depending on material properties, manufacturing tolerances and nut and head size. In the UK the three most commonly used classes of bolts are black, precision and high strength friction grip bolts. The strength grade is given by two figures separated by a point (in accordance with the ISO system). The first figure is one-tenth of the minimum ultimate stress in kgf/mm^2. The second is one-tenth of the percentage of the ratio of minimum yield stress to minimum ultimate strength. Black bolts are normally of grade 4.6; precision bolts are generally grade 8.8. Detailed information on bolts is provided by Kulak *et al.* (1987). Bolts may transfer loads by means of shear, tension or a combination of the two; they are usually installed in clearance holes, e.g. 2 mm oversize up to M24 bolts. In many simple joints the bolts are considered to act in shear only, and the transfer of force through the connection is achieved by bearing of the plates on the bolt and so no bolt preloading is necessary. The bolt may act in single or double shear (Fig. 1.7) depending on the joint detail. Bolts may also be used in direct tension, for example in a hanger as illustrated in Fig. 1.8. The bolts in the tension region of an extended endplate connection are sometimes considered as acting in direct tension, with the vertical shear force being carried by the lower row of bolts. In many connections the bolts are subjected to a combination of tension and shear, although often the two forces are assumed to be carried by different parts of the joint; see for example the T-stub connection in Fig. 1.8.

   In joints in which bolts are loaded in shear, slip may occur as the structure is loaded and the bolts move from their installed position into bearing against the edges of the clearance holes (Fig. 1.9). In some cases this

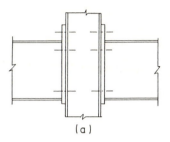

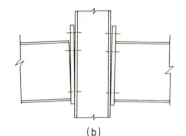

(a)   (b)

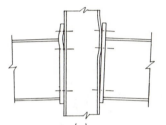

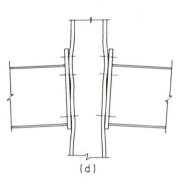

(c)   (d)

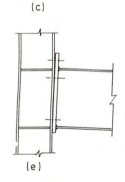

(e)

FIG. 1.6. Failure modes of an extended endplate: (a) original condition; (b) weld failure/bolt failure; (c) plate/column flange bending; (d) web yielding/web buckling; (e) shear failure of web panel.

slip is not acceptable, for example if the structure is to be subjected to vibrations or load reversal, or if the slip would produce large deflections in the connected member. In such cases slip-resistant joints may be produced by preloading the bolts in order to clamp the parts of the connection together, thus developing sufficient frictional force between the plates to resist the applied loads.

Welding is extensively used in structural engineering to produce neat

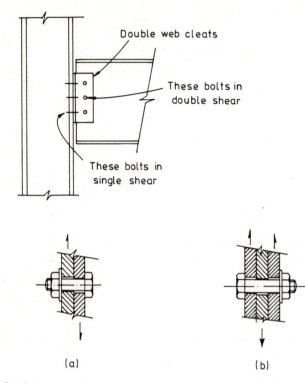

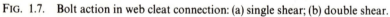

FIG. 1.7.   Bolt action in web cleat connection: (a) single shear; (b) double shear.

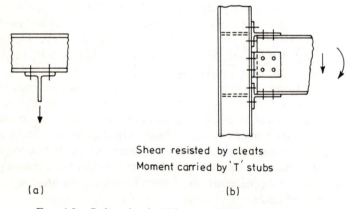

FIG. 1.8.   Bolt action in (a) hanger, (b) T-stub connection.

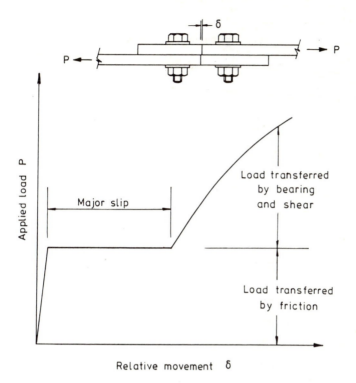

FIG. 1.9.   Load against slip of a bolted lap splice.

joints. Arc welding, in which a high current is passed through an electrode causing it and the parent metal to melt, is the predominant method used in structural fabrication. The process may be manual or automatic. Descriptions of the particular welding processes normally used in the fabrication of structural steelwork are given in Pratt (1979). Generally, welded joints require tighter tolerances than bolted ones, along with skilled labour for fabrication and inspection. Furthermore, devices such as the use of an additional seating cleat attached to columns to act as a temporary seat during erection will often be required. Moreover, during fabrication, jigs may be required to hold parts in position for tack welding before the full joints are made. Such considerations tend to redress the balance between bolted and welded connections, the former appearing to involve more operations but being generally simpler to produce and use.

Two types of weld are common in structural steelwork: the fillet weld in

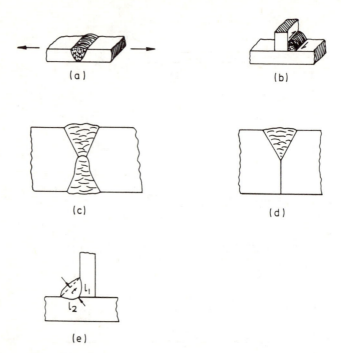

FIG. 1.10. Typical weld details: (a) single sided butt weld; (b) fillet weld; (c) full penetration butt weld; (d) partial penetration butt weld; (e) fillet weld size (t = throat thickness, l_1 = vertical leg length, l_2 = horizontal leg length).

which the weld material is placed on the faces of the joint plates, with loads transmitted by the welds in shear, and butt welds in which the weld material is placed between the edges and the welds are subjected to tension (Fig. 1.10). Butt welds may be either full penetration or partial penetration. The former are structurally very efficient, since the full strength of the original cross-section may be utilised, but they are expensive to produce because of the amount of edge preparation required and therefore should be used only when necessary. Fillet welds are extensively used in producing structural connections, for example with end plates, base plates, gusset plates and tubular joints. Correct weld detailing in tubular joints is of great importance and is covered in Chapter 6. The strength of the weld is calculated as the product of the weld design strength and the throat area of the weld. The strength of fillet welded connections under complex loading is discussed in Chapter 5.

The development of welding techniques for on-site welding of shear studs to the top flange of beams through galvanised metal decking (see Fig. 1.4(a)) has contributed to the increase in popularity of composite construction. In the past, shear studs were welded to the beams before the decking was placed, and the fitting of the decking around the shear studs was time-consuming. However, now the decking can be placed with the minimum of delay and the shear studs added afterwards. Slightly different welding techniques are employed to avoid problems due to the zinc coating on the sheet; these are explained by Pratt (1979).

1.3.2 Standardisation

The design of connections is often regarded as a fabrication detail. In an attempt to reduce unnecessary duplication of design effort, some fabricators have compiled, over a period of time, their own standard connections for the most popular arrangements. The details reflect the fabricator's preference as determined by available equipment and past experience. Increases in labour costs (both in fabrication and in design) and reductions in the price of steel mean that the cheapest solution may not necessarily be that which uses the least material. In the matter of connections it is not so important to use the minimum amount of material, but to reduce the time spent in designing and fabricating the connection, to ease subsequent erection and to include reasonable tolerance for possible misalignment. Several national institutions now present standard connection details in their steel design manuals. Of these the most comprehensive is the Australian Institute of Steel Construction's standard connection details (Hogan & Firkins, 1981). Tables of preferred sizes for common arrangements of beams and columns are presented, enabling the designer to select a connection with great ease, and to supplement the tables a volume of design principles and standard design approaches is also available to assist the designer when unusual arrangements outside the scope of the tables are encountered (Hogan & Thomas, 1981).

1.4 RESEARCH INTO THE STRENGTH OF CONNECTIONS

Assessment of the strength of a particular connection depends upon correctly identifying the weakest of the potential failure modes and then being able to determine the capacity in this mode. In some connections it is straightforward to identify failure modes and to quantify the resistance of each, thereby determining the connection strength. In more complex connections, the number of possible failure modes—or the exact mechanism of load transfer—is more difficult to ascertain and the only satisfactory method of obtaining an indication of the strength is by a programme of experimental research. Most of the common forms of connection (beam-to-column, beam-to-beam, truss and tubular joints) have at some time been the subject of research; some are still receiving attention in order to verify, or improve, design approaches. In several cases more than one accepted design model exists.

The strength and behaviour of fasteners is discussed in detail by Fisher & Struik (1974). A comparison of the strengths of the various grades of bolts used in the UK was undertaken by Godley & Needham (1982). Similar work has also been reported by Stark *et al.* (1987) and Valtinat (1987).

An area which has received considerable attention is that of prying action. Prying occurs when the force in a bolt is increased over that due to the applied loading because of the effects of plate deformation as illustrated in Fig. 1.11. Prying action may be accounted for by estimating the prying force and adding this to the primary loads in the bolts (Stark *et al.*, 1987), or the allowable bolt strength may be reduced in order that the effect of prying does not overload the bolt (BSI, 1985). Research on this problem has been reported by Granstrom (1979).

Probably the most popular form of beam-to-column connection nowadays is the endplate of Figs 1.2(b) and 1.2(c). The strength of endplate connections, both flush and extended, has been researched widely. Notable work was conducted in the Netherlands by Zoetemeijer (1983), in the UK by Packer & Morris (1977) and recently by Jenkins *et al.* (1986). The important feature of these studies was the identification of the various modes of failure and presentation of methods for checking the adequacy of a connection detail. The performance of endplate connections to columns

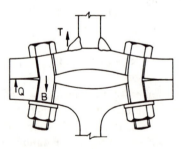

FIG. 1.11.   Prying forces (Granstrom, 1979).

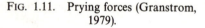

B = T + Q

stiffened with backing plates rather than conventional stiffeners was reported by Moore & Sims (1986).

Design of endplate connections is often based on the yield line method. This method equates the work done by the external loads to the energy absorbed in a series of yield lines associated with an assumed failure mechanism. Testing of other types of beam-to-column connections has been extensive and a summary is provided by Nethercot (1985b). A special issue of the Journal of Constructional Steel Research (Chen, 1988) provides up-to-date information on steel beam-to-column building connections.

1.5 PERFORMANCE OF BEAM-TO-COLUMN CONNECTIONS

Joints in structural steel frameworks are commonly assumed to behave in one of two ways, as pins or as fully rigid connections. A by-product of tests on the strength of connections has been an appreciation of the fact that even the most flexible of connections possess some ability to resist rotational movement and, at the other extreme, rigid connections have some slight flexibility. Recognition of this has led to a class of connection termed 'semi-rigid'. Usually this is taken to mean connections which can resist small but significant moments, or those which can sustain a fairly high moment but with appreciable rotation. Many studies of the rotational capacity of beam-to-column connections and column base plates have been undertaken and a large body of test data is available (Goverdhan, 1984; Picard & Beaulieu, 1985; Kishi & Chen, 1986; Nethercot, 1988) although not always readily accessible. Consideration of these test data enables the various types of connection to be graded in terms of restraint characteristics and the most significant parameters affecting rotational stiffness to be identified.

Figure 1.12 shows a typical range of moment–rotation characteristics ($M–\phi$) for a variety of connection types. The spread is very large, from very flexible web cleat connections to extended endplates and T-stubs which approach full rigidity. $M–\phi$ curves are usually non-linear over most of the range, although the stiffer connections often have an initial phase which approximates to a straight line. The non-linearity arises from softening in some component within the connection. The stiffest connections tend to be those in which the moment is resisted by components carrying axial loads, for example the T-stub and welded top plate, since axial deformations prior to yield are generally small. However, connections in which the forces are resisted by members in bending, for example the flange cleated joint or end-plate to unstiffened thin column flanges, or those in which the moment is transferred through a connection to the beam web, are much more flexible.

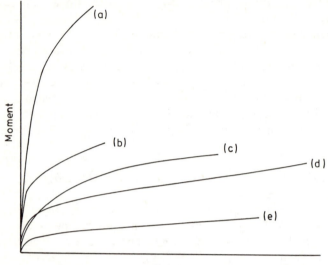

FIG. 1.12. Moment–rotation characteristics of beam-to-column connections: (a) extended endplate; (b) flush endplate; (c) seat and web cleats; (d) flange cleats; (e) web cleats.

Since joint flexibility is dependent on the behaviour under load of individual parts, attempts have been made to identify the force–deformation relationships of the major sources of flexibility (plate bending, bolt elongation, web compression etc.) and to sum these to predict the overall response of the connection (Tschemmernegg, 1988; Zandonini & Zanon, 1988). Considerable effort has been expended in this direction and a review is presented in Chapter 2.

Much of the research work conducted to date has concentrated on the in-plane response of connections. Structural frames will also contain joints in which members frame in from the third dimension. Though structural design usually considers only in-plane response and prevents out-of-plane action wherever possible, members (particularly those under axial load) respond in three dimensions and hence the response of joints in all directions is of some importance (Bennets *et al.*, 1982; Jones *et al.*, 1983; Celikag & Kirby, 1988; Janss *et al.*, 1988; Wang *et al.*, 1987). This is an area in which relatively little research has been conducted but, as interest in the overall response of building frames increases, more attention seems likely.

The recent popularity of composite construction for multi-storey frames has opened up another area of research—the performance of composite joints. Before the advent of composite construction the assumption that the building frame acted independently of the flooring system was acceptable, though still probably not correct. However, in composite construction the floor and the steel beams are designed to complement each other and work together to form a very efficient structural system although at the beam-to-column connections the composite action is usually ignored and the joints assumed to behave as pins. This assumption may be rationalised since in a braced frame the concrete deck will be in tension over the support, and will therefore crack. However, in many cases reinforcement is provided to control cracking, and the few tests that have been conducted on composite joints suggest that the $M-\phi$ response is considerably enhanced over the bare steel skeleton. Chapter 3 reviews completed work on composite joints; additional tests are known to be in progress in several centres.

1.6 INFLUENCE OF CONNECTION PERFORMANCE ON FRAME BEHAVIOUR

Structural design and analysis is simplified by the assumption that the connections between beams and columns behave as pins or as rigid joints but, since joints conform to neither extreme, the influence of the real behaviour of joints on frame action has been under investigation for many years (Steel Structures Research Committee, 1931, 1934, 1936; Jones et al., 1983; Anderson et al., 1987). Interest in the subject is still high and a compilation of work has recently been published in a special issue of the Journal of Constructional Steel Research (Chen, 1987).

In frames in which the joints are assumed to act rigidly, the flexibility of the joints leads to increased deformations (Gerstle, 1985). A study of the effects of joint flexibility on the performance of notionally rigid frames is presented in Chapters 8 and 9 of this volume. In 'simple' frames, i.e. those in which the connections are assumed to function as pins, the real behaviour of the joints is of benefit to the frame in a number of ways (Nethercot, 1988). The influence of end restraint on column stability has been examined by several researchers and found to have a beneficial effect (Chen, 1987). Modest moment–rotation stiffness may enable slender columns to carry significantly greater loads than those indicated by designs which assume pinned ends. In many cases the inherent joint stiffness may be accounted for in column design by estimating an effective length based on an assessment of the degree of restraint provided at the column's ends. Test results suggest that effective lengths shorter than those currently adopted can be justified in 'simple' braced frames (Bergquist, 1977; Davison *et al.*, 1987a).

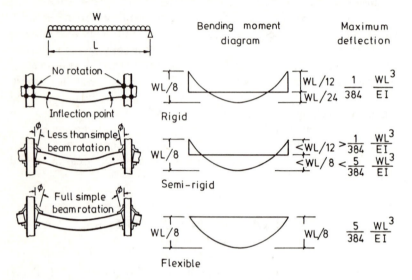

FIG. 1.13.   Effect of end restraint on moments and deflections for elastic response.

Figure 1.13 shows the change in bending moment distribution for a beam under uniform loading when the ends of the beam are pinned, semi-rigidly connected, and fully fixed. In simple design, the beam would be designed to carry a moment of $wL^2/8$ at its midspan. If it were encastré, the design moment would be $wL^2/12$ at the supports. For a semi-rigid connection, the end and span moments are somewhere in between. Hence, in simple frames the beams are designed for a moment in excess of that which occurs in practice. Depending on the type of connection, reductions in the midspan moment can lead to useful savings in beam weight. A further benefit is the reduction of midspan deflections. The ratio of midspan deflections for simply supported and fully fixed beams is 5:1 (see Fig. 1.13), indicating that the potential for reductions in deflection as a result of semi-rigid action is greater than that in design moments. Larger spans have become more common in steel frames (to allow greater flexibility for future changes of use), and serviceability rather than strength is often the controlling limit state. Reductions in deflection due to the inherent stiffness of the joint may well permit a reduction in beam weight, and it should be noted that this benefit is already present in the frame and needs only to be taken into account, no change in construction detail being necessary.

Joint flexibility in tubular structures has also received considerable study and a recent report (UEG, 1984) deals with the effects of node flexibility on offshore jacket structures. DeJong & Wardenier (1987) have considered the behaviour of tubular joints and the effect of joint rigidity on the buckling behaviour of tubular members in trusses and frames. Further information is presented in Chapter 6 which deals with welded joints between hollow sections.

1.7 LACK OF FIT IN STRUCTURAL CONNECTIONS

During the erection of steel frames some degree of lack of fit in the structure may arise due, for example, to fabrication deviations or foundation misalignment, and therefore it is necessary that joints where possible are tolerant to slight adjustments. In general, bolted cleated type connections have some adjustment by virtue of the use of bolts in clearance holes. Endplate connections and welded joints have little or no tolerance and designers must bear this in mind when selecting these types of connection. The effects of the various types of lack of fit in steel structures on the performance of both joints and the overall frame were studied in a report by Mann & Morris (1981). Precautions to be taken to avoid lack of fit problems were also presented.

The influence of lack of fit on the rotational capacity of bolted beam-to-column connections has been reported (Davison et al., 1987b). Tests showed that the lack of fit in endplate connections of the type arising from plate distortion during welding had no effect on the moment–rotation response. In cleated connections the effect of enlarging bolt holes to accommodate lack of fit permitted larger rotations to occur in the joint under loading than in an equivalent 'perfect' connection. Clearly, if the connected members had been designed on the assumption that the joints functioned as pins, this type of lack of fit would not be detrimental to the structure but, if the semi-rigid nature of the connection had been relied on in design, the implications would have to be considered carefully. Although this subject is still under study, some evidence does exist (Nethercot, 1988) to suggest that the variations in notionally identical connections likely to be encountered in practice will have only relatively small effects on the response of complete structures.

1.8 CONCLUSIONS

Research into the behaviour of structural steelwork connections may conveniently be considered under two headings. The traditional line is concerned with the performance of the connections themselves, e.g. work that results in design models for the load-carrying capacity of particular forms of connection. The second category is concerned with the ways in which connection behaviour influences the performance of the whole structure. A prerequisite for such studies is, of course, an understanding of the load–deformation behaviour of the connection—specifically its stiffness and deformation capacity. One means of obtaining such information is from the first type of study, although this might well have to be augmented so as to provide additional information. Thus both aspects of the problem are essentially complementary and should be treated under a common theme covering both the behaviour of connections themselves and their influence on the performance of the structure.

This opening chapter has attempted to provide the reader with an introduction to the general area of research into the behaviour of steelwork connections. By covering details such as individual fasteners, examples of structural actions taking place within connections such as the development of prying forces, and the importance of M–ϕ curves when incorporating considerations of connection behaviour into assessments of the performance of complete frames, it has highlighted areas that will be considered in greater detail in subsequent chapters.

REFERENCES

ANDERSON, D., BIJLAARD, F., NETHERCOT, D. A. & ZANDONINI, R. (1987) Analysis and Design of Steel Frames with Semi-Rigid Connections. IABSE Survey No. 4/1987, S-39-87.

BENNETS, I. D., THOMAS, I. R. & GRUNDY, P. (1982) Torsional stiffness of some standard shear connections. *Civil Engng Trans., Inst. Engrs* (Australia), 254–9.

BERGQUIST, D. J. (1977) Tests on Columns Restrained by Beams with Simple Connections. Department of Civil Engineering, University of Texas at Austin.

BRITISH STANDARDS INSTITUTION (1985) BS5950: Structural Use of Steelwork in Building, Part 1. BSI, London, clause 6.3.6.2.

CELIKAG, M. & KIRBY, P. A. (1988) Standardised method for measuring three-dimensional response of semi-rigid joints. In *Connections in Steel Structures: Behaviour, Strength & Design* (ed. R. Bjorhovde et al.). Elsevier Applied Science Publishers, London, pp. 203–10.

CHEN, W. F. (Guest ed.) (1987) Joint flexibility in steel frames. *J. Construct. Steel Res.*, 8 (Special Issue), 1–290.

CHEN, W. F. (Guest ed.) (1988) Steel beam-to-column building connections. *J. Construct. Steel Res.*, **10** (Special Issue.), 1–482.
DAVISON, J. B., KIRBY, P. A. & NETHERCOT, D. A. (1987a) Column behaviour in PR construction: experimental behaviour, *J. Struct. Engng, ASCE*, **113**(9), 2032–50.
DAVISON, J. B., KIRBY, P. A. & NETHERCOT, D. A. (1987b) Effect of lack of fit on connection restraint, *J. Construct. Steel Res.*, **8**, 55–69.
DEJONG, H. & WARDENIER, J. (1987) The effect of joint rigidity on the buckling behaviour of compressed tubular members in trusses and frames. In *Steel Structures: Advances, Design and Construction* (ed. R. Narayanan). Elsevier Applied Science Publishers, London, pp. 270–8.
GERSTLE, K. H. (1985) Flexibly connected steel frames. In *Steel Framed Structures: Stability and Strength* (ed. R. Narayanan). Elsevier Applied Science Publishers, London, pp. 205–40.
GODLEY, M. H. R. & NEEDHAM, F. H. (1982) Comparative tests on 8.8 and HSFG bolts in tension and shear. *Structural Engineer*, **60A**(3), 94–101.
GOVERDHAN, A. V. (1984) A Collection of Experimental Moment-Rotation curves and Evaluation of Predicting Equations for Semi-Rigid Connections. Doctoral Dissertation, Vanderbilt University, Nashville, Tennessee.
GRANSTROM, A. (1979) The Strength of Bolted End-Plate Connections. Report 15:13, Swedish Institute of Steel Construction.
GUY, R. G. (1987) Offshore tubular structures. *Steel Construction Today*, **1**(4), 115–23.
HOGAN, T. J. & FIRKINS, A. (1981) *Standardised Structural Connections. Part A, Details and Design Capacities*, 2nd edn. Australian Institute of Steel Construction.
HOGAN, T. J. & THOMAS, I. R. (1981) *Standardised Structural Connections. Part B, Design of Structural Connections*, 2nd edn. Australian Institute of Steel Construction.
JANSS, J., JASPART, J. P. & MAQUOI, R. (1988) Strength and behaviour of in-plane weak axis joints and of 3-D joints. In *Connections in Steel Structures: Behaviour, Strength & Design* (ed. R. Bjorhovde et al.). Elsevier Applied Science Publishers, London, pp. 60–80.
JENKINS, W. M., TONG, C. S. & PRESCOTT, A. T. (1986) Moment-transmitting endplate connections in steel construction, and a proposed basis for flush endplate design. *Structural Engineer*, **64A**(5), 121–32.
JONES, S. W., KIRBY, P. A. & NETHERCOT, D. A. (1981) Modelling of semi-rigid connection behaviour and its influence on steel column behaviour. In *Joints in Structural Steelwork* (ed. J. H. Howlett et al.). Pentech Press, London, pp. 5.73–5.87.
JONES, S. W., KIRBY, P. A. & NETHERCOT, D. A. (1983) The analysis of frames with semi-rigid connections: a state-of-the-art report. *J. Construct. Steel Res.*, **3**(2), 2–13.
KISHI, N. & CHEN, W. F. (1986) Data Base on Steel Beam-to-Column Connections. CE-STR-86-26, School of Civil Engineering, Purdue University, Lafayette, Indiana.
KULAK, G. L., FISHER, J. W. & STRUIK, J. H. A. (1987) *Guide to Design Criteria for Bolted and Riveted Joints*, 2nd edn. John Wiley and Sons, New York.
MANN, A. P. & MORRIS, L. J. (1981) Lack of Fit in Steel Structures. CIRIA Report 887.

MOORE, D. B. & SIMS P. A. C. (1986) Preliminary investigations into the behaviour of extended end plate steel connections with backing plates. *J. Construct. Steel Res.*, **6**, 59–122.

NETHERCOT, D. A. (1985a) Utilisation of experimentally obtained connection data in assessing the performance of steel frames. In *Connection Flexibility and Steel Frames* (ed. W. F. Chen). ASCE, pp. 13–37.

NETHERCOT, D. A. (1985b) Steel Beam to Column Connections: A Review of Test Data and their Application to the Evaluation of Joint Behaviour on the performance of Steel Frames. CIRIA Project Record 338, London.

NETHERCOT, D. A. (1986) The behaviour of steel frame structures allowing for semi-rigid joint action. In *Steel Structures: Recent Research Advances and their Application to Design* (ed. M. N. Pavlovic). Elsevier Applied Science Publishers, London, pp. 135–52.

NETHERCOT, D. A. (1988) Connection flexibility and beam design in non-sway frames. *American Institute of Steel Construction Engineering Journal*, **25**(3), 99–108.

PACKER, J. A. & MORRIS, L. J. (1977) A limit state design method for the tension region of bolted beam-to-column connections. *Structural Engineer*, **55** (10), 446–58.

PICARD, A. & BEAULIEU, D. (1985) Behaviour of a simple column base connection. *Canad. J. Civil Engng*, **12**, 126–36.

PRATT, J. L. (1979) *Introduction to the Welding of Structural Steelwork.* Constrado.

STARK, J. W. B., BIJLAARD, F. S. K. & SEDLACEK, G. (1987) Bolted and welded connections in steel structures. In *Steel Structures: Advances, Design and Construction* (ed. R. Narayanan). Elsevier Applied Science Publishers, London, pp. 366–75.

STEEL STRUCTURES RESEARCH COMMITTEE (1931, 1934, 1936) First, Second and Final Reports. Department of Scientific and Industrial Research, HMSO, London.

TSCHEMMERNEGG, F. (1988) On the nonlinear behaviour of joints in steel frames. In *Connections in Steel Structures: Behaviour, Strength & Design* (ed. R. Bjorhovde *et al.*). Elsevier Applied Science Publishers, London, pp. 158–67.

UNDERWATER ENGINEERING GROUP (UEG) (1984) Node Flexibility and Its Effects on Jacket Structures: Pilot Study on Two-Dimensional Frames. Report UR22, Research and Information Group for the Underwater and Offshore Engineering Industries, a part of CIRIA.

VALTINAT, G. (1987) DIN 18 1800, Part 1, New German basic standard for steel construction connections. Workshop on Connections and the Behaviour, Strength and Design of Steel Structures, Cachan, France.

WANG, Y. C., EL-KHENFAS, M. A. & NETHERCOT, D. A. (1987) Lateral-torsional buckling of end-restrained beams. *J. Construct. Steel Res.*, **7**(5), 335–62.

ZANDONINI, R. & ZANON, P. (1988) Experimental analysis of end plate connections. In *Connections in Steel Structures: Behaviour, Strength & Design* (ed. R. Bjorhovde *et al.*). Elsevier Applied Science Publishers, London, pp. 41–51.

ZOETEMEIJER, P. (1983) Summary of Research on Bolted Beam-to-Column Connections. Report 6-85-7, Technical University of Delft, Stevin Laboratory.

Chapter 2

METHODS OF PREDICTION OF JOINT BEHAVIOUR: BEAM-TO-COLUMN CONNECTIONS

D. A. Nethercot
Department of Civil and Structural Engineering, University of Sheffield, UK
&
R. Zandonini
Department of Engineering, University of Trento, Italy

SUMMARY

Incorporation of the effects of joint flexibility in assessments of the structural performance of steel frame structures requires a knowledge of the connection moment–rotation (M–ϕ) characteristics. Available methods for the prediction of M–ϕ curves are identified and techniques for representing them in mathematical and/or analytical form are reviewed. These embrace empirical curve fitting of experimental data, the use of simplified analytical, behavioural and mechanical models, and full numerical analysis.

NOTATION

a, b, c	Coefficients
B	Bolt force
C	Joint 'coefficient'; see eqn (2.11)
C_b	Value of C for the bolts; see Fig. (2.10)
C_c	Value of C for the column flange; see Fig. (2.10)
C_p	Value of C for the endplate; see Fig. (2.10)
d	Depth, distance
d_b	Depth of beam
d_c	Depth of column between root fillets; see Fig. (2.11)

E	Young's modulus
g	Gauge length
h	Height
k	Coefficient
K	Joint stiffness
K_i	Initial stiffness of joint
K_p	Plastic stiffness of joint
K_1	$K_i - K_p$; see eqn (2.8)
m	Number of parts in a B-spline curve; see eqn (2.4)
M	Moment at connection
M_p	Plastic moment of connection
M_u	Ultimate moment of connection
M_0	Initial moment
n	System factor
Q	Prying force
t	Thickness
x, y	Coordinates
Z	Semi-rigid connection factor; see eqn (2.1)
α	Power index
ϕ	Joint rotation
ϕ_0	Reference value of ϕ; see eqn (2.3)

2.1 INTRODUCTION

Chapter 1 identified the three requirements for satisfactory connection performance: strength, stiffness and deformation capacity. It also explained how these may all be obtained directly in the case of the in-plane response of a beam-to-column connection if the moment–rotation or $M-\phi$ curve is available. Knowledge of the $M-\phi$ curve, or at least the ability to approximate the key parts of the curve adequately, is a prerequisite for performing any sort of frame analysis that seeks to include semi-rigid joint behaviour. Thus it is not surprising to find numerous studies, particularly of late, in which the objective has been to provide methods for predicting moment–rotation behaviour. These range from purely empirical curve fitting of test data, through ingenious behavioural, analogy and semi-empirical techniques, to comprehensive finite element analysis.

Despite the fact that several national codes for the design of steel structures permit semi-rigid joint action to be accounted for in design, this facility has rarely been employed, designers opting to use one of the more basic approaches of 'simple construction' or 'continuous construction'. In the former, joints are assumed to function as pins with no transfer of bending moments; in the latter, full continuity of rotations and moments is assumed. When compared with the true in-plane behaviour of beam-to-column connections as discussed in Chapter 1, it is clear that most practical arrangements fall somewhere between these two extremes, with very flexible or very stiff joint types approximating to the ideal cases. If the semi-rigid nature of the majority of connection types is to be correctly allowed for, either in detailed research studies or in a more approximate fashion in design, then the $M-\phi$ characteristic must be available. For research purposes this will form part of the input data for analytical work or for the interpretation of tests, whilst in design it may be used in an indirect fashion as a means of distinguishing between different classes of behaviour, or an approximate form of $M-\phi$ curve may actually feature in the design calculations. Thus an important input to work on the *effects* of connection behaviour on the performance of components and frames is a knowledge of and ability to handle analytically joint $M-\phi$ data. Such data may either have been generated by physical testing or be the result of properly checked theoretical approaches.

Early studies of the effect of semi-rigid joint action relied on representations of test data as the most appropriate means of including the contribution of the joints. Whilst this has led to an improved understanding of the role of connection stiffness, it is, of course, limited by the availability of good quality, carefully documented test data. Despite the large number of joint tests conducted world-wide and recent attempts to assemble these data into usable collections, the number of different connection types and the scope for variation within each type means that only a patchy coverage will ever be available. Although careful study of these test data and selective additional testing can ensure that their value is maximised in terms of interpolation between cases, identification of similarities etc., comprehensive coverage really requires the availability of analytical techniques that can be used to generate parametric studies. It is the purpose of this chapter to review the available methods for the prediction of beam-to-column $M-\phi$ behaviour, dealing with methods based on curve fitting of test data, behavioural and mechanical models, and various types of numerical simulation. Present limits for each method, as well as limits inherent to the very nature of the approach, are discussed.

2.2 PREDICTION USING MATHEMATICAL EXPRESSIONS

Several representative $M-\phi$ curves are shown in non-dimensional form in Fig. 2.1. Any attempt to describe these curves by means of mathematical expressions must be capable of recognising the typical shape of an initial fairly straight portion, followed by a region of gradually reducing slope,

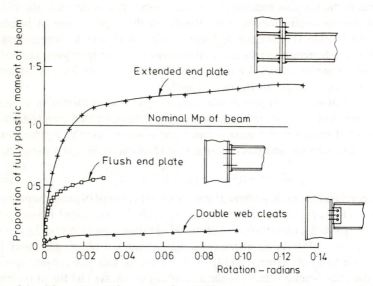

FIG. 2.1.   Moment–rotation curves for steel beam-to-column connections (beam 305 × 127 UB 48 and column 406 × 178 UB 74).

leading to a shallow final part. Although tests have been conducted in which joints have been taken to quite large rotations (more than 0·1 radian), studies for both frames and individual restrained members (Nethercot *et al.*, 1986) of the joint rotations required at maximum load have shown that behaviour at rotations beyond 0·05 radian—often much less—has little practical significance. Thus, in those joint types for which direct bearing of the beam lower flange against the column face eventually occurs due to beam rotation, e.g. web cleats or header plates, only that part of the $M-\phi$ curve at lower rotations is of real interest.

The first attempt at fitting a mathematical representation to connection $M-\phi$ curves dates back to the work of Baker (1934) in the UK and Rathbun (1936) in the USA in the 1930s. In this pre-computer era, analytical capability was severely limited and a single straight-line tangent to the initial slope was therefore all that was used. This leads to the notion of a semi-rigid connection factor Z, defined as the angle change per unit moment

$$Z = \phi/M \qquad (2.1)$$

which may be introduced directly into the slope–deflection equations or the moment distribution method (Jones et al., 1983). It was not until the 1970s that greater sophistication was introduced through the use of bilinear representations (Lionberger & Weaver, 1969; Romstad & Subramanian, 1970), which recognised the reduced stiffness at higher rotations, and polynomial representations (Kennedy, 1969; Sommer, 1969; Frye & Morris, 1975), which recognised the curved nature.

The polynomial representation uses a standardised format to express rotation in terms of moment via several constants obtained by a combination of straightforward least-squares curve fitting for the c terms and consideration of a family of experimental M–ϕ curves for the k parameter:

$$\phi = c_1(kM) + c_2(kM)^3 + c_3(kM)^5 \qquad (2.2)$$

k depends on the main geometrical parameters of the particular connection type under consideration. The technique required to evaluate k is explained by Morris & Packer (1987) or in more detail by Sommer (1969) and by Frye & Morris (1975). As an alternative, the polynomial of eqn (2.2) may be replaced (Ang & Morris, 1984) by a Ramberg–Osgood (1943) type of exponential function that has the advantage of always yielding a positive slope, which corresponds to the rotational stiffness of the connection:

$$\frac{\phi}{\phi_0} = \frac{kM}{[kM]_0}\left[1 + \left(\frac{kM}{[kM]_0}\right)^{n-1}\right] \qquad (2.3)$$

in which ϕ_0 and $[kM]_0$ are defined in Fig. 2.2 and the value of n controls the shape of the curve.

As numerical analysis capable of dealing with restrained members (Nethercot et al., 1987) and whole frames with semi-rigid connections (Anderson et al., 1987) developed, so these models were further refined. Multilinear representations were proposed by Poggi & Zandonini (1985) to overcome the obvious limitation of the bilinear model in that it could not deal with continuous changes in stiffness in the knee region, whilst B-spline techniques were suggested by Jones et al. (1981) as an alternative to polynomials as a means of avoiding possible negative slopes despite a good

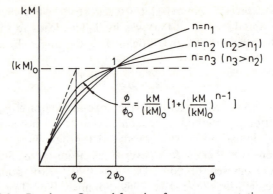

FIG. 2.2.   Ramberg–Osgood function for moment–rotation curves.

fit to the actual points:

$$\phi = \sum_{j=0}^{3} a_j M_j + \sum_{j=1}^{m} b_j (\langle M - M_j \rangle)^3 \qquad (2.4)$$

in which m is the number of knots (junctions of multi-part curve) and

$$\langle M - M_j \rangle = M - M_j \quad \text{for} \quad (M - M_j) > 0$$
$$= 0 \quad \text{for} \quad (M - M_j) < 0$$

with M_j upper bound moment in the jth part of the curve, and a_j and b_j coefficients obtained by least-squares curve fitting. An exponential representation has been used in several studies by Lui & Chen (1986):

$$M = M_0 + \sum_{j=1}^{n} c_j [1 - \exp(|\phi|/2ja)] + K_b |\phi| \qquad (2.5)$$

in which M_0 is the initial moment, K_p is the strain hardening type connection stiffness, and a and c_j are modelling parameters. Although at first sight complex, such schemes can readily be incorporated in analytical computer programs (Lui & Chen, 1986; Nethercot et al., 1987).

Although it is now possible to fit extremely closely virtually any shape of M–ϕ curve, purely empirical methods of this type possess the disadvantage that they cannot be extended outside the range of the calibration data. This is particularly important for joints such as endplates where the change in geometrical and/or mechanical properties of the connection may lead to substantially different behaviour and collapse mechanisms. Despite an attempt by Sommer (1969), Kennedy (1969) and Frye & Morris (1975) to link the coefficients of the polynomial with physical parameters of the joints, extrapolation has been found to lead to some curious results; it is not therefore recommended. This limitation has led to the linking of more recent curve fitting approaches to some form of behavioural model as proposed by Yee & Melchers (1986) and by Kishi et al. (1988a,b) and Chen & Kishi (1987).

In a somewhat different vein, Richard et al. (1980) have used a type of formula already developed by Richard & Abbott (1975) to represent data generated by finite element analyses (see Section 2.2.5 for a description of the analytical techniques used) in which the constitutive relations of certain of the joint components, e.g. bolts in shear, have been obtained directly from subsidiary tests. A power expression of the form

$$\phi = cM^\alpha \qquad (2.6)$$

in which c depends on the joint properties, and $\alpha = 1 \cdot 58$ for the extended endplate connections studied, has been proposed by Krishnamurthy and his associates (1979) on the basis of curve fitting finite element results (see Section 2.2.5). The same type of approach and of expression was applied very recently by Murray and associates (Kukreti et al., 1987) to the case of flush endplate connections.

Whilst the use of numerical data as a basis for the development of prediction formulae has certain advantages in terms of the range of joint parameters included, it is, of course, essential that the numerical analysis receive very careful prior checking so as to ensure its ability to provide accurate analysis over the range of practical interest. Even then some doubt must remain of the ability of purely empirical formulae to account for the different forms of behaviour encountered within even a single connection type, as its main parameters, e.g. plate thicknesses, bolt arrangements etc., are varied over the full range of possibilities.

Table 2.1 presents a compendium of past attempts to represent in a mathematical form connection $M-\phi$ data. This shows a range of sophistication and complexity, with the best schemes being capable of providing an almost perfect fit to any available data set. Selection of a particular scheme should take due account of the task for which the representation is required.

All of the foregoing relates only to connection behaviour under a single application of a gradually increasing load. However, now that studies of sub-assemblages (Nethercot et al., 1987) and complete frames (Poggi

TABLE 2.1
REPRESENTATIONS OF M–ϕ CURVES: STATIC BEHAVIOUR

Model	Eqn	References	Comments
M Linear	(2.1)	Baker (1934) Rathbun (1936) Lothers (1951)	Overestimates connection stiffness at finite rotations
M Bilinear	— —	Lionberger & Weaver (1969) Romstad & Subramanian (1970)	Acceptable for certain types and for applications where only small joint rotations are likely
M Multilinear	— —	Moncarz & Gerstle (1981) Poggi & Zandonini (1985)	Trilinear; initial, secondary and final slopes k_1, k_2, k_3 and elastic limit and yield moments M_{el}, M_y No formula; only suitable for numerical work
M Nonlinear	(2.2) (2.4) (2.8) (2.3) (2.5) (2.12) (2.6)	Sommer (1969) Kennedy (1969) Frye & Morris (1975) Jones et al. (1981) Richard et al. (1980) Kishi et al. (1988a,b) Chen & Kishi (1987) Ang & Morris (1984) Lui & Chen (1986) Yee & Melchers (1986) Krishnamurthy et al. (1979) Kukreti et al. (1987)	Polynomial Cubic B-spline Richard formula Ramberg–Osgood Exponential Power } All require mathematical curve fitting

& Zandonini, 1985) are being undertaken, it is clear that connections will be subjected to unloading and reloading even though the frame itself may not be subjected to any actual load reversals. Thus the ability to represent these other aspects of joint behaviour is now recognised as vital if full simulations are to be undertaken. At present, development is hampered by a lack of

TABLE 2.2

REPRESENTATIONS OF M–ϕ CURVES: CYCLIC BEHAVIOUR

Models	References	Comments
	Moncarz & Gerstle (1981) Altman *et al.* (1982)	Extension of Moncarz & Gerstle (1981) trilinear (see Table 2.1)
	Mazzolani (1988)	$\phi = \phi_0 + \phi_1 + \phi_2$ in which $\phi_0 =$ residual rotation of previous cycle $\phi_1 =$ Ramberg–Osgood type term $\phi_2 =$ incremental rotation due to slip

actual data on the performance of connections under these more complex load paths. Clearly many of the models of Table 2.1 are, at least in principle, capable of adaptation in this way, and some have already been used to represent the performance of certain connection types under cyclic loading as indicated in Table 2.2. Compared with the behaviour covered in Table 2.1, however, this topic has received far less attention.

2.3 PREDICTION BY SIMPLIFIED ANALYTICAL MODELS

Several authors have applied the basic concepts of structural analysis—equilibrium, compatibility and material constitutive relations—to simplified models of the key components in various types of beam-to-column connections. The usual approach has been:

(i) Close observation of test behaviour to identify the major sources of deformation in the connection

(ii) Elastic analysis of the initial loading phase, concentrating on the key component(s) to predict initial connection flexibility

(iii) A plastic mechanism analysis for the key component(s) to predict ultimate moment capacity

(iv) Verification of the resulting equations against test data
(v)   Description of connection $M-\phi$ behaviour by curve fitting using the calculated initial stiffness and ultimate moment capacity values in suitable expressions

Figure 2.3 illustrates in diagrammatic form the application of the technique. To date this form of approach appears to have been most successful and most widely applied to the more flexible forms of connection, particularly those involving the use of angle cleats. A common theme in such work has been to consider only the deformations of the cleats, other sources of connection flexibility, e.g. column flange bending, bolt slip etc., being neglected.

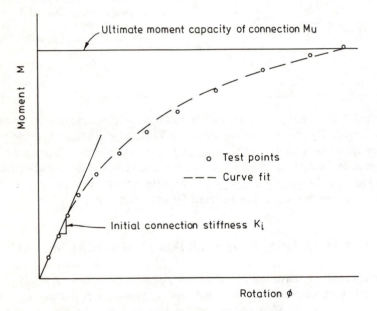

FIG. 2.3.   Construction of semi-empirical $M-\phi$ curve.

Following an initial suggestion by Beaufoy & Moharram (1948) that the behaviour of web cleat connections be studied by treating the cleats as a series of short lengths in either tension or compression, Lewitt et al. (1969) produced a comprehensive study of the behaviour of double web cleat connections. Concentrating on the behaviour of the parts of the angles in tension, they provided formulae for the load–deformation behaviour in both the initial elastic and the final plastic phases. These need to be used in conjunction with a knowledge of the centre of rotation of the connection (the point within the angle length at which there is no deformation due to the applied moment). From tests it was concluded that, whilst such a point will initially be located towards the centre of the angle, under increasing load due to changes in the stiffnesses of different parts of the connection resulting from local yielding etc., this will gradually move down towards the lowest row of fasteners; a final location of 0·8 times the length of the angle from its tension end was proposed. Figure 2.4 compares the predictions of this approach with some of the authors' experimental $M-\phi$ curves.

A few years previously, Lothers (1951) presented an elastic analysis for the initial flexibility (Z of eqn (2.1)) of double web cleat connections, leading to the expression

$$Z = \frac{6g^3}{Eht^3y^2} \frac{g+g_1}{4g+g_1} \tag{2.7}$$

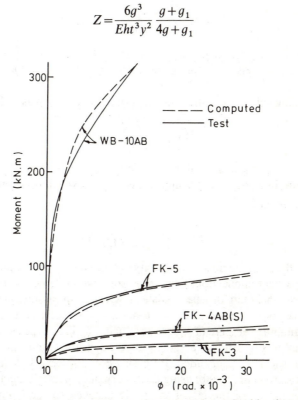

FIG. 2.4. Comparison of moment–rotation curves determined by theory and by test (Lewitt *et al.*, 1969).

in which g and g_1 define the bolt positions on the cleat legs of thickness t, and y relates the neutral axis to the depth h of the connection. The analysis ignores all deformations other than bending of the cleats but was nonetheless able to predict the initial stiffness of the tests of Rathbun (1936) quite well.

Chen and his associates in a series of three recent papers (Chen & Kishi, 1987; Kishi *et al.*, 1988a,b) have considered the behaviour of web cleats (single or double sided), flange cleats and combined web and flange cleat connections using the general type of approach described at the beginning of this section. In each case the resulting values of initial connection stiffness and ultimate moment capacity were utilised in a Richard type of power expression (Richard & Abbott, 1975) to represent the resulting $M-\phi$ curve as

$$M = \frac{K_1 \phi}{[1 + (\phi/\phi_0^n)]^{1/n}} + K_p \phi \qquad (2.8)$$

in which K_p is the plastic connection stiffness, $K_1 = K_i - K_p$, K_i is the initial connection stiffness, ϕ_0 is the reference plastic rotation, and n is the shape parameter.

Providing this is simplified into its elastic–perfectly plastic form

$$M = \frac{K_i \phi}{[1 + (\phi/\phi_0)^n]^{1/n}} \qquad (2.9)$$

then the Chen approach requires only one parameter (n) derived from test data to produce the curve fitting expression from which rotations ϕ can be obtained directly as

$$\phi = \frac{M}{K_i [1 - (M/M_u)^n]^{1/n}} \qquad (2.10)$$

with M_u the ultimate moment capacity determined by plastic analysis. For the flange cleat connection, Chen & Kishi (1987) treated the top cleat as a cantilever including the effects of shear deformation, assuming rotation to take place about the heel of the bottom cleat as shown in Fig. 2.5. For the plastic analysis the pair of hinges producing a shear type of mechanism illustrated in Fig. 2.6 was assumed for the top angle and once again the effects of shear were included. Both single and double web angles were treated (Kishi *et al.*, 1988b) using the theory of moderately thick plates for the deformation of the leg of the angle fastened to the column flange, followed by the assumption of a pair of yield lines along this same part of the

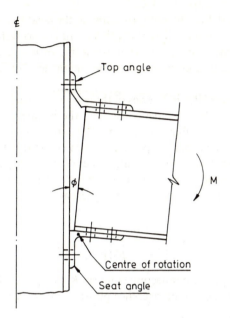

FIG. 2.5.   Deflected configuration of top and seat angles at the elastic condition
(Chen & Kishi, 1987).

cleat(s) as illustrated in Figs 2.7 and 2.8 respectively. For the combined form
of connection, the two separate approaches were simply used together
(Chen & Kishi, 1987). Figure 2.9 provides examples of the application of
these techniques to one set of test data (Altman *et al.*, 1982).

   These studies focus their attention on the steel connection, which is

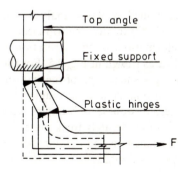

FIG. 2.6.   Mechanism of the top angle
at the ultimate condition (Chen &
Kishi, 1987).

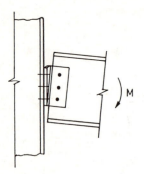

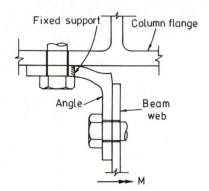

(a) General deformation pattern of the angle of web-angle connections

(b) Deformation of the angle during initial loading

FIG. 2.7.   Assumed elastic deformation of web angles.

implicitly assumed to lie on a rigid support. In most cases, however, deformation of the column components (flange and web) takes place, contributing significantly to the overall joint flexibility. If it is assumed that the interaction between different joint components only negligibly affects the response of each single component considered in isolation, the

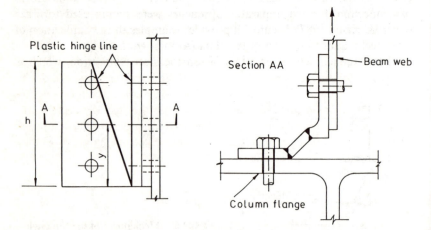

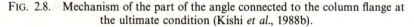

FIG. 2.8.   Mechanism of the part of the angle connected to the column flange at the ultimate condition (Kishi *et al.*, 1988b).

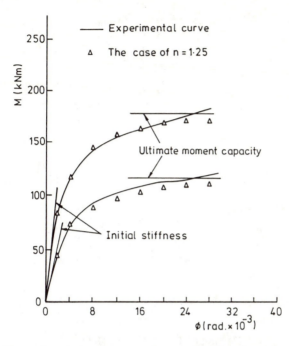

FIG. 2.9. Comparison between proposed power model and experimental results
(Chen & Kishi, 1987).

behaviour of the whole joint may be obtained simply by superimposing the
flexibilities of the components of the joint (member elements, connecting
elements, fasteners).

This approach was first used by Johnson & Law (1981) who proposed
a method for the prediction of the initial stiffness and plastic moment
capacity of flush endplate connections. The fairly crude assumption of an
ideal bilinear $M-\phi$ curve was justified because the steel connection was
studied just as a component, and not the governing one, of the composite
joint in Fig. 2.10(a) (the complete method is presented in Chapter 3). For the
initial stiffness, a 'joint coefficient'

$$C = \frac{1}{0.5[(1/C_b)+(1/C_c)](d_b/d)^2 + 1/C_p}$$ (2.11)

which is a function of the coefficients for the connecting elements defined as
in Fig. 2.10(b), was introduced. The elastic stiffness of the overall joint is
then $K = Cd_b^2$. Simple behavioural models were assumed for evaluating the

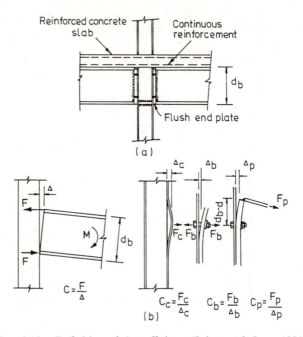

FIG. 2.10.   Definition of C coefficients (Johnson & Law, 1981).

various C coefficients, and these were calibrated against available test data. However, no comparison was conducted against experimental results for the whole endplate connection.

More recently, Yee & Melchers (1986) developed a method, based on the same philosophy, as part of an extensive study of bolted endplate eaves connections (Fig 2.11(a)). The exponential representation

$$M = M_p \left[1 - \exp\left(\frac{-(K_i - K_p + c\phi)\phi}{M_p}\right) \right] + K_p\phi \qquad (2.12)$$

was assumed, which depends on four parameters: M_p related to the joint plastic resistance, K_i and K_p defining the stiffness in the initial and strain hardening ranges, and c which is an empirical coefficient permitting a calibration of eqn (2.12) against test data. For the computation of the plastic moment, reference was made to methods already available in the literature for the different possible failure modes. The determination of the stiffness parameters required the development of mathematical expressions to compute the deformation of simple behavioural models, which nonethe-

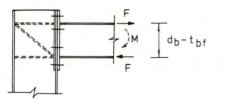

(a)

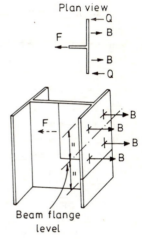

Plan view

(b)

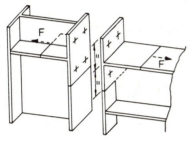

Stiffened column

Unstiffened column

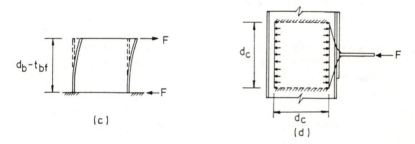

(c)

(d)

FIG. 2.11. Behavioural models for the single components of an extended end-plate eaves connection (Yee & Melchers, 1986).

less accounted for all the major factors affecting the joint response, i.e. deflection of plate components for both stiffened and unstiffened columns (T-stub models in Fig. 2.11(b)), bolt extension, shear deformation of the column panel zone (column stub model in Fig. 2.11(c)) and compression deformation of the column web (plate model in Fig. 2.11(d)). The effect of bolt preloading and of the presence of doubler plates was also included. The plastic stiffness K_p was then determined based on the assumption that it is a consequence of strain hardening or post-buckling resistance of the column web. The same models of Figs 2.11(c) and 2.11(d) were used for these two contributions. Finally the empirical coefficient c was defined from a correlation study between the mathematical model (eqn (2.12)) and experimental $M-\phi$ curves obtained from 16 tests conducted by the same authors. Three values of c were so determined, i.e. $c=0$ for stiffened connections with torqued bolts, $c=3\cdot5$ for stiffened connections with snug tight bolts and $c=1\cdot5$ for unstiffened connections. The agreement then obtained with the test data was most satisfactory.

The connections tested were in effect of a very particular type and the range of the geometrical and mechanical parameters investigated rather limited. Nevertheless the results obtained indicate that the 'superposition' approach is feasible in principle, although the actual limits of its applicability should be investigated.

More generally we can conclude that methods based on simplified analyses of the behaviour of key components of connections show that it is possible to approximate the form of $M-\phi$ curves without resort to testing. However, as they rely on the prediction of a few key parameters, such as the initial stiffness and the ultimate moment capacity, such analyses still require empirical curve fitting to generate the full curve; this often involves selecting values for certain free parameters, and some use of test data is normally required. Moreover, since only limited checking of $M-\phi$ curves generated in this way against experimentally obtained connection characteristics has so far been conducted, it is considered unwise at present to apply the available techniques outside the range for which such validations have been completed.

2.4 PREDICTION BY MECHANICAL MODELS

The availability of models which enable the joint response to be directly predicted through the whole range appears to be advantageous. The actual shape of the $M-\phi$ curve would be obtained, without the need to constrain it to follow predetermined patterns.

To achieve this objective, mechanical models were developed by several researchers for the sole connection as well as for the whole joint. The complexity of the connection/joint behaviour, however, makes it quite difficult to set up simple but comprehensive models. This approach has therefore been pursued only for connections/joints where the number of physical governing parameters is rather limited. Generally the connection/

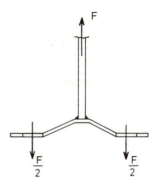

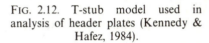

FIG. 2.12. T-stub model used in analysis of header plates (Kennedy & Hafez, 1984).

joint is conceived as a set of rigid and deformable components, representing the behaviour of 'elemental' parts. The nonlinearity of its response is then accounted for by inelastic constitutive laws adopted for the deformable elements, obtained from test data or from analytical models.

Kennedy & Hafez (1984) used a rather similar technique of connection discretisation to that of Lothers (1951) to describe the behaviour of header plate connections (partial depth endplates). In this case T-stub models of the type illustrated in Fig. 2.12 were used to represent the tension and compression parts of the connection. Analytical representations of their behaviour were developed and validated against test data on elemental T-sections. A trial and error location of the instantaneous neutral axis was then used to trace the moment–rotation relationship. Comparisons against the authors' own tests provided good agreement for ultimate moment capacities but rather more erratic predictions of the corresponding rotations. It was suggested that this was due to a greater sensitivity of rotations to the exact location of the instantaneous neutral axis, and an empirical modification to the predicted value at which the lower flange came into contact with the column face was therefore suggested if the method was to be used as a direct check on connection deformation capacity in design.

A similar approach was used by Wales & Rossow (1983) to develop a model for double web cleat connections. The model, whose main features are presented in Fig. 2.13, idealises the joint as two rigid bars connected by a homogeneous continuum of independent nonlinear springs. The values of the parameters defining the trilinear load–deformation law adopted for the springs are obtained via the analysis of numerical models for the whole connection considered as being subject to simple tension or compression.

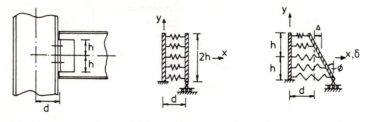

(a) Actual connection   (b) Model (Undeformed)   (c) Model (Deformed)

FIG. 2.13.   Mechanical model of web cleat connections (Wales & Rossow, 1983).

The cleat and column flange flexural deformations as well as the bolt elongations are accounted for under tension, while the column web deformation is the sole factor assumed to contribute in compression. No allowance is made for other factors such as bolt slip, local deformations due to bolt bearing and strain hardening. Both bending moment and axial force are considered to act on the connection, and coupling effects between the two stress resultants are then included in the stiffness matrix which defines the instantaneous response of the joint.

The comparison presented with a single test by Lewitt *et al.* (1969) has the limited aim of validating only the philosophy of the approach. Nevertheless, an important feature of the model lies in its ability to account for the presence of the axial force, presence which may exert a non-negligible influence on the whole M–ϕ characteristic. Although axial forces in the beams generally are not large, the results obtained indicate that greater attention should be given to such forces, as a factor affecting the response of beam-to-column connections.

This model has recently been extended by Richard and his associates (Chmielowiec & Richard, 1987) to predict the behaviour of all types of cleated connections but subject only to bending and shear (Fig. 2.14 shows the case of a connection with flange and web cleats). Mathematical expressions of the form of eqn (2.8) were adopted for the force–deformation relationships of the double angle segments and were then calibrated by curve fitting against experimental results obtained by the same author. A rather extensive comparison with experimental data from different series of connection tests in general confirms the validity of the method (see for example Fig. 2.15), at least when the deformation of the column components and slip of the bolts are negligible. These factors might, however, be included quite simply without modifying the basic features of the approach.

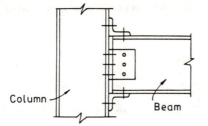

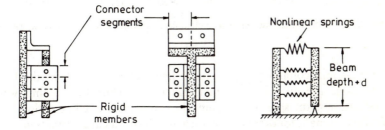

FIG. 2.14. Mechanical model for a flange and web cleated connection (Chmielowiec & Richard, 1987).

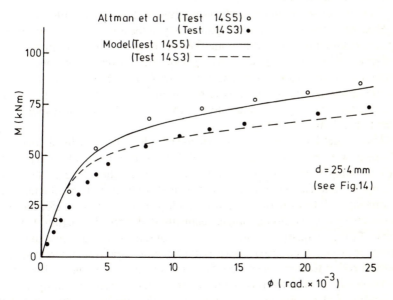

FIG. 2.15. Comparison of moment–rotation curves determined by the model of Fig. 2.14 and by tests (Chmielowiec & Richard, 1987).

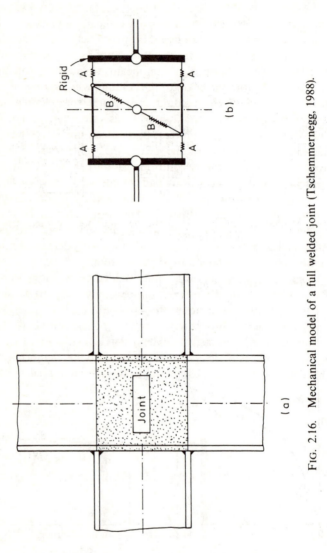

FIG. 2.16. Mechanical model of a full welded joint (Tschemmernegg, 1988).

Beam-to-column welded moment connections are generally assumed to act as rigid joints. However, if the costly column web stiffeners are avoided, the joint stiffness as well as the strength may be substantially reduced and joint behaviour may affect significantly the overall structural response. In order to set up suitable design methods, one extensive investigation into the response of fully welded connections has been conducted by Tschemmernegg and his associates (1988). They represent the joint by the mechanical model of Fig. 2.16(b), where springs A are meant to account for the load introduction effect from the beam to the column, while springs B simulate the shear flexibility of the column web panel zone. Three series of supplementary experiments for a total of 30 tests were carried out. The first on column stubs subject to transverse point loads simulated the sole load introduction mechanism from the beam, the other two on full joints employed either cruciform (second series) or cantilever (third series) arrangements. A wide range of beam and column sections was investigated, making possible a calibration of the mathematical models assumed to describe the spring element properties. The spring characteristic defined, the two contributions to the joint $M-\phi$ curve due to the load transfer and to the shear panel deformation may be straightforwardly determined and then the overall behaviour obtained by superposition.

The moment–rotation curves for fully welded connections were determined via the model for all possible combinations of beams and columns made of European rolled sections IPE, HEA and HEB, and design tables prepared gathering the main parameters defining such curves (SZS, 1987). In principle the model can easily be extended as shown in Fig. 2.17 to allow the additional sources of deformation present in bolted connections to be taken into account (springs C). Research in this direction is currently being

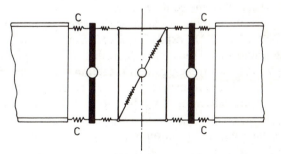

FIG. 2.17. Mechanical model of a bolted joint (Tschemmernegg, 1988).

conducted by the same author, with particular reference to extended endplate connections and including the presence of backing plates.

Mechanical models have been confirmed as an adequate and promising tool for the study of steel connections. They are, however, not 'self contained' approaches and their accuracy relies on the degree of refinement and accuracy of the assumed load–deformation laws for the principal connection components. The determination of such characteristics requires a full understanding of the behaviour of single components, as well as of the way in which they interact, as a function of the geometrical and mechanical factors of the complete connection. Such knowledge, which is required for a proper model assumption for each component, is at present available only for joints with rather simple physical behaviour. A large amount of experimental and/or numerical work is still required in order to allow mechanical models to be used with confidence for predicting the $M-\phi$ curves of connections involving a more complex interaction between the single elements.

2.5 PREDICTION BY FINITE ELEMENT ANALYSIS

Moment–rotation curves are the final product of a very complex interaction between the member components (webs, flanges), the connection components (cleats, plates) and the fasteners (bolts, welds). As already pointed out, the basic mechanism of this interaction needs to be fully understood as the fundamental background for any simpler approach to joint behaviour.

Whilst the experimental measure of displacement components and strains provides valuable insight into the problem, in many cases important local effects either cannot be measured at all or cannot be measured with the necessary accuracy, e.g. bolt local deformations in threaded parts, prying forces and extension of the contact zone, contact forces between the bolt and the connection components, because the necessary measuring process is either not feasible or too expensive. Experimental studies, although of paramount importance, thus provide rather limited information and possess a low cost-effectiveness ratio. Furthermore, the number of geometrical and mechanical parameters which can reasonably be expected to influence the joint behaviour is significant, even for simple connections. Thus the extensive parametric study, which should be the basis for the development of simpler prediction approaches, can only realistically be carried out by means of numerical simulation.

The finite element technique represents, in principle, the most suitable tool presently available for conducting such exhaustive investigations. Nevertheless, it should be recognised that, despite substantial and continuous progress, some of the requirements for the accurate simulation of joint response appear, as yet, to be unsolved. Further advances are therefore needed before the technique can be used with confidence. In this section the main problems relating to the numerical analysis of the behaviour of beam-to-column joints are identified and different approaches that have been used highlighted. A detailed discussion of the actual formulations is beyond the scope of this chapter; a complete presentation of the various methods is, however, available in the referenced literature.

In general, the analysis of steel joints requires the modelling of:

(a) geometrical and material nonlinearities of the various plate components of the members and of the connection;
(b) bolt pre-load and behaviour under a general stress distribution resulting in a combination of moment, shear and tension;
(c) bolt interaction with the plate components of the member and of the connection, i.e. contact between the shank and the hole surface and contact at the head and/or the nut due to the bolt preload or to the compatibility conditions with the adjacent elements;
(d) compressive interface stresses due to bolt pre-tensioning and consequent friction resistance;
(e) possibility of slip due to bolt-to-hole clearance;
(f) variability of the zones of contact between component elements under loading;
(g) behaviour of weldments under complex loading;
(h) presence of initial imperfections (residual stresses, lack of fit, etc.).

The analysis of isolated plates has already reached a significant degree of refinement, allowing both the in-plane and out-of-plane response to be simulated with a high degree of accuracy, including the respresentation of large strains and/or displacements and accounting for the spread of plasticity over the surface and through the thickness as well as for strain hardening and instability effects. Thus requirement (a), which is perhaps the most important for welded joints, may be met.

The first study into joint behaviour making use of the FEM (Bose et al., 1972) was indeed related to welded beam-to-column connections of the type shown in Figs 2.18(a) and 2.18(b). The connections were characterised by the web being the critical component. This element was then studied in isolation as a plate strength problem using a load pattern simulating the moment and shear transmitted by the beam. An incremental analysis was

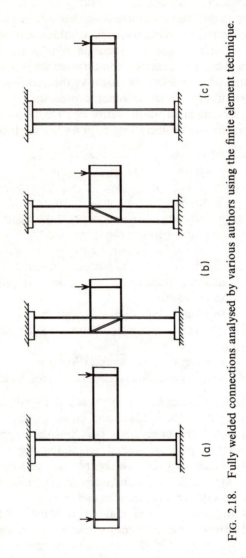

FIG. 2.18. Fully welded connections analysed by various authors using the finite element technique.

performed, including in the formulation plasticity, with strain hardening, and buckling. The comparison with available experimental results showed satisfactory agreement, but only the critical load levels were considered.

Patel & Chen (1984) also investigated, as part of a wider study, welded two-way connections (Fig. 2.18(a)), where the beam was either fully welded to the column or welded only at the flanges. The full joint assembly was in this case modelled using the general purpose program NONSAP (Bathe *et al.*, 1974). Considering the fact that only a two-dimensional analysis was conducted by means of plane stress isoparametric elements, the agreement on the load–deflection curve was found to be fairly good, as indicated in Fig. 2.19 for the fully welded specimen, at least when the presence of initial imperfections such as residual stress was recognised. More recently, Atamiaz Sibai & Frey (1988) studied the one-way unstiffened joint configuration in Fig. 2.18(c). One of the tests conducted by Tschemmernegg was actually simulated under various loading conditions, pointing out the significant role played by strain hardening on the plastic shear deformation of the column web panel.

Though the number of analyses is still limited, the available results are consistent in indicating close agreement between numerical and experi-

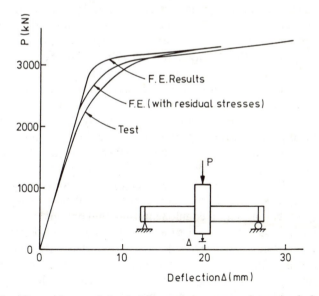

FIG. 2.19. Comparison of load–deformation curves determined by finite element analysis and by test (Patel & Chen, 1984).

mental data. It may therefore be concluded that the finite element technique already represents a tool sufficiently accurate for welded beam-to-column joints, though refinements might be necessary in the modelling of the weldments and of the heat-affected zones before reliable predictions of the joint rotation capacity can be achieved.

The numerical analysis of bolted connections is significantly more difficult, requiring the modelling of the bolt behaviour as well as of quite complex boundary conditions designed to simulate friction, slip and unilateral contact (see points (b)–(f)). Furthermore, all these factors are generally interacting in a way which in some cases is not yet thoroughly understood.

The recent advances in finite element formulations to tackle problems such as unilateral contact and friction *per se* have certainly been substantial. Nevertheless the resulting approaches do not yet seem suitable for a direct complete analysis of bolted steel connections, even in the simplest cases where bolts are acting in shear.

As a consequence, simplified, though sometimes ingenious, approaches have usually been adopted. It is possible in general to classify the approaches by the way they include bolt action in the numerical analysis, i.e. if indirectly by force or displacement boundary conditions, by *ad hoc* developed finite elements or by equivalent structural systems or, directly, by a finite element discretisation of the bolt itself. Because of the different inherent problems, it seems however more convenient not to follow this classification, but rather to organise this review using the basic mode of action of the bolts in the connection, distinguishing between connections where all the bolts act primarily in shear and connections where at least some of the bolts act in tension or in tension and shear.

The study by Lipson & Hague (1978) was actually not directly concerned with prediction of the M–ϕ curves. It had the main aim of improving the understanding of the behaviour of single angle bolted–welded connections (Fig. 2.20(a)), of a type already studied experimentally by the first author (Lipson, 1977). Nevertheless, the approach used is of more general interest, because it may be a useful tool where a more complete set of data on the behaviour of the connection components than that obtainable from tests is essential to the development of simplified methods of prediction.

The connection is modelled as a rigidly supported elastic-plastic plate (Fig. 2.20(b)) subject to a load distribution simulating the bolt plate interaction (Fig. 2.20(c)). Such a distribution, as well as the loading history, was determined by an evaluation of the experimental data, supplemented by load–deformation test data obtained for a single high-strength bolt

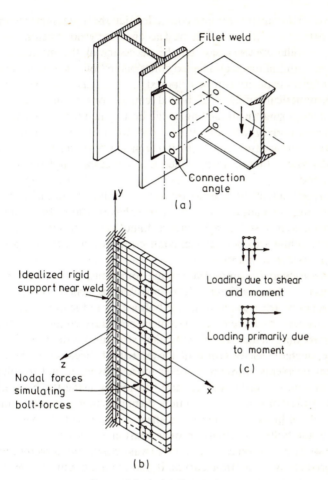

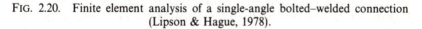

FIG. 2.20. Finite element analysis of a single-angle bolted–welded connection (Lipson & Hague, 1978).

connecting two plates. The analysis allowed the stress state and the progression of plasticity in the plate to be followed in detail under both monotonic and cyclic loading.

The numerical work by Richard and his associates (1980) on single web plate connections was conceived as a preliminary step towards the calibration of mathematical expressions aimed at predicting the whole range of the moment–rotation curve. To that end, the finite element model included part of the beam as well as the whole connection system. An inelastic finite element was developed to simulate bolt action, whose load–deformation relationship was determined by a statistical evaluation of a series of single bolt single shear tests conducted *ad hoc*. The connection model was then validated against available experimental results, before carrying out a parametric study which led to a mathematical expression in the form presented in eqn (2.9).

A very simple equivalent bar system was adopted by Patel & Chen (1985) in order to account for the bolt action, when simulating the response of the fully bolted moment connection of Fig. 2.21(a), using NONSAP. Plane stress isoparametric elements were selected for modelling the beam, column and connection plates, while three bar elements were used to simulate the bolt behaviour (Fig. 2.21(b)): elements 1 and 2 account for the pre-tension in the bolts, while element 3 simulates the shear-carrying behaviour. Piecewise linear stress–strain characteristics were assumed for the bars, whose parameters were calibrated against experimental results related to bolts subject to tension or shear. The proposed system does not, however, take into account the possibility of slip. This factor is suggested as the main reason for the discrepancies found between numerical results and test data in the inelastic range.

An improved bar system model with regard to this particular aspect has been suggested very recently by Beaulieu & Picard (1988), where a fourth bar element is placed in series with the shear element 3 (Fig. 2.22). This element is capable of representing perfect slip or friction, and it is presently under development by the same authors.

However, the equivalent truss models only allow bolt action to be represented rather crudely, and their scope must be thoroughly checked by comparison and calibration studies against an extensive range of tests on bolted plates and full connections.

When the joint arrangement requires the bolts to act in tension, or in shear and tension, such forces are transmitted from the members to the bolts through plate components, which usually deform in shear and bending. The contact forces between such components (e.g. between an endplate and the column flange), in zones whose extension changes during the loading (i.e. the so-called prying forces), significantly affect the connection behaviour. Interface contact must then be adequately modelled in the analysis, which must also recognise the more complex form of bolt action.

Richard and his associates (1983), in order to reduce substantially the

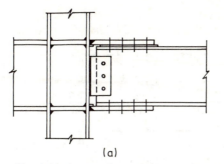

(a)

The bolted moment connection analysed

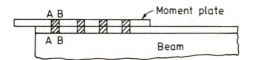

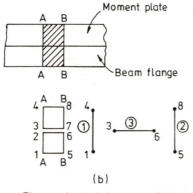

(b)

The equivalent truss system

FIG. 2.21.   Finite element analysis of a bolted moment connection using an equivalent truss system to simulate bolt behaviour (Patel & Chen, 1985).

complexity of the problem, applied to double web cleat connections the same methodology as for the single plate connections, i.e. based on the development of *ad hoc* finite elements. As already mentioned in Section 2.2.4 with reference to the mechanical model proposed by the same author for cleated connections, a series of tests on single bolted double angle

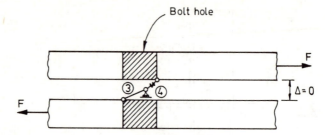

FIG. 2.22.   Equivalent truss system including friction and slip effects (Beaulieu & Picard, 1988).

segments formed the basis for mathematical expressions of the type of eqn. (2.8) to represent the anisotropic behaviour of this elemental system (see also the yield surface in Fig. 2.23). These expressions were assumed to define the constitutive law of a special inelastic element to be implemented in a finite element program. The comparison with the M–ϕ curve for

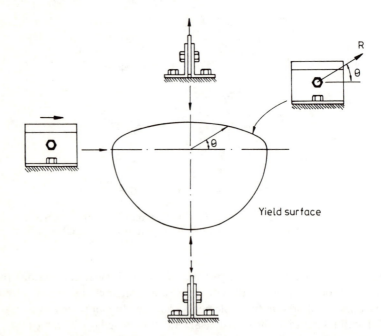

FIG. 2.23.   Yield surface for a double-angle segment (Richard et al., 1983).

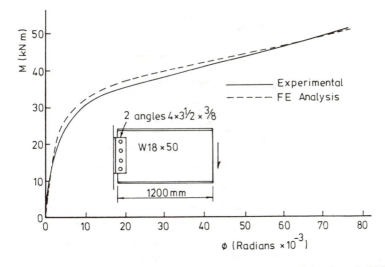

FIG. 2.24.   Comparison between finite element analysis by Richard *et al.* (1983) and tests of Lewitt *et al.* (1969).

a cantilever test by Lewitt *et al.* (1969) exhibited very good agreement (Fig. 2.24), indicating that the methodology by 'elemental finite elements' which integrates experimental and numerical capabilities may be the most suitable to tackle the problem, at least for a broad category of connections. Besides, it avoids the significant increase in the size and complexity of the numerical problem resulting from direct modelling of the bolts.

The direct modelling of the bolts, on the other hand, seems to represent the only adequate approach to the study of those connections for which it is difficult to single out 'elementary component elements', as in the case of endplate connections.

The most sophisticated formulation for this type of joint was developed by Krishnamurthy (1980); its main features are:

(a) an iterative solution procedure to follow the change in the zone of contact between the endplate and the support (considered rigid), which initially assumes full contact as in the mesh of Fig. 2.25(a);

(b) a technique for simulating bolt pre-load, highlighted in Fig. 2.25(b) (the initial bolt forces B_i are applied and the bolt extensions δ_i determined; in the subsequent loading phases the clamping effect is represented by imposing the bolt stretch δ_i as a specified displacement condition).

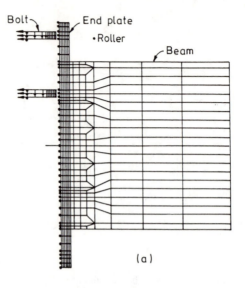

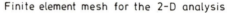

Finite element mesh for the 2-D analysis

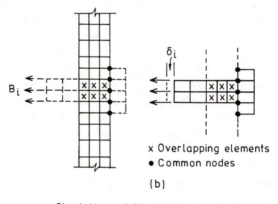

x Overlapping elements
● Common nodes

(b)

Simulation of the bolt pretensioning

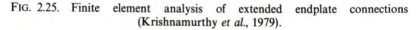

FIG. 2.25. Finite element analysis of extended endplate connections (Krishnamurthy *et al.*, 1979).

Both 3-D and 2-D models were developed, though the study was mainly conducted by means of the 2-D model after calibration work between the two was carried out. Some comparisons with experiments conducted as part of the same research programme illustrated the important role played

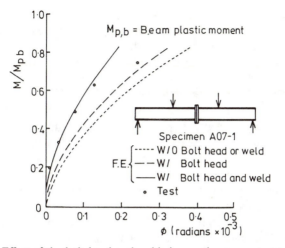

FIG. 2.26.   Effect of the bolt head and weld size on the moment–rotation curve of an extended endplate (Krishnamurthy & Oswalt, 1981).

by the bolt heads and by the finite size of the weldments (Fig. 2.26), both of which should be included in numerical analyses. Recently, Murray and his associates (Kukreti *et al.*, 1987) used basically the same formulation in an investigation into the behaviour of flush endplate connections. Since both researches were aimed at the development of mathematical expressions for the M–ϕ curves (see Section 2.2.2), the information published is not sufficient to state the actual level of accuracy of the numerical approach in predicting the overall and local behaviour of the connection.

In any case, the formulation, though sophisticated, may still be considered rather approximate in the modelling of bolt action and possesses the significant limitation of being based on the assumption that the endplate is attached to a rigid flange. A complete understanding of the whole joint, including the actual interaction between the endplate and the supporting element, which recognises that interaction may be influenced by the relative stiffness of both elements and of the bolts, would require more refined formulations, which at present are not available.

2.6 CONCLUDING REMARKS

As a result of a number of studies into the influence of joint flexibility on frame performance, there is an increasing interest in incorporating semi-rigid action in the analysis and design of steel frames, both braced and unbraced. The capability of predicting with adequate accuracy the connection moment–rotation curve then becomes a fundamental requirement. This chapter has attempted to provide the reader with an appraisal of the present status of the techniques currently available. The results of this review may be summarised as follows:

(i) *Mathematical expressions.* These have the capability of representing with extreme accuracy any shape of M–ϕ curve; the methods of prediction are, however, purely empirical and their use cannot be extended outside the range of the data used for their calibration. A further inherent difficulty in the development of adequate expressions is due to their inability to recognise that, depending on the geometrical and mechanical parameters, the type of connection behaviour as well as the contribution of each component to the overall joint response may change significantly.

(ii) *Simplified analytical models.* Behavioural models permit the determination of some characteristic parameters defining the M–ϕ curve. The generation of the full curve still requires some empirical curve fitting, which results in the same basic disadvantage mentioned in (i) with reference to range of applicability. The variation in behaviour (and contribution) of each component might however be included.

(iii) *Mechanical models.* The few studies using this approach show that they are, in principle, the most suitable, provided that a knowledge of the load–deformation curve of the key components of the connection is available.

(iv) *Finite element analysis.* While this technique already seems to be suitable for predicting the response of welded connections or components, a direct analysis of bolted connections requires the ability to model bolt action and unilateral contact at a level of refinement not yet attained.

We may therefore conclude that at present the ability to predict the moment–rotation curve with good accuracy is rather limited. Furthermore test data are not usually readily available to designers, despite the recent attempts to assemble them in usable collections.

This situation thus represents a severe handicap for semi-rigid frame action to become a viable alternative design option. The fundamental features of the way the joint behaviour affects the response of the whole structure are already understood. Suitable methods for the analysis and design of this type of structure have already been set up and used for parametric frame studies (see also Chapters 8, 9 and 10). Therefore, it may be expected that research in the near future will be concentrated mainly in the area of joint behaviour prediction, including the unloading and cyclic response, whose representation has proved to be vital for an adequate frame analysis.

It is felt by the authors that mechanical models represent the most suitable tool. These possess the added advantage of being easy for implementation in frame analysis programs (Driscoll, 1987); they then represent also a suitable tool towards the development of CAD approaches for semi-rigid frame design. Models of component behaviour, based on a full understanding gained from a combination of experimental and numerical studies, should be established; when properly combined, they allow the overall joint model to be constructed. Since it is not feasible to cover all possible joint arrangements, the study should at first be restricted to the most popular connection types.

It should, however, be noted that the prediction of the joint behaviour is not important *per se* but as input data to incorporate joint action in the frame analysis. The adequacy of a prediction method should then be judged not merely on the basis of the level of accuracy achieved in approximating the actual $M-\phi$ curve, but rather on the basis of the influence that this accuracy level has on the overall frame performance.

Studies of the sensitivity of frame response to the variation of the joint rotational characteristic should therefore be carried out as a preliminary step. The results already available (Nethercot *et al.*, 1986) suggest that, as the structure under consideration becomes more extensive, so the need for very precise $M-\phi$ representations decreases.

Thus, simplified representations of the $M-\phi$ curve, such as the trilinear and bilinear representations recently proposed (Zandonini & Zanon, 1988), may well be acceptable in many instances. Prediction methods capable of handling only the key aspects of connection behaviour could therefore be used, thereby simplifying the acceptance of semi-rigid design in practice.

ACKNOWLEDGEMENTS

This material was prepared in the Department of Civil and Structural Engineering at the University of Sheffield whilst Professor Zandonini was working there as an SERC Senior Visiting Fellow.

REFERENCES

ALTMAN, W. G., AZIZINAMINI, A., BARDBURN, J. H. & RADZIMINSKI, J. B. (1982) Moment-Rotation Characteristics of Semi-Rigid Steel Beam-Column Connections. Civil Engineering Department, University of South Carolina.

ANDERSON, D., BIJLAARD, F. S. K., NETHERCOT, D. A. & ZANDONINI, R. (1987) *Analysis and Design of Steel Frames with Semi-Rigid Connections*. International Association for Bridge and Structural Engineering Surveys, No. 4/1987, S-39-87.

ANG, K. M. & MORRIS, G. A. (1984) Analysis of 3-dimensional frames with flexible beam-column connections. *Canad. J. Civil Engng*, **11**, 245–54.

ATAMIAZ SIBAI, W. & FREY, F. (1988) Numerical simulation of the behaviour up to collapse of two welded unstiffened one-side flange connections, In *Connections in Steel Structures: Behaviour, Strength and Design* (ed. R. Bjorhovde *et al.*). Elsevier Applied Science Publishers, London, pp. 85–92.

BAKER, J. F. (1934) Second Report, Steel Structures Research Committee, Department of Scientific and Industrial Research. HMSO, London.

BATHE, K. J., WILSON, E. L. & IDING, R. H. (1974) NONSAP: A Structural Analysis Program for Static and Dynamic Response of Nonlinear Systems. Struct. Eng. Lab., University of California, Berkeley.

BEAUFOY, L. A. & MOHARRAM, A. (1984) Derived Moment-Angle Curves for Web-Cleat Connections. Preliminary Publication, 3rd Congress IABSE, Liege, pp. 105–18.

BEAULIEU, D. & PICARD, A. (1988) Finite element modelling of connections. In *Connections in Steel Structures: Behaviour, Strength and Design* (ed. R. Bjorhovde *et al.*). Elsevier Applied Science Publishers, London, pp. 96–103.

BOSE, S. K., MCNEICE, G. M. & SHERBOURNE, A. N. (1972) Column webs in steel beam to column connections. Part I, Formulation and verification, *Computers and Structures*, **2**(February), 253–72.

CHEN, W. F. & KISHI, N. (1987) Moment-Rotation Relation of Top and Seat Angle Connections. Department of Structural Engineering, Purdue University, Report CE-STR-87-4, p. 16.

CHMIELOWIEC, M. & RICHARD, R. M. (1987) Moment Rotation Curves for Partially Restrained Steel Connections. Report to AISC, University of Arizona, p. 127.

DRISCOLL, G. C. (1987) Elastic-plastic analysis of top and seat connections, *J. Construct. Steel Res.* (Special Issue on Joint Flexibility in Steel Frames), **8**, 119–36.

FRYE, M. J. & MORRIS, G. A. (1975) Analysis of flexibility connected steel frames, *Canad. J. Civil Engng*, **2**, 280–91.

JOHNSON, R. P. & LAW, C. L. C. (1981) Semi-rigid joints for composite frames. In *Joints in Structural Steelwork* (ed. J. H. Howlett, *et al.*). Pentech Press, London, pp. 3.3–3.19.

JONES, S. W., KIRBY, P. A. & NETHERCOT, D. A. (1981) Modelling of semi-rigid connection behaviour and its influence on steel column behaviour. In *Joints in Structural Steelwork* (ed. J. H. Howlett *et al.*). Pentech Press, London, pp. 5.73–5.87.

JONES, S. W., KIRBY, P. A. & NETHERCOT, D. A. (1983) The analysis of frames with semi-rigid connections: a state-of-the-art report, *J. Construct. Steel Res.*, **3**(2), 1–13.

KENNEDY, D. J. L. (1969) Moment-rotation characteristics of shear connections, *Engng J.*, *Amer. Inst. Steel Constr.*, October, 105–15.

KENNEDY, D. J. R. & HAFEZ, M. (1984) A study of end-plate connections for steel beams, *Canad. J. Civil Engng*, **11**(2), 139–49.

KISHI, N. CHEN, W. F., MATSUOKA, K. G. & NOMACHI, S. G. (1988a) Moment-rotation relation of top- and seat-angle with double web-angle connections. In *Connections in Steel Structures: Behaviour, Strength and Design* (ed. R. Bjorhovde *et al.*). Elsevier Applied Science Publishers, London, pp. 121–34.

KISHI, N., CHEN, W. F., MATSUOKA, K. G. & NOMACHI, S. G. (1988b) Moment-rotation relation of single/double web-angle connections. *Connections in Steel Structures: Behaviour, Strength and Design* (ed. R. Bjorhovde *et al.*). Elsevier Applied Science Publishers, London, pp. 135–49.

KRISHNAMURTHY, N. (1980) Modelling and prediction of steel bolted connection behaviour, *Computers and Structures*, **11**(2), 75–82.

KRISHNAMURTHY, N. & OSWALT, R. E. (1981) Bolt head and weld effects in steel connection behaviour. In *Joints in Structural Steelwork* (ed. J. H. Howlett, *et al.*). Pentech Press, London, pp. 2.158–2.176.

KRISHNAMURTHY, N., HUANG, H. T., JEFFREY, P. K. & AVERY, L. K. (1979) Analytical M-ϕ curves for end-plate connections, *ASCE, J. Struct. Div.*, **105**(ST1), 133–45.

KUKRETI, A. R., MURRAY, T. M. & ABOLMAALI, A. (1987) End-plate connection moment-rotation Relationship, *J. Construct. Steel Res.*, **8** (Special Issue on Joint Flexibility in Steel Frames), 137–57.

LEWITT, C. W., CHESSON, E. & MUNSE, W. (1969) Restraint Characteristics of Flexible Riveted and Bolted Beam to Column Connections. Bulletin No. 500, Engineering Experiment Station, University of Illinois, Chicago.

LIONBERGER, S. R. & WEAVER, W. (1969) Dynamic response of frames with non-rigid connections, *J. Engng Mech. Div., ASCE*, **95**(EM1), 95–114.

LIPSON, S. L. (1977) Single-angle welded-bolted connections, *ASCE, J. Struct. Div.*, **103**(ST3), 559–71.

LIPSON, S. L. & HAGUE, M. I. (1978) Elasto-plastic analysis of single-angle bolted-welded connections using the finite element method, *Computers and Structures*, **9**(6), 533-45.

LOTHERS, J. E. (1951) Elastic restraint equations for semi-rigid connections, *Trans. ASCE*, **1**, 480–502.

LUI, E. M. & CHEN, W. F. (1986) Analysis and behaviour of flexibly jointed frames, *Engng Struct.*, **8**(2), 107–15.

MAZZOLANI, F. M. (1988) Mathematical model for semi-rigid joints under cyclic loads. In *Connections in Steel Structures: Behaviour, Strength and Design* (ed. R. Bjorhovde *et al.*). Elsevier Applied Science Publishers, London, pp. 112–20.

MONCARZ, P. D. & GERSTLE, K. H. (1981) Steel frames with nonlinear connections, *J. Struct. Div., ASCE*, **107**(ST8), 1427–41.

MORRIS, G. A. & PACKER, J. A. (1987) Beam to column connections in steel frames, *Canad. J. Civil Engng*, **14**, 68–76.

NETHERCOT, D. A., DAVISON, J. B. & KIRBY, P. A. (1986) Connection flexibility and beam design in non-sway frames. American Society of Civil Engineers Structural Convention, New Orleans, September.

NETHERCOT, D. A., KIRBY, P. A. & RIFAI, A. M. (1987) Design of columns in PR construction: analytical studies, *Canad. J. Civil Eng*, **14**(4), 485–97.

PATEL, K. V. & CHEN, W. F. (1984) Nonlinear analysis of steel moment connections, *ASCE, J. Struct. Engng*, **110**(8), 1861–75.

PATEL, K. V. & CHEN, W. F. (1985) Analysis of a fully bolted moment connection using NONSAP, *Computers and Structures*, **21**(3), 505–11.

POGGI, C. & ZANDONINI, R. (1985) Behaviour and Strength of Steel Frames with Semi-Rigid Connections. In *Connection Flexibility and Steel Frame Behaviour* (ed. W. F. Chen). American Society of Civil Engineers.

RAMBERG, W. & OSGOOD, W. R. (1943) Description of Stress-Strain Curves by 3 Parameters. Technical Report 902, National Advisory Committee for Aeronautics.

RATHBUN, J. (1936) Elastic Properties of Riveted Connections, *Trans. Amer. Soc. Civil Engrs*, **101**, 524–63.

RICHARD, R. M. & ABBOTT, B. J. (1975) Versatile elastic-plastic stress-strain formula, *ASCE, J. Eng. Mech. Div.*, **101**(EM4), 511–15.

RICHARD, R. M., GILLETT, P. E., KRIEGH, J. D. & LEWIS, B. A. (1980) The analysis and design of single plate framing connections, *Engng J.*, *Amer. Inst. Steel Constr.*, **17**(2), 38–52.

RICHARD, R. M., RABERN, D. A., HORNBY, D. E. & WILLIAMS, G. C. (1983) Analytical models for steel connections. In *Behaviour of Metal Structures* (Proc. W. H. Munse Symposium, May) (ed. W. J. Hall, & M. P. Gaus). American Society of Civil Engineers. May.

ROMSTAD, K. M. & SUBRAMANIAN, C. V. (1970) Analysis of frames with partial connection rigidity, *ASCE, J. Struct. Div.*, **96**(ST11), 2283–2300.

SOMMER, W. H. (1969) Behaviour of Welded Header Plate Connections. Master's Thesis, University of Toronto, Ontario, Canada.

SZS (Scheiwerische Zentralstelle fur Stahlbau) (1987) *Rahmentragwerk in Stahl unter besonderer Berucksichtigung der steifenlosen Bauweise*. Zurich.

TSCHEMMERNEGG, F. (1988) On the nonlinear behaviour of joints in steel frames. In *Connections in Steel Structures: Behaviour, Strength and Design* (ed. R. Bjorhovde *et al.*). Elsevier Applied Science Publishers, London, pp. 158–65.

WALES, M. W. & ROSSOW, E. C. (1983) Coupled moment-axial force behaviour in bolted joints, *ASCE, J. Struct. Engng*, **109**(5), 1250–66.

YEE, K. L. & MELCHERS, R. E. (1986) Moment-rotation curves for bolted connections, *ASCE, J. Struct. Engng*, **112**(3) 615–35.

ZANDONINI, R. & ZANON, P. (1988) Experimental analysis of end plate connections. In *Connections in Steel Structures: Behaviour, Strength and Design* (ed. R. Bjorhovde *et al.*). Elsevier Applied Science Publishers, London, pp. 41–51.

Chapter 3

SEMI-RIGID COMPOSITE JOINTS

R. ZANDONINI

Department of Engineering, University of Trento, Italy

SUMMARY

Recent studies indicate that the cost effectiveness of steel structures may be improved if the degree of continuity provided by nominally simple joints is recognised in design. Potentially this seems to be of even greater interest for composite steel–concrete structures, where significant stiffness and strength can be provided to the joints, simply by placing reinforcing bars (or mesh) continuous around the column. Though this was first suggested back in 1970, very few studies are available on the behaviour, analysis and design of semi-rigid composite joints. The results of all known studies are reviewed in this chapter and topical problems still requiring investigation are identified, with the aim of providing a background for further research and practical applications.

NOTATION

A_c	Area of concrete slab
A_f	Area of single flange of steel beam: $A_f = b_f t_f$
A_r	Area of reinforcement
A_s	Area of steel beam
b_c	Breadth of concrete slab
b_{ef}	Effective breadth of concrete slab
b_f	Width of steel section flange
C_0, C_1	Constants

63

d	Total depth of composite beam
d_c	Depth of concrete slab
d_F	Lever arm of force F
d_s	Depth of steel section
d_w	Depth of steel section web
D	Distance between steel section and concrete slab centroids
E	Young's modulus
$f_{y,r}$	Yield strength of reinforcing bars
$f_{y,s}$	Yield strength of structural steel
F	Force
H	Horizontal load
I	Moment of inertia
k	Short-term stiffness of a stud connector
K_i	Initial joint stiffness
K_l	Elastic joint stiffness (loading)
K_s	Elastic stiffness of steel connection
K_{unl}	Elastic joint stiffness (unloading)
M_{cr}	Moment at first slab cracking
M_e	Elastic limit moment
M_p	Plastic moment of resistance of joint
$M_{p,c}^-$	Negative plastic moment of composite beam
$M_{p,d}$	Design value of joint plastic moment
$M_{p,s}$	Plastic moment of steel section
M_u	Ultimate moment capacity of joint
P	Vertical load
s	Connector spacing
t_f	Thickness of steel flange
t_w	Thickness of steel section web
v	Deflection
V	Shear force
γ	Interface slip
Δ	Displacement
ε_y	Elastic strain at yield
θ	Absolute rotation
ρ	Slab reinforcement ratio (%)
ρ_F	Semi-rigid force factor $= A_r f_{y,r}/A_f f_{y,s}$
ϕ	Relative rotation; rotation of joint
ϕ_u	Rotation capacity of joint

3.1 INTRODUCTION

The stiffness and strength of the connections may influence substantially the response and stability of steel framed constructions. The joint behavioural characteristics are therefore, in principle, parameters whose value may be properly selected in order to achieve the desired performance of the structure. Traditional, and generally used, methods of frame design, however, disregard the actual joint behaviour and assume the ideal models of perfectly rigid or pinned connections. Such an assumption may lead to a non-conservative assessment of the structural reliability of sway frames, where the rigid joint model involves an underestimation of the frame flexibility, and to an overconservative assessment of the strength of braced frames, where the simple design approach (hinged joints) is adopted.

The need for more realistic design methods and, mainly, the recognition of possible non-negligible advantages in terms of the construction cost effectiveness created an increasing interest in the behaviour, and eventually in the design, of flexibly connected (semi-rigid) steel frames (Anderson *et al.*, 1987). Studies already pointed out that the rotational characteristic of joints, even with fairly simple details, may be used to achieve the goal of more economic, and then more competititve, construction (Van Douwen, 1981). This is likely to be of potentially greater importance in the field of composite steel–concrete structures, as indicated by Owens & Echeta (1981). The trend towards larger open areas in buildings with increasing intensity of servicing requirements, the greater importance of the construction speed, together with several technological improvements, have made composite construction increasingly popular in the USA as well as in Europe. However, composite action is generally taken as giving advantages solely in the sagging moment region of the beams, which are assumed as simply supported. Rigid beam-to-column connections (Fig. 3.1(a)) present several disadvantages; in particular they are expensive to fabricate and they require very tight b/t ratios to be satisfied by the steel section (tighter than for bare steel structures) in order to apply the advantageous plastic design approach (Climenhaga & Johnson, 1972; Johnson, 1985). On the other hand, in simple construction (Fig. 3.1(b)), serviceability may often govern the design. Moreover, some reinforcing steel should in many cases be placed around the column for crack control. By a proper selection of the amount of such longitudinal reinforcement, a semi-rigid composite joint is easily obtained, and almost at no cost, the stiffness and strength of which may substantially improve the frame performance with respect to both serviceability and ultimate limit states. Moreover, the joint can easily be detailed

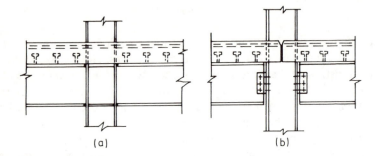

FIG. 3.1.   Beam-to-column composite joint: (a) a rigid joint; (b) a simple joint.

to avoid local and lateral buckling of the steel sections, making it possible to relax local slenderness requirements for plastic beam design.

The proposal of taking advantage of less than rigid (semi-rigid) joints dates back to 1970 (Barnard). Even though the results obtained since the very early investigations were highly encouraging and confirmed the basic expectations, only a few studies were conducted since then into the semi-rigid joint action and its effect on frame stability. As a consequence, there is a lack of background information vital to the development of sensible design criteria and related specifications, which is well reflected in the recently proposed draft of Eurocode 4 (EEC, 1984). Semi-rigid joints are expressly allowed but '... detailed recommendations of this Eurocode are limited to structures with simple, rigid or monolithic joints'. It is then left to the designer to assess 'the effect of joint rotation on the overall structural behaviour ... from the expected moment–rotation characteristics of the joint'. This task appears to be in effect extremely difficult; not only is the present knowledge limited, as already mentioned, but most of it is not readily available, even to researchers.

It is the purpose of this chapter to review in detail the known research into semi-rigid composite joint action. The characteristics of the behaviour of semi-rigid composite joints under monotonic as well as under cyclic loading are highlighted and the key factors affecting joint response identified. Approaches to the prediction of the joint moment–rotation curves either by full numerical analysis or simplified models are also discussed, and eventually an appraisal of the problems related to frame design is presented. Topical areas also requiring further investigation to obtain a better understanding of semi-rigid action in composite frames and to take full advantage of it in practice are identified.

The complexity of the problem makes it necessary that full consistency is achieved through the research studies in order to maximise the scope of their findings. To that purpose it would be extremely useful if a standard definition was agreed for the key parameters describing the joint constitutive law, as well as (on the experimental side) for the testing and reporting procedures. This aspect is also briefly discussed and possible criteria to approach the problem are indicated.

3.2 SEMI-RIGID COMPOSITE JOINTS

The terms rigid and pinned joints refer to ideal models which can be easily defined, whilst the term semi-rigid joint, which applies to the actual joint behaviour, cannot be defined straightforwardly and, more importantly, univocally. In fact, a joint should not in principle be classified *per se* but on the basis of the influence its behaviour has on the response of the whole structure. Such an influence, however, is very dependent upon the frame type, loading and configuration. Therefore the same joint, but in different structures, may be classified in a different category (rigid, semi-rigid, flexible) and different models then adopted in the structural analysis.

The purpose of this chapter requires that some criterion for a broad classification of semi-rigid composite joints is adopted. Following an assumption made, at least implicitly, in most studies of this topic, reference will be made to the steel beam-to-column connection, then distinguishing semi-rigid joints (Fig. 3.2), in which the steel connection is realised with rather simple detailing and the continuity under negative moments is

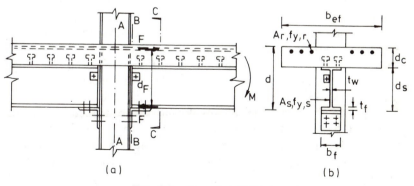

FIG. 3.2. A semi-rigid joint.

basically assured by the concrete slab, from rigid joints, where the steel connection also is able to provide a substantial degree of continuity (Fig. 3.1(a)) to the framework.

However, it should be emphasized that this criterion is adopted only to define the range of joint configurations to appear in this review. It is not intended as a criterion for 'labelling' the joint.

Within this classification the semi-rigid in plane rotational joint action can be schematically modelled, as in Fig. 3.2, by two balanced forces F, the tension action at the reinforcement level and the compression action at the bottom flange level, which give a bending moment of $M = Fd_F$. Although this simple model tends to become less adequate as soon as the steel connection stiffness increases, it is still useful for a basic understanding of the semi-rigid joint behaviour and of the related governing parameters.

3.3 THE JOINT CHARACTERISTIC

3.3.1 Defining the Moment–Rotation Relationship

A complete account of joint behaviour would need to recognise its three-dimensional nature and to include six stress resultants associated with six generalised displacement components. However, the presence in composite frames of a rather stiff continuous floor slab usually allows out-of-plane and torsional deformations of the joint to be neglected. Moreover, with reference to the in-plane behaviour, the rotational flexibility is the most important joint characteristic affecting the global structural response, while investigations (Echeta & Owens, 1981) seem to indicate that the interaction of the various effects may be neglected in practical applications and each may be treated independently. These considerations enable the joint behaviour to be described by its in-plane moment–rotation $(M–\phi)$ characteristic. All the research work has therefore been focused on the determination of such a relationship.

The definition of the two parameters M and ϕ is, however, not straightforward, as also pointed out by the fact that different researchers have reported different quantities for them, implying different assumptions. With the growing interest in semi-rigid composite construction, it seems important that a standard definition is agreed. Such a definition, together with that of standard testing procedures, would allow experimental results to be fully consistent and comparable. Moreover, it would give a common background to the development of methods suitable for the prediction of joint behaviour and to the analysis of semi-rigid composite frames.

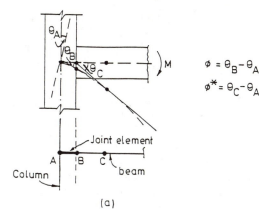

$$\phi = \theta_B - \theta_A$$
$$\phi^* = \theta_C - \theta_A$$

(a)

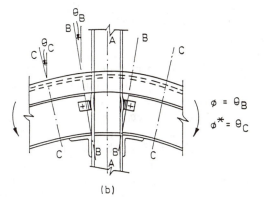

$$\phi = \theta_B$$
$$\phi^* = \theta_C$$

(b)

FIG. 3.3. The joint rotation ϕ: (a) general definition; (b) the symmetrical case.

It would be convenient in effect actually to define the constitutive law of the joint with reference to its incorporation into traditional approaches to frame analysis. The 'joint element' in Fig. 3.3(a) (whatever its actual formulation) should simulate the overall effect of the additional source of flexibility (i.e. besides member deformation) due to the local interaction between the column and the beam(s). This flexibility mainly causes the end cross-section of the beam to rotate with respect to the column. Joint rotation ϕ might hence be properly represented by the change in angle of the tangent to the axis of the beam at its end B relative to the tangent to the column axis at the intersection point A, i.e. $\phi = \theta_B - \theta_A$. In the particular case of an internal column symmetrically loaded (Fig. 3.3(b)) the joint rotation would therefore coincide with the rotation of the end cross-section of the beam, i.e. $\phi = \theta_B$. The compatibility with frame analysis formulations based on the classical beam theory requires that the rotation θ_B is defined assuming that the end cross-section of the beam remains plane in the deformed beam state. In composite members, longitudinal interface slip between the steel beam and the concrete slab arises and a discontinuity in the displacement field along the cross-section is usually present at the steel–concrete interface. Reference should then be made to the sole steel section when determining θ_B. This assumption is consistent with traditional approaches to the analysis of composite structures, and it recognises that the steel connection represents the actual lower bound of joint behaviour.

The above definition of joint rotation implies specific requirements to be met by tests intended to establish the joint characteristic. In particular, if the rotation at a point C along the beam is measured instead of the end beam rotation at B (θ_C in Fig. 3.3), measurements should be taken to single out the contribution to this rotation due to curvature of the beam between B and C.

The value of the bending moment varies along the beam axis. It seems appropriate to refer to the value at the column outer face, which may be considered to govern the joint rotational response. Moreover, this moment is generally used to check the capacity of joint components.

The above definition of the joint characteristic, which presents practical advantages for incorporating joint flexibility in frame analysis, implicitly defines a 'joint zone'. It should be borne in mind that the load-shedding mechanism between the columns and the beams via the joints is quite complex in composite structures. Joint behaviour may hence be substantially affected by a number of factors which 'lie' outside this zone, e.g. by the degree of shear interaction in the composite beam and by the local ductility of the steel section plate components. The moment–rotation characteristic does not therefore depend solely on joint parameters. This fact must be properly recognised when either determining or predicting such a relationship.

3.3.2 Parameters Affecting the Moment–Rotation Behaviour

The moment–rotation relationship of a composite joint is the end product of a complex interaction, between the composite beam(s) and the column, through the steel connection and the concrete slab. A significant number of variables play a role in the development of the joint action and hence affect the M–ϕ curve. The following list attempts to identify the main factors which in principle influence the joint response under negative moment (Fig. 3.2):

(i) Factors affecting the concrete slab action:
— effective width of the concrete slab;
— amount, distribution and yield strength of the steel reinforcement;
— type of shear connection (full or partial) and degree of interaction (complete or partial) with the steel beam section;
— details of the slab 'anchorage' to the column (for joints to external columns);
— type of slab (i.e. solid concrete or with metal decking);
— relative stiffness of the slab to the steel section;
— tensile strength of the concrete.

(ii) Factors affecting the action of the steel connection:
— type of connecting elements (e.g. cleats or endplates);
— size and strength of connecting elements and fasteners;
— connection configuration, and in particular details in the tension zone;
— slippage of bolts.

(iii) Factors affecting the column and steel beam contributions:
— local deformation and strength of the column plate components (load transfer mechanism);
— shear deformation and resistance capacity of the web panel zone;
— presence of column encasement;
— presence of an axial load in the column;
— local plastic deformation of beam components (basically in the lower flange and adjacent part of the web).

(iv) Factors affecting the joint rotation capacity:
— plastic deformation capacity of the reinforcing bars;
— local buckling of the column web;
— local buckling of the beam steel section plate components (bottom flange and web).

Furthermore, the loading conditions and the loading path can have a non-negligible influence and should be considered in a proper assessment of the joint response. The continuity of the slab, for example, might make the joints at the two sides of an internal column interact (Law, 1983; Benussi et al., 1986).

3.3.3 Determining the M–ϕ Curves

Chapter 2 has attempted to highlight the various approaches to the prediction of the behaviour of joints with reference to bare steel connections.

Three types of approaches can be identified: by direct experimental analysis, by full numerical analysis, and by use of simplified models.

Although some research work on this topic has been carried out also for semi-rigid joints in composite structures (and will be presented in Sections 3.4.2 and 3.4.3), interest in this type of joint is recent and, as a consequence, only a few studies have been conducted so far and were mainly aimed at assessing (experimentally) the basic features of the joint response. Therefore the available data are too limited to be considered adequate for a proper calibration of methods of prediction.

The number of variables would in principle suggest numerical approaches, such as the finite element technique, to be the most suitable methods for undertaking comprehensive parametric studies. Present formulations seem, however, not yet capable of accounting in a proper way for both the behaviour of the single joint components and their complex interaction. Results by Leon & Lin (1986) would suggest that a high degree of accuracy is actually not required in the simulation of the response of the steel connection, because the slab action is the most important factor governing joint response. However, the slab behaviour in the uncracked and cracked range, as well as its interaction with the steel beam and the columns, must be adequately simulated.

The basic and most reliable tool available at present to determine the moment–rotation curves is direct experimental analysis. Experimental research is nevertheless a costly approach and may give only a patchy coverage of the problem. The goal should therefore be to achieve an improved understanding of the mechanism of joint action and to build a sufficiently comprehensive set of data against which adequate finite element formulations and simplified models of prediction could be developed and validated. To this aim it is important that testing and reporting procedures are optimised. On the one hand, tests should be designed and measurements taken so that the influence of each governing parameter can be singled out; on the other hand, past experience indicates that the degree of usefulness of a test is maximised if a complete report is provided, which includes (in addition to the moment–rotation curves):

(i)   all the data that would allow, at least in theory, an identical test to be conducted in another laboratory (geometrical and material parameters as well as supporting and loading conditions, loading history, measurement system and location of measurement points etc);

(ii) the records of the deformation and displacement components measured, which would allow the influence of the various factors to be determined;

(iii) the stiffness values and level of moments, which characterise the different phases of the overall joint behaviour (see Fig. 3.8) under loading and unloading.

The research work in this field would hence benefit greatly if international standard testing and reporting procedures were agreed, which give the same type of guidance that is already available for tests on materials or on structural members. This, as previously mentioned with reference to the definition of the M and ϕ variables, would allow the experimental work by different research groups to be fully consistent and directly comparable.

3.4 JOINT BEHAVIOUR UNDER MONOTONIC LOADS

The degree of continuity offered by semi-rigid joints can be expected to be of particular advantage in braced frames. With the present trend towards large spans, the serviceability limit state of deflection tends to govern the beam design in 'simple' frames. Semi-rigid joint action may be seen as a low-cost parameter which allows a better balance to be obtained in design with respect to different limit states; besides the increase in the ultimate resistance of the beam due to the joint moment capacity, the joint stiffness significantly affects the beam elastic response, enabling deflections to be controlled and a most effective use of the material strength to be therefore achieved.

The more immediate interest in the use of semi-rigid joints in braced structures is well reflected by the current state of knowledge, the response of joints to monotonically increasing loads being until very recently the only aspect of joint behaviour to be studied. Most of the investigations were experimental, but a few attempts to simulate the joint characteristic by full numerical analysis and to set up simplified methods of prediction were also carried out.

The relatively small number of studies allows the research work so far conducted to be reviewed in detail. This seems appropriate because the great majority of the work has been reported in conference papers or just in doctoral dissertations and therefore most of the information is not readily available even to researchers.

3.4.1 Experimental Research

3.4.1.1 Main Studies

All the studies had the common aim of investigating the feasibility of achieving an advantageous degree of continuity via composite joints which still maintain a reasonable degree of simplicity in the steel detailing. The single researches were, however, initiated in the context of considerations remarkably different.

Several studies on the behaviour of continuous rigid jointed composite beams pointed out at the end of the 1960s that severe limitations (indeed more restrictive than for bare steel beams) were to be applied to the slenderness ratios of the web and the compression flange in order to guarantee the composite beam a rotation capacity in hogging moment regions adequate to allow the full plastic strength of the member to be developed (Climenhaga & Johnson, 1972; Johnson *et al.*, 1966). This is due partly to the greater moment redistribution needed in a composite beam because of the uneven distribution of strength along the beam and partly to the fact that the presence of the slab reinforcement shifts the plastic neutral axis closer to the upper flange of the steel section and so requires a greater portion of the web to undergo plastic deformation in compression.

As a possible alternative to rigid joints, Barnard (1970) first suggested the use of semi-rigid joints, as a mean to provide a still significant degree of continuity, while substantially reducing the importance of local buckling. This stems from the consideration that the chance of web buckling is practically eliminated (see in Fig. 3.2(a) the basic way semi-rigid joint action is developed), whilst flange buckling might be controlled by a proper selection of steel reinforcement.

An experimental check on the feasibility and validity of such a proposal was then conducted by Johnson & Hope-Gill (1972). The type of joint in Fig. 3.4(a), with two angles located symmetrically about the bottom flange of the steel section, was selected in order to match different requirements: simplicity in detailing, high frictional resistance at the compression side, and capability of stabilising the beam flange. Five specimens were tested with a cruciform configuration (Fig. 3.5(a)) and under symmetrical loading (Fig. 3.6(a)). They were designed on the basis of the simple model of joint action shown in Fig. 3.2. Joint plastic capacity was assumed to be controlled by the yield strength of the reinforcement (i.e. $M_{p,d} = F_y d_F = A_r f_{y,r} d_F$) and specimens details (steel and shear connection, slab transversal reinforcement) designed on the basis of this value. The parameters investigated were the steel section web slenderness (with d_w/t_w ranging from 32·4

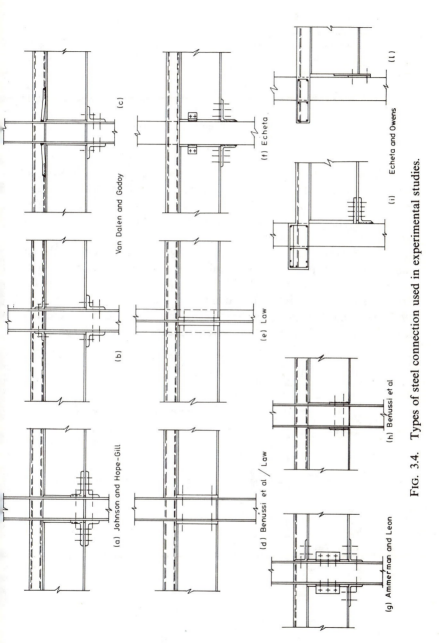

FIG. 3.4. Types of steel connection used in experimental studies.

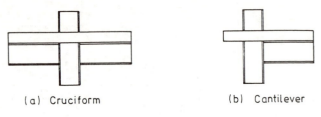

(a) Cruciform   (b) Cantilever

FIG. 3.5.   Specimen configuration.

to 56·4) and the 'force ratio' defined as the ratio $A_r f_{y,r}/A_s f_{y,s}$ between the axial yield strengths of the reinforcement bars and of the overall steel section. The higher this ratio the more critical web buckling in rigid jointed beams was found to be (Climenhaga & Johnson, 1972). Values as high as 0·44 were included in this study.

The results obtained were very satisfactory with reference to all the key components of joint behaviour, i.e. stiffness, strength and rotation capacity. Nevertheless other studies were not performed until the beginning of this decade. The growing interest in composite construction since the early 1980s has enhanced interest in the joint action and its possible effect on the cost effectiveness of the structure. Several researchers worked then on this

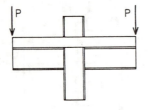

(a) Symmetrical

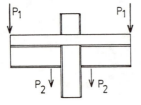

(b) Symmetrical- Variable
     Moment/Shear ratio

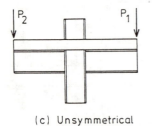

(c) Unsymmetrical

FIG. 3.6.   Loading conditions.

topic in Canada (Van Dalen & Godoy, 1982) and in the United Kingdom (Johnson & Law, 1981; Owens & Echeta, 1981; Echeta, 1982; Law, 1983).

Developments in current practice in these countries influenced the way the problem was approached. Johnson & Hope-Gill (1972) were basically concerned about the rotation capacity in the hogging moment region and considered semi-rigid joints as an alternative to fully rigid connections. As a consequence they designed specimens with a significant slab reinforcement ratio (see Table 3.2). The research work carried out in the 1980s conceived semi-rigid joint action as a factor to be used to 'improve' the cost effectiveness of 'simple' frame construction. The principal aim was therefore to investigate the response of joints with rather simple steel detailing and a moderate amount of steel reinforcement, often not too dissimilar from the one that might be present in any case around the column to control slab cracking.

The two steel connections of Figs 3.4(b) and 3.4(c) were selected by Van Dalen and Godoy (1982) as being typical details for a 'flexible' and 'semi-rigid' connection in practice. The latter would not actually fall in the definition of 'semi-rigid' composite joints given in Section 3.2, a substantial degree of continuity being assured to the steel structure in the tension zone by the presence of the welded plate and of the column web stiffener. The influence of the reinforcement ratio was also checked by adopting two values of ρ for each joint (0·46% and 0·80%), which were considered to bound the range of practical interest. Specimens had again a cruciform arrangement and were tested under symmetrical loading. Supplementary tests on rigidly jointed composite beams as well as on bare steel specimens were conducted in order to single out respectively the influence of the steel connection flexibility and of the concrete slab action on the overall joint behaviour. Slippages developed in the flexible connections at the early stages of the $M-\phi$ characteristic (tests CB1 and CB2 in Fig. 3.10), pointing out the importance, for bolted cleat connections, of controlling this factor. In subsequent tests (CB4 and CB5) the cleats were hence welded to the beam flange.

Endplate connections represent a convenient alternative, which at the same time provides greater restraint to the beam web. Flush endplates were then selected for the tests carried out at Warwick as part of a study on partially restrained frames (Law, 1983). This investigation is the most comprehensive so far conducted as to the number of tests, the range of variables and the amount of measured data. Strains and displacements were in effect monitored in the slab, reinforcing bars and ties as well as in the steel section in order to allow the main features of the joint action to be

singled out. Six cruciform specimens (Figs 3.4(d) and 3.4(e)) were tested for
a total of 12 joints designed to allow the effect of several interesting
parameters to be investigated: (a) distribution of shear connectors (uniform
or bunched away from the column); (b) encasement of the column; (c) axis of
the column the beam is framed to (i.e. major or minor); (d) slab-to-beam
depth ratio; (e) presence of an axial load in the column. In order to simulate
the checkerboard loading conditions, two of the tests were conducted by
applying first the load on one side only (P_1) (Fig. 3.6(c)) and increasing it up to
the attainment of the plastic resistance of the relevant joint. The load P_2 was
then applied and increased while load P_1 was kept constant until P_1 and P_2
were equal. Finally both loads were increased together up to collapse.

The research work at Imperial College (Owens & Echeta, 1981; Echeta,
1982) was basically aimed to check the feasibility of meeting the requirements of a novel plastic design approach (see Section 3.6). Only one of the
specimens had a cruciform arrangement simulating an internal column
(Fig. 3.4(f)) and was subject to symmetrical loads, while four tests were on
cantilever arrangements simulating the external column conditions; these
are the only tests so far conducted on semi-rigid joints to an external
column. Different steel connections (Fig. 3.4(f)(i)(l)) and different details of
the concrete slab behind the column were selected (Fig. 3.12), whilst the
same hoop detailing of Fig. 3.7 was used to anchor the longitudinal
reinforcing bars. Very low slab reinforcement ratios (0·38–0·51%) were
adopted as a consequence of the limited moment capacity required by the
proposed design method. The loading arrangement was as in Fig. 3.6(b).
The relative values of P_1 and P_2 were controlled so that the V/M ratio in
the joint zone was varying, while the moment at the column face was kept

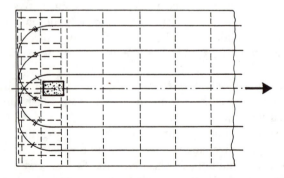

FIG. 3.7. Hoop detailing for anchoring longitudinal reinforcement at an
external column (Echeta, 1982).

constant in order to simulate the changes in the shear/moment ratio when the moment redistribution is occurring in the beam after the joint plastic moment is achieved.

The stiffness and strength observed even for composite joints with simple steel connections suggest that semi-rigid composite action may be sufficient to allow moderate horizontal actions to be sustained by the frame, without the need of bracing systems. In order to check the suitability of semi-rigid composite joints for sway frames, even in regions with low seismicity, a research programme is being carried out at the University of Minneapolis (Leon & Ammerman, 1986; Ammerman & Leon, 1987; Leon, 1987). Most of the experimental work was related to the response to horizontal cyclic forces and it will be reviewed in Section 3.5. Nevertheless, one preliminary test was conducted with monotonically increasing vertical loads. In the same (cruciform) specimen two different steel connections were adopted (Fig. 3.4(g)), to check the influence of the degree of continuity given by the top flange cleat. The selection of the steel connection details was done so that the advantage given in terms of both stiffness and strength by the presence of the slab continuity was easily pointed out by a comparison with already available results on bare steel specimens (Altman *et al.*, 1982). In order to keep the detailing as simple as possible, the column web was not stiffened.

Quite recently a research project has started in Italy (Benussi *et al.*, 1986, 1987) on the behaviour of composite semi-rigid non-sway frames. On the experimental side, four cruciform specimens were tested up to collapse under slightly unsymmetrical loading. On the basis of the results of the previous investigations, endplate connections were considered the most suitable ones in order to ensure proper restraint to the beam web and to avoid bolt slippage. Besides the flush endplate, a connection with a header plate welded to the web in its lower part was also selected (Fig. 3.4(h)), in order to point out the steel connection contribution. Values of ρ slightly higher than in the previous studies (0·71% and 1·21%) were adopted to investigate practical bounds imposed on this parameter by local buckling.

The main characteristics of the tests so far carried out are summarised in Tables 3.1 and 3.2. It can be noted that a fairly limited range of conditions and governing factors is actually covered. A sufficient set of data for an assessment of joint response is achieved only for the cruciform arrangement under symmetrical loading. Besides other shortcomings, symmetrical loading practically washes out the interaction between the concrete slab and the column, which is quite an important and complex factor in composite joint action.

3.4.1.2 Appraisal of Test Results

The experimental M–ϕ characteristics reported in the studies presented in the previous section are plotted in Figs 3.9–3.17. Though non-negligible differences between test results are apparent, a typical M–ϕ relationship can be defined, which is presented in Fig. 3.8, together with the key parameters which describe it.

Three regimes can basically be identified, although in the case of cleated steel connections slippages may arise which affect the M–ϕ curve by introducing a 'slip' plateau. The first, elastic range is characterised by two different values of the stiffness (K_i and K_1) associated respectively with uncracked and cracked slab conditions. Yielding of reinforcing bars, or in the steel connection and members, as well as interface slip and shear lag make the joint enter a second nonlinear inelastic phase. A plastic regime then follows up to the attainment of the ultimate moment capacity M_u.

Moment levels and corresponding rotations can be defined which bound each of these phases (Fig. 3.8). A further parameter should, however, be considered to describe the M–ϕ curve fully, i.e. the unloading stiffness K_{unl}. The importance of this component was overlooked in the past, but recent studies indicate (Nethercot *et al.*, 1987) that the ability to recognise also this aspect in the analysis is vital if frame simulations have to be undertaken.

Single behavioural phases will be dealt with separately in the review of the experimental results, and an attempt will be made to point out the influence the factors investigated have on the key components of the joint response. Most of the tests are reported just in a qualitative way, without any attempt to report the values of the stiffness and strength parameters (even the ultimate capacity in some cases should be deduced from the M–ϕ plots). Moreover, rotations include the effect of bending over a length (variable) of beam (ϕ^* in Fig. 3.3); results hence are not directly comparable. This situation does inevitably affect the following considerations.

(1) Elastic Range

(i) Uncracked conditions. All the joints showed fairly linear elastic behaviour before the development of the first cracks in the concrete slab, which meant generally up to moments about 20–25% of the ultimate moment capacity. Very high values of the initial stiffness were recorded in all cases, also when the steel connection used was rather flexible. The values reported by Ammerman & Leon (1987) are 255 000 kN m/rad for the right connection with a top flange angle and 226 000 kN m/rad without the top

TABLE 3.1
JOINT TESTS: MAIN CHARACTERISTICS

	Johnson & Hope-Gill	Van Dalen & Godoy	Law	Law	Echeta & Owens	Ammerman & Leon	Benussi et al.
Specimens							
Number	5	4	4	2	1 4	1	4
Arrangement[a]	(a)	(a)	(a)	(a)	(a) (b)	(a)	(a)
Loading[b]	(a)	(a)	(a)	(c)	(b) or (a)	(a)	(a)
Column[c]							
Type	WF	WF	WF/EWF	EWF	RHS filled	WF	WF
Axis	S	S	S/W	S	S	S	S
Web stiffener	yes	yes	yes	—	—	no	yes
Beam[d]							
Shear connection[e]	F/UD	F/UD	F/UD and F/C	F/UD	F/UD	F/UD	F/UD
Steel connection[f]	(a)	(b),(c)	(d),(e)	(f)	(i),(l)	(g)	(d),(h)

[a] See Fig. 3.5.
[b] See Fig. 3.6.
[c] WF = wide flange section; E = encased; RHS = rectangular hollow section; S = strong axis; W = weak axis.
[d] All beams do have a solid concrete slab shear connected via stud connectors to a steel section.
[e] F = full shear connection; UD = stud connectors uniformly distributed; C = stud connectors concentrated near the point of contraflexure.
[f] See Fig. 3.4.

TABLE 3.2
JOINT TESTS: GEOMETRICAL AND MECHANICAL CHARACTERISTICS OF SLAB AND STEEL SECTION

Author Specimen	Slab						Steel section			
	b_c (mm)	$\dfrac{b_c}{d_c}$	$\dfrac{d_c}{d_s}$	$f_{y,r}$ (N/mm²)	$\rho(\%)$	ρ_F	Shape	$\dfrac{d_w}{t_w}$	$\dfrac{b_f}{t_f}$	$f_{y,s}$ (N/mm²)
Johnson & Hope-Gill										
HB50	760	9·2	0·40	363	1·42	1·011	203 × 133 UB 25	32·4	16.6	310
HB51	760	8·5	0·29	390	0·84	0·479	305 × 165 UB 40	46·4	16·5	277
HB52	760	8·5	0·29	404	1·78	1·060	305 × 165 UB 40	46·0	16·4	277
HB53	760	8·5	0·29	402	1·97	1·148	305 × 165 UB 40	43·4	17·1	293
HB54	760	8·5	0·22	391	2·01	1·380	406 × 140 UB 39	56·4	17·0	315
Van Dalen & Godoy										
CB1–CB4	1 220	12·0	0·49	483	0·46	0·709	W8 × 20	29·8	14·0	310
CB2–CB5	1 220	12·0	0·49	483	0·80	1·233	W8 × 20	29·8	14·0	310

Echeta & Owens										
1B	1050	14·0	0·29	540	0·51	0·716	254 × 102 UB 28	37·6	10·2	311
2BS	1050	14·0	0·29	415	0·38	0·413	254 × 102 UB 28	37·6	10·2	311
3BS	1050	14·0	0·29	555	0·38	0·369	254 × 102 UB 28	37·6	10·2	460
4BS	1050	14·0	0·29	555	0·38	0·369	254 × 102 UB 28	37·6	10·2	460
5BS	1050	14·0	0·46	550	0·38	0·269	152 × 152 UC 37	17·1	13·4	366
Law										
JX/JY/JC1	1400	11·2	0·28	461	0·72	0·892	457 × 191 UB 67	50·4	14·9	267
JC2	1400	7·0	0·44	461	0·45	0·875	457 × 191 UB 67	50·4	14·9	272
Leon										
SRCC1M	1524	14·9	0·28	435	0·67	0·684	4WF14 × 38	42·2	13·1	293
Benussi et al.										
SJA-10/SJB-10	1000	8·3	0·40	495	0·71	0·912	IPE 300	39·2	14·0	288
SJA-14/SJB-14	1000	8·3	0·40	413	1·21	1·297	IPE 300	39·2	14·0	288

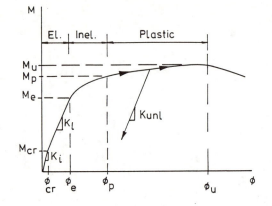

FIG. 3.8.   Typical moment–rotation characteristic.

flange angle (see Fig. 3.4(g)), i.e. approximately ten times the stiffness observed by Altman *et al.* (1982), on a flange and web cleated steel connection identical to the right connection (but without the concrete slab). This clearly indicates that the initial response is, as can be reasonably expected, governed by the axial stiffness in tension of the concrete slab. The contribution of the top flange angle in the right connection then tends to be

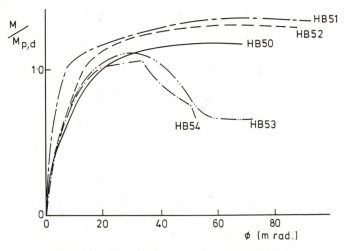

FIG. 3.9.   Tests by Johnson & Hope-Gill (1972).

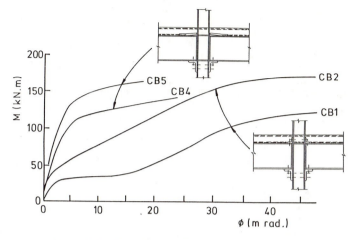

FIG. 3.10. Tests by Van Dalen & Godoy (1982).

modest. Similar indications come from other studies; Benussi *et al.* (1986), for example, found only moderate differences in the initial slope of the $M-\phi$ curves related to the weaker and stronger endplate connection (Fig. 3.17). The steel connection contribution, in order to become significant, requires

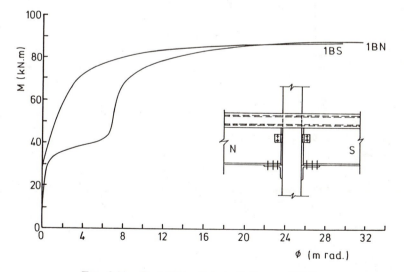

FIG. 3.11. Test 1B by Echeta & Owens (1981).

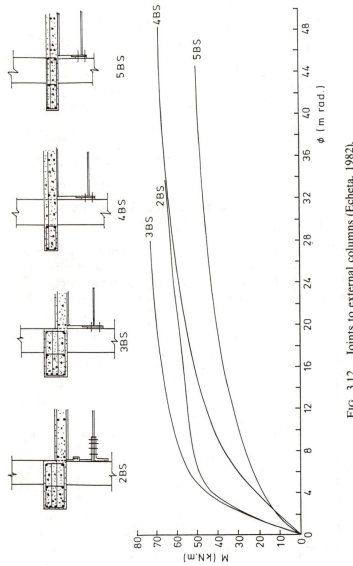

FIG. 3.12. Joints to external columns (Echeta, 1982).

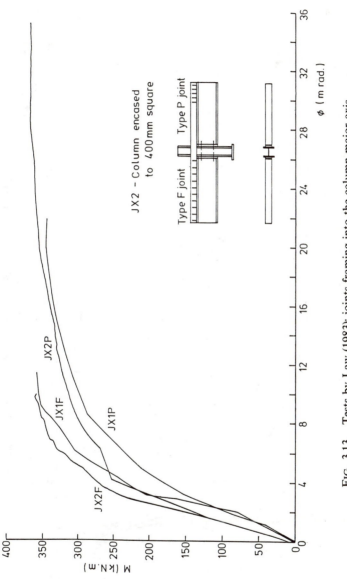

FIG. 3.13. Tests by Law (1983); joints framing into the column major axis.

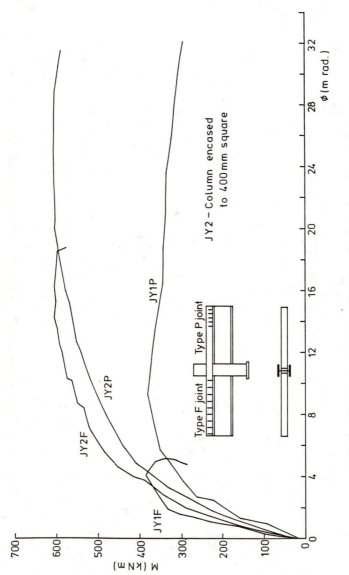

FIG. 3.14.   Tests by Law (1983); joints framing into the column minor axis.

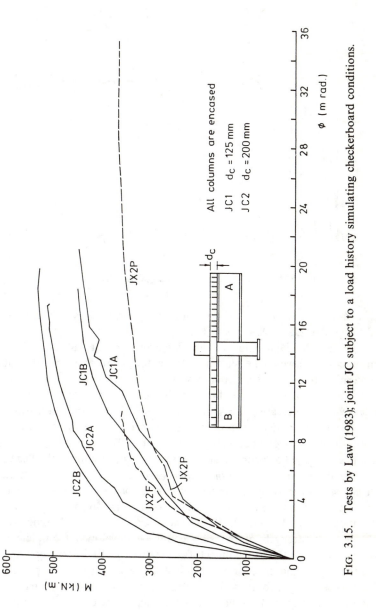

FIG. 3.15. Tests by Law (1983); joint JC subject to a load history simulating checkerboard conditions.

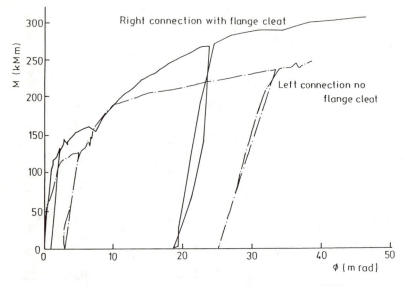

FIG. 3.16.   Test SRCC1M by Ammerman & Leon (1987).

a substantial degree of continuity on the tension side, as in tests CB4 and CB5 by Van Dalen & Godoy (Fig. 3.10).

The factors which influence the effectiveness of the slab action and the interaction between the slab and the column are therefore the factors governing this first elastic uncracked regime: (a) *The distribution of the steel reinforcement*: due to the shear lag in the slab the reinforcing bar effectiveness decreases as its distance from the column increases. This would suggest bunching most of the reinforcement near to the column, within the limits of practicality. Hope-Gill (1974) reported increases of stiffness obtained by concentrating the bars near the column. (b) *The degree of interaction realised by the shear connection, i.e. if the connector layout and behaviour assure complete or partial interaction between the slab and the steel section*: an insight into the problem is given by Law's tests JX and JY (Figs 3.13 and 3.14). The shear connection was designed so that the tension strength of the slab could be developed (complete shear connection), but the stud connectors were distributed differently in the two cantilevers of the cruciform specimens to realise either complete shear interaction (F-type joints with uniformly distributed studs) or partial shear interaction (P-type joints with studs bunched at the end of the cantilever). Although differences in the behaviour of these two types of joints tend to

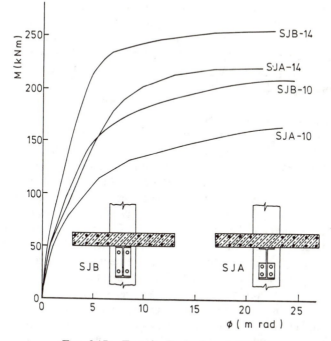

FIG. 3.17. Tests by Benussi *et al.* (1986).

become significant in the latest nonlinear phases, the degree of interaction in the beam affects also the early stages of the response. (c) *The presence of column encasement also has a non-negligible influence, due to the stiffening of the zone around the column, and to the 'support' given to the steel connection, i.e. improving in many instances the beam-to-column interaction:* the tests conducted by Law on encased columns (see Figs 3.13–3.15) confirm the importance of this factor, and in work dealing with joint behaviour prediction, and based mainly on these results, Johnson & Law (1981) suggest that column encasement is sufficient to allow the joint to be assumed to act as 'rigid' up to half of its ultimate strength when a full shear connection with studs distributed uniformly along the beam is adopted. (d) *The way the slab is 'anchored' to the column plays a major role, in particular for joints to external columns:* the results of Echeta plotted in Fig. 3.12 show that joint elastic flexibility can be practically controlled by a proper selection of the details in the anchorage zone. (e) *The presence of moment imbalance at two sides of the column:* because of the continuity of the slab the response of the two joints at an internal column is not fully independent. The JC tests by Law (Fig. 3.15), where the joints were loaded in sequence as described previously, and the tests by Benussi et al., where the moment at the joints was kept slightly different, suggest the more heavily loaded joint (JC1A and JC2A in Fig. 3.15) has a sort of stiffening effect on the less heavily loaded one.

(ii) *Cracked conditions*. Cracks are usually initiated at the column face and rapidly spread to the outer edges of the slab. The crack pattern depends on the type of shear flow in the slab, i.e. on the stiffness of the steel connection (Benussi et al., 1986) and on the distribution of the shear connectors in the beam (Law, 1983). More flexible steel connections and less effective shear connections (e.g. P-type connection in Law's test) lead to almost straight cracks running transversely across the slab. More stiff connections increase the shear lag (Fig. 3.18) and this is reflected in the inclined pattern of the cracks. Results by Van Dalen & Godoy also indicate that increasing the amount of slab reinforcement ensures a more uniform distribution of cracking in the slab. On this basis the same authors suggest a value of the reinforcing ratio of at least 0·8% should be recommended.

When cracking is developed in the region close to the column, the rotational behaviour of the joint enters a second phase. This phase is still fairly linear, though it is characterised by a stiffness (K_1 in Fig. 3.8) substantially lower than the initial uncracked value.

The axial rigidity of the slab is substantially reduced by cracking; nevertheless slab action is a key component of the joint response. The factors already identified for the uncracked phase then continue to have a significant influence on joint behaviour. In particular, the amount and distribution of steel reinforcement constitute a major parameter affecting the stiffness in the cracked phase (see, for example, tests CB4 and CB5 in Fig. 3.10 and tests SJA-10 and SJA-14 in Fig. 3.17). Anyway, the greater slab flexibility allows the steel connection also to contribute to a greater extent. Increases of the average stiffness of about 2–2·5 times were reported by Benussi et al., passing from the header plate (SJA in Fig. 3.17) to the flush endplate connection (SJB). Similar results were reported by Van Dalen & Godoy (Fig. 3.10).

On the other hand, the steel connection may also be the cause of early loss of stiffness. This is typically the case with cleated connections which experienced in most cases bolt slippage even at an early stage of loading. This happened either rather gradually (tests HB50 and HB52 by Johnson & Hope-Gill; Fig. 3.9) or suddenly as in tests CB1 by Van Dalen & Godoy

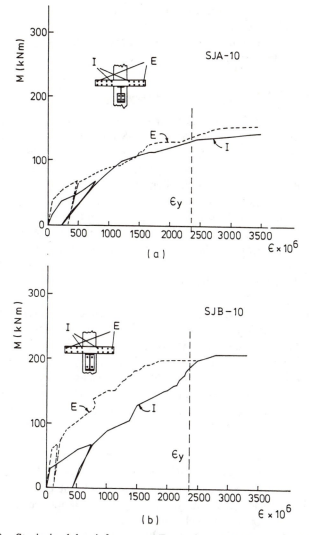

FIG. 3.18. Strain in slab reinforcement (Benussi *et al.*, 1986): (a) flexible header plate connection; (b) semi-rigid flush endplate connection.

(Fig. 3.10), 1BS by Echeta & Owens (Fig. 3.11) and in Leon's test (3.16). The possibility exists of delaying, or even eliminating, this phenomenon through an appropriate design of the connection (see, for example, the additional plate used by Echeta (Fig. 3.4(i)) in test 2BS to improve the frictional resistance of the connection with respect to test 1BS). A reliable control of this event, which is certainly undesirable in the range of service loads, however, might require the use of rather conservative design criteria for the HSFG bolts, due to the uncertainty in the prediction of the friction factor.

(2) Inelastic Range

Nonlinearity is generally developed in composite joints, due to numerous sources and of different nature. A general distinction can be made between nonlinearities inherent in the material behaviour (e.g. yielding of reinforcing bars, steel members, connecting elements and fasteners, increase in size and extension of cracks in either the concrete slab or the column encasement), nonlinearities caused by inelastic phenomena (e.g. slippages at the beam-to-column steel connection or, along the beam, between the slab and steel section), and nonlinearities due to changes in the mode of action of different components (e.g. changing of the contact zones in endplated connections, decrease in the shear lag due to slab cracking, etc). Moreover, mechanical imperfections, such as locked in residual stresses due to the fabrication process, which affect both the onset and the spreading of yielding in the steel section, may also play a major role.

As a consequence, the extent of the inelastic range as well as the rate of the stiffness deterioration are quite variable. Besides, the available data are not sufficient to enable any evaluation of the contribution of each source to be conducted. It is, however, of interest to note that the degree of shear interaction in the composite beam has an increasing influence and might become a major factor governing joint response in this phase, as clearly indicated by Law's tests (Figs. 3.13 and 3.14).

(3) Plastic Range

Though a value for the joint plastic moment M_p has never been reported, an evaluation of the $M-\phi$ curves indicates that the onset of the plastic phase ranged from 75% to 90% of the ultimate moment capacity. It was the result of significant yielding of one of the key joint components, i.e. of the reinforcing bars or of the steel section lower flange.

It should be pointed out that in the tests conducted so far the column contribution to both the stiffness and the strength of the joint had little, if any, importance. With reference to the joint plastic resistance, the loading conditions (mainly symmetrical) and the presence of web stiffeners in bare H-sections or of concrete encasement (Law) or infill (Echeta) were practically preventing the column web failure in shear and in compression. Column stiffeners are, however, costly details and the tendency in practice is to omit them. The column web then becomes very likely the weakest component of the joint and governs its plastic resistance, as evidenced experimentally by Law's test JX1. This joint was in fact first tested without column web stiffeners, and yielding (and subsequent buckling) of the web was observed at an applied moment of about 200 kN m, i.e. only 55% of the moment capacity achieved by the same joint when re-tested with stiffeners welded on.

After the plastic moment was achieved, most joints sustained further increases of moments as a consequence of strain hardening of the yielded reinforcement bars and the possible contribution of the steel connection, which tends to develop its inherent strength for relatively high rotations. Besides the unevenness in the steel bars strain distribution tends to reduce substantially, and the bars farther from the column increasingly contribute to the slab force. The measurements of the strains in the rebars showed in all cases that the bars all yielded at the attainment of the ultimate moment capacity (Fig. 3.18), even when the width/thickness ratio of the slab (b_c/d_c in Table 3.2) was as high as 14·9 (test SRCC1M by Leon). These results then confirm the significant shear transfer ability of the slab in hogging moment regions, already observed in tests on continuous beams with rigid joints (Johnson, 1975).

Besides these general considerations, the available results make possible a first evaluation of some factors, such as presence of column encasement, degree of shear interaction and contribution of the steel connection.

The presence of column encasement, unlike that of stiffness, seems to have a substantial influence only for the joints framing into the column minor axis. Test JY2 (Fig. 3.14) exhibited an ultimate moment capacity 55% higher than that of test JY1 with a bare steel column, whilst maximum strengths of joints JX1 and JX2 to the column major axis were practically the same (Fig. 3.13). The thickness of the encasement at the outer face of the column flange is modest in effect when compared with the same thickness at the web sides. In major axis joints then the concrete cover undergoes severe cracking under increasing loads, which make its effectiveness almost vanish.

A comparison of the $M-\phi$ relationships obtained by Law for the F-type and P-type joints (Figs 3.13 and 3.14) stresses again the fact that the degree of interaction is a major factor governing joint flexibility. In both cases, however, the number of stud connectors was equal and was selected so that a full shear connection was realised. They then attained almost the same ultimate moment of resistance, though separation between the slab and the steel beam occurred in the vicinity of the P-joints at the final stage, confirming that slip and shear lag have a small influence on the joint strength if a full connection is provided in the hogging region of the beam.

A semi-rigid steel connection is always somewhat flexible and tends to develop a significant part of its resistance at rather high rotations, i.e. for values of rotation for which the composite joint already entered its plastic phase. Test results seem, however, to indicate that the rotation capacity of the joint is usually sufficient to make the steel connection contribute nearly its whole moment capacity, even when flexible connections were used, as the top and seat cleated connection in CB1 and CB2 tests by Van Dalen & Godoy (Fig. 3.10).

Table 3.3 presents the moment and rotation capacity as well as the mode of failure observed. Useful comparisons with the plastic moment of resistance of both the steel section and the composite beam are also included.

The joints in general exhibited a remarkable strength. Values of the ultimate moment capacity up to 1·72 of the plastic moment $M_{p,s}$ of the steel section, and 1·15 of the plastic moment $M_{p,c}$ of the composite beam were attained. Besides, rather low reinforcement ratios (of about 0·5%) may be sufficient for the joint to develop a moment of resistance of the order of, or even greater than, the plastic moment of the steel section (see results by Van Dalen & Godoy, Echeta & Owens, and Law). This is partly the result of the favourable internal lever arm of semi-rigid composite action, which therefore tends to become more effective as the ratio between depths of the slab and the steel beam increases (d_c/d_s in Table 3.2).

Within the same joint geometry an appropriate choice of the reinforcement area (A_r) and yield strength ($f_{y,r}$) and/or of the steel connection details allows a significant range of strength to be covered. The former factor is certainly the most effective. The amount, or better the strength, of the reinforcing bars is, however, bounded by the local buckling strength of the steel sections (i.e. the column web or the beam flange). Benussi et al. report ultimate moment capacities ranging from 165 to 261 kN m, passing from a joint with $\rho = 0\cdot71\%$ and a header plate connection (test SJA-10) to a joint with $\rho = 1\cdot21\%$ and a flush endplate connection (test SJB-14). Buckling of the beam flange detected at the end of this last test suggests that no further increases could be obtained.

The advantages given by semi-rigid action can only be fully exploited if the beams are designed plastically (Anderson et al., 1987; Van Douwen, 1981). As the joint strength is always lower in composite structures than the positive plastic moment of the composite beam, the use of plastic design requires the joint to possess 'adequate ductility'. In order to determine the ductility of a joint, its plastic moment should be defined and the

TABLE 3.3
JOINT TESTS: MOMENT AND ROTATION CAPACITY[a]

Author Specimen	Beam				Joint				
	$M_{p,s}$	$M_{p,c}^-$	$M_{p,d}$	M_u	$\dfrac{M_u}{M_{p,d}}$	$\dfrac{M_u}{M_{p,s}}$	$\dfrac{M_u}{M_{p,c}^-}$	ϕ_u^b	Fail[c]
Johnson & Hope-Gill									
HB50	81	120	86	101	1·17	1·24	0·84	>60	B
HB51	187	226	78	105	1·35	0·56	0·47	>70	A
HB52	184	249	171	222	1·30	1·21	0·89	>65	A
HB53	175	285	229	254	1·11	1·45	0·89	30	C
HB54	225	339	286	303	1·06	1·35	0·89	33	D
Van Dalen & Godoy									
CB1	95	123	70	120	1·71	1·26	0·98	47	A
CB2	95	142	127	163	1·28	1·72	1·15	36	A
CB4	95	123	70	138	1·97	1·45	1·12	22	A
CB5	95	142	127	162	1·28	1·71	1·14	14	A
Echeta									
1B	105	139	68	111	1·63	1·06	0·80	>32	A
2BS	105	126	39	65	1·67	0·62	0·52	>34	F
3BS	157	185	52	72	1·38	0·46	0·39	>30	A
4BS	157	185	52	68	1·31	0·43	0·37	>50	G
5BS	110	130	35	50	1·43	0·45	0·38	>45	A
Law[d]									
JX1	409	541	295	354	1·21	0·87	0·66	24	A
JX2	409	541	295	370	1·25	0·90	0·68	35	A
JY1	409	541	295	384	1·30	0·94	0·71	10	A
JY2	409	541	295	600	2·03	1·47	1·11	88	D
JC1	411	541	295	449	1·52	1·10	0·83	19	F
JC2	411	564	317	530	1·67	1·30	0·94	18	F
Ammerman & Leon									
SRCC1ML	295	392	190	235	1·24	0·80	0·60	39	A
SRCC1MR	295	392	190	305	1·61	1·03	0·78	47	E
Benussi et al.									
SJA-10	181	248	156	165	1·06	0·91	0·67	>21	A
-14	181	273	227	221	0·97	1·22	0·81	>23	A
SJB-10	181	248	156	208	1·33	1·15	0·84	>22	A
-14	181	273	227	261	1·15	1·44	0·96	24	D

[a]Moments in kN m; rotations in mrad.
[b]Includes also the contribution of a length of the beam (ϕ^* in Fig. 3.3).
[c]Failure modes: (A) test terminated for excessive joint deformation; (B) failure of the shear connectors; (C) fracture of the slab in shear; (D) local buckling of the steel beam (flange and/or web); (E) shear fracture of the bolts connecting the bottom cleat and the beam flange; (F) fracture of the slab reinforcement; (G) crushing of the slab against the column.
[d]Rotations for tests JX and JY refer to the P-joints.

moment–rotation curve should be known through all the range including the post-ultimate unloading branch (Johnson, 1975; Kemp, 1988). Moreover, the rotation capacity required of the joint depends upon the frame configuration and loading. A quantitative assessment of semi-rigid joint ductility, and of its adequacy, is therefore not feasible simply on the basis of the available data. However, the joints tested in general showed a fairly high rotation capacity (ϕ_u in Table 3.3), which the limited checks conducted (Bridge *et al.*, 1981; Benussi *et al.*, 1987) indicate as sufficient to meet in many instances the structural requirements at the plastic ultimate limit state.

Care should be taken to prevent brittle behaviour in the composite beam region adjacent to the joint due to secondary failures in the slab (such as failure of the shear connectors and longitudinal shear fracture of the slab) and to local buckling. The problem then arises of the prediction of the moment capacity of the joint on which the design of the slab detailing should be based. The value $M_{p,d} = A_r f_{y,r} d_F$ determined by adopting the simple scheme shown in Fig. 3.2 for the joint action was used by several researchers in the past. Although it gives a good approximation of the joint plastic resistance, at least for joints with very flexible steel connections (Fig. 3.9), it may represent a too conservative assessment of the joint ultimate strength (see the ratio $M_u/M_{p,d}$ for the tests of Johnson & Hope-Gill and of Echeta & Owens), mainly because of the significant contribution of the rebars strain hardening. This should be borne in mind to avoid failures, such as the one observed in test HB53 by Johnson & Hope-Gill where transverse reinforcement was designed with reference to $M_{p,d}$.

As to local buckling, the results indicate that less severe rules than for rigid joints can be adopted to prevent it. In particular, they confirm that the more favourable way the joint develops its strength tends substantially to reduce the importance of web buckling. Hence flange instability becomes the critical factor on which attention should be focused. In most of the known tests, however, this element can be classified as plastic, also under Eurocode 4. Little information can therefore be deduced about the actual local slenderness requirements to be met in semi-rigid joints.

The ratio ρ_F between the yield strengths of the reinforcing bars and the bottom beam flange, i.e. $\rho_F = A_r f_{y,r}/A_f f_{y,s}$, may be appropriate in design to control beam local buckling. The value of this ratio (a sort of 'semi-rigid force ratio') in the tests is reported in Table 3.2. A possible design criterion might be bounding ρ_F to be lower than 1. This would allow the use of more slender sections (e.g. compact sections) in plastic beam design, whilst joint ductility would be reliably provided by the plastic deformation of the reinforcement. The results by Johnson & Hope-Gill suggest that this criterion might, however, be rather conservative, and that values of ratio ρ_F greater than 1 might be acceptable also when the steel flange is compact (under Eurocode 4).

3.4.1.3 Concluding Remarks

The set of experimental data available has already pointed out that semi-rigid composite joints can be designed to possess high elastic stiffness, remarkable ultimate moment of resistance and substantial rotation capacity. Moreover, they show that these characteristics may be achieved at a rather low additional cost, with respect to simple construction, maintaining very simple details of the steel connection and just increasing the amount of slab reinforcement around the column. Stiffer steel connections can give further advantage by increasing the elastic stiffness after the slab has cracked and hence the joint effectiveness under service loads. Furthermore, semi-rigid composite action develops basically in a simple way, which makes rather easy the control of the parameters affecting joint strength and ductility.

A better understanding of the role played by some factors should, however, be achieved, with particular reference to the following:

(i) *Joint–column interaction:* the mechanism of interaction between the beams and the columns via the concrete slab and the steel connections is very complex and it has not been adequately studied. Even though this factor is of interest also for joints at internal columns, where moment transfer is likely to happen caused by uneven spans and for loading conditions, it becomes of paramount importance for joints framing to external columns. The limited number of tests so far conducted on this type of joint pointed out unexpected aspects of such a mechanism, related in particular to the slab–column interaction along the column sides. Echeta's test 4BS failed by crushing of the concrete on the lateral faces of the hollow column section. This led the same author to define an 'anchorage zone' in the slab which includes column depth (see details of test 5BS in Fig. 3.12 and design scheme in Fig. 3.19). Leon, in a cyclic test on a whole frame, which will be discussed in Section 3.5, found a non-negligible capacity of the slab to transfer force via the concrete located inside the column flanges of an H-section.

(ii) *The moment gradient and interaction between moment and shear force:* the tests by Echeta & Owens, which included the shear/moment ratio as a parameter (see Section 3.4.1.1 and Fig. 3.6), did not point out any noticeable effect of moment gradient. The joints tested cannot, however, be

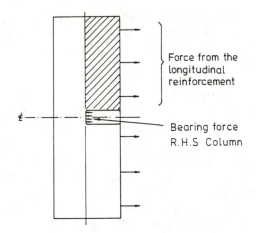

FIG. 3.19.   Scheme for the design of the anchoring zone of the slab to an external column (Echeta, 1982).

considered conclusive due to the very low moments of resistance (see Table 3.3). In joints with strength comparable with the plastic moment of the beam, the moment–shear interaction might also become significant. Attention should also be drawn to the shear flow when the steel connection does not restrain the web (see connections used by Johnson & Hope-Gill, Echeta & Owens, Benussi *et al.*); it tends in fact to subject the beam web to vertical compression, triggering off web buckling (test HB54 by Johnson & Hope-Gill).

(iii) *Local buckling:* adequate design criteria to prevent local buckling in both the beam and the column section have to be defined which avoid undue conservatism in the member sections. Ductility requirements to be met by plate components should hence be determined. To that purpose the way compressive forces are transmitted from the beam to the column should also be properly assessed as a function of the different connection arrangements. Some tests (Johnson & Hope-Gill, Van Dalen & Godoy) indicate the ability of bottom cleats to restrain locally the beam flange, which should also be further investigated.

(iv) *Longitudinal shear connection:* flexibility and strength of the connectors, as well as their distribution, are important factors requiring a systematic study. The P-type joints tested by Law, where practically there was no interaction in the vicinity of the column, represent a lower bound condition for full shear connections, while all other tests used stud connectors uniformly spaced, practically realising a complete shear interaction.

(v) *The loading sequence:* it has already been noted that the continuity of the slab makes the behaviour of the joints located at the two sides of a column not completely independent. Results by Benussi *et al.* pointed out that this interrelation increases with the flexibility of the steel connection. Moreover, Law reports that loading sequence influences substantially the stress state in the slab around the column. Besides other effects, this might imply high strain hardening in the rebars which affects the joint moment capacity (compare in Fig. 3.15 test JCA and JX2). Finally, a proper selection of loading sequence makes possible the contribution of column web panel shear deformation to be investigated, which might be a significant component of joint flexibility in the presence of unbalanced moments.

More generally, the fact that joint behaviour in composite structures depends also upon the beam behaviour raises the fundamental question of the inherent limits of joint tests and points out the need for experimental research on limited and full scale frames.

3.4.2 Numerical Analysis

Although experimental analysis is essential to establish the fundamental background, against which all theoretical approaches should be validated, it has by its very nature a limited scope. The necessary parametric investigations are made possible only by numerical simulation which, besides, allows the influence of each factor to be singled out.

The difficulties to be overcome when developing numerical formulations capable of predicting the behaviour of bare steel connections have already been discussed in Chapter 2. As a further requirement, the simulation of joint action in composite frames should properly model the behaviour of the concrete slab under tension, as well as the mechanism by which it sheds force into the steel beam and the column. The lack of sufficient experimental data, enabling a full understanding of the slab–beam–column interactive behaviour in the presence of flexible steel connections, has in fact hampered the development of comprehensive numerical formulations.

The research work so far conducted (Echeta, 1982; Leon & Lin, 1986) neglected slab–column interaction, concentrating on the particular condition typical of two-way joints subject to symmetrical loading, as in Fig. 3.6(a). Moreover, crude models were adopted for the concrete behaviour in tension (i.e. no resistance model) and for the shear lag in the slab (disregarded by Echeta and accounted for by the selection of equivalent 'effective' areas of the reinforcing bars by Leon & Lin).

Echeta used a finite difference formulation, and modelled the steel connection merely by displacement boundary conditions, while on the other hand the model of the composite beam allowed the shear connector flexibility as well as material and geometrical nonlinearities and initial imperfections to be taken into account. A comparison with the experimental $M-\phi$ curves obtained by the same author indicates the need for a further refinement. Discrepancies are suggested to be related to (a) the slip between the slab and the beam being overestimated (e.g. resistance to longitudinal shear by interface steel–concrete friction was ignored) and (b) the tensile resistance of the concrete on the one hand and the flexibility of the beam anchoring the slab to the column on the other being neglected. The crude way of modelling the steel connection can also be considered an additional possible cause.

Leon & Lin approached the problem by using the finite element technique, via the general purpose program ADINA (1981). They analysed a joint tested by the first author (the right joint in Fig. 3.4(g)) with flange and web cleats (i.e. test SRCC1MR in Fig. 3.16). A two-step procedure was adopted. First, three-dimensional finite element models were developed for the behaviour of angle cleat segments subject to either a tension or a compression force acting along one leg, which included the effect of slip due to the bolt–hole clearance. Multilinear stress–strain constitutive laws

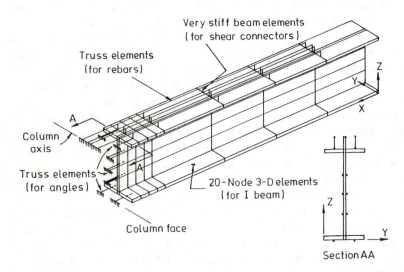

FIG. 3.20.   Finite element mesh for the joint and the beam (Leon & Lin, 1986).

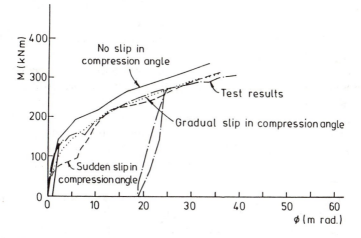

FIG. 3.21. Comparison between test results and numerical M–ϕ curves for different slip models (Leon & Lin, 1986).

were then determined via this component model for the equivalent truss elements used, in the model of the overall system (joint and beam) shown in Fig. 3.20, to simulate the steel connection. The contributions due to deformation of the bolts and of the column components, as well as to the shear connectors flexibility, were neglected; nonetheless, comparison with the experimental M–ϕ curve (Fig. 3.21) showed fairly close agreement. Although a wider validation is necessary, the procedure adopted seems correct and the formulation used adequate. The results in Fig. 3.21 indicate a great sensitivity to the slip in the steel connection, suggesting that a proper assessment of this factor is a preliminary to any simulation of the behaviour of composite joints with bolted connections. It is interesting, however, to note that the same approach was used to simulate tests by Altman *et al.* (1982) on bare steel cleated connections, and the agreement was less satisfactory. This suggests that high accuracy might not be actually required in the model of the steel connection, slab action being the governing factor. On the other side, it stresses the necessity of developing comprehensive formulations allowing slab action and slab–column inter-action to be accurately modelled before any systematic studies into semi-rigid composite joints may be undertaken.

3.4.3 Prediction by Simplified Models
Both experimental and numerical analysis are basically research tools,

although in some cases the importance of the structure may justify their use in design. Simplified methods to approximate at least the key components of the rotational response of the joint should be available, in a form suitable for everyday design practice.

The substantial research being carried out for semi-rigid steel connections was reviewed in Chapter 2, where different approaches to the problem were also identified.

Semi-rigid composite joints have, so far, received limited attention. Semi-rigid composite joints were, and in some instances still are, a quite new 'world' to be explored. The first studies had to concentrate just on the appraisal of the main characteristics of semi-rigid action, as a preliminary step to evaluate their possible structural effectiveness. Furthermore, the number of parameters governing the joint response and the interaction with the beam behaviour make the development of a prediction method quite a complex problem, for which the solution requires a level of understanding, not yet achieved, of the way joint action is developing, as is clear from the previous review of the experimental and numerical work.

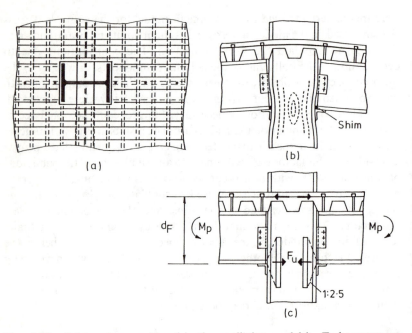

FIG. 3.22.   Joint action considered in the prediction model by Tschemmernegg
(SZS, 1987).

In the framework of the studies conducted by Tschemmernegg and his associates (1988) to set up mechanical models of steel connections (see Chapter 2), the particular composite joint of Fig. 3.22 has also been considered, and a simple model for the prediction of the key stiffness and strength parameters included in a recent document on design of semi-rigid frames published by the Swiss Centre for Steel Construction (SZS, 1987). The two-way node is subject to balanced moments and the slab arranged with a hole around the column (Fig. 3.22(a)) so that the beam–column interaction is developing only via the steel web cleated connections. Shims are used at the bottom cleat (Fig. 3.22(b)) to prevent slip. The column web is unstiffened and it is assumed to be the component actually governing overall joint behaviour, i.e. the initial stiffness, the ultimate moment capacity and the rotation capacity. This allows the composite joint to be dealt with by means of a mechanical model almost identical to that set up for bare steel welded connections (see Fig. 2.16(b) of Chapter 2). The behavioural models of column web already developed and calibrated (Tschemmernegg, 1988) to determine the load–deflection characteristic of the springs simulating the load introduction effect may then be used (see for example Fig. 3.22(c) for the determination of the spring ultimate buckling resistance F_u).

This approach therefore concentrates fully on the column side and assumes that the contribution to the joint response by the steel connection as well as the effect of interface slip between steel and concrete and shear lag in the composite beam are negligible. Although no reference is given to the validation of the model, it may in effect be expected that these parameters do have a modest influence, when the joint is designed to have the column web as the critical component, and full shear connections are adopted in the beams. If the column web on the contrary is stiffened, its deformation under symmetrical loading can be neglected. Attention should then concentrate on the sources of flexibility which lie outside the column, as in the approach by Johnson & Law (1981), which can therefore be considered as 'complementary' to Tschemmernegg's work.

The method of prediction is based on a trilinear representation of the M–ϕ curve (Fig. 3.23(b)) and makes use of simplified analytical and behavioural models to determine the elastic stiffness K_1 and the plastic moment capacity of the joint M_p.

The contributions of the slab action and the steel connection are both taken into account. The respective shares of the applied moment resisted by the slab and the steel connection are dependent upon the degree of shear connection in the composite beam. Interface slip may then affect substan-

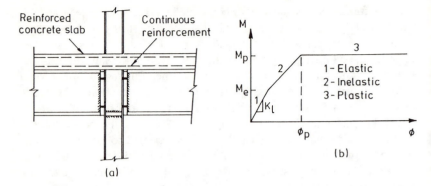

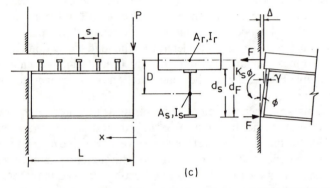

FIG. 3.23. Prediction of the joint characteristic by Johnson & Law (1981): (a) the joint; (b) the trilinear representation; (c) the model for determining the elastic stiffness.

tially the response of the joint, from an early stage, as already discussed (Section 3.4.1.2). To account properly for this factor, the beam (or at least the part under negative moment) should be included in the analytical model.

Johnson & Law therefore determined the elastic stiffness of the joint by elastic partial interaction analysis of the cantilever in Fig. 3.23(c), under the assumption that the end cross-section of the steel beam rotates about its bottom edge (which lies on a rigid support). They adopt the theory developed by Newmark *et al.* (1951) and hence neglect the tensile resistance of the concrete and the shear lag effect. Within this approach, the general solution for the axial force F in the slab gives

$$F = C_0 \sinh \sqrt{R}x + C_1 \cosh \sqrt{R}x + PQx/R \tag{3.1}$$

where (see Fig. 3.23(c)) k is the short-term stiffness of a stud connector, γ is the interface slip, and

$$R = k\overline{EI}/(s\overline{EA}\Sigma EI)$$
$$Q = kD/(s\Sigma EI)$$
$$\overline{EA} = 1/(1/EA_r + 1/EA_s)$$
$$\overline{EI} = \Sigma EI + \overline{EA}D^2$$
$$\Sigma EI = EI_r + EI_s$$

Let K_s indicate the (known) stiffness of the steel connection; equilibrium and compatibility conditions at the column face $(x = L)$ are then respectively

$$PL = M = Fd_F + K_s\phi \tag{3.2}$$

$$\phi d_s = \Delta d_s/d_F + \gamma \tag{3.3}$$

while the equilibrium at $x = 0$ imposes $F = 0$, which results in $C_1 = 0$. The slip is linked to the derivative of F along x and then may be written from eqn (3.1) as

$$\gamma = s(C_0\sqrt{R} \cosh \sqrt{R}L + QP/R)/k \tag{3.4}$$

Equations (3.2)–(3.4) allow one to define C_0, and finally the joint rotation is determined as

$$\phi = \frac{M}{K_s}\left(1 - \frac{Qd_F}{R}\right) - \frac{C_0 d_F \sinh \sqrt{R}L}{K_s} \tag{3.5}$$

Equation (3.5) assumes that the shear connection is continuous along the length of the beam. It does not hold when joints have not uniformly distributed connectors as in Law's P-type joints. Similar relations can, however, be obtained for this case by appropriate methods of analysis.

In order to apply eqn. (3.5), the elastic stiffness K_s of the steel connection needs to be known. With reference to the joints tested by Law (Fig. 3.4(d)), which used flush endplate connections, a method was set up by the authors (presented in detail in Chapter 2) which uses behavioural models to determine the contribution to the connection flexibility of each component

108   R. ZANDONINI

(i.e. endplate, bolts and column flange). The overall connection flexibility is
then obtained by superimposing the effect of each contribution.

On the strength side, the ultimate capacity of the joint is determined
simply by adding the moment capacity of the steel connection $M_{p,s}$ to the
moment of resistance given by the yield strength of the rebars, i.e.

$$M_p = M_{p,s} + A_r f_{y,r} d_F$$

The elastic stiffness and the plastic moment do not completely define the
trilinear $M-\phi$ characteristic; knowledge of the elastic limit moment M_e and
of the value of the rotation ϕ_p at the onset of the plastic regime is also
required. The authors indicate values of M_e and ϕ_p (i.e. $M_e = 0.5M_p$ and
$\phi_p = 10$ mrad for F-type joints and $\phi_p = 20$ mrad for P-type joints) deduced
from the tests conducted by Law (1983) and by Johnson & Hope-Gill (1972)
and used them when checking the accuracy of the method, but do not
provide any general procedure for their determination.

The comparison between the theoretical and experimental results is
presented in Fig. 3.24 for the test JX1. The agreement of the elastic stiffness
and plastic moment capacity was found to be good, and the discrepancies
mainly attributable to the trilinear representation adopted.

The available test data (Figs 3.9–3.17) would indicate that quite different
values of M_e and ϕ_p should be assumed depending on the different joint

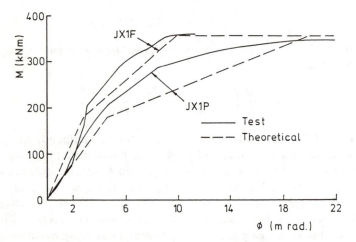

FIG. 3.24. Comparison by Johnson & Law (1981); prediction and experimental
results of test JX1 by Law (1983).

characteristics, even when the steel connection is a flush endplate connection (Fig. 3.17). It should therefore be remarked that, although a further check, against the test results by Johnson & Hope-Gill, confirmed the basic validity of the approach, its actual applicability seems to depend on the development of simple criteria for the computation of such variables.

Moreover, the scope of the method is limited; sources of flexibility due to deformation of the column and of the slab in the joint zone as well as of the system anchoring the slab to the column (important factors in joints to external columns) are ignored, which may contribute significantly to joint behaviour.

More comprehensive methods need to be developed. It should anyway be borne in mind that joint behaviour is not important *per se* but because it influences the overall performance of the frame. Studies of the behaviour of semi-rigid frames should hence be conducted in order to assess the accuracy requirements to be met by a prediction method.

3.5 BEHAVIOUR UNDER CYCLIC LOADS

The incremental analysis of semi-rigid braced steel frames (Nethercot *et al.*, 1987) pointed out that unloading and reloading may take place at the joints, even though the frame is subject to increasing loads. The ability to approximate all the components of the joint behaviour is therefore important if a numerical simulation of the response of a braced frame is undertaken. This becomes vital in the case of unbraced frames where wind loads may cause the joint to experience full load cycles, and obviously even more important if the frame is subject to seismic forces.

The studies related to the performance under monotonic loads showed that semi-rigid composite joints do possess stiffness, strength and rotation capacity at a level which makes them, potentially, an adequate solution also for unbraced frames, at least in the case of low-rise buildings. This possibility, and consequently the cyclic behaviour of composite semi-rigid joints, has received practically no attention until very recently when Leon and his associates (Leon, 1987) started a research project into this topic, to which the monotonic test already presented represents a preliminary and supplementary part.

Three cyclic tests have so far been carried out: two on specimens with a cruciform arrangement (Fig. 3.5(a)) and one on a complete two-bay limited frame (Fig. 3.27).

The first joint test (Ammerman & Leon, 1987) was conducted on

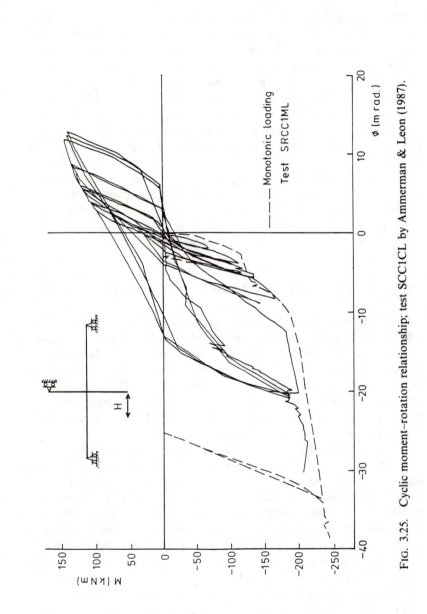

FIG. 3.25. Cyclic moment–rotation relationship; test SCC1CL by Ammerman & Leon (1987).

a specimen identical to the one tested under monotonic loads (SRCC1M in Section 3.4.2), but both steel connections were without the top flange cleat (i.e. equal to the left connection in test SRCC1M). A horizontal load H was applied quasi-statically at the bottom end of the column as schematically illustrated in Fig. 3.25. The deflection, v, at the bottom end of the column was then used to control the amplitude of the load cycles. In each cycle a predetermined value of this deflection was achieved. Two cycles were performed for each value, except for the maximum deflection attained, for which three cycles were performed to check the possible tendency towards incremental damage. The moment–rotation curve obtained for the right connection is presented in Fig. 3.25, which was eventually brought to collapse under gradually increasing load.

The joints showed a modest nonlinearity for displacements up to values corresponding to a storey drift equal to 0·68%; as v increased further, the hysteresis increased and the loops assumed the typical pinched form in Fig. 3.26. Pinching is mainly due to the presence of cracks in the slab and of significant plastic deformations in the bottom cleat. Even though the joint is completely unloaded, the cracks in the slab are still open (if the previous moment was negative, point 1) or the cleat is still pulled away from the column face (previous moment positive, point 2). Therefore, if the load is reversed, the joint initially exhibits a very low stiffness, until the crack is closed or the cleat comes into contact (points 1′ and 2′).

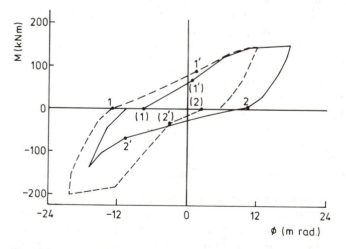

FIG. 3.26. Typical hysteresis loops (Ammerman & Leon, 1987).

The plastic strength of the joint is controlled essentially by the yield strength respectively of the reinforcement bars for negative moments and of the bottom flange cleat for positive moments, which causes a significant dissymmetry. This dissymmetry does not imply the response is dependent upon the loading history (i.e. upon the sign of the moment which first makes the joint undergo inelasticity); the $M-\phi$ curves obtained for the joints at the two sides of the column agree closely.

The envelope of the moment–rotation curve of the connection tested to failure compared very closely to the one determined in the monotonic loading test (Fig. 3.25), indicating that cyclic loading had a limited influence on key joint properties. Finally, there was no sign of increase of damage in the subsequent cycles at the same deflection v.

Joint tests in a cruciform arrangement cannot simulate the actual stress state history in a complete frame, where moment gradient, points of contraflexure and moment/shear ratio are varying during loading, depending on the vertical–lateral loads ratio. The two-bay limited frame shown in Fig. 3.27 (Leon, 1987) was then tested under combined gravity and lateral loads. At the external columns the slab was extended 610 mm beyond the centre-line of the column and reinforced respectively with one and three 13 mm transverse bars, in order to check the adequacy of very simple detailing in the slab anchoring zone.

Gravity loading P was first applied up to a value (280 kN in total) assumed to simulate typical service conditions in an office building; the lateral load was then applied, quasi-statically, in successive cycles. The deflection at the loading point (i.e. the top of the columns) was assumed to control the amplitude of each cycle, and the testing procedure was as in the previous joint test. The internal joints showed a very similar behaviour to that observed in the joint test, with a stiff elastic range up to inter-storey drifts of about 0·75% and subsequent pinched inelastic cycles. The test was finally stopped at 3·5% drift when failure was attained in a bottom flange cleat by low-cycle fatigue.

Besides a general confirmation of previous results, the frame tests allowed further aspects of particular interest to be pointed out, which stress the importance of an adequate understanding of the slab–column inter-action:

(a) The column web panel experienced substantial yielding in shear and contributed significantly via its shear deformation to the overall joint rotation in the final cycles. This happened although the web met the relevant AISC specifications (AISC, 1980) for fully welded steel moment connections.

(a)

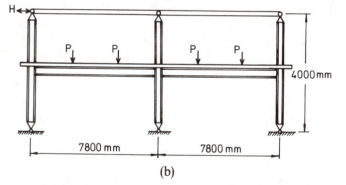

(b)

Fig. 3.27. The limited frame test (Leon, 1987): (a) a frame view; (b) the frame geometry.

(b) The exterior connection with one transverse bar failed at a drift of 1·25%, with a very large crack (up to 5 mm in size) propagating in the slab from the edge of the column flange to the end of the slab. A different mechanism of slab–column interaction, by bearing of the concrete on the internal column flange, was then activated and the joint regained strength and attained a moment greater than the value at the previous 'failure'.

A further joint test (SRCC3C) was conducted (Leon, 1987) in order to investigate the possibility of improving the joint performance in the region of positive moments by adopting a thicker flange cleat (12·5 mm instead of 9·5 mm). The increase of the positive moment capacity of about 24% reduced in effect the difference with respect to the negative moment capacity to less than 5%. The increased joint strength, however, caused more severe yielding of the column panel zone. Slip of the bolts at the bottom cleats was also found to be a factor contributing significantly to the overall joint flexibility in the inelastic range.

These results already indicate that composite semi-rigid joints can be designed to possess stiffness, strength and ductility at a level which makes them a structural solution adequate for use in unbraced frames. Furthermore, the significant energy dissipation capacity would suggest also their suitability for low-rise frames in zones of moderate seismicity.

Design criteria and recommendations need to be established, which require systematic research studies to be carried out to assess the influence of the main factors. The following aspects in particular, seem important and should be addressed: (i) slab–column interaction; (ii) type of slab (solid or with metal decking having different rib configurations); (iii) flexibility and strength of longitudinal shear connection in the beam; (iv) type and detailing of the steel connection; (v) low cycle fatigue of the steel connection; (vi) local buckling of steel member component elements under cyclic loads; (vii) type of column (if bare steel, concrete encased or infilled).

Models capable of representing with satisfactory accuracy the cyclic behaviour of a composite joint should then be developed, as for steel connections (Mazzolani, 1988), which would also allow full simulation of semi-rigid composite frames to be conducted, including seismic analysis.

3.6 SEMI-RIGID COMPOSITE FRAMES

Joint and frame behaviour are more interdependent in composite than in bare steel construction. However, studies into the behaviour of semi-rigid composite frames, seeking to supplement and validate joint test results as well as to develop semi-rigid frame design methods, have not yet been undertaken, except the test on a limited frame carried out by Leon.

Benussi *et al.* (1987) analysed composite beams under uniform loading with end-restraints simulating the joint action. Multilinear $M-\phi$ relationships were used to represent the behaviour obtained in the joint tests

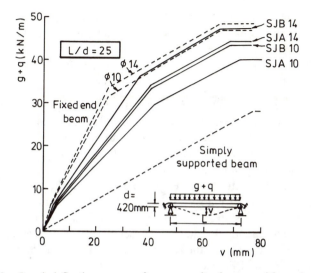

FIG. 3.28. Load–deflection curves for composite beams with end restraints simulating semi-rigid joint action (Benussi *et al.*, 1987).

conducted by the same authors (Fig. 3.17). The analysis confirmed that the degree of continuity assured by simple semi-rigid joints (SJA-10) is already sufficient to improve substantially the beam performance through all the range, with the load–deflection curve lying close to the one for the fixed end condition (Fig. 3.28). These results may only approximate the actual response of an internal beam of a braced frame with columns significantly stiffer and stronger than the beams, and their scope is hence rather limited. Even when attention is drawn to the beam behaviour, the interaction between beams and columns should be properly recognised.

Studies on the stability of braced steel frames indicated that the nonlinearity of connection response affects the effectiveness of the restraint offered by the beam to the column, whilst the nature of moment shedding may change with the load level. Significant, not yet solved, difficulties then arise related to the definition of both the value of the column effective length and of the moment to be used in column and beam design (Nethercot *et al.*, 1987; Snijder *et al.*, 1986). The very nature of joint action and of beam–column interaction in composite semi-rigid frames may be expected to increase further the complexity of the problem.

The present state of knowledge of the behaviour of semi-rigid composite frames does not allow design methods such as the one proposed by Owens

& Echeta (1981) to be fully validated. Nevertheless it seems useful to outline the general philosophy of this method, which represents basically an engineering approach to the problem.

Performance criteria to be met during erection, and at serviceability and ultimate limit state conditions, are first identified:

(i)   Erection. The steel beam should act as simply supported under factored dead and construction loads. This reduces the difference between the hogging and sagging moments of resistance of the composite beam and then the ductility required to the joint.

(ii) Serviceability limit state. The joint should behave elastically up to load levels greater than the service ones (the authors propose up to 1·1 times service loads), so that elastic analysis may be used.

(iii) Ultimate limit state. The composite beam should be able to carry the factored dead and live loads in presence of the plastic end moments of the joints M_p, and the column should carry the combined action of the factored axial load and the joint moments.

These criteria then allow the requirements to be met by the joints to be subsequently identified, which should (a) behave closely to a hinge before concreting (steel connection alone), (b) be very stiff and elastic up to a predetermined moment value, and (c) be capable of undergoing significant rotation in the plastic range. Furthermore, economy requires the joints to be cheap to fabricate and straightforward to erect on site.

Even though the degree of reliability of the procedure adopted for member checking needs to be assessed against full frame analyses, this approach has the significant merit of possessing inherent clarity and simplicity, which is mainly a consequence of the attempt to relate each design step closely to the structural behaviour. Actually to fulfil this objective, methods for the joint behaviour prediction and for inelastic column design are necessary and not yet available. The assumption implicitly made by the authors of an ideally elastic-plastic joint behaviour may be too crude and the practical consequences of this approximation should also be evaluated.

It is finally worth noting that the method enabled the authors to conduct comparative design studies of a long-span building which clearly pointed out the benefits, in terms of planning flexibility, floor steelwork density and beam depth, made possible by accounting for semi-rigid action. Besides, the results obtained by Leon (1987) in the pilot frame test indicate that the inherent high elastic stiffness of composite semi-rigid joints may make them an advantageous solution also in unbraced frames, to which more attention should be given in future investigations.

3.7 CONCLUDING REMARKS

An appraisal of the present state of knowledge in the behaviour of semi-rigid composite joints is given in this chapter. A comprehensive review of the experimental and analytical studies so far conducted, as well as an account of the methods developed for the prediction of the joint behaviour, have been presented, and the main areas to which future research work should be addressed have been suggested. Even though the number of studies is limited, the following conclusions may already be drawn:

(i)   Semi-rigid composite joints may be designed to possess high stiffness and ultimate strength. Moment capacities of the order of the negative plastic moment of the composite beam may be achieved, while maintaining simple detailing in the steelwork.

(ii) The rotation capacity is generally significant and sufficient for a plastic beam mechanism to be activated. Moreover, proper selection of the amount of steel reinforcement in the slab allows local buckling of steel members to be easily controlled. It is then possible to adopt less strict requirements than for rigid jointed members with respect to slenderness ratios of the steel plate components.

(iii) The single major factor governing the behaviour of the joint is the slab action. Numerical formulations have to be capable of adequately simulating slab action as well as the slab–column interaction. On the other hand, high accuracy might not be required for the steel connection model, though such factors as slip in bolted connections should be included (Leon & Lin, 1986).

(iv) The moment–rotation characteristic does not depend solely on joint parameters. Methods of prediction of the $M-\phi$ curve should account for the way the composite action is developed in the beam (and in particular for the influence of the shear connection flexibility and strength). Methods are already available (Johnson & Law, 1981) for the particular case of joints subject to symmetrical loads, which proved sufficiently accurate, and might be extended to make their scope more comprehensive.

Furthermore, the behaviour observed under cyclic loads (Leon, 1987) indicates that semi-rigid composite joints might represent a suitable alternative to resist lateral loads in low-rise sway frames.

All the investigations so far have been conceived mainly as pilot studies with the aim of gaining an insight into basic features of joint behaviour and to identify the governing parameters. The state of knowledge seems now mature for extensive parametric studies to be undertaken, which would make possible the development of criteria for the design of both joints and frames. In order to maximise the outcome of experimental analyses, it is important that tests are consistent and adequately reported. Standard definitions of the force and displacement components describing joint behaviour, as well as of testing and reporting procedures, should then be agreed. Some aspects of this problem have also been discussed in this chapter.

ACKNOWLEDGEMENT

This chapter was prepared in the Department of Civil and Structural Engineering at the University of Sheffield whilst Professor Zandonini was working there as an SERC Senior Visiting Fellow.

REFERENCES

ADINA (1981) A Finite Element Program for Automatic Dynamic Incremental Nonlinear Analysis. Report AE81-1, ADINA Engineering.

AMERICAN INSTITUTE OF STEEL CONSTRUCTION (AISC) (1980) Steel Construction Manual, 8th edn, Chicago.

AMMERMAN, D. & LEON, R. T. (1987) Behaviour of semi-rigid composite connections, AISC, Engng J., 42 (June).

ALTMAN, W. G., AZIZINAMINI, A., BRADBURN, J. H. & RADZIMINSKI, J. B. (1982) Moment–Rotation Characteristics of Semi-Rigid Steel Beam-Column Connections. Technical Report, Dept. of Civil Engineering, University of South Carolina.

ANDERSON, D., BIJLAARD, F., NETHERCOT, D. A. & ZANDONINI, R. (1987) Analysis and Design of Steel Frames with Semi-Rigid Connections. IABSE Survey No. S-39/87.

BARNARD, P. R. (1970) Innovations in composite floor systems. Paper presented at the Canadian Structural Engineering Conference, Canadian Steel Industries Construction Council, p. 13.

BENUSSI, F., PUHALI, R. & ZANDONINI, R. (1986) Experimental analysis of semi-rigid connections in composite frames. Proc. Int. Conf. on Steel Structures: Recent Research Advances and Their Applications to Design, Budva, Yugoslavia, September.

BENUSSI, F., PUHALI, R. & ZANDONINI R. (1987) Composite braced frames with semi-rigid joints. Proc. Int. Symposium on Composite Steel Concrete Structures, Bratislava, May.

BRIDGE, R. Q., SPENCER, J. A. & ANTARAKIS, M. K. (1981) Acceptable moment-rotation capacities for semi-rigid connections. *Proc. Int. Conf. on Joints in Structural Steelwork* (ed. J. H. Howlett *et al.*). Pentech Press, London, pp. 2.26–2.39.

CLIMENHAGA, J. J. & JOHNSON, R. P. (1972) Local buckling in continuous composite beams, *Structural Engineer*, **50**(9), 180–97.

ECHETA, C. B. (1982) Semi-rigid Connections between Concrete Filled Steel Columns and Composite Beams. PhD Thesis, University of London.

ECHETA, C. B. & OWENS, G. W. (1981) A semi-rigid connection for composite frames: initial test results, *Proc. Int. Conf. on Joints in Structural Steelwork* (ed. J. H. Howlett *et al.*). Pentech Press, London, pp. 3.20–3.38.

EUROPEAN ECONOMIC COMMUNITY (EEC) (1984) Eurocode 4: Composite Steel and Concrete Structures, 1st draft, October.

HOPE-GILL, M. C. (1974) The Ultimate Strength of Continuous Composite Beams. PhD Thesis, University of Cambridge.

JOHNSON, R. P. (1975) *Composite Structures of Steel and Concrete*, Vol. 1, *Beams, Columns, Frames and Applications in Building*. Constrado Monographs, Granada Publishing, London, p. 210.

JOHNSON, R. P. (1985) Continuous composite beams for buildings. Report of IABSE-ECCS symposium, Steel in Buildings, Luxembourg, pp. 195–202.

JOHNSON, R. P. & HOPE-GILL, M. C. (1972) Semi-rigid joints in composite frames. IABSE, Ninth Congress, Prelim. Report, Amsterdam, May, pp. 133–44.

JOHNSON, R. P. & LAW, C. L. C. (1981) Semi-rigid joints for composite frames. *Proc. Int. Conf. on Joints in Structural Steelwork* (ed. J. H. Howlett *et al.*). Pentech Press, London, pp. 3.3–3.19.

JOHNSON, R. P., VAN DALEN, K. & KEMP, A. R. (1966) Ultimate strength of continuous composite beams. British Construction Steelwork Association, Conference on Structural Steel, London, pp. 27–35.

KEMP, A. R. (1988) Quantifying ductility in continuous composite beams. *Composite Construction in Steel and Concrete* (eds. C. D. Buckner & I. M. Viest). ASCE, New York, pp. 107–21.

LAW, C. L. C. (1983) Planar No-sway Frames with Semi-Rigid Beam-to-Column Joints. PhD Thesis, University of Warwick.

LEON, R. T. (1987) Behaviour of semi-rigid composite frames. In *Composite Steel Structures: Advances, Design and Construction* (ed. R. Narayanan). Elsevier Applied Science, London, pp. 145–53.

LEON, R. T. & AMMERMAN, D. (1986) Seismic performance of composite semi-rigid subassemblages. *Proc. 8th ECEE*, Vol. 4, Libson, pp. 25–32.

LEON, R. & LIN, J. (1986) Towards the Development of an Analytical Model for Composite Semi-Rigid Connections. Report to AISC, Struct. Eng. Rep. No. 86-06, University of Minnesota, Minneapolis, p. 83.

MAZZOLANI, F. M. (1988) Mathematical model for semi-rigid joints under cyclic loads. In *Connections in Steel Structures: Behaviour, Strength and Design* (ed. R. Bjorhovde *et al.*). Elsevier Applied Science Publishers, London, pp. 112–20.

NETHERCOT, D. A., KIRBY, P. A. & RIFAI, A. M. (1987) Columns in partially restrained construction: analytical studies. *Canad. J. Civil Engng*, **14**(4), 485–97.

NEWMARK, N. M., SIESS, C. P. & VIEST, I. M. (1951) Tests and analysis of composite beams with incomplete interaction. *Proc. Soc. Exp. Stress Anal.*, **9**(1), 75–92.

OWENS, G. W. & ECHETA, C. B. (1981) A semi-rigid design method for composite frames. *Proc. Int. Conf. on Joints in Structural Steelwork* (ed. J. H. Howlett *et al.*). Pentech Press, London, pp. 3.20–3.38.

SNIJDER, H. H., BIJLAARD, F. S. K. & STARK, J. W. B. (1983) Use of the elastic effective length for stability checks of columns and consequences for checks on beams in braced frames. In *Instability and Plastic Collapse of Steel Structures* (ed. L. J. Morris). Granada, pp. 152–63.

SZS (Schweizerische Zentralstelle fur Stahlbau) (1987) Rahmentragwerk in Stahl unter besonderer Berucksichtigung der steifenlosen Bauweise. Zürich, p. 167.

TSCHEMMERNEGG, F. (1988) On the nonlinear behaviour of joints in steel frames. In *Connections in Steel Structures: Behaviour, Strength and Design* (ed. R. Bjorhovde *et al.*). Elsevier Applied Science Publishers, London, pp. 158–65.

VAN DALEN, K. & GODOY, H. (1982) Strength and rotational behaviour of composite beam-to-column connections, *Canad. J. Civil Engng*, **9**, 313–22.

VAN DOUWEN, A. A. (1981) Design for economy in bolted and welded connections, *Proc. Int. Conf. on Joints in Structural Steelwork* (ed. J. H. Howlett *et al.*). Pentech Press, London, pp. 5.18–5.35.

Chapter 4

INFLUENCE OF JOINT CHARACTERISTICS ON STRUCTURAL RESPONSE OF FRAMES

P. Zoetemeijer
Mannesmann Nederland BV, Fijnaart, The Netherlands

SUMMARY

The strength and stability of steel frames are very much influenced by the strength and stiffness of the connections if these are lower than those of the connected beams. In this chapter a design method is discussed based on the assumption that all structural parts behave in a linear way, whereas the strength and stiffness of the connections are so low that the non-linear moment–rotation curve of the connections should be used. The influence of the joint characteristics on the structural behaviour of frames is shown by using the Merchant–Rankine formula which makes use of the first-order plastic bearing capacity and the linear Euler buckling load of the frame. It is shown that a bilinear approximation of the moment–rotation curve gives a safe value for the load-bearing capacity of the frame, provided that the assumed rigidity and strength of the connection remain below the actual value. As the actual moments in the frame may become higher than calculated, it is advisable to design the welds in the connections in such a way that they are able to transfer a moment that is a factor higher than the design value. This factor depends on the design method of the connections, but is 1·4 for braced frames and 1·7 for unbraced frames if a design method for connections is used based on the theory of plasticity.

121

NOTATION

a	Optional distance
c	Rotational stiffness of connection
EI	Flexural stiffness
EI_b	Flexural stiffness of beam
EI_c	Flexural stiffness of column
EI_v	Flexural stiffness of connection
F	Applied axial load
F_c	Ultimate limit load of frame
F_E	Euler buckling load of frame
F_p	First-order plastic load of frame
h	Beam depth
H	Applied horizontal load
k	Relative stiffness of connection
l	Span of beam
l_c	Length of column
M	Bending moment
M_{action}	Moment caused by applied loads
M_{eb}	Elastic limit moment of beam
M_{ec}	Elastic limit moment of column
M_p	Plastic moment capacity of beam
M_{pb}	Plastic moment capacity of beam
M_{pc}	Plastic moment capacity of column
$M_{reaction}$	Moment in connection
$\hat{M}_v$	Calculated moment capacity of connection
P	Applied vertical load
q	Uniformly distributed load on beam
$\hat{q}$	Ultimate load on beam
R	Factor
α	Factor
Δ	Deformation
ϕ	Rotation

4.1 INTRODUCTION

4.1.1 Relevance of Joint Characteristics

The joint characteristics are of importance only if the strength and/or stiffness of the connection between beams and columns are less than the strength and stiffness of the beams. If this is not the case one speaks of full-strength and rigid connections and it is not necessary to incorporate joint characteristics in the computation. Thus an investigation into the influence of the joint characteristics on the structural response of frames is only necessary if semi-rigid or partial-strength connections are used and the actual characteristics of these connections are not known exactly or are not taken into account correctly. The latter may be the case because the tools for a proper computation are not available or the time necessary for a good computation fails as often happens in a professional environment. In that case knowledge of the influence of the joint characteristics is necessary to estimate incorrectness in the approach.

4.1.2 Aspects to be Discussed

In order to get an idea as to which parameters influence a proper design, first a computation method will be explained by which the actual behaviour of the frame is predicted correctly. Due to the low strength and/or stiffness of partial restraint connections it appears necessary to take into account the non-linear behaviour of these connections until failure.

In the following it will be shown how this is possible with linear elastic theory (theory based on Hooke's law). Many designers assume it necessary to know the behaviour of the connection exactly before they will apply it in the structure. In that case tests are proposed to determine the moment–rotation curves. At present, efforts from various sources are beginning to make such information available, both in the form of experimental data and predictive equations as shown in the other chapters of this book. However, it is not always certain that the moment–rotation curves determined by tests will also occur in the actual structure. This is especially true for bolted connections, where the tightening of the bolts and the initial form of the connected parts have a great influence on the final behaviour of the connection in the structure. That is why it is advisable to use a lower-bound approximation of the stiffness of the connection. It appears that a lower stiffness of the connections causes greater bending moments due to side-sway of unbraced frames. On the other hand it will be shown that lower stiffness of the connection causes smaller bending moments due to gravity loads of the beams. The conclusion is that elastic theory is not suited for determining the ultimate strength of the frame. It should be used for the computation of the deformations under working loads but the ultimate strength capacity should be determined by means of the plastic hinge method. The latter is only possible if the connections have sufficient rotation capacity. These aspects will be discussed in the next sections.

4.2 DESIGN METHODS AND INFLUENCES

4.2.1 Design Methods

Figure 4.1 gives an indication of the problems which are encountered by the designer if he wants to use partial restraint connections in frames. This figure gives the moment–rotation curves of beam, column and connection over the same distance a. For frames with rigid and full-strength connections the values K_e and M_{ev} of the connection characteristic are greater than the stiffness and strength values of the beam.

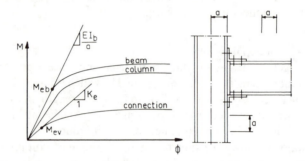

FIG. 4.1.   Moment–rotation curves of beam and connection over the same distance.

With rigid and full-strength connections the designer has only to take into account the moment–rotation relations of the beams and columns. Furthermore it is possible to use only the linear elastic part of the moment–rotation curves, because experience has shown that steel structures have sufficient safety if the linear part is not exceeded under working loads. In that case one speaks of a linear elastic computation of the frame.

If partial-restraint connections are used, the moment–rotation curves of the connections should be incorporated in the computation model. In that

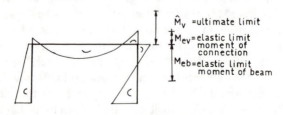

FIG. 4.2.   Typical bending moment distribution in a frame.

case the computation cannot be restricted to the linear part of the moment–rotation curve of the connection. The use of beam and column capacity would be very inefficient because the bending moments in the frame tend to have large values in the connections, whereas the elastic capacity at that point is only a fraction of that of beams and columns (see Fig. 4.2). For that reason the non-linear part of the moment–rotation curve of the connection should be used.

4.2.2 Connection Stiffness

As already explained with Fig. 4.1, the moment–rotation relations are valid for a specific length of the beam. There are two methods to incorporate the moment–rotation characteristics of the connection in the computation model. Both methods are schematically shown in Fig. 4.3.

(a)   (b)

FIG. 4.3. Connection stiffness incorporation: (a) reduced stiffness; (b) spring constants.

The first method is based on a reduction of the beam stiffness over a length equal to half the column depth.

Most of the computer programmes now available have the possibility of incorporating spring constants at the end of the beams or columns. The spring constants can be assumed as equal to the connection stiffness.

4.2.3 Tangent Stiffness Method

In principle the available computation methods are all based on the linear elastic relations of forces and deformations. Theoretically a non-linear computation can only be carried out by increasing the loads in such small steps that the load–deformation relationship can be assumed to remain linear in this step. This is indicated in Fig. 4.4 where the moment–rotation relation of the connection of Fig. 4.1 is shown in detail together with that of the beam.

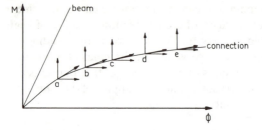

FIG. 4.4.   Tangent stiffness method indicated in the moment–rotation curve of
the partial-restraint connection of Fig. 4.1.

It is assumed that the increments of loading on the frame are such that this gives the load situations a–e in the moment–rotation curve of the connection. At each loading step a new construction model is computed in which the stiffness of the connection is taken as being equal to the tangent value of the curve then available.

The computed load distribution due to the loading step is added to those of the previous loading steps. If the designer has not a computer program at his disposal which automatically uses this algorithm he will not be able to apply this method. It is too laborious and expensive and not suited for a professional environment. In that case it is better to use the secant stiffness method.

4.2.4 Secant Stiffness Method

This is an iterative process in which the ultimate or factored load is taken into account at each computational step and the computation is continued until the assumed connection stiffness coincides with the secant stiffness of the connection at the factored load (see Fig. 4.5). The secant stiffness is the

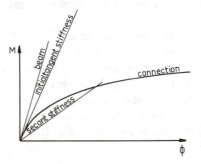

FIG. 4.5.   Secant stiffness.

linear relation between the moment and the rotation at the bending moment considered.

4.2.4.1 Initial Estimate of Secant Stiffness

This stiffness is not known when the computational process starts, because the ultimate moment in the connection is not known. A good estimate can be made by using the beam-line concept. For a simply supported beam acted upon by a uniformly distributed load and equal moments at its ends, a formula can be derived for the rotation of the ends of the beam (see Fig. 4.6(a)). This formula is a linear relationship between the moments and the rotation at the ends of the beam, and this relationship has been plotted in Fig. 4.6(b). This beam-line intersects the vertical axis at a moment value

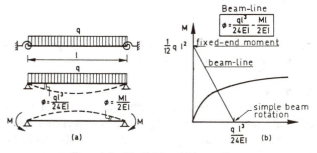

FIG. 4.6.   Definition of beam-line.

equal to the end moment of a fully clamped beam, and the horizontal axis at a rotation value equal to the rotation at the end of a simply supported beam. The point of intersection between the beam-line and the actual moment–rotation characteristic gives the moment and rotation of the connection for a given loading. In Fig. 4.6 the beam-line is defined for a uniformly distributed load but this can be done in the same way for any type of loading.

4.2.4.2 Choice of Secant Stiffness in Next Iteration

A further computation is necessary as long as the resulting moments in the connection do not agree with the moments assumed with the estimate of the secant stiffness. In order to accelerate the convergence of the computation it is advisable to use a weighted average of the old secant stiffness and a new secant stiffness as shown in Fig. 4.7. The new secant stiffness is the value found at the rotation in the connection resulting from the computation.

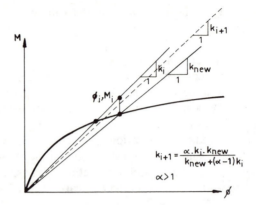

FIG. 4.7. Choice of secant stiffness in next iteration.

Figure 4.7 gives a formula with the weight factor α. It appears that a weight factor 3 gives convergence after 5 or 6 iterations.

4.2.5 P–Δ Effects

Due to the relative displacements of the columns, extra moments are introduced in the frame as shown in Fig. 4.8. The P–Δ effect is not a specific property of frames with semi-rigid connections, if the restrictions with respect to lateral displacements of the frame are identical for frames with rigid and semi-rigid connections. With both types of connections the P–Δ effect should be taken into account. However, the frames with partial-restraint connections reach the permissible deformations or allowable stress at a lower load than frames with rigid connections. This can easily be shown by using the Merchant–Rankine formula as indicated in Fig. 4.9.

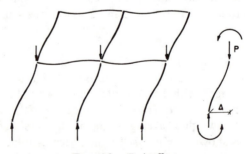

FIG. 4.8. P–Δ effect.

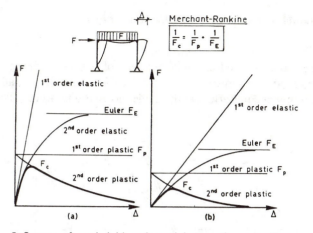

FIG. 4.9. Influence of semi-rigid and partial-strength connections on the calculated bearing capacity of an unbraced frame with (a) rigid and full-strength connections, (b) semi-rigid and partial-strength connections.

Figure 4.9(a) shows the behaviour of an unbraced frame with rigid and full-strength connections, while Fig. 4.9(b) depicts the behaviour of the same frame but with semi-rigid and partial-strength connections. In this figure, the load–deformation curves are plotted using the various methods for calculating the force distribution. The curves plotted with the thick line indicate the real behaviour. Due to the flexibility of the connections, the Euler buckling load of the frame will decrease. As a result of the partial strength of the connection, the bearing capacity, based on the first-order plastic theory, will decrease. Both phenomena, with respect to the same frame but now with rigid and full-strength connections, will lead to a lower ultimate bearing capacity of the frame. This will be explained with some examples computed for the frame shown in Fig. 4.10.

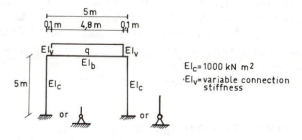

FIG. 4.10. Example portal frame.

4.2.6 Examples of Influences on Unbraced Frames

4.2.6.1 Euler Buckling Loads of Frames
The computation of the Euler buckling load of this frame is executed with a Shanley model as shown in Fig. 4.11. The Euler buckling load follows from the moment equilibrium at the hinge shown in Fig. 4.11(b). The spring

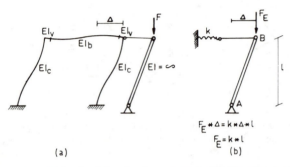

$$F_E * \Delta = k * \Delta * l$$
$$F_E = k * l$$

FIG. 4.11.   Euler buckling load computed with Shanley model.

constant k represents the lateral resistance of the frame. Buckling occurs when the vertical load is equal to the product of the spring constant and the height of the frame. Table 4.1 gives the results of the computations. It appears that the Euler buckling load determined with the Shanley model for a portal frame with an infinitely stiff beam deviates 21% from the exact known Euler buckling load of this frame.

For an investigation into the influence of the joint characteristic this deviation is acceptable. The results for frames with slight connection stiffness and different beam stiffness (cases 8 and 9) show that the beam stiffness is not relevant for the Euler buckling load if the connection stiffness is very small. This situation is almost identical to that of two columns connected by a hinged infinitely stiff beam (cases 10 and 11). Furthermore it is evident that the influence of connection stiffness is greater if the stiffness of the structure as a whole is smaller; compare, for example, cases 3 and 6 (clamped column feet) with cases 14 and 16 (hinged column feet). In the latter case the stability of the frame is entirely furnished by the connection stiffness.

4.2.6.2 First-Order Plastic Bearing Capacity of Frames
The bearing capacity of the example portal frame of Fig. 4.10 is computed

TABLE 4.1
EULER BUCKLING LOADS OF THE FRAME OF FIG. 4.10

Case	EI_c $(kN\,m^2)$	EI_b $(kN\,m^2)$	EI_v $(kN\,m^2)$	Supports type	F_E (kN)	Remarks
1	1 000	∞	∞	Clamped	790	Theoretical
2	1 000	∞	∞	Clamped	960	Shanley
3	1 000	5 000	5 000	Clamped	646	Shanley
4	1 000	5 000	1 000	Clamped	632	Shanley
5	1 000	1 000	1 000	Clamped	552	Shanley
6	1 000	5 000	100	Clamped	525	Shanley
7	1 000	1 000	100	Clamped	481	Shanley
8	1 000	5 000	1	Clamped	250	Shanley
9	1 000	1 000	1	Clamped	250	Shanley
10	1 000	∞	0	Clamped	240	Shanley
11	1 000	∞	0	Clamped	198	Theoretical
12	1 000	∞	∞	Hinged	198	Theoretical
13	1 000	∞	∞	Hinged	240	Shanley
14	1 000	5 000	5 000	Hinged	152	Shanley
15	1 000	5 000	1 000	Hinged	147	Shanley
16	1 000	5 000	100	Hinged	112	Shanley
17	1 000	1 000	100	Hinged	96	Shanley
18	1 000	5 000	1	Hinged	4	Shanley
19	1 000	5 000	0	Hinged	0	Shanley

on the basis of the first-order plastic theory with the values given in Fig. 4.12. From a comparison of cases 2 and 3 of Table 4.2 it follows that it is not always necessary for the strength of the connection to equal that of the beam because a plastic hinge will form in the column if its strength is lower than that of the beam.

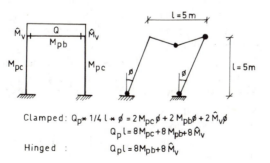

Clamped: $Q_p * 1/4\, l * \phi = 2 M_{pc}\phi + 2 M_{pb}\phi + 2 \hat{M}_v\phi$
$Q_p l = 8 M_{pc} + 8 M_{pb} + 8 \hat{M}_v$

Hinged : $Q_p l = 8 M_{pb} + 8 \hat{M}_v$

FIG. 4.12. Example portal frame.

TABLE 4.2
BEARING CAPACITIES OF THE FRAME OF FIG. 4.12

Case	M_{pc} (kN m)	M_{pb} (kN m)	$\hat{M}_v$ (kN m)	Bearing capacity F_p (kN)	
				Clamped	Hinged
1	20	20	20	96	64
2	20	60	60	160	128
3	20	60	20	160	128
4	20	60	10	144	112
5	20	60	5	136	104
6	20	60	1	130	98

4.2.6.3 Ultimate Bearing Capacity
Table 4.3 shows the interaction of the stiffness and the strength of the connection on the second-order load-bearing capacity of the portal frame. Especially cases 3 and 4 show that the influence of the partial-restraint connection on the structural behaviour of the frame may be small if the stability of the frame is provided for by clamped feet.

With hinged feet of the columns the reduction of the bearing capacity is about 50% due to the second-order effect. As the bearing capacity of the frame with rigid and full-strength connections is already low, the influence of the partial-restraint connections is relatively high in that case.

4.2.7 Classification of Connections
If the stability of the frame depends completely on the stiffness of the connections, it appears that three types of connections in relation to their influence can be distinguished. This will be explained with reference to Fig. 4.13 where the relationships between loading, moments and deformations are given for frequently occurring situations in braced and unbraced frames. All relationships are expressed by the relation scheme described for the situation with rigid connections multiplied by a reduction factor R which is a function of the factor k. This factor k is the ratio between the rotational spring stiffness of the connection and the bending stiffness of the beam. Therefore $k = cl/EI$, where c is the calculated value of the rotational spring stiffness of the connection.

In all cases, the reduction factor R increases from zero to 1 with increasing k. The last two columns of the scheme give the reduction factor R with respect to the situation where $k = \infty$. These ratios are shown in the form of curves in Fig. 4.13(b) for cases 1, 3 and 4. It appears that at $k = 1000$

TABLE 4.3
BEARING CAPACITY OF THE FRAME OF FIG. 4.12 IF STIFFNESS IS TAKEN INTO ACCOUNT

Case	EI_c (kN m²)	EI_b (kN m²)	EI_v (kN m²)	F_E (kN)	M_{pc} (kN m)	M_{pb} (kN m)	$\bar{M}_v$ (kN m)	F_p (kN)	F_c (kN)	Columns feet
1	1 000	1 000	1 000	552	20	20	20	96	82	Clamped
2	1 000	1 000	100	481	20	20	20	96	80	Clamped
3	1 000	5 000	5 000	646	20	60	60	160	128	Clamped
4	1 000	5 000	1 000	632	20	60	20	160	128	Clamped
5	1 000	5 000	100	525	20	60	10	144	113	Clamped
6	1 000	5 000	1	250	20	60	1	130	86	Clamped
7	1 000	5 000	5 000	152	20	60	20	160	78	Hinged
8	1 000	5 000	1 000	147	20	60	20	128	68	Hinged
9	1 000	5 000	100	112	20	60	10	112	56	Hinged
10	1 000	5 000	1	4	20	60	5	104	4	Hinged

	c — EI — c, l	Relation scheme $R = f(k = \frac{cl}{EI})$		$\dfrac{I_c l}{Ih}$	$\dfrac{R(k=\ )}{R(k=\infty)}$	
					0.5 $\quad k \quad$ 25	
1	M $\overset{q}{\longleftrightarrow}$ M	$\dfrac{M}{q} = R\,\dfrac{l^2}{12}$	$R = \dfrac{k}{k+2}$		0.20	0.93
2	M $\overset{\downarrow F}{\longleftrightarrow}$ M	$\dfrac{M}{F} = R\,\dfrac{l}{8}$	$R = \dfrac{k}{k+2}$		0.20	0.93
3	$\downarrow F \quad \updownarrow \delta \quad F\uparrow$	$\dfrac{F}{\delta} = R\,\dfrac{12EI}{l}$	$R = \dfrac{k}{k+6}$		0.08	0.81
4	$\overset{)M}{\phi}$	$\dfrac{M}{\phi} = R\,\dfrac{4EI}{l}$	$R = \dfrac{k^2+3k}{k^2+8k+12}$		0.10	0.84
5	$\triangle \quad \overset{)M}{\phi}$	$\dfrac{M}{\phi} = R\,\dfrac{3EI}{l}$	$R = \dfrac{k}{k+3}$		0.14	0.89
6	$\phi \overset{)M}{\underset{M}{}} \phi$	$\dfrac{M}{\phi} = R\,\dfrac{6EI}{l}$	$R = \dfrac{k}{k+6}$		0.08	0.81
7	$\downarrow F_k \quad \downarrow F_k$, h, EI_o	$F_k = R\,\dfrac{\pi^2 EI_c}{4h^2}$	$R = \dfrac{1}{1 + \dfrac{k+6}{k}\,\dfrac{I_c\cdot l}{I\cdot h}\,\dfrac{\pi^2}{24}}$	10 2 1 0.5 0.1	0.09 0.16 0.22 0.33 0.68	0.84 0.90 0.93 0.96 0.99
8	$\downarrow F_k \quad \downarrow F_k$, h, EI_o	$F_k = R\,\dfrac{\pi^2 EI_c}{8h^2}$	$R = \dfrac{1}{1 + \dfrac{k+3}{k}\,\dfrac{I_c l}{I\cdot h}\,\dfrac{\pi^2}{12}}$	10 2 1 0.5 0.1	0.16 0.21 0.27 0.36 0.69	0.90 0.93 0.95 0.97 0.99

(a)

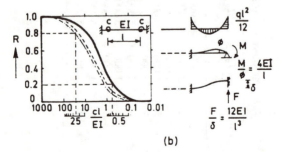

(b)

FIG. 4.13. Relation scheme for the reduction factor R for forces and deflections as a function of the relative connection stiffness.

the value for R approaches 1, and the connection can be classified as rigid.

For cases where $k > 25$ the reduction factor becomes $R \geqslant 0.80$. From cases 7 and 8 of the scheme of Fig. 4.13(a), it appears that the Euler buckling load at $k > 25$ deviates by less than 10% from the Euler buckling load at $k = \infty$. It can be concluded that a connection can be considered to be rigid when the value of k exceeds 25. From Fig. 4.13(b) it can also be concluded that a connection can be considered to be a hinge when the value of k is less than 0.5. When the k value lies between 0.5 and 25, the connection is to be classified as semi-rigid, and flexibility is to be taken into account in calculating the force distribution and the stability of the frame.

4.2.8 Limitation of Secant Stiffness Approach

The use of the secant stiffness of the connections is a safe approximation to the connection behaviour in calculating the stability of the frame as long as the ultimate moment capacity of the connection is not assumed to be greater than the point of intersection of the secant stiffness with the actual moment–rotation characteristic. This is shown by the following simplified example.

Assume a vertical bar with infinite bending stiffness, connected to the ground by a rotational spring, as shown in Fig. 4.14(b). At the top of the bar a horizontal and a vertical load act, producing an overturning moment

$$M_{\text{action}} = Hl + Fl\phi \qquad (4.1)$$

In the rotational spring a reaction moment

$$M_{\text{reaction}} = c\phi \qquad (4.2)$$

is activated in the case of a linear rotational spring characteristic (see Fig. 4.14(c)). Equilibrium is achieved when the following holds:

$$Hl + Fl\phi = M_{\text{reaction}} \qquad (4.3)$$

From Fig. 4.14(c) it can be seen that equilibrium is possible when

$$c > Fl \qquad (4.4)$$

The possibility of reaching equilibrium is also dependent on the value of the ultimate moment capacity $\hat{M}_v$. In Fig. 4.14(d) the lines a–c indicate three different values for Hl. Line 'b' indicates the maximum value for Hl at a cut-off value for Fl for which equilibrium is possible. In the case of a non-linear rotational spring characteristic, the same procedure holds (see Fig. 4.14(e)). The maximum load line 'b' does not reach the ultimate moment capacity $\hat{M}_v$ of the connection characteristic, but touches that

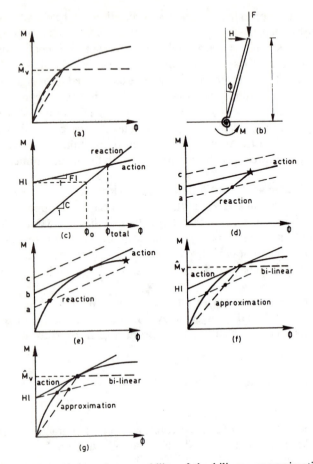

FIG. 4.14.   Influence upon frame stability of the bilinear approximation to the
moment–rotation characteristics of a connection.

curve. Figure 4.14(f) shows a non-linear rotational spring characteristic and
a bilinear approximation to this curve. It can be seen that the use of the
bilinear approximation leads to a safe calculation of the stability of the
frame, because it produces a lower value for Hl than in the case of a constant
value of Hl (see Fig. 4.14(g)). In that case, use of the bilinear approximation
leads to a lower value for Fl than in the case of the non-linear curve.

It can be concluded that it is safe to use a bilinear approximation to
the non-linear moment–rotation characteristic in semi-rigid and partial-
strength connections for purposes of calculating the stability of frames.

4.2.9 Reduction of Connection Stiffness Advised

Until now it has been assumed that the moment–rotation characteristics of the partial-restraint connections are known when the frame is designed. In the past this seemed to be the bottleneck of analysis techniques that took connection flexibility into account. Recently, however, efforts from various sources are beginning to make such information available in the form of both experimental data and predictive equations. However, for bolted connections it will be difficult to predict the actual stiffness of the connection even if tests are carried out. The secant stiffness depends largely on the tightening of the bolts and the initial form of the end plates and flanges as shown in Fig. 4.15.

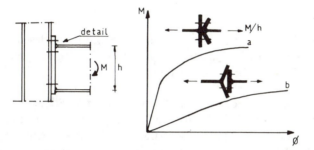

FIG. 4.15. The initial form of connection parts and the tightening influences the moment–rotation characteristics.

With the initial form of case 'a', the elastic deformations of the end plate are negligible as long as there is contact pressure between flanges and end plate, because a tensile load on the connection is transferred by reduction of the contact pressure. Figure 4.16 illustrates this phenomenon. The load on the connection reduces the contact pressure and increases the tensile load depending on the stiffness ratio of plates and bolts. In case 'b' of Fig. 4.15, the tensile load on the connection causes more deformations because the stiffness of the plates is low with respect to the stiffness of the bolt. This situation is indicated with broken lines in Fig. 4.16.

If no special attention is given to this effect during manufacture, the actual moment–rotation curve can have the form of case 'b' whereas in the preliminary tests case 'a' was present. In order to be on the safe side with respect to frame stability it is advisable to give special attention to this factor or else to use a low secant stiffness. However, the latter advice has the consequence that the connections may have to transmit higher bending

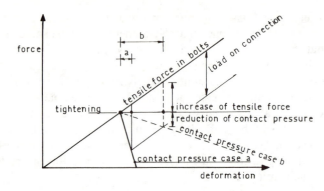

FIG. 4.16.   Influence of initial plate form and tightening of the bolts.

moments due to gravity loads than accounted for in the design. This may have consequences for the connecting parts like bolts and welds. That is why this effect will be considered further in Fig. 4.17.

4.2.10 Consequences of the Reduction of Connection Stiffness

In the graph of Fig. 4.17, the moment capacity of the connection has been plotted on the horizontal axis as a fraction of the plastic moment of the beam. On the vertical axis, the ratio between the uniformly distributed

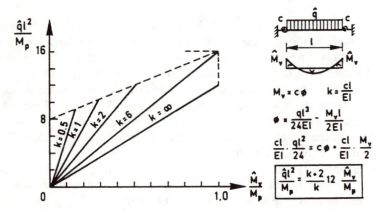

FIG. 4.17.   Calculated strength of a beam in braced frame as a function of the computed moment capacity and the relative stiffness $k = cl/EI$ for relatively stiff connections.

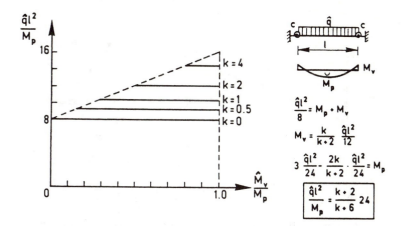

FIG. 4.18. Calculated strength of a beam in a braced frame as a function of the computed moment capacity and the relative stiffness $k = cl/EI$ for relatively weak connections.

loading $\hat{q}$ (multiplied by the square of the beam length) and the plastic moment of the beam is plotted. The straight lines, passing through the origin, give relations between the calculated strength of the beam and the moment capacity of the connections. The slopes of these lines depend on the ratio between the rotational stiffness of the connection and the bending stiffness of the beam. From the graph it can be seen that the bearing capacity of the beam decreases when the rotational stiffness of the connection increases. In this graph, however, the situation where the connection is so flexible that the plastic moment capacity of the mid-section of the beam is reached prior to the attainment of the moment capacity of the connection is not yet taken into account. Such a situation is accounted for in Fig. 4.18. The points of intersection of the horizontal lines in Fig. 4.18 and the lines in Fig. 4.17 all lie on a straight line. This particular line represents the situation where the plastic moment capacity of the mid-span section of the beam and the moment capacity of the connection are reached at the same time (see Fig. 4.19). Theoretically, a beam mechanism occurs at that stage, which is the starting point of the first-order plastic theory. This situation can always be reached, whatever the rotational stiffness of the connection, provided the connection has sufficient rotational capacity. This can be illustrated with an example.

Suppose that a connection has a rotational spring characteristic as indicated in Fig. 4.20. Suppose also that, on the basis of the calculated

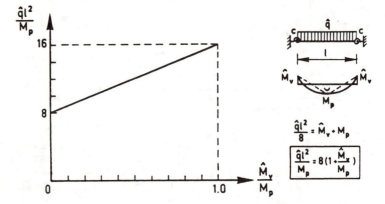

FIG. 4.19.   Calculated strength of a beam in a braced frame as a function of the
moment capacity computed using plastic theory.

moment capacity and the calculated stiffness of the connection, the moment
capacity $\hat{M}_v = 0.4\,M_p$ and the relative stiffness $k = 6$. (The actual stiffness of
the connection can be higher.) It will be shown that this is of no importance
by using the so-called beam-line concept. When the actual moment–
rotation characteristic of the connection is known, it is possible to
investigate the moment and rotation of the connection for various loading
conditions on the beam. This has been done for the moment–rotation
characteristic of Fig. 4.20(a).

The values of the uniformly distributed loads are chosen so that the
moment in the connection just reaches the calculated moment capacity
$\hat{M}_v = 0.4\,M_p$. The levels of the uniformly distributed loads can be read off
from the graph in Fig. 4.20(b) for various rotational stiffnesses of the
connections. This graph summarizes Figs 17–19 inclusive.

The vertical line at $\hat{M}_v = 0.4\,M_p$ first intersects the line $k = \infty$ leading to
$\hat{q}l^2/M_p = 4.8$, and next intersects the lines corresponding to the stiffnesses
and load levels summarized in Table 4.4. The values found in this way are
indicated by circles in Fig. 4.20(a). It appears that the highest value for the
uniformly distributed load $\hat{q}$ can be reached for the stiffness factor $k = 1.5$.
For this stiffness ratio in the beam, an elastic moment distribution exists
which corresponds to the moment distribution according to the first-order
plastic theory, namely $0.4\,M_p$ at the mid-span section of the beam. If
one wants to perform the calculations by means of elastic theory only, but
uses a rotational stiffness of the connection so that $k = 1.5$ (while the actual
stiffness is higher), one is actually using plastic theory. This need

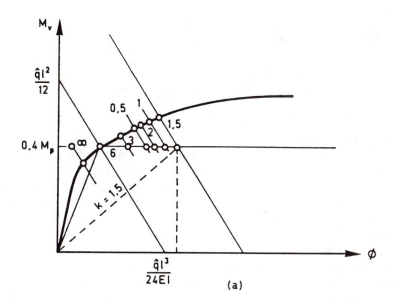

(a)

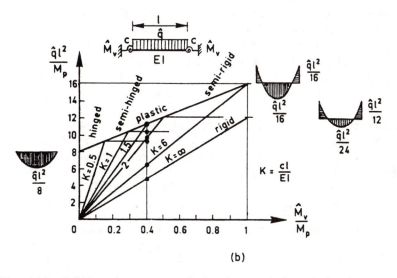

(b)

FIG. 4.20. Relations between actual situations and the calculated moment capacity and rotational stiffness of connections.

TABLE 4.4

LOAD-BEARING CAPACITY OF BEAM IN RELATION TO THE CONNECTION STIFFNESS FOR CONNECTIONS WITH A MOMENT CAPACITY $\hat{M}_v = 0.4\,M_p$ (M_p IS MOMENT CAPACITY OF BEAM)

k	∞	6	3	2	1·5	1	0·5	0
$\hat{q}l^2/M_p$	4·8	6·4	8	9·6	11·2	10·3	9·2	8

not be dangerous, provided that the connection has sufficient rotational capacity to undergo the deformation corresponding to the assumed stiffness at $k = 1.5$ (see the dashed line in Fig. 4.20(a)). In other words, in calculating the ultimate strength of a beam in a braced frame, the connection stiffness is irrelevant provided that the connections have sufficient rotational capacity for the assumed failure mechanism to be reached.

For an unbraced frame the same conclusion is valid with the addition that a lower assumed connection stiffness gives higher $P-\Delta$ effects and thus more rotation capacity is needed. It is possible to make the design rules in such a way that sufficient rotational capacity is assured. In the Netherlands, for example, this is done by checking all the test results with the beam-line concept. From this, specific requirements are derived. This will be explained in the next section. The stiffness of the connection is of relevance in calculating the deflection of the beam under service load. In establishing the rules to determine the moment capacity, a separate check for controlling the deflection of the beam is avoided by setting limits to the span of the beam. This will also be explained in the following section.

4.2.11 Simplifying Rules for the Calculation of Braced Frames

In braced frames it is not necessary that the connections transfer moments. It is possible to use beams with nominally pinned connections as shown in Fig. 4.21. These connections are assumed to transfer only the end reaction of the beam (vertical shear force) to the column. Nevertheless these connections can give some restraint against rotation. Bjorhovde (1988)

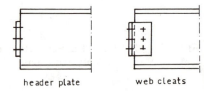

FIG. 4.21. Nominally pinned connections.

header plate   web cleats

proposes the use of this restraint for stability of the column. To facilitate the incorporation of the method into current design procedures, he uses the effective length concept, modified to reflect the actual restraints at the column ends. Another possibility is that the restraining effect of the connection is used for increasing the beam strength. In the following sections both methods will be described. In both methods it is necessary that the structural part behind the connection can give the restraining effect. This means that column collapse should characterize the frame behaviour if the restraining effect of the beams is used in the design of the column. In the method where beam collapse characterizes the frame behaviour, other types of connections, for example with end plates and top and seat angles, are used too.

4.2.11.1 Connection Restraint Used for Beam Strength

In the preceding section it was shown that the rotational stiffness of the connections is irrelevant in calculating the ultimate bearing capacity of beams in braced frames, provided that the connections have sufficient rotational capacity. This rotational capacity has to be large enough to ensure the occurrence of the failure mechanism which is assumed in the calculation. Another condition is that the connection should have sufficient stiffness under service load, so that the mid-span deflection of the beam is within limits.

In checking the accuracy of the rules for the moment capacity of connections against test results, the two conditions mentioned above are taken into account. In the moment–rotation characteristic determined, for instance, by a test on a connection (see Fig. 4.22) the beam-line is drawn corresponding to a loading based on a beam mechanism and a certain beam span-to-depth ratio l/h. The loading is $\hat{q} = 8(\hat{M}_v + M_p)l^2$. The moment–rotation characteristic has to intersect the beam line, otherwise there is insufficient rotational capacity available.

Next, the beam-line is drawn corresponding to a load level which is a factor 1·5 lower than $\hat{q}$, namely $q = 8(\hat{M}_v + M_p)/1·5\,l^2$. The moment–rotation characteristic has to intersect this last beam-line at a rotation which is smaller than, or equal to, the rotation corresponding to the permissible deflection of the beam under service load. It is assumed that this permissible deflection equals $0·004\,l$. The requirement for the deflection can also be represented as a line, called the rotation line, in the graph of Fig. 4.22.

The moment–rotation characteristic has to pass the intersection between the beam-line and the rotation line (point G in Fig. 4.22) on the left-hand

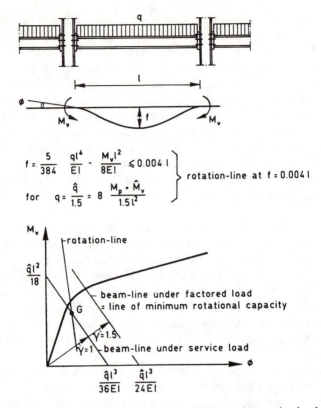

$$f = \frac{5}{384} \frac{ql^4}{EI} - \frac{M_v l^2}{8EI} \leqslant 0.004\, l$$

$$\text{for} \quad q = \frac{\hat{q}}{1.5} = 8 \frac{M_p + \hat{M}_v}{1.5\, l^2}$$

rotation-line at $f = 0.004\, l$

FIG. 4.22. The requirement for minimum stiffness under service load is determined by point G in the moment–rotation diagram.

side. If this is not the case, it means that the beam deflection exceeds the deflection limit at a load level calculated on the basis of the formulae for the moment capacity of the connection and the occurrence of the beam mechanism. In that case the structure does not meet the requirement for stiffness under service load. This can be avoided by choosing a lower load level or a shorter beam span. In both cases, point G moves towards the origin of the graph and so does the beam-line for the rotational capacity. This is shown by comparing the graphs in Fig. 4.23. In these graphs, the requirements for the moment–rotation characteristics are shown for beam spans of 20, 25, 30 and 40 times the beam depth and are based on the theory explained in this section.

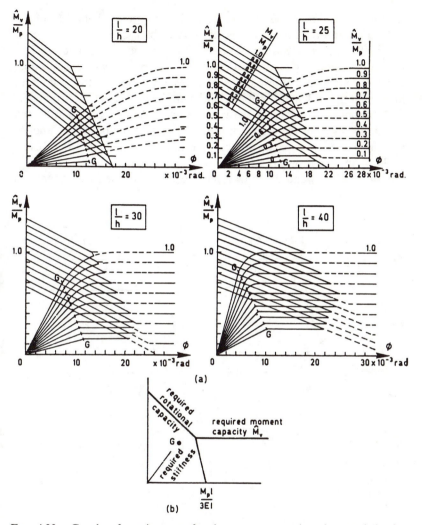

FIG. 4.23.   Graphs of requirements for the moment–rotation characteristics for braced frames.

The curves in these graphs belong to load levels based on the occurrence of beam mechanisms with end moments equal to the moment capacities of the connections. These moment capacities are given on the vertical axis as a fraction of the plastic moment of the beam. The graphs are determined by

146   P. ZOETEMEIJER

the location of point G, the calculated moment capacity $\hat{M}_v$ of the connection and the beam-line, which have to be passed in order to have sufficient rotational capacity (see Fig. 4.23(b)). Besides these lines, there is another line valid for small span-depth ratios of beams, when connections with low stiffness are allowed. In such cases, it can happen that the plastic moment at the mid-span section of the beam occurs prior to the attainment of the moment capacity in the connections. The line representing this situation goes from the intersection point between the beam line and the calculated moment capacity of the connection to the point $\phi = M_p l/3EI$ on the horizontal axis, where $\hat{M}_v = 0$.

Figures 4.24 (a) and (b) show typical examples of the requirements for

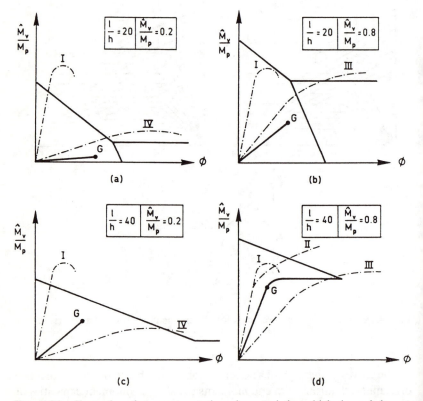

FIG. 4.24. Examples of moment–rotation characteristics which do and do not meet the requirements: (a) I and IV meet the requirements; (b) III meets the requirements; (c) I meets the requirements; (d) II meets the requirements.

small beam spans, which are also contained in Fig. 4.23. Figures 4.24 (c) and (d) show representative examples of the requirements for large beam spans. In Fig. 4.24(c) it is surprising that, in order to pass point G on the left-hand side, the moment–rotation characteristic has to reach a moment higher than the calculated moment capacity. This means that, even under service load, the calculated moment capacity of the connection is exceeded. To avoid this situation, it is necessary to limit the span-to-depth ratio of the beam to the values given in Table 4.5. These values can be read off from Fig. 4.23.

TABLE 4.5
SPAN-TO-DEPTH RATIO OF BEAM IN RELA-
TION TO ULTIMATE MOMENT CAPACITY OF
CONNECTION

$\hat{M}_v/M_p$	l/h
$<0\cdot1$	<20
$<0\cdot2$	<25
$<0\cdot3$	<30
$<0\cdot4$	<35
$<0\cdot5$	<40

Also in Fig. 4.24, four moment–rotation characteristics (I to IV) are drawn, and these will now be discussed. Connection I, with $\hat{M}_v = 0\cdot8\,M_p$, is a typical connection designed for elastic calculations. Assuming $\hat{M}_v = 0\cdot8\,M_p$ and the occurrence of a beam mechanism, this connection has insufficient rotational capacity for small and large beam spans, as is shown in Figs 4.24 (b) and (d). The connection, however, does have sufficient rotational capacity if one calculates the loading based upon $\hat{M}_v = 0\cdot2\,M_p$ (see Fig. 4.24(a)). In such a case, it is assumed in the calculation that a moment of $0\cdot2\,M_p$ exists in the connection and a moment M_p at the mid-span of the beam. Actually, however, in the connection a moment of $0\cdot8\,M_p$ would occur, while at the mid-span section of the beam there would be a moment of $0\cdot4\,M_p$. This is the moment distribution according to the elastic theory. From this one can conclude that, in spite of the fact that one assumes a moment capacity of the connection $\hat{M}_v = 0\cdot2\,M_p$ in the calculations, the connecting parts, such as welds, need to be designed to transfer a higher moment. In such a case, the real moment is $0\cdot8\,M_p$. This is, however, an extreme example. From test results it appeared that the welds of connections, which have to develop sufficient rotational capacity to allow a beam mechanism in a braced frame to occur, need to be designed to transfer a moment equal to 1·4 times the calculated moment capacity. For connections in unbraced frames the welds should be designed to transfer a moment equal to 1·7 times the calculated moment capacity.

However, in both of the above cases (braced as well as unbraced frames), this moment need not be higher than the plastic moment M_p of the beam, although it appears from Fig. 4.23 that it is possible for a very stiff connection, with a calculated moment capacity of M_p, to intersect the line for sufficient rotational capacity at a moment level of 1·33 M_p.

This situation can occur when the yield stress level of the beam material is 33% above the guaranteed yield stress level, which is quite possible. The moment distribution is in accordance with the elastic theory, with the ultimate loading $\hat{q} = 16 M_p/l^2$, 1·33 M_p in the connections and 0·67 M_p in the mid-span section, and actually the connections need not be designed for sufficient rotational capacity. So, for practical cases, it is sufficient to design the welds for a moment of 1·4 times $\hat{M}_v$ and 1·7 times $\hat{M}_v$, respectively, with a maximum of M_p. Connection II in Fig. 4.24(d) is an example of a connection which meets all requirements. Connection III meets the requirement for sufficient rotational capacity, but not the requirements for stiffness for a large span-to-depth ratio (40) of the beam. Connections like connection IV with a calculated moment capacity $\hat{M}_v = 0·2 M_p$ which is acceptable at $l/h = 20$ and at $l/h = 25$, but not at $l/h = 40$, do exist. Such a connection is, for instance, a connection with a flush end plate, designed to produce sufficient rotational capacity.

4.2.11.2 Connection Restraint Used for Column Strength

Figure 4.25 gives the maximum strength column curves for members with three types of connections and the middle of the SSRC column curve (Johnston, 1976) as reported by Bjorhovde (1988). The vertical axis in Fig. 4.25 gives the relative maximum column strength, and the horizontal one is based on the non-dimensional slenderness term.

Also shown is the Euler curve, as well as the ranges of practical slenderness values for two common steel grades (yield stresses of 36 ksi = 248 MPa and 50 ksi = 345 MPa) that are in extensive use in North America. The strength of the end-restrained columns is significantly higher than that of the pinned-end member. The benefits are clear, and advantage should be taken of this contribution to the performance of the structure. Bjorhovde (1988) proposes the use of the simplified frame stability solution that makes use of the effective length or k-factor concept which was originally

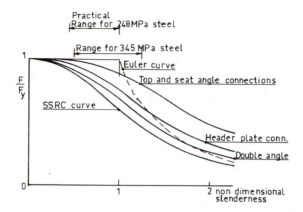

FIG. 4.25.   Column curves for members with different end connections.

developed from considering a sub-assembly of an elastic frame, using rigid beam-to-column connections (Johnston, 1976). With semi-rigid connections Bjorhovde proposes replacement of the relative stiffness distribution factor G, given as

$$G = \frac{E_c I_c / L_c}{E_b I_b / L_b}$$

by

$$G_r = \frac{E_c I_c / L_c}{C^*}$$

where C^* is the effective rotational restraint of the connection. It is noted that a single C^* is to be used for each column end. The reason is shown in Fig. 4.26. As the column buckles, two of the connections of the interior column will unload elastically (stiffness $= C$) and the other two will continue loading with a stiffness equal to the slope of the moment–rotation curve at a point equal to the beam moment before buckling.

Following the above evaluation of the behaviour of an interior column prior to and during buckling, it is clear that when an exterior column fails one end connection will load and the other will unload.

The values of G_r to be used should be based on one C^* at one end of the exterior column, and at the other end a pin could be assumed as the support.

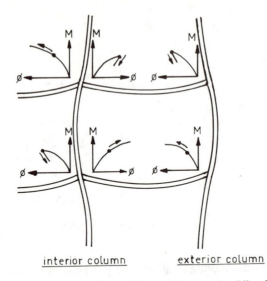

interior column   exterior column

FIG. 4.26.   Deformations of braced frame at buckling load.

4.3. FINAL OBSERVATIONS

Dependent on the rigidity against side-sway, a distinction can be made between braced and unbraced frames. The force distribution in both braced and unbraced frames can be calculated on the basis of either the elastic theory or the plastic theory. In all cases, appropriate code-checking rules are available to determine the bearing capacity, starting from the first-order force distribution which, in most cases, is influenced by plastic behaviour and second-order effects. The bearing capacity of an unbraced frame can be approximated by using the Merchant–Rankine formula which makes use of the first-order plastic bearing capacity and the linear Euler buckling load of the frame. The behaviour of semi-rigid and partial-strength connections influences the outcome of these calculations.

A semi-rigid connection has a calculated rotational stiffness which is smaller than the bending stiffness of the beam over a fictitious length equal to half the depth of the column section. A partial-strength connection has a calculated moment capacity which is smaller than that of the connected beam.

In determining the force distribution in a frame based upon the elastic theory, the calculated rotational stiffness of connections is only of importance for cases with a stiffness ratio $k = cl/EI < 25$. Connections with $k > 25$ can be considered as rigid connections.

From calculations on braced frames, it appears that the calculated ultimate load of the beam increases when the calculated rotational stiffness of the connections decreases. In reality, the actual rotational stiffness of the connection can be larger, but this is not harmful provided that the connection has sufficient rotational capacity for the expected force distribution to be reached. If one designs a frame by means of the elastic theory taking the actual rotational stiffness of the connections into account, and considers all load combinations (including all uneven settlements which can be expected to occur), then theoretically the connections need not have rotational capacity. However, it is too complicated to calculate the exact connection behaviour and it is not realistic to assume that one has taken all the possible load cases and settlements into consideration. Therefore, it is always necessary, even in using elastic theory, to use connections which possess rotational capacity. An exception can be made for connections with a calculated moment capacity which is larger than that of the connected beam. In that case rotational capacity can develop in the beam next to the connection.

A maximum value for the calculated strength of a frame will be reached if the frame is designed on the basis of the first-order plastic theory. In that case the rotational stiffness of the connections is not relevant either for braced frames or for unbraced frames, but the connections must have sufficient rotational capacity. However, the rotational stiffness of the connections is relevant with regard to the stability of the frames. In unbraced frames it influences the second-order effects due to sway, and in braced frames it can be used to reduce the elastic effective length of the columns.

Partial-strength connections can only produce sufficient rotational capacity if the welds in the connection are designed to transfer a moment which is 1·4 times the calculated moment capacity of the connection for braced frames, and 1·7 times for unbraced frames, but not higher than the moment capacity of the connected beam.

Partial-strength connections, which remain elastic up to failure, are not suitable for frames designed according to the plastic theory because of lack of rotational capacity.

Connections designed according to the plastic theory can freely be used in frames designed according to the elastic theory. The rotational stiffness of semi-rigid connections influences the force distribution and the stability of the frames.

REFERENCES

BJORHOVDE, R. (1988) Simplified design approach for end-restrained columns in frames. In *Connections in Steel Structures: Behaviour, Strength and Design* (ed. R. Bjorhovde *et al.*). Elsevier Applied Science Publishers, London, pp. 263–71.

JOHNSTON, B. G. (ed.) (1976) *Guide to Stability Design Criteria for Metal Structures*, 3rd edn. Wiley-Interscience, New York.

Chapter 5

THE STRENGTH OF IN-PLANE FILLET WELDED CONNECTIONS

A. G. KAMTEKAR

Department of Civil Engineering, University of Birmingham, UK

SUMMARY

The ideas of plasticity theory are used to analyse the strengths of two basic planar fillet weld groups subjected to an eccentric coplanar shearing force. The internal loads in the welds are simplified for performing the analysis and the strength of each of the basic weld groups is obtained in terms of the weld group geometry, the load orientation and eccentricity and the weld metal ultimate tensile strength. The effect of residual stresses in the welds is considered. The strength curves for the basic weld groups are used to derive similar curves for other weld groups made up by suitably combining the basic groups. The strength curves can be used directly in design.

NOTATION

a	Spacing between pairs of parallel welds
e	Defined as $(r + a/2)$; see Fig. 5.14
L	Weld length
M_i	Moment on weld i
M_0	Pure couple causing weld group failure
p	Principal stress (p_1, p_2, p_3 are the three principal stresses)
P	Applied external load (suffices c and s denote components $P \cos \theta$ and $P \sin \theta$ respectively)
r	Load eccentricity; Fig. 5.3
w	Weld leg length

X	Longitudinal residual stress in weld
x, y, z	Co-ordinate axes
α	Defined as $\beta\psi + 1/2$
β	(Weld length/spacing) for parallel welds (suffices v and h denote values for welds for which $\theta = 0$ and $90°$ respectively)
η	Defines position of plane of discontinuity
$\bar{\eta}$	Defined as $\eta(1 - \eta)$
η^*	Defined as $[\eta^2 + (1 - \eta)^2]/(1 - 2\eta)$
θ	Weld orientation; Fig. 5.3
κ	Fraction of applied load P carried by one of a pair of parallel welds with $\theta = 0$
λ	Defined as $2 \sin \theta/[3(1 - 2\eta)^2]$
μ_i	Defined as $2M_i/wL^2$
ξ	Defined as e/L
σ	Defined as P/wL (suffices x, y, z denote stresses in co-ordinate directions; suffices c and s denote $\sigma \cos \theta$ and $\sigma \sin \theta$ respectively)
$\bar{\sigma}$	Defined as $P/\sigma_u wL$
σ_u	Ultimate tensile strength of weld metal
τ	Shearing stress (suffices xy, yz, zx denote stresses in yz, zx and xy planes respectively)
χ	Defined as $2\beta[\psi - (\bar{\eta} \sin \theta/(1 - 2\eta))]$
ψ	Defined as (eccentricity/weld length) (suffices v and h denote values of ψ for weld orientations of 0 and $90°$ respectively)
ψ^*	Defined as $\psi/\bar{\eta}$

5.1 INTRODUCTION

Steel structures are made up of a number of discrete elements connected together. If the structure is to act as one unit, the connections have to be designed to transfer load from one element to another. To achieve this it must be possible to determine the maximum load that each connection can transmit.

Many structural elements transfer their loads to other elements through fillet welded connections. Generally, the group of welds that makes up each connection is required to transmit a shearing force and a moment. Frequently it is possible to assume that the group of welds making up a connection all lie in one plane and that the load that the connection is

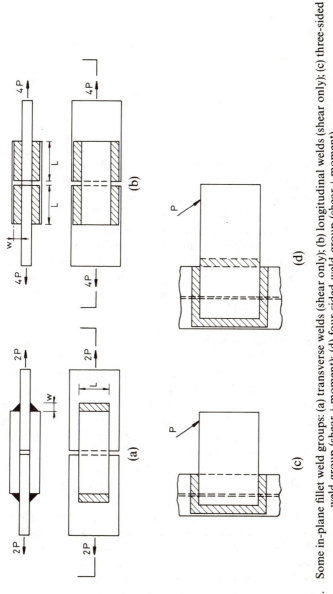

FIG. 5.1.   Some in-plane fillet weld groups: (a) transverse welds (shear only); (b) longitudinal welds (shear only); (c) three-sided weld group (shear + moment); (d) four-sided weld group (shear + moment).

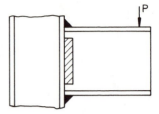

FIG. 5.2.   An out-of-plane weld group.

required to transfer can be idealised as an eccentric shearing force which is applied either in the plane of the weld group (in-plane welds) or in a plane normal to the one containing the welds (out-of-plane welds). Examples of such welds are given in Figs 5.1 and 5.2 respectively.

Figures 5.1(a) and 5.1(b) are the simplest types of fillet welded connections since they transmit a shearing force only. Each weld of Fig. 5.1(a) transmits a shearing force P applied in a direction normal to its length (transverse welds) while each weld of Fig. 5.1(b) transmits a shearing force P applied parallel to its length (longitudinal or shear welds). The in-plane weld groups of Figs. 5.1(c) and 5.1(d), however, transmit both an inclined shearing force and a moment. These weld groups can be considered to be made up of two sub-groups each of which transmits a part of the applied load. The weld group of Fig. 5.1(c) consists of a sub-group containing a single vertical weld and another consisting of a pair of parallel welds whereas that of Fig. 5.1(d) consists of two pairs of parallel welds. If the weld metal is ductile, the capacity of each of these weld groups can be obtained by summing the capacities of its two component sub-groups. Most practical in-plane weld groups can be sub-divided in this way into either single welds or pairs of parallel welds, each sub-group being required to transmit an eccentrically applied shearing force. The strength of such weld groups can, therefore, be assessed if the strengths of the two basic weld groups of Fig. 5.3 can be determined. The problem of assessing the strengths of such weld groups is considered in this chapter.

The analysis of out-of-plane weld groups (Fig. 5.2) is not considered here. It is noted that the strength of the vertical weld in Fig. 5.2 is exactly the same as that of the weld in Fig. 5.3(a) with $\theta = 0$. The analysis of the horizontal welds has been considered elsewhere (Kamtekar, 1984).

The approach described above assumes that the strength of the connection is governed by the failure load of the weld group making up the connection. This will be true only if the connected members are themselves strong enough to carry the load that the weld group is capable of transmitting. The possibility that the connected members might fail before

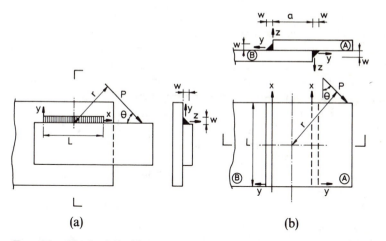

FIG. 5.3.   The basic weld groups: (a) weld group (i); (b) weld group (ii).

the weld group must always be checked, but is not considered in this chapter.

In assessing such connections, it is generally assumed that the connected members remain rigid when the weld group fails so that the relative displacement between them consists of a rotation about some centre of rotation, C (Fig. 5.4). Both the displacement and the resisting force at any point in the weld group are directed along the normal to the line joining the point to C. When the weld group is subjected to a shearing force only (Fig. 5.3, with $r = 0$), C is at infinity so that the resisting force at every point in the weld acts in the same direction (parallel to the line of action of the applied force). When the weld group is subjected to a combination of a shearing force and a moment, however, the direction of the resisting force changes from point to point in the weld (Fig. 5.4).

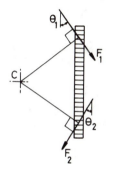

FIG. 5.4.   Direction of displacement and resisting force (F) at points in a weld at failure.

Koenigsberger (1951) suggested that, at failure, the shearing stress caused on the throat by the resisting force at any point in the weld should be set to the ultimate shearing stress of the weld metal, which was to be determined by performing tests on longitudinal welds of the type shown in Fig. 5.1(b). Strength curves could then be drawn for specified weld configurations using the equilibrium equations for the connections.

Butler *et al.* (1972), Clark (1972) and Swannell & Skewes (1979) found, from tests on fillet welds subjected to a shearing force only, that both the load and the deformation in the weld at collapse depended upon the angle θ ($0 \leqslant \theta \leqslant 90°$) between the line of action of the applied force and the direction of the weld length. They assumed that the weld group would fail when the deformation at any point within it reached its ultimate value. Because the orientation of the resisting force in a weld group subjected to both a shearing force and a moment changes along the weld length (Fig. 5.4), the ultimate deformation at each point is different, and it is necessary to determine the point that reaches its ultimate deformation first. Once this point has been located, the deformations of all other points can be calculated. The resisting force at any point can then be obtained from the load–deformation curve corresponding to the angle θ at that point. Again, the magnitude and line of action of the failure load can be calculated from the equilibrium equations for the connection. To apply this approach, however, it is necessary to have available load–deformation curves corresponding to different weld orientations, θ.

Either of the above approaches can be used to calculate the failure loads of weld groups easily if the position of C (Fig. 5.4) is known. The converse (design) problem, in which the line of action of the external force is specified and the magnitude of the failure load is to be calculated (together with the position of C), is much more difficult to solve because the equilibrium equations become non-linear. That is why the available solutions have been presented in either tabular (Butler *et al.*, 1972) or graphical (Koenigsberger, 1951; Clark, 1972; Swannell & Skewes, 1979) form.

A different approach is developed in this chapter for predicting the strength of weld groups. The strengths of the basic groups (Fig. 5.3) are derived in terms of the load eccentricity (r) and orientation (θ), the weld group geometry and the weld metal ultimate tensile strength (σ_u). A pair of parametric equations is obtained to relate the weld group strength to the load eccentricity. These equations can be simplified in some practically important cases to a single equation which directly relates the applied shearing force to its eccentricity. The whole range of loading cases from a pure shearing force to a pure moment is considered. The strength curves that are obtained can be used directly in design.

5.2 THE METHOD

The ideas of plastic theory are used to assess the strengths of the basic weld groups of Fig. 5.3. It is assumed that the weld metal is ductile so that the whole weld length will have yielded at failure.

The analysis begins by determining the internal loads in the welds; these must be in equilibrium with the external loads and must also keep the weld in equilibrium. The internal loads will, in general, consist of direct and shearing forces and moments acting on the weld legs. Each moment is replaced by a pair of equal and opposite forces (i.e. a couple) which is equivalent to it in a static sense. The resulting force system consists only of direct and shearing forces on the weld legs. At failure, these are assumed to give rise to uniform stresses on the areas over which they act. The weld length can then be divided into regions in each of which the stress system is uniform. The strength of the weld group when it is subjected to this revised stress system is determined and this is assumed to be a good estimate of its strength when it is subjected to the actual load system.

When determining the stresses in the welds it must be remembered that there are residual stresses locked into the weld metal when it is deposited. In the as-welded condition the major residual stress acts in the direction parallel to the weld length, is tensile and initially (i.e. when there is no external load) has a magnitude approximately equal to the yield stress of the weld metal (Kamtekar, 1987a). There are other stresses present in the weld but these are generally small and are neglected in the analysis. The longitudinal stress (say X) is assumed to remain constant along the weld length. Thus, unless the welds are initially stress-relieved, the weld metal is at yield even before it is subjected to any external load. As the external load (P) is applied, the internal stresses redistribute themselves to enable the weld to carry the applied load but the weld metal remains at yield. Thus the value of X changes as P is increased but remains constant along the weld length at every stage. Its value at collapse has to be determined.

When this approach is applied to welds subjected to a shearing force only the entire weld length is subjected to a uniform stress state at failure (Kamtekar, 1987a). When the applied force is eccentric, however, the weld has to transmit a moment and its length is divided into two regions in each of which the stress system is uniform (Kamtekar, 1984). The stress system is, therefore, discontinuous at the (plane) boundary between the two regions. The stresses in these regions must be chosen to ensure that they satisfy the equilibrium conditions at the plane of discontinuity. Kamtekar (1984) has shown that this will happen if all the stresses acting in the direction normal to the plane of discontinuity have the same values in the two regions; stresses acting in a direction parallel to the plane of discontinuity can have different values in the two regions without affecting equilibrium.

It is assumed that the weld group will fail when all the weld metal is stressed to its ultimate tensile stress (UTS), σ_u. To express this condition analytically it is convenient to determine the principal stresses in each region of the weld. An orthogonal set of axes (x, y, z) is selected and the stresses in each region are expressed in terms of the stresses $\sigma_x, \sigma_y, \sigma_z$, $\tau_{xy} (=\tau_{yx})$, $\tau_{yz}(=\tau_{zy})$ and $\tau_{zx}(=\tau_{xz})$ acting in the co-ordinate directions. The principal stresses p_1, p_2 and p_3 in each region can then be calculated (Timoshenko & Goodier, 1982) as the roots of the following cubic equation in p:

$$\begin{vmatrix} (\sigma_x - p) & \tau_{yx} & \tau_{zx} \\ \tau_{xy} & (\sigma_y - p) & \tau_{zy} \\ \tau_{xz} & \tau_{yz} & (\sigma_z - p) \end{vmatrix} = 0 \tag{5.1}$$

To find the stresses σ_x etc. in terms of the applied load, it is convenient to treat the weld cross-section as the y, z plane, with the y and z axes coinciding with the weld legs, and the weld root as the x axis. It should be noted that the sloping face of the weld, being a free surface, has neither shear nor direct stresses on it. It is therefore a principal plane and one principal stress is always zero. $p = 0$ is a root of eqn (5.1) so that it is only necessary to determine the other two roots by solving a quadratic equation.

The weld metal is assumed to obey the von Mises yield criterion (Mendelson, 1968) which can be written as

$$2\sigma_u^2 = (p_1 - p_2)^2 + (p_2 - p_3)^2 + (p_3 - p_1)^2 \tag{5.2}$$

Substituting the principal stresses calculated from eqn (5.1) into eqn (5.2) leads to a relationship between P, its eccentricity (r), the weld group geometry and those variables which cannot be determined from the equilibrium equations for the connection. These variables are chosen as follows. The approach adopted is similar to that used when the lower bound theorem is applied in the theory of structures (Neal, 1977). In that case a value of the external load which is in equilibrium with any internal load distribution which satisfies the static boundary conditions of the problem and which does not violate the yield criterion anywhere is a lower bound on the exact collapse load. In the approach described for calculating the strength of weld groups, stress distributions which are in equilibrium with the external load and which satisfy the yield condition everywhere are used. Hence, the external load calculated from the assumed internal stress distribution would be expected to be a lower bound on the failure load of the connection so that the undetermined variables should be chosen to *maximise* the failure load. It turns out that the stress distributions adopted sometimes require shearing forces to act on the end cross-sections of the weld. Since these cannot be present in reality, the calculated failure loads will only be estimates of the actual failure loads.

5.3 ANALYSIS OF THE WELD GROUPS

5.3.1 Assumptions
The following assumptions are made in the analysis:

(i)   Moments acting on the welds can be replaced by statically 'equivalent' couples.

(ii)   The strength of the weld when subjected to this revised load system is a good estimate of its actual strength.

(iii)   The residual stress system in the welds consists of a longitudinal tensile stress only; this stress remains constant along the weld length.

(iv)   The weld metal is ductile and all of it yields before failure occurs.

(v)   The weld metal obeys the von Mises yield criterion.

(vi)   The yield stress at collapse is the weld metal UTS, σ_u.

(vii)   The welds have equal legs, each of length w.

(viii) Failure occurs in the weld metal only.

5.3.2 Analysis of Basic Weld Group (i)
The loads on plates A and B and on the connection are shown in Fig. 5.5. The externally applied force P is transferred to the weld as a tensile force $P_s (= P \sin \theta)$, a shearing force $P_c (= P \cos \theta)$ and a moment Pr applied on the face in contact with plate A. The weld transfers the load to plate B as shearing forces of magnitude P_s and P_c and a moment Pr on the leg in contact with that plate.

The forces P_s and P_c give rise to uniform stresses σ_s and σ_c repectively on the faces on which they act, where $\sigma = P/wL$ (Fig. 5.6(a)). The moment Pr

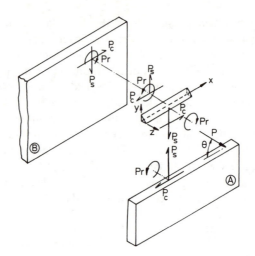

FIG. 5.5. Loads of components of weld group (i).

will give rise to stresses that act in the direction of P_s and vary along the
weld length. Pr is replaced by a couple, the tensile and compressive forces
leading to corresponding direct stresses on the weld leg in contact with plate
A (i.e. the x, z plane). Since these give rise to uniform stresses on the areas of
the leg over which they act, there will be a discontinuity in the normal
stresses that act on the x, z plane at the plane where the stresses due to the
moment change from tensile to compressive. Suppose that this plane of
discontinuity, which divides the weld length into two regions, is defined by
$x = \eta L$ (Fig. 5.6(a)). The (uniform) normal stress (σ_{11}) on the x, z plane in
region 1 consists of the stress $\sigma \sin \theta$ together with the tensile stress due to
the moment Pr, and the tensile stress (σ_{12}) in region 2 consists of the stress
$\sigma \sin \theta$ superimposed on the compressive stress due to the moment Pr. From
equilibrium, the stresses due to the moment in regions 1 and 2 are
$2\sigma\psi/(1-\eta)$ and $-2\sigma\psi/\eta$ respectively, so that

$$\sigma_{11} = \sigma \sin \theta + 2\sigma\psi/(1-\eta) \tag{5.3a}$$

$$\sigma_{12} = \sigma \sin \theta - 2\sigma\psi/\eta \tag{5.3b}$$

From a similar argument it follows that shearing stresses σ_{11} and σ_{12} act in
the y direction on the x, y plane in regions 1 and 2 respectively (Fig. 5.6(a)).

There are some out-of-balance moments present in the weld. By taking
moments about the co-ordinate axes, it is found that moments of
magnitude $0.5\,wP \cos \theta$ act about each of the y and z axes, and moments

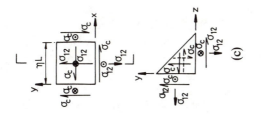

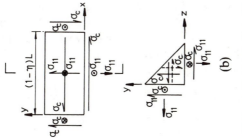

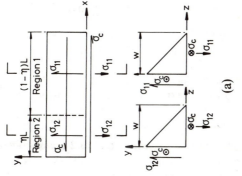

Fig. 5.6.   Stresses in group (i) welds.

$0.5(1-\eta)w^2L\sigma_{11}$ and $0.5\eta w^2L\sigma_{12}$ act about the x axis in regions 1 and 2 respectively. All these moments are replaced by statically 'equivalent' couples, as before. The moment about the y axis is replaced by shearing forces of magnitude $(wP\cos\theta)/2L$ on the triangular end faces of the weld in the z direction, and that about the z axis gives rise to shearing forces of the same magnitude on the end faces in the y direction. These forces give rise to stresses $\sigma\cos\theta$ in both y and z directions on the two end faces. The moment about the x axis in region 1 is replaced by a couple consisting of forces of magnitude $(1-\eta)wL\sigma_{11}$, one acting as a tensile force on the x,y plane and the other as a shearing force in the z direction on the x,z plane, giving rise to corresponding stress σ_{11} on these planes (Fig. 5.6(b)). Similarly, the moment in region 2 is equivalent to a tensile stress σ_{12} on the x,y plane and a shearing stress in the z direction on the x,z plane (Fig. 5.6(c)).

In addition to the stresses shown in Figs 5.6(b) and 5.6(c), there is a longitudinal tensile residual stress (X) present in the weld. The weld is in equilibrium under this set of stresses, which satisfies the required conditions at the plane of discontinuity. The stresses in each region are uniform and those in region 1 can be defind using the standard convention for stress (see Timoshenko & Goodier, 1982) as

$$\sigma_x = X, \ \sigma_y = \sigma_z = \sigma_{11}, \ \tau_{xy} = -\sigma\cos\theta, \ \tau_{yz} = -\sigma_{11}, \ \tau_{zx} = \sigma\cos\theta$$

The stress field in region 2 is obtained by replacing σ_{11} by σ_{12} in the above set of stresses.

Using the stresses in region 1, eqn (5.1) reduces to

$$p[(X-p)(2\sigma_{11}-p)-2(\sigma\cos\theta)^2]=0$$

whence the principal stresses in this region become

$$p_1=0, \ p_{2,3}=(X+2\sigma_{11})\pm R$$

where $R^2=(X-2\sigma_{11})^2+8(\sigma\cos\theta)^2$.

At failure, the principal stresses in region 1 satisfy eqn (5.2). Hence

$$\sigma_u^2 = X^2 - 2X\sigma_{11} + 4\sigma_{11}^2 + 6(\sigma\cos\theta)^2 \qquad (5.4a)$$

Noting that the principal stresses in region 2 are obtained by replacing σ_{11} by σ_{12} in the stress system in region 1, the stresses in region 2 must satisfy the following equation at failure (for yielding):

$$\sigma_u^2 = X^2 - 2X\sigma_{12} + 4\sigma_{12}^2 + 6(\sigma\cos\theta)^2 \qquad (5.4b)$$

The problem has now been reduced to finding the value of the failure load (σ) from eqns (5.4a) and (5.4b). σ is a function of X and η; one of these variables can be eliminated from eqns (5.4) to leave σ as a function of the other. This undetermined variable can then be chosen to maximise σ, as discussed earlier.

Subtracting eqn (5.4b) from eqn (5.4a) gives

$$0 = (\sigma_{11} - \sigma_{12})[2(\sigma_{11} + \sigma_{12}) - X]$$

Either $\sigma_{11} = \sigma_{12}$ or $X = 2(\sigma_{11} + \sigma_{12})$. Substituting from eqns (5.3), the first possibility can be shown to imply the special case $\psi = 0$. In general, therefore, the second possibility governs, whence

$$X = 4\sigma[\sin\theta - \psi^*(1 - 2\eta)] \qquad (5.5)$$

where $\psi^* = \psi/\bar{\eta}$ and $\bar{\eta} = \eta(1 - \eta)$. Using this value in eqn (5.4a) gives

$$\bar{\sigma} = \sigma/\sigma_u = 0 \cdot 5[3 \sin^2\theta - 6\psi^*(1 - 2\eta)\sin\theta +$$
$$4\psi^{*2}(1 - 3\bar{\eta}) + 1 \cdot 5 \cos^2\theta]^{-0 \cdot 5} \qquad (5.6)$$

The failure load (σ) has now been obtained as a function of η, which must be chosen to allow the weld to transmit the maximum possible load. Differentiating eqn (5.6) and setting $d\sigma/d\eta = 0$ gives

$$2\psi(1 - 2\eta)(2 - 3\bar{\eta}) = 3\bar{\eta}(1 - 2\bar{\eta})\sin\theta \qquad (5.7)$$

η cannot easily be eliminated between eqns (5.6) and (5.7) in all cases to obtain a direct relationship between $\bar{\sigma}$ and ψ. The general results can be presented as strength/eccentricity curves for different values of θ. These are obtained by noting that, as the loading varies from pure shear ($\psi = 0$) to a pure couple, $M_0(P \to 0, r \to \infty$ but $Pr = M_0)$, eqn (5.7) requires η to vary in the range $(0, 0 \cdot 5)$ so long as P acts in the direction shown in Fig. 5.3(a). For a specified value of θ, values of η can be chosen in this range and corresponding values of ψ and $\bar{\sigma}$ can be obtained from eqns (5.7) and (5.6) respectively. Strength curves for $\theta = 0, 30°, 60°$ and $90°$ are given in Fig. 5.7.

It is worth noting some interesting points that emerge from the analysis and can be observed in Fig. 5.7:

(i) Figure 5.7 shows that, when the weld is subjected to a shearing force only ($\psi = 0$), transverse welds ($\theta = 90°$) are considerably stronger than longitudinal ones ($\theta = 0$). When $\psi = 0$, eqn (5.7) requires $\eta = 0$ but

$$\psi^* = \frac{3}{2} \frac{(1 - 2\bar{\eta})\sin\theta}{(1 - 2\eta)(2 - 3\bar{\eta})} \to \frac{3}{4}\sin\theta \text{ when } \eta \to 0$$

Equation (5.5) now gives $X = \sigma \sin\theta$ and eqn (5.6) becomes

$$\bar{\sigma} = 1/\sqrt{3(2 - \sin^2\theta)} \qquad (5.8)$$

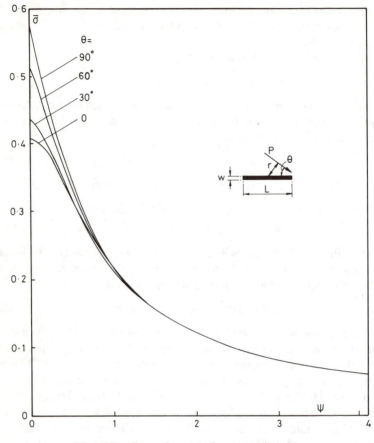

FIG. 5.7.   Strength curves for group (i) welds.

Thus, $\bar{\sigma}$ for transverse and longitudinal welds in $1/\sqrt{3}$ and $1/\sqrt{6}$ respectively, so transverse welds are $\sqrt{2}$ times stronger than similar longitudinal welds. The values of X at collapse for the two welds are σ and zero respectively, so the strength of a transverse weld would be affected if it is stress relieved and loading does not induce a longitudinal stess in it, but that of a longitudinal weld would not be.

(ii) When $\theta = 0$, eqn (5.7) requires $\eta = 0.5$. Then $\psi^* = 4\psi$, whence eqn (5.6) gives

$$\bar{\sigma} = 1/\sqrt{6 + 64\psi^2} \qquad (5.9)$$

Thus, when $\psi = 0$ and when $\theta = 0$, the weld strength is directly related to the weld metal properties and the load eccentricity.

(iii) The slope of the curve for $\theta = 90°$ for small ψ is much steeper than that for the curve for $\theta = 0$ (Fig. 5.7). Hence, in experiments, small eccentricities would be expected markedly to affect the strength of transverse welds but not that of longitudinal welds. For example, if $\psi = 0.05$, the strength of a transverse weld will be more than 10% lower than its strength when $\psi = 0$, whereas the strength of a longitudinal weld will change by only about 1% (eqn (5.9)).

(iv) If the external load consists of a pure moment, M_0, eqn (5.7) requires $\eta = 0.5$ (since $\psi \to \infty$), whence, noting that $\sigma \to 0$ and that $\sigma\psi = M_0/wL^2$, eqn (5.6) gives the value of M_0 at failure as

$$M_0 = \sigma_u wL^2/8 \qquad (5.10)$$

The ultimate value of M_0 is therefore independent of the weld orientation, as may be expected. This is why all the curves in Fig. 5.7 merge for higher values of ψ when the moment becomes the dominant load effect. Further, since $\eta = 0.5$, eqn (5.5) requires $X = 0$, so M_0 is not affected by the presence of residual stresses.

(v) The effect of stress-relieving the weld can be studied by setting $X = 0$ in the analysis. The relationship between ψ and η is obtained directly from eqn (5.5) as

$$\psi(1 - 2\eta) = \eta(1 - \eta)\sin\theta \qquad (5.11)$$

Equation (5.6) again gives the failure load. If $\theta = 0$, $\eta = 0.5$, confirming that the strength of a longitudinal weld is not affected by stress relieving (eqn (5.5)). Generally the strength *is* affected, being slightly lower when the weld has initially been stress relieved. The effect on the strength of a transverse weld is shown in Fig. 5.8 where it is seen that the maximum reduction in strength is about 15% ($1/\sqrt{3}$ compared to 0.5). When ψ increases, the effect of the longitudinal stress decreases, becoming negligible when $\psi > 1$.

5.3.3 Analysis of Basic Weld Group (ii)

The externally applied force (P) is shared between the two parallel welds making up this group, and the aim of the analysis is to find the load distribution which will enable the weld group to transmit the maximum possible load.

In general, each weld will be subjected to a horizontal and vertical force and a moment on each face in contact with the component plates (Fig. 5.9). The six loads shown in Fig. 5.9 are related by the equilibrium equations for

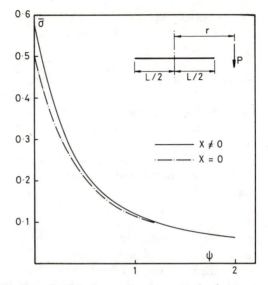

FIG. 5.8.   The effect of residual stress on the strength of an eccentrically loaded transverse weld.

the component plates. Considering plate A, for example (Fig. 5.10), and using the notation $\sigma_i = P_i/wL$, $\mu_i = 2M_i/wL^2$ $(i = 1, 2)$ and $\beta = L/a$, the equilibrium equations can be written as

$$\sigma_1 + \sigma_2 = \sigma \cos \theta \tag{5.12a}$$

$$\sigma_3 + \sigma_4 = \sigma \sin \theta \tag{5.12b}$$

$$2\sigma_1 + \beta(\mu_1 + \mu_2) = \sigma(2\beta\psi + \cos \theta) \tag{5.12c}$$

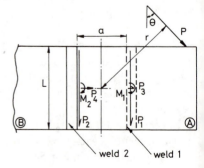

FIG. 5.9.   Internal loads on group (ii) welds.

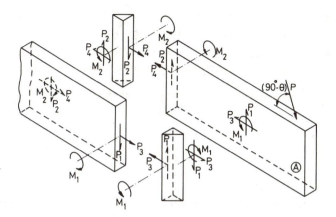

FIG. 5.10.   Loads on components of group (ii) welds.

The moments M_1 and M_2 can be replaced by couples, as before. The equal and opposite forces on the weld legs that make up these couples will again give rise to a discontinuity in the stress field in each weld. It is assumed that the discontinuity in each weld occurs at the same distance ηL from an end (Fig. 5.11). The stresses caused by the couples act in the y direction and,

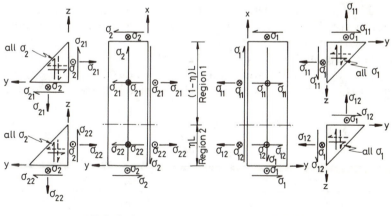

WELD 2   WELD 1

FIG. 5.11.   Stresses caused by the external force in group (ii) welds (stresses on far end of each region shown dashed on sections).

from considerations of equilibrium, have magnitudes $\mu_i/(1-\eta)$ and μ_i/η in regions 1 and 2 respectively of weld i $(i=1, 2)$. When these are superimposed on the uniform stresses caused on the weld legs by the forces in the y direction $(P_3$ and $P_4)$, the stresses σ_{ij} in the y direction in region j of weld i become

$$\sigma_{11} = \sigma_3 + \mu_1/(1-\eta) \qquad (5.13a)$$

$$\sigma_{12} = \sigma_3 - \mu_1/\eta \qquad (5.13b)$$

$$\sigma_{21} = \sigma_4 + \mu_2/(1-\eta) \qquad (5.13c)$$

$$\sigma_{22} = \sigma_4 - \mu_2/\eta \qquad (5.13d)$$

These stresses act as tensile stresses on the x, z planes and as shearing stresses on the x, y planes of the welds (Fig. 5.11).

As in the case of group (i) welds, there are out-of-balance moments present in the weld. In weld 1 these are

(a) moments $0.5\,wP$, about each of the y and z axes
(b) a moment $0.5(1-\eta)w^2 L\sigma_{11}$ about the x axis in region 1
(c) a moment $0.5\eta w^2 L\sigma_{12}$ about the x axis in region 2

The moments on weld 2 are obtained by replacing σ_{11} and σ_{12} by σ_{21} and σ_{22} respectively.

The moments (a) above can be replaced by couples in the y and z directions on the end faces, the forces making up these couples being of magnitude $0.5\,wP_1/L$; these lead to stresses σ_1 in each of these directions on the end faces. The moment (b) is replaced by a couple of forces of magnitude $(1-\eta)wL\sigma_{11}$ in region 1, and the moment (c) is replaced by a couple of forces of magnitude $\eta wL\sigma_{12}$ in region 2, one force acting as a tension on the x, y plane and the other as a shearing force in the z direction on the y, z plane in each region; these forces give rise to corresponding stresses σ_{11} and σ_{12} in

TABLE 5.1
FINAL STRESS FIELDS

Stress component	σ_x	σ_y	σ_z	τ_{xy}	τ_{yz}	τ_{zx}
Weld 1, region 1	X_1	σ_{11}	σ_{11}	$-\sigma_1$	$-\sigma_{11}$	σ_1
Weld 1, region 2	X_1	σ_{12}	σ_{12}	$-\sigma_1$	$-\sigma_{12}$	σ_1
Weld 2, region 1	X_2	σ_{21}	σ_{21}	σ_2	$-\sigma_{21}$	$-\sigma_2$
Weld 2, region 2	X_2	σ_{22}	σ_{22}	σ_2	$-\sigma_{22}$	$-\sigma_2$

the two regions. Similarly, stresses of magnitude σ_2 act in the y and z directions on the end faces of weld 2, and stresses σ_{21} and σ_{22} act in the z direction in regions 1 and 2 of that weld. The stresses due to the external load are as indicated in Fig. 5.11. In addition to these stresses, longitudinal tensile residual stresses X_1 and X_2 are present in welds 1 and 2 respectively at failure. The final stress fields are given in Table 5.1.

The principal stresses in each region are obtained by substituting the sets of stresses (Table 5.1) in eqn (5.1) in turn. The principal stresses in weld i, region j ($i, j = 1, 2$), are

$$p_1 = 0; \quad p_{2,3} = 0 \cdot 5[(X_i + 2\sigma_{ij}) \pm R_{ij}] \tag{5.14}$$

where $R_{ij}^2 = (X_i - 2\sigma_{ij})^2 + 8\sigma_i^2$

Since all the weld metal has to yield at failure, the principal stresses in each region must satisfy eqn (5.2). This requires

$$\sigma_u^2 = X_1^2 - 2X_1\sigma_{11} + 4\sigma_{11}^2 + 6\sigma_1^2 \tag{5.15a}$$

$$\sigma_u^2 = X_1^2 - 2X_1\sigma_{12} + 4\sigma_{12}^2 + 6\sigma_1^2 \tag{5.15b}$$

$$\sigma_u^2 = X_2^2 - 2X_2\sigma_{21} + 4\sigma_{21}^2 + 6\sigma_2^2 \tag{5.15c}$$

$$\sigma_u^2 = X_2^2 - 2X_2\sigma_{22} + 4\sigma_{22}^2 + 6\sigma_2^2 \tag{5.15d}$$

Subtracting eqn (5.15b) from eqn (5.15a) and eqn (5.15d) from eqn (5.15c) gives

$$0 = -2X_1(\sigma_{11} - \sigma_{12}) + 4(\sigma_{11} - \sigma_{12})(\sigma_{11} + \sigma_{12}) \tag{5.16a}$$

$$0 = -2X_2(\sigma_{21} - \sigma_{22}) + 4(\sigma_{21} - \sigma_{22})(\sigma_{21} + \sigma_{22}) \tag{5.16b}$$

Equation (5.16a) leads to the conclusion that either $\sigma_{11} = \sigma_{12}$ or $X_1 = 2(\sigma_{11} + \sigma_{12})$.

Similarly, from eqn (5.16b), either $\sigma_{21} = \sigma_{22}$ or $X_2 = 2(\sigma_{21} + \sigma_{22})$.

Using eqns (5.13), the solution $\sigma_{11} = \sigma_{12}$ implies that $\mu_1 = 0$. This means that M_1 and therefore η are both zero, whence M_2 (and μ_2) must also be zero (i.e. $\sigma_{21} = \sigma_{22}$) and neither weld is subjected to a moment. Consider this case first.

Since $\mu_1 = \mu_2 = 0$, eqns (5.15a) and (5.15b) become identical, as do eqns (5.15c) and (5.15d). From eqn (5.12c)

$$\sigma_1 = \sigma(\beta\psi + 0 \cdot 5 \cos \theta) \tag{5.17a}$$

whence eqn (5.12a) gives

$$\sigma_2 = \sigma(0 \cdot 5 \cos \theta - \beta\psi) \tag{5.17b}$$

Using eqns (5.12b) and (5.17), eqns (5.15a) and (5.15c) become

$$\sigma_u^2 = X_1^2 - 2X_1\sigma_3 + 4\sigma_3^2 + 6\sigma^2(\beta\psi + 0{\cdot}5\cos\theta)^2 \qquad (5.18a)$$

$$\sigma_u^2 = X_2^2 - 2X_2(\sigma\sin\theta - \sigma_3) + 4(\sigma\sin\theta - \sigma_3)^2 + 6\sigma^2(0{\cdot}5\cos\theta - \beta\psi)^2 \quad (5.18b)$$

σ_3 can be eliminated from eqns (5.18) to give σ as a function of X_1 and X_2, which can be chosen to maximise σ. It is in fact easier to differentiate eqns (5.18) with respect to X_1 and X_2 in turn (remembering that σ_3 is a function of these two variables) and setting $\partial\sigma/\partial X_1 = \partial\sigma/\partial X_2 = 0$. Equation (5.18a) gives

$$(X_1 - 4\sigma_3)\frac{\partial\sigma_3}{\partial X_1} = X_1 - \sigma_3 \qquad (5.19a)$$

and

$$(4\sigma_3 - X_1)\frac{\partial\sigma_3}{\partial X_2} = 0 \qquad (5.19b)$$

while eqn (5.18b) requires that

$$[X_2 - 4(\sigma\sin\theta - \sigma_3)]\frac{\partial\sigma_3}{\partial X_1} = 0 \qquad (5.19c)$$

and

$$[X_2 - 4(\sigma\sin\theta - \sigma_3)]\frac{\partial\sigma_3}{\partial X_2} = \sigma\sin\theta - \sigma_3 - X_2 \qquad (5.19d)$$

Equation (5.19b) shows that either $X_1 = 4\sigma_3$ or $\partial\sigma_3/\partial X_2 = 0$, and eqn (5.19c) requires that either $X_2 = 4(\sigma\sin\theta - \sigma_3)$ or $\partial\sigma_3/\partial X_1 = 0$. These values of X_1 and X_2 do not satisfy eqns (5.19a) and (5.19d), so the only possible solution is $\partial\sigma_3/\partial X_1 = \partial\sigma_3/\partial X_2 = 0$. When these conditions are applied to eqns (5.19a) and (5.19d) respectively, the values of X_1 and X_2 are obtained as

$$X_1 = \sigma_3, \quad X_2 = \sigma\sin\theta - \sigma_3 \qquad (5.20)$$

and σ_3 is obtained as

$$\sigma_3 = \sigma(0{\cdot}5\sin\theta - 2\beta\psi\cot\theta) \qquad (5.21)$$

provided that $\theta \neq 0$. By substituting eqns (5.20) and (5.21) into either of the equations (5.18) the weld strength can now be calculated as

$$\bar{\sigma} = \sigma/\sigma_u = \{0{\cdot}75[(1 + \cos^2\theta) + 8\beta^2\psi^2(1 + 2\cot^2\theta)]\}^{-0{\cdot}5} \qquad (5.22)$$

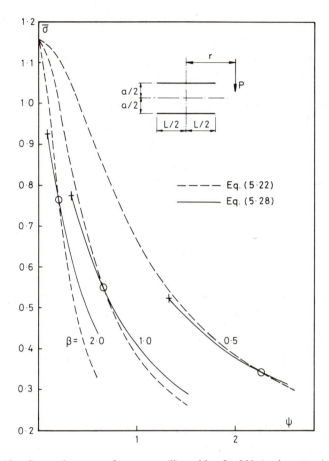

FIG. 5.12.   Strength curves for group (ii) welds, $\theta = 90°$ ($+$ denotes ψ_{min} and ◯ denotes point of intersection of curves of eqns (5.22) and (5.28)).

$\theta = 0$ is a special case and is considered later. Equation (5.22) is shown plotted as the dashed curves in Fig. 5.12 for $\theta = 90°$ and three values of β.

Consider now the second solution of eqn (5.16). Substituting for $\sigma_{11}, \sigma_{12}, \sigma_{21}$ and σ_{22} from eqns (5.13), X_1 and X_2 become

$$X_1 = 2\sigma_3 - [\mu_1(1 - 2\eta)/\bar{\eta}] \tag{5.23a}$$

$$X_2 = 2\sigma_4 - [\mu_2(1 - 2\eta)/\bar{\eta}] \tag{5.23b}$$

Using these expressions for X_1 and X_2 in eqns (5.15a) and (5.15c) provides two equations which, together with eqns (5.12), form five equations from which the eight remaining variables of the problem (σ, σ_1 to σ_4, μ_1, μ_2 and η) have to be determined. This problem proved to be difficult to solve. Noting that residual stresses did not significantly affect the strength of group (i) welds for higher values of ψ, the analysis was continued by *setting* $X_1 = X_2 = 0$. Then σ_3 and σ_4 can be obtained from eqns (5.23) and substituted into eqn (5.12b) to give

$$(1 - 2\eta)(\mu_1 + \mu_2) = \bar{\eta}\sigma \sin\theta \qquad (5.24)$$

When $\theta = 0$, the left-hand side of eqn (5.24) is zero for all μ_1 and μ_2. Hence $\eta = 0.5$. When $\theta \neq 0$, $(\mu_1 + \mu_2)$ can be eliminated from eqns (5.12c) and (5.24) to obtain

$$2\sigma_1 = \sigma(\chi + \cos\theta) \qquad (5.25a)$$

where $\chi = 2\beta[\psi - (\bar{\eta}\sin\theta/(1 - 2\eta))]$. Now σ_2 is obtained from eqn (5.12a) as

$$2\sigma_2 = -\sigma(\chi - \cos\theta) \qquad (5.25b)$$

Using these values of σ_1 and σ_2, eqns (5.13a) and (5.13c) give $\sigma_{11} = \mu_1/2\bar{\eta}$ and $\sigma_{21} = \mu_2/2\bar{\eta}$, whence the yield conditions become

$$\sigma_u^2 = (\mu_1/\bar{\eta})^2 + 6\sigma_1^2 = (\mu_2/\bar{\eta})^2 + 6\sigma_2^2 \qquad (5.26)$$

μ_1 and μ_2 can now be calculated from eqns (5.24) and (5.26) as

$$2\mu_1 = -3\bar{\eta}\sigma(1 - 2\eta)(\chi \cot\theta - \lambda) \qquad (5.27a)$$

$$2\mu_2 = 3\bar{\eta}\sigma(1 - 2\eta)(\chi \cot\theta + \lambda) \qquad (5.27b)$$

where $\lambda = 2\sin\theta/[3(1 - 2\eta)^2]$. The strength of the connection can be obtained from eqns (5.25a), (5.26) and (5.27a) as

$$\bar{\sigma} = \sigma/\sigma_u = \{[3/(2\lambda \sin\theta)][\lambda \sin\theta + \cos^2\theta][\chi^2 + \lambda \sin\theta]\}^{-0.5} \quad (5.28)$$

σ is now a function of η only. The value of η to be used in eqn (5.28) for any specified load eccentricity, ψ, is chosen to maximise σ. By differentiating eqn (5.28) it is found that σ becomes a maximum when η satisfies the equation

$$\chi^2 \cot^2\theta + \chi\beta\eta*(\cos\theta \cot\theta + \lambda) - \lambda^2 = 0 \qquad (5.29)$$

where $\eta* = \{[\eta^2 + (1 - \eta)^2]/(1 - 2\eta)\}$. Strength curves for specified values of θ are easily obtained by choosing values of η in the range $(0, 0.5)$, calculating χ (and hence ψ) from eqn (5.29) for each chosen value of η, and thence the corresponding value of $\bar{\sigma}$ from eqn (5.28). Curves for $\theta = 90°$ and three β values are shown by the full lines in Fig. 5.12. It is not possible significantly to simplify eqns (5.28) and (5.29) for specific values of θ.

If the connection has to transmit a pure couple M_0, $\sigma \to 0$, $\psi \to \infty$ and $\sigma \psi = M_0/wL^2$ $(= \bar{M}$ say). Equations (5.12) require $\sigma_1 = -\sigma_2$, $\sigma_3 = -\sigma_4$ and $2\sigma_1 + \beta(\mu_1 + \mu_2) = 2\beta\bar{M}$. Assuming that $X_1 = X_2 = 0$, σ_3 and σ_4 are obtained from eqns (5.23). Since $\sigma_3 = -\sigma_4$, either $\eta = 1/2$ or $\mu_1 = -\mu_2$. Consider first that $\eta = 0.5$; then, $\sigma_3 = \sigma_4 = 0$ from eqns (5.23) and $\sigma_{11} = -\sigma_{12} = 2\mu_1$ and $\sigma_{21} = -\sigma_{22} = 2\mu_2$ from eqns (5.13). Since $\sigma_1 = -\sigma_2$, the yield conditions (eqns (5.15)) become

$$\sigma_u^2 = 4(2\mu_1)^2 + 6\sigma_1^2 = 4(2\mu_2)^2 + 6\sigma_1^2 \tag{5.30}$$

so that $\mu_1 = \mu_2$, since it has been assumed that $\mu_1 \neq -\mu_2$. Equation (5.12c) now gives $\sigma_1 = \beta(\bar{M} - \mu_1)$. Substituting this into eqn (5.30), the equation for determining M at collapse is obtained as

$$\sigma_u^2 = 16\mu_1^2 + 6\beta^2(\bar{M} - \mu_1)^2 \tag{5.31}$$

μ_1 is chosen to maximise $\bar{M}$, which happens when

$$\mu_1 = 3\bar{M}\beta^2/(3\beta^2 + 8) \tag{5.32}$$

The failure moment is obtained from eqn (5.31) as

$$M_0 = \sigma_u \frac{wL^2}{4\beta} \sqrt{\frac{3\beta^2 + 8}{3}} \tag{5.33}$$

To complete the analysis it is necessary to show that this moment is always greater than the failure moment that will be predicted if $\mu_1 = -\mu_2$. In this case, eqn (5.12c) gives $\sigma_1 = \bar{M}\beta$, eqns (5.23) give $\sigma_3 = -\sigma_4 = \mu_1(1 - 2\eta)/2\bar{\eta}$ and the yield condition becomes

$$\sigma_u^2 = (\mu_1/\bar{\eta})^2 + 6\bar{M}^2\beta^2$$

Clearly $\bar{M}$ is maximum when $\mu_1 = 0$ and the maximum moment is predicted to be $\sigma_u wL^2/(\beta\sqrt{6})$. This is always less than the failure moment predicted by eqn (5.33). Since eqn (5.33) does not have terms in θ, the failure moment is independent of the weld orientation.

The analysis has provided two expressions (eqns (5.22) and (5.28)) for the failure load when $\theta \neq 0$, and it is necessary to decide which of these is to be used. It can be seen from eqn (5.29) that $\psi \neq 0$ when $\eta = 0$, so the analysis that leads to eqn (5.28) allows the weld to carry a moment when $\eta = 0$. The strength curve obtained from eqn (5.28) will not reach the $\bar{\sigma}$ axis; this can be seen in Fig. 5.12 for $\theta = 90°$. The value (ψ_{min}) of ψ obtained from eqn (5.29) with $\eta = 0$ decreases as θ decreases (Fig. 5.13). Clearly, eqn (5.22) predicts the strength when $\psi < \psi_{min}$. Since the aim is to provide the largest possible

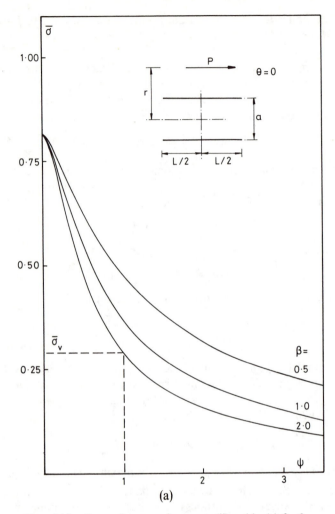

FIG. 5.13.   Strength curves for group (ii) welds. (a) $\theta = 0$.

failure load for the weld group, the expression to be used when $\psi > \psi_{min}$ is the one which gives the higher value of $\bar{\sigma}$. Reference to Fig. 5.12 shows that for $\theta = 90°$ there is a small range of values of $\psi > \psi_{min}$ for which eqn (5.22) predicts a higher failure load than eqn (5.28). For higher ψ values, eqn (5.28) always leads to the higher load. The strength curve is therefore discontinuous (Fig. 5.12) where the curves obtained from eqns (5.22) and (5.28)

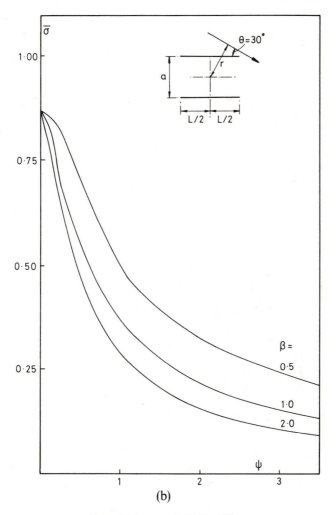

FIG. 5.13.—contd. (b) $\theta = 30°$.

intersect. Strength curves for values of θ other than $\theta = 0$ are similar; curves for $\theta = 30°$, $60°$ and $90°$ are shown in Fig. 5.13 for three β values.

The above analysis applies provided that $\theta \neq 0$. Equations (5.12)–(5.20) remain valid when $\theta = 0$. However, since $X = 0$ for such welds when $\psi = 0$, the analysis is developed assuming that the residual stress in each weld at collapse is zero. Further, since there is no horizontal force, $\sigma_3 = \sigma_4 = 0$. The

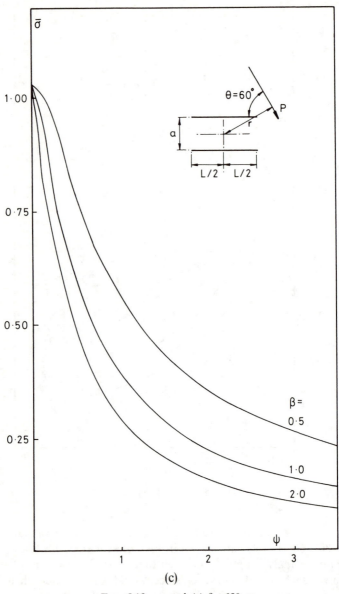

FIG. 5.13.—*contd.* (c) $\theta = 60°$.

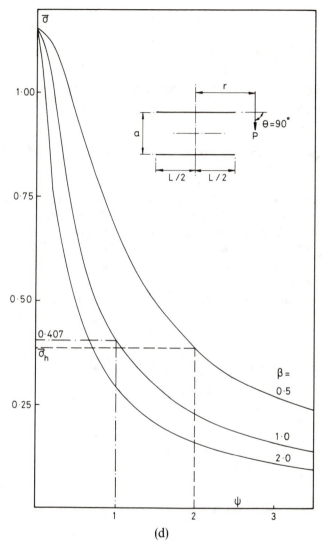

(d)

FIG. 5.13.—*contd.* (d) $\theta = 90°$.

stresses $\sigma_{ij}(i, j = 1, 2)$ are obtained from eqns (5.13) and substituted into eqns (5.15). It is now found that $\eta = 1/2$, so the yield conditions become

$$16\mu_i^2 + 6\sigma_i^2 = \sigma_u^2 \qquad (i = 1, 2) \tag{5.34}$$

Using eqn (5.34) with $i = 1$ and 2 respectively

$$16(\mu_1 - \mu_2)(\mu_1 + \mu_2) + 6(\sigma_1 - \sigma_2)(\sigma_1 + \sigma_2) = 0 \tag{5.35}$$

The analysis becomes more compact by putting $\sigma_1 = \kappa\sigma$ and $\alpha = (\beta\psi + 0.5)$. Equations (5.12a) and (5.12c) then give $\sigma_2 = (1 - \kappa)\sigma$ and

$$\beta(\mu_1 + \mu_2) = 2\sigma(\alpha - \kappa) \tag{5.36}$$

Using eqn (5.36) and the expressions for σ_1 and σ_2 in eqn (5.35) leads to

$$16(\mu_1 - \mu_2)(\alpha - \kappa) + 3\beta\sigma(2\kappa - 1) = 0 \tag{5.37}$$

Two possibilities now arise—either $\alpha = \kappa$ or $\alpha \neq \kappa$. In the former case, eqn (5.37) requires $\kappa = 0.5$, which corresponds to the special case of a pair of longitudinal welds subjected to a shearing force only. Since $\alpha = \kappa = 0.5$, $\sigma_1 = \sigma_2 = 0.5\sigma$ (eqn (5.12a)) so that to obtain the maximum value of σ eqns (5.34) require $\mu_1 = \mu_2 = 0$; the failure load is then obtained as $2\sigma_u/\sqrt{6}$, as would be expected.

If $\alpha \neq \kappa$ eqns (5.36) and (5.37) can be solved to give

$$\mu_1 = \frac{\sigma}{4}\left[\frac{4(\alpha - \kappa)}{\beta} + \frac{3}{8}\beta\frac{1 - 2\kappa}{\alpha - \kappa}\right] \tag{5.38}$$

The failure load for the weld group is now obtained from eqn (5.34) as

$$\bar{\sigma} = \sigma/\sigma_u = \left\{\left[\frac{4(\alpha - \kappa)}{\beta} + \frac{3}{8}\beta\frac{1 - 2\kappa}{\alpha - \kappa}\right]^2 + 6\kappa^2\right\}^{-0.5} \tag{5.39}$$

The unknown factor κ is to be chosen to maximise σ, as before. It is found, by differentiating eqn (5.39), that the required value of κ is the solution of the equation

$$\kappa = \frac{1}{2} + \frac{8}{3}\frac{\alpha - \kappa}{\beta^2} + \frac{3}{128}\beta^2\frac{(1 - 2\kappa)(2\alpha - 1)}{(\alpha - \kappa)^3} \tag{5.40}$$

For a given weld group, β is known. For specified values of α (or ψ), κ is obtained from eqn (5.40) and used in eqn (5.39) to give corresponding values of $\bar{\sigma}$. Strength curves plotted in this way are given in Fig. 5.13(a).

An analysis similar to that used for $\theta \neq 0$ shows that the pure couple that the connection can transmit is again given by eqn (5.33).

Equation (5.28) was developed by ignoring the effect of the residual stresses that are present. The effect of allowing for these stresses in the special case $\theta = 90°$ was considered by Kamtekar (1987b) and it was found that the strength curves obtained were nearly coincident. Since residual stresses appear to have the most effect on transversely loaded weld groups, the curves of Fig. 5.13 are unlikely to alter much if these stresses are included in the analysis.

5.3.4 Analysis of Other Weld Groups

Assumption (iv) can be utilised to obtain the failure load of other weld groups which are made up by combining the two basic weld groups already considered. Two weld groups that occur frequently in practice are the ones indicated in Figs 5.1(c) and 5.1(d) with P parallel to the vertical weld. The strengths of these weld groups can be obtained as follows.

The weld group of Fig. 5.1(c) consists of a group (i) weld with $\theta = 0$ and a group (ii) weld with $\theta = 90°$. The strength of the group corresponding to a load applied at an eccentricity $e(= r + a/2;$ Fig. 5.14) is obtained by summing the strengths of the two component sub-groups. The best way to obtain a curve of load against eccentricity is by assuming various values of η in the range $(0, 0.5)$ for the pair of horizontal welds. The eccentricity, r, to which each value of η corresponds is calculated using eqn (5.29). Noting that the length of each horizontal weld is a, the contribution $(\bar{\sigma}_h)$ of this sub-group to the weld group strength is then the higher of the values calculated from eqns (5.22) and (5.28) with $\psi = r/a$. The contribution $(\bar{\sigma}_v)$ of the vertical weld to the failure load is calculated directly using eqn (5.9) with $\psi = e/L$. The forces carried by these welds at failure are $\bar{\sigma}_h(\sigma_u w a)$ and $\bar{\sigma}_v(\sigma_u w L)$ respectively. The failure load of the weld group (P) is the sum of these two contributions, whence $\bar{\sigma} \ (= P/\sigma_u w L)$ is defined by

$$\bar{\sigma} = \bar{\sigma}_v + \beta_h \bar{\sigma}_h \qquad (5.41)$$

where $\beta_h = a/L$. The procedure is repeated for the other chosen values of η to produce the strength curves of Fig. 5.14 in which $\xi = e/L$.

If the applied load is orientated at a different angle, θ, the same procedure can be used, but the calculation is a little more involved because, once the value of r is calculated for a chosen η for the horizontal welds, e (and e/L) becomes fixed and the corresponding value of η for the vertical weld has to be obtained by solving eqn (5.7) before $\bar{\sigma}_v$ can be calculated from eqn (5.6). However, this second calculation becomes unnecessary if curves of the type given in Fig. 5.7 are available for the appropriate angle, θ. In this case, $\bar{\sigma}_v$ can immediately be read off from the $\bar{\sigma}$ axis once ψ has been determined.

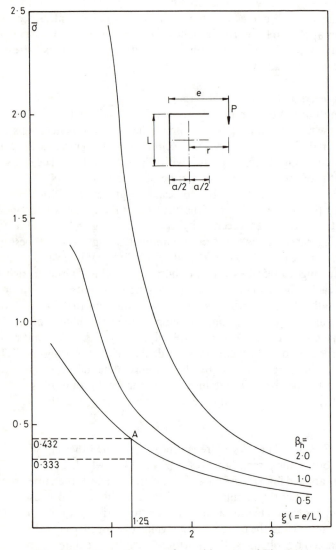

FIG. 5.14.   Strength curves for weld group of Fig. 5.1(c).

The weld group of Fig. 5.1(d) consists of two group (ii) welds, one with $\theta = 0$ and the other with $\theta = 90°$. The calculation of the strength becomes easy if strength curves like those in Fig. 5.13 are available. For a given value of r (Fig. 5.15), the contribution of the horizontal welds ($\bar{\sigma}_h$) to the weld group strength is obtained from Fig. 5.13(d) with $\psi = r/a$ (since the weld length is a), and that of the vertical welds ($\bar{\sigma}_v$) is obtained from Fig. 5.13(a) with $\psi = r/L$. Equation (5.41) again defines the weld group strength when $\bar{\sigma} = P/\sigma_u wL$. The procedure for obtaining $\bar{\sigma}_h$ and $\bar{\sigma}_v$ for the special case $L = r = 2a$ is indicated in Figs 5.13(a) and 5.13(d). For this geometry, the values of β for the vertical (β_v) and horizontal (β_h) welds are 2 and 0·5, and those of ψ are 1 and 2 respectively. Figure 5.15 shows strength curves for three weld geometries.

The curves for weld groups having geometrically similar welds (i.e. one group can be obtained by rotating the other through $90°$) are interesting. The curves begin at widely different positions along the $\bar{\sigma}$ axis when $\psi = 0$. This reflects the fact that transverse welds loaded by a shearing force only are much stronger than similar longitudinal ones. For the cases shown in Fig. 5.15, for example, $\bar{\sigma}_v = 2/\sqrt{6}$ and $\bar{\sigma}_h = 2/\sqrt{3}$ when $\psi = 0$, so that, using eqn (5.41), $\bar{\sigma}$ equals 1·394 ($= 2/\sqrt{6} + 1/\sqrt{3}$) when $\beta_h = 0·5$, and 3·125 ($= 2/\sqrt{6} + 4/\sqrt{3}$) when $\beta_h = 2$. As ψ increases, the moment becomes the dominant load effect and the strength becomes independent of the weld orientation. That is why the two curves merge for increasing values of ψ.

A similar approach can be used to obtain strength curves for such weld groups for different values of θ.

5.3.5 Comparisons with Test Results

A number of important assumptions have been made in deriving expressions for the strengths of the weld groups analysed, and it is necessary to establish that their predictions are in reasonable agreement with test results. This has been done for all the weld groups considered (Kamtekar, 1982, 1984, 1987a,b; Kamtekar & Sanaei, 1986), and it has been found that

(i) the theoretical strength predictions for welds with $\psi = 0$ are generally no more than 15% lower than the experimental results, and

(ii) when the weld metal UTS determined from tension tests on specimens obtained from the deposited weld metal is used in the calculation for group (ii) welds, the theoretical predictions tend to be about 15% lower than the experimental results. If the value of σ_u deduced from either tension or shear fillet welds (Figs 5.1(a) and

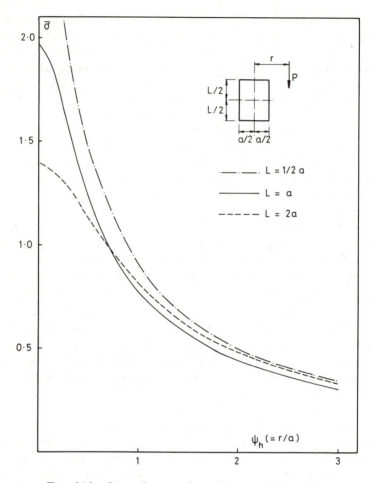

FIG. 5.15. Strength curves for weld group of Fig. 5.1(d).

5.1(b)) is used in the calculation, the agreement between theory and experiment improves,

(iii) the theory makes no allowance for any root penetration that might be achieved. This penetration effectively increases the weld size and can be allowed for by a suitable increase in the value of w. However, it must be possible to guarantee the penetration if it is to be used in assessing the weld group strength.

Since the theoretical predictions generally provide conservative strength estimates, the curves of Figs 5.7, 5.13, 5.14 and 5.15 (and similar curves obtained for other θ and β values) can be used directly in design. The only material property required (σ_u) is readily available since it is supplied by electrode manufacturers.

5.4 APPLICATION TO DESIGN

In design it is necessary either (i) to check whether a guessed solution is satisfactory or, (ii) given the weld group geometry, to determine the minimum weld size required or, (iii) given the weld size, to determine the weld lengths required.

To see how Figs 5.7, 5.13, 5.14 and 5.15 can be used, consider the bracket connection of Fig. 5.16(a). Assuming that $\sigma_u = 500 \text{ N/mm}^2$, it is necessary to check whether the weld group of Fig. 5.16(b) with $w = 6$ mm will carry the applied load, and also to determine the minimum weld size required for this weld group to be satisfactory.

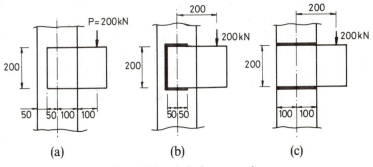

FIG. 5.16.   A design example.

The eccentricity e to be used in Fig. 5.14 is found to be $200 + 50 = 250$ mm. $a = 100$ mm, $L = 200$ mm, $P = 200$ kN and $w = 6$ mm, so $\xi = 250/200 = 1.25$, $\beta_h = 100/200 = 0.5$ and $\bar{\sigma} = 200 \times 10^3/(500 \times 6 \times 200) = 0.333$. Lines drawn parallel to the axes from $\xi = 1.25$ and $\bar{\sigma} = 0.333$ in Fig. 5.14 intersect at a point below the curve for $\beta_h = 0.5$. Hence the weld group will carry the applied load. The load-carrying capacity is given by the ordinate of the point A in Fig. 5.14 ($\bar{\sigma} = 0.432$). The minimum weld size required to enable the group to carry the load is then given by $P/(0.432\sigma_u L) = 4.6$ mm.

Suppose that the alternative design of Fig. 5.16(c) is to adopted. Now

$a = r = L = 200$ mm, so $\beta = \psi = 1$. The value of $\bar{\sigma}$ at collapse is obtained from Fig. 5.13(d) as 0·407, whence the minimum weld size required for this design is $P/(0·407\sigma_u L) = 4·91$ mm. For this example, therefore, there is very little difference in the weld sizes required for the two designs considered.

5.5 CONCLUSIONS

An analysis based on the application of the ideas of plastic theory to a simplified force distribution in eccentrically loaded in-plane fillet welded connections has been used to obtain the strength of the two basic weld groups of Fig. 5.3 in terms of the weld group geometry (β, w, L), the load orientation (θ) and eccentricity (r) and the weld metal UTS (σ_u). The results for the basic groups can be combined to obtain strength curves for other weld groups made up by combining the basic groups. Strength curves for particular combinations of the basic groups have been obtained using the curves for the basic groups; those for other combinations can be obtained in the same way. Since the expressions developed for predicting the weld group strength agree reasonably well with experimental results, the strength curves given can be used directly in design.

The effect of welding residual stresses has been examined in some cases, and it is found that, surprisingly, they can increase the strength of statically loaded weld groups. The effect is only significant for small eccentricities in transversely loaded ($\theta = 90°$) weld groups; as the load eccentricity increases or θ decreases, the effect becomes negligible.

REFERENCES

BUTLER, L. J., PAL, S. & KULAK, G. L. (1972) Eccentrically loaded welded connections, *Proc. Amer. Soc. Civ. Engrs, J. Struct. Div.* **98**(ST5), 989–1005.

CLARK, P. J. (1972) Basis of design for fillet welded joints under static loading, Proc. Conf. on Improving Welding Product Design (Paper 10). Welding Institute, Abingdon, UK, pp. 85–96.

KAMTEKAR, A. G. (1982) A new analysis of the strength of some simple fillet welded connections, *J. Construct. Steel Res.*, **2**(2), 33–45.

KAMTEKAR, A. G. (1984) The strength of planar fillet weld groups subjected to a shearing force applied outside their planes, *J. Construct. Steel Res.*, **4**(3), 163–99.

KAMTEKAR, A. G. (1987a) The strength of inclined fillet welds, *J. Construct. Steel Res.*, **7**(1), 43–54.

KAMTEKAR, A. G. (1987b) The strength of planar fillet weld groups subjected to an eccentric shearing force in their planes, *J. Construct. Steel Res.*, **7**(3), 155–87.

KAMTEKAR, A. G. & SANAEI, E. (1986) The strength of some arbitrarily loaded in-plane fillet weld groups, Proc. Int. Conf. on Steel Structures: Recent Research Advances and Their Application to Design, Part I, Budva, pp. 335–44.

KOENIGSBERGER, F. (1951) Design stresses in fillet weld connexions, *Proc. Inst. Mech. Engrs.* **165**, 148–64 (WEP Nos. 63–9).

MENDELSON, A. (1968) *Plasticity: Theory and Applications.* Macmillan Co., New York.

NEAL, B. G. (1977) *The Plastic Methods of Structural Analysis*, 3rd edn. Chapman and Hall, London.

SWANNELL, P. & SKEWES, I. C. (1979) The Design of Welded Brackets Loaded In-plane: Elastic and Ultimate Load Techniques. AWRA report p6-8-77, Australian Welding Research, Jan., pp. 28–59.

TIMOSHENKO, S. P. & GOODIER, J. N. (1982) *Theory of Elasticity*, 3rd edn. McGraw-Hill Book Co., Japan, Ch. 7.

Chapter 6

WELDED JOINTS BETWEEN HOLLOW SECTIONS

J. WARDENIER

Department of Mechanics and Structural Engineering,
Delft University of Technology, Delft, The Netherlands

SUMMARY

After describing the various aspects which determine the economical use of circular or square hollow sections as structural elements, this chapter concentrates on the behaviour of welded hollow section joints in lattice girders.

The strength criteria and the various modes of failure are discussed. The governing parameters on the joint strength are determined with simple analytical models which relate to the particular failure modes. Based on these simplified models and the experimental evidence, ultimate strength formulae have been developed by various researchers.

Sub-cie XV-E of the International Institute of Welding and the Working Group 'Welded Joints' of CIDECT have agreed about a unified approach for the evaluation to design rules. The resulting design formulae, now also adopted in Eurocode 3, have been included in this chapter.

NOTATION

a	Throat thickness of a fillet weld
A_i	Cross-sectional area of member i ($i = 0, 1, 2$)
A_Q	Effective cross-sectional area of chord for shear
b	Width (general)
b_e	Effective width for brace to chord connection
$b_{e(ov)}$	Effective width for overlapping brace to overlapped brace connection
b_{ep}	Effective punching shear width

b_i	External width of a square or rectangular hollow section (RHS) for member i ($i=0,1,2$)
b_m	Effective width for web of chord
B_e	Effective ring length in ring model
c, c_1, c_2	Coefficients
d	Diameter (general)
d_i	External diameter of a circular hollow section (CHS) for member i ($i=0,1,2$)
e	Eccentricity of a joint
E	Elastic modulus of steel
f_{cr}	Critical buckling stress
f_u	Ultimate tensile strength
f_y	Yield stress
f_{yeq}	Equivalent yield stress
f_{yi}	Design value for yield stress in member i ($i=0,1,2$)
f_0	Maximum compressive stress in chord due to axial force and bending moment
f_{0p}	Maximum compressive stress in chord excluding stress due to horizontal brace load components
g	Gap between braces of a K- or N-joint
g'	Gap g divided by wall thickness of chord
h_i	External depth of a section for member i ($i=0,1,2$)
h_w	Depth of web of an I- or H-section chord
i	Integer used to denote member of joint; $i=0$ designates chord and $i=1,2$ the brace members (normally $i=1$ refers to strut and $i=2$ to tie)
k_a	Angle function in punching shear model
l_i	Length of a yield line i
m_{pi}	Plastic moment per unit length
n, n'	$n=f_0/f_{y0}$; $n'=f_{0p}/f_{y0}$
$\hat{N}_i$	Joint design strength capacity based on load in member i ($i=1$ or 2)
N_k	Characteristic strength (95% survival)
$\hat{N}_{wl}$	Allowable joint design strength capacity under working load conditions
N_{0gap}	Axial load in cross-section of chord at gap
(ov)	Index used for overlapped brace
O_v	Overlap
Q	Shear force ($Q=N_i \sin \theta_i$)
Q_p	Shear yield capacity of a section
r_0	Radius of an I- or H-section

S	Loading (general)
t_i	Wall thickness of member i ($i = 0, 1, 2$)
t_w	Web thickness of an I- or H-section
v_p	Punching shear
α	Factor giving the effectiveness of the chord flange for shear
β	(Average) brace to chord diameter ratio or width ratio: d_1/d_0, $(d_1 + d_2)/2d_0$, b_1/b_0, $(b_1 + b_2)/2b_0$
γ	Half chord width or half chord diameter to wall thickness ratio ($d_0/2t_0$ or $b_0/2t_0$)
γ_m	Joint coefficient
γ_s	Load factor
δ	Displacement
θ_i	Included angle between a brace member ($i = 1$ or 2) and the chord
ϕ_i	Angle

6.1 INTRODUCTION

Structural hollow sections have excellent strength properties with regard to loading in compression, torsion and bending in all directions. These advantageous strength properties, combined with an aesthetically pleasing shape, make the hollow section an attractive structural element. The circular hollow section has proved to be the best shape for elements subjected to wind or wave loading. The smaller painting surface, the omission of sharp corners and the smooth change-over from one section to another at the joints decrease the painting costs and increase the protection time. In some applications the inner space can be used for strength, fire protection, heating or for conveying liquids.

In steel structures, the members have to be jointed and it is a well known fact that joints of circular hollow sections are more expensive than those of rectangular hollow sections or those between open sections. Consequently, circular hollow sections are used mainly for applications subjected to wind or wave loading, and further for columns or for architectural reasons. Square and rectangular hollow sections are now used widely for many structural applications such as columns and lattice girders.

Due to the complex load transfer in hollow section joints, many research programmes have been carried out to investigate the behaviour. Based on analytical models and experimental results, design rules have been established for the basic types of joints.

After describing briefly the properties and applications of hollow sections, this chapter concentrates on the behaviour of welded hollow section joints in lattice girders.

6.2 HOLLOW SECTIONS

6.2.1 Applications

The selection of a particular section in a steel structure is determined by many factors: it is a comparison of the pros and cons with regard to strength properties, unit material costs, and the costs of fabrication, erection, painting and protection. The effects of other aspects have also to be included in the evaluation. The experiences of architects, designers and manufacturers sometimes determine the choice. In this respect it is very important that the designer understands the behaviour of hollow section joints.

The joint behaviour and joint strength should be considered in the initial design stage for the member selection to avoid expensive stiffening plates and bad experiences afterwards.

Figure 6.1 shows a qualitative comparison of the pros and cons of various aspects of the use of hollow sections as compared to open sections. The selection of the structural member shape depends on the various aspects. Sometimes combinations with open sections offer more advantages, e.g. trusses with SHS diagonals and bottom chord and a wide flange section for the top chord. In this way purlins can be easily bolted to the top chord.

Many examples in practice, and also actual cost calculations, show that the use of hollow sections can result in very economical steel structures.

Hollow sections are nowadays used for many structures or structural elements, e.g.

—columns and frames
—trusses and triangular lattice
  girders
—space structures
—domes, barrel vaults
—radio telescopes
—towers, masts
—jibs
—pedestrian bridges

—transport bridges
—piles
—chimneys
—gantries
—dolphins
—road signs
—offshore jacket structures
—mechanical equipment
—agricultural equipment

Aspect	○	□	Explanation
Mechanical properties	0/+	0/+	
Geometrical properties			
Sectional shape	+	+	Wind/wave loading
Tolerances	+	+	Smaller than for open sections
Tension loading	0	0	Cross-sectional area related
Compression loading	+	+	Buckling/buckling length
Torsional loading	+	+	Torsional rigidity
Bending	−/0	−/0	Only profit for bending in more directions or for long spans (lateral buckling)
Fabrication			
End preparation	−/+	+	End cutting
Bending	+	+	Shape stability
Weld preparation	+	0	Automatically for CHS
Welding	0	0	
Transport	0	0	
Erection	0/+	0/+	Better lateral stability of trusses; bolted connections more difficult
Use internal void			
Strength	+	+	Concrete filling
Fire protection	+	+	Concrete filling
Heating, air-conditioning	+	+	Air or water
Cable tray	+	+	Simple to use
Transport fluids	+	+	e.g. Transport bridges
Maintenance			
Corrosion sensitivity	+	+	No sharp corners
Painting area	+	+	Smaller painting area
Unit material cost	−	−	Manufacturing more expensive
Aesthetics	+	+	Architectural

+ advantage compared to open sections
0 about the same
− disadvantage compared to open sections

FIG. 6.1. Qualitative comparison between structural hollow sections (SHS) and open sections.

6.2.2 Geometrical and Mechanical Properties

The geometrical properties and the tolerances of hollow sections are given in the relevant ISO Standards ISO 657/14 and ISO/4019.

Depending on the manufacturing process, hollow sections can be hot- or cold-formed. Hot-formed hollow sections can be seamless or longitudinally welded. In application and mechanical properties no difference is made between hot-formed seamless and longitudinally welded hollow sections. Cold-formed hollow sections have higher residual stresses but also an increased yield stress due to cold forming.

If the residual stresses are taken into account by a lower buckling curve (e.g. the European curve 'c' instead of curve 'a'), an increased equivalent yield stress $f_{y\,eq}$ may be used:

$$f_{y\,eq} = f_y + 4ct(f_u - f_y) \leqslant 1 \cdot 25 f_y$$

where $c = 7$, t is the wall thickness, L is the perimeter hollow section, f_y is the design value for the yield stress of the parent material, and f_u is the design value for the ultimate tensile stress of the parent material.

Other codes state that the same buckling curve as for hot-formed hollow sections may be used, provided that the design value for the yield stress of the parent material before cold-forming is taken into account.

The corner radii of cold-formed square and rectangular hollow sections should not be too small to prevent strain ageing after welding or after galvanizing. On the other hand, large corner radii complicate welding at the saddles of connections between sections of the same width. Hollow sections used as single sections loaded in compression provide the best overall buckling behaviour if the diameter (or width) to thickness ratio (d/t or b/t) is high. This ratio is, on the other hand, limited by the local buckling criteria. It should furthermore be kept in mind that the joint behaviour may further limit the ratio d/t or b/t.

6.3 SECTIONAL REQUIREMENTS

In plastic design, the members and/or joints must be able to resist the governing plastic moment after a certain plastic rotation. The required rotation capacity κ/κ_p (see Fig. 6.2) depends on the structure.

Figure 6.2 shows four moment–rotation curves. A hollow section with a behaviour like curve 'a' is suitable for plastic design because the strength exceeds the plastic moment M_p and the rotational capacity is large. The other curves show no or less deformation capacity. Sections with properties like curve 'b' may only be used for plastic design if no deformation capacity

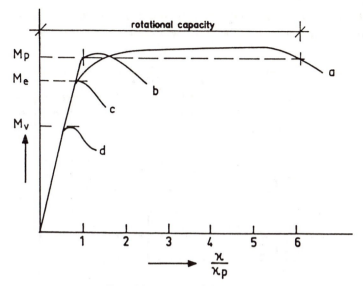

FIG. 6.2. Rotational capacity.

is required. Sections with properties like curves 'c' and 'd' may only be used for elastic design.

Based on discussions in working groups of international organizations such as IIW-XV-E, CIDECT and ECCS, the classification for hollow sections given in Table 6.1 has been adopted. For large hollow sections

TABLE 6.1
MEMBER CLASSIFICATION FOR HOLLOW SECTIONS

Section	○	□	*Fig. 6.2 curve*
Plastic design sections	$\dfrac{d}{t} \leqslant 50\varepsilon^2$	$\dfrac{b}{t} \leqslant 33\varepsilon$	a
Compact sections	$\dfrac{d}{t} \leqslant 70\varepsilon^2$	$\dfrac{b}{t} \leqslant 37\varepsilon$	b
Elastic design sections	$\dfrac{d}{t} \leqslant 100\varepsilon^2$	$\dfrac{b}{t} \leqslant 45\varepsilon$	c
	Local buckling check for sections with larger d/t or b/t ratios		d

$\varepsilon = \sqrt{235/f_y}$

made from plates such as large diameter tubes in offshore and box sections, more stringent values may be used due to welding deformations.

6.4 TYPES OF JOINTS

Hollow sections are mainly used in truss or lattice type structures. Connectors as used in space structures are not within the scope of this

CLASSIFICATION JOINTS		
BRACE	CHORD	TYPE OF JOINT
◯	◯	CC
◯	▢ ▢ ▢	CR
▢ ▢ ▢	▢ ▢ ▢	RR
◯	I I	CI
▢ ▢ ▢	I I	RI
◯	⌐⌐	CU
▢ ▢ ▢	⌐⌐	RU

FIG. 6.3.   Combinations of sections.

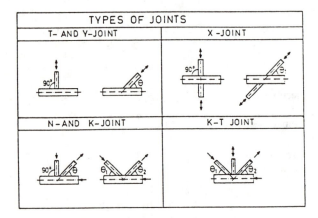

FIG. 6.4.   Basic types of joints.

chapter. Here special attention will be paid to welded hollow section joints in plane trusses under predominant static loading.

Figure 6.3 shows the most relevant combinations of sections used for chords and braces, while Fig. 6.4 shows the most common types of joints. The geometry of the joints is described by the main parameters shown in Fig. 6.5.

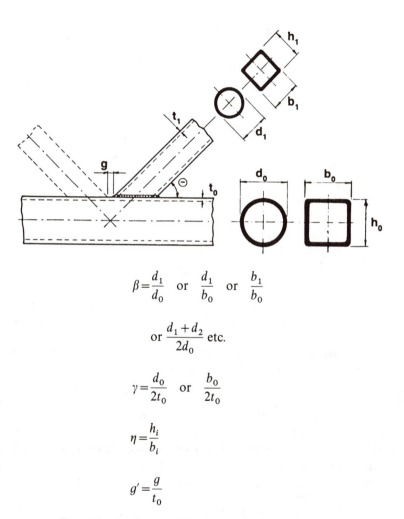

$$\beta = \frac{d_1}{d_0} \quad \text{or} \quad \frac{d_1}{b_0} \quad \text{or} \quad \frac{b_1}{b_0}$$

$$\text{or} \; \frac{d_1 + d_2}{2d_0} \; \text{etc.}$$

$$\gamma = \frac{d_0}{2t_0} \quad \text{or} \quad \frac{b_0}{2t_0}$$

$$\eta = \frac{h_i}{b_i}$$

$$g' = \frac{g}{t_0}$$

FIG. 6.5. Symbols used for the main joint parameters.

6.5 STATIC STRENGTH CRITERIA

6.5.1 Criteria of Failure

In general, the static strength can be characterized by the criteria shown in Fig. 6.6, i.e.

—Ultimate load capacity (5)
—Deformation criteria (2) or (3)
—Visual observed crack initiation (4)

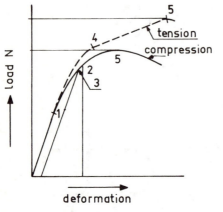

1 = elastic limit

2 = deformation limit

3 = remaining deformation limit

4 = crack initiation

5 = ultimate load

FIG. 6.6.   Criteria of failure.

The ultimate load capacity is well defined for joints loaded in compression and chosen as the basis for the determination of the static strength. Because of the non-linear load–deflection behaviour, there is no international agreement regarding the deformation criterion or the determination of the yield load for joints made of hollow sections.

For T-, Y- or X-joints loaded in tension, the deflection at ultimate load is rather high for joints with low β ratios; on the other hand, the deformation capacity decreases for high β ratios. This is the reason why the higher ultimate load capacity as compared to joints loaded in compression is generally not taken into account. The strength for similar joints loaded in compression agrees approximately with the kink in the load–deformation curve. This means that the ultimate load for joints in compression nearly agrees with the 'yield load' for joints loaded in tension.

To avoid too high deformations or, on the other hand, to include additional safety for joints with a lower deformation capacity, it is advisable to adopt for joints loaded in tension the same strength as for joints loaded in compression.

6.5.2 Modes of Failure

Depending on the type of joint, joint parameters and loading condition, several basic modes of failure can occur, as illustrated in Fig. 6.7:

(a) Plastic failure of the face or cross section of the chord
(b) Rupture of the bracings from the chord (punching shear)
(c) Cracking of the bracings near the joint
(d) Weld failure
(e) Shear failure of the chord
(f) Local buckling in compressive areas of the joint members

Lamellar tearing (more probable for heavy wall thicknesses) can be avoided by choosing suitable material qualities (low sulphur content) and suitable welding procedures (restraint).

On many occasions failure occurs by combinations of the basic types mentioned above. For each type of failure, principal models can be developed to describe the joint behaviour.

6.5.3 Analytical Models

Analytical models which take account of all influencing parameters are generally too complicated. More simplified models are used to determine the governing joint parameters for the ultimate strength and to give insight into the joint behaviour.

For joints between circular hollow sections, the ring model and the punching shear model are mainly used. The behaviour of joints between rectangular hollow sections is generally described by yield line models and effective width models.

6.5.3.1 Ring Model

In the ring model (shown in Fig. 6.8) first used by Togo, the joint is simplified to a ring with an effective length B_e. The stresses in the brace are concentrated at the saddles; therefore, in the ring model, the brace load is schematized to two line loads at a distance $c_1 \cdot d_1$, in which c_1 is a constant somewhat smaller than 1·0.

By neglecting the influence of shear stresses on the plastic moment, the plastic failure load for the ring model of an X-joint can be determined as

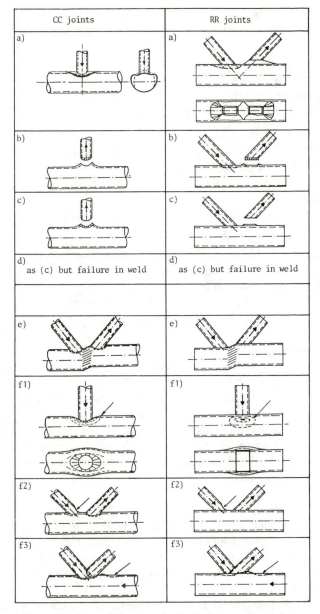

FIG. 6.7. Some failure modes for hollow section joints.

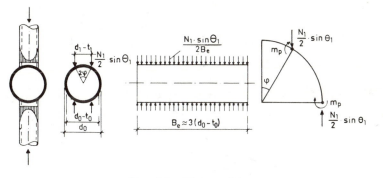

FIG. 6.8.   Ring model.

follows:

$$2m_p = \frac{N_{1y} \sin \theta_1}{2}(1 - \sin \phi)\left(\frac{d_0 - t_0}{2}\right) \tag{6.1}$$

with

$$m_p = \frac{B_e t_0^2}{4} f_{y0}$$

$$\sin \phi \simeq c_1 \beta$$

$$\frac{d_0 - t_0}{2} \approx \frac{d_0}{2}$$

$$N_{1y} = \frac{2B_e}{d_0} \frac{1}{1 - c_1 \beta} \frac{f_{y0} t_0^2}{\sin \theta_1} \tag{6.2}$$

The effective length has been determined experimentally ($B_e \approx 3d_0$). The resulting formula for X-joints used in recommendations is

$$\hat{N}_1 = \frac{c_2}{1 - c_1 \beta} \frac{f_{y0} t_0^2}{\sin \theta_1} f(n) \tag{6.3}$$

in which c_1 and c_2 are coefficients determined experimentally, and $f(n)$ gives the influence of additional loading in the chord, e.g. $f(n) = 1.0$ for tension loading and $f(n) \leqslant 1.0$ for compression loading in the chord.

For T-joints, but especially K- and N-joints, the load transfer becomes considerably more complicated, resulting in the following basic formula for

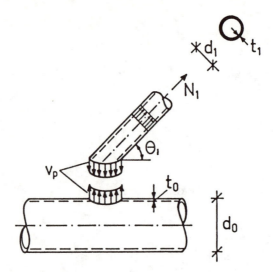

FIG. 6.9. Punching shear model for circular hollow sections.

the strength of joints between hollow sections:

$$\hat{N}_1 = f(\beta)f(\gamma)f(g)f(n)\frac{f_{y0}t_0^2}{\sin\theta_1} \qquad (6.4)$$

in which the functions for β, γ, g and n are mainly determined experimentally.

6.5.3.2 Punching Shear Model
In the punching shear model for circular hollow section joints, shown in Fig. 6.9, the punching shear stress v_p is assumed to be uniformly distributed over the punching shear area:

$$N_1 \sin\theta_1 = k_a \pi d_1 t_0 v_p \qquad (6.5)$$

with

$$v_p = 0\!\cdot\!58f_{y0} \quad \text{and} \quad k_a \simeq \frac{1+\sin\theta_1}{2\ \sin\theta_1}$$
$$\hat{N}_1 = 0\!\cdot\!58f_{y0}\pi d_1 t_0 \frac{1+\sin\theta_1}{2\ \sin^2\theta_1} \qquad (6.6)$$

In general this criterion may only be critical for joints with small β ratios. Initially this model was generally used as the basis for the offshore recommendations in the USA. In these recommendations the active punching shear had to be calculated with

$$v_p = \frac{N_1 \sin \theta_1}{k_a \pi d_1 t_0} \quad \text{or}$$

$$v_p \simeq \frac{\pi d_1 t_1 f_a \sin \theta_1}{k_a \pi d_1 t_0} \quad \text{or}$$

$$v_p = \frac{\tau f_a}{k_a} \sin \theta_1 \tag{6.7}$$

The acting punching shear v_p had to be compared with the allowable $\bar{v}_p$. Since this model was used for all types of tubular joints, the functions for the allowable $\bar{v}_p$ had to compensate for the k_a effect which is not generally valid because actually plastic failure of the chord ring was governing. In the most recent offshore recommendations, the formulae are given in terms of loads, or a fictitious punching shear v_p is used according to eqn (6.7) with $k_a = 1 \cdot 0$. This agrees with the ring model.

For joints with square or rectangular hollow sections (see Fig. 6.10) the stiffness at the sides of the bracings is considerably higher than at the centres of the chord face. Especially for joints with width ratios β close to $1 \cdot 0$, the whole perimeter cannot be taken as effective. The associated punching shear strength v_p for a T-, Y- or X-joints can be expressed as

$$N_{1u} = v_p t_0 \left(\frac{2h_1}{\sin \theta_1} + 2b_{ep} \right) \frac{1}{\sin \theta_1} \tag{6.8}$$

When both the b_0/t_0 ratio of the chord and the width ratio β are low, the perimeter can be fully effective.

The effective punching shear width b_{ep} is generally determined in an experimental way. In joints with more than one bracing member, the internal stiffness distribution at the intersection between bracings and chord face determines the effective punching shear area. To avoid too small effective widths, limitations have to be put on the gap size in relation to the width ratio.

6.5.3.3 Effective Width Model
The previously described punching shear model may be governing for joints with relatively thick-walled bracings; for joints with thin-walled bracings the effective width of the bracings may become critical. The model

J. WARDENIER

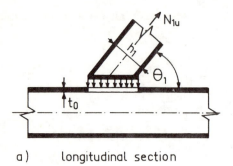

a)   longitudinal section   b)   cross section

$$l_{eff} = 2\left(\frac{h_1}{\sin\theta_1} + 2b_e\right)$$

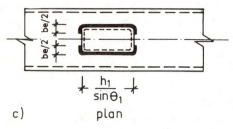

c)   plan

FIG. 6.10. Punching shear model for a RR-joint.

looks similar to that for punching shear. For example, for a T-, Y- or X-joint:

$$N_{1u} = f_{y1}t_1(2h_1 - 4t_1 + 2b_e) \tag{6.9}$$

The effectiveness becomes larger when the parameters b_0/t_0 and t_1/t_0 decrease.

Up to now conservatively no angle function has been included although some tests show an influence, depending on the loading and the type of joint.

6.5.3.4 Yield Line Model
The yield line model is mainly used for joints between square or rectangular hollow sections. Figure 6.11 shows a simplified yield line pattern which can be used for an estimation of the yield strength of a T-, Y- or X-joint with a width ratio $\beta \leqslant 0.8$.

The yield line method gives an upper bound of the yield strength; therefore various yield line patterns have to be examined. In the simplified yield line models, the effects of membrane action and strain hardening have

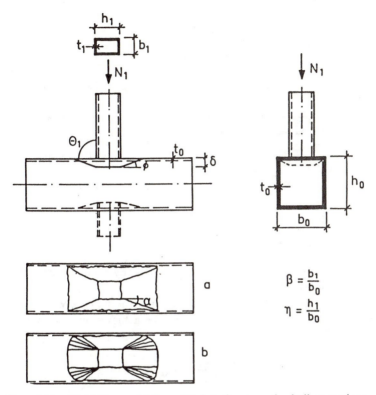

FIG. 6.11. Yield line model for a T-joint of rectangular hollow sections.

been neglected, resulting in a conservative estimation of the actual strength. This is especially true for joints with low β ratios which have a very high deformation at ultimate load. For T-, Y- and X-joints the yield strength is used to avoid large deformations in actual design.

For K- and N-joints the membrane action has been included in the yield line models as used by Packer *et al.*, 1984. The method consists in equating the work of the external forces and the work by the plastic hinge system. For example, for a Y-joint:

$$N_i(\sin\theta_1)\delta = \Sigma l_i\phi_i m_{pi} \qquad (6.10)$$

with

$$m_{pi} = \frac{f_{y0}t_0^2}{4}$$

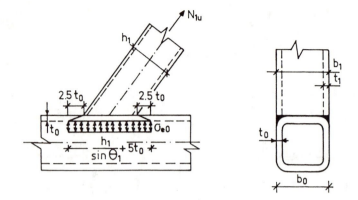

FIG. 6.12.   Chord side wall bearing.

δ is the displacement of load N_i, l_i is the length of yield line i, and ϕ_i is the rotation of yield line i.

Equation (6.10) can be written as a function of the angle between the yield lines. The minimum for the load N_1 can be achieved by differentiation, resulting in

$$N_{1y} = \frac{f_{y0}t_0^2}{1-\beta}\left(\frac{2\eta}{\sin\theta_1} + 4\sqrt{1-\beta}\right)\frac{1}{\sin\theta_1} \tag{6.11}$$

For K- and N-joints, semi-empirical formulae are used in the design recommendations since the theoretical equations become too complicated.

6.5.3.5 Chord Wall Bearing Models
T-, Y- and X-joints with a high β ratio may fail by yielding or buckling of the chord side walls, as shown in Fig. 6.12.

In principle the same method is used as for beam-to-column connections between I-shaped sections. For equal width joints, the strength follows directly from the model shown in Fig. 6.12:

$$N_{1y} = 2f_{y0}t_0\left(\frac{h_1}{\sin\theta_1} + 5t_0\right)\frac{1}{\sin\theta_1} \tag{6.12}$$

For joints loaded in compression, the yield stress in eqn (6.12) is replaced by a critical buckling stress f_{cr}:

$$N_{1y} = 2f_{cr}t_0\left(\frac{h_1}{\sin\theta_1} + 5t_0\right)\frac{1}{\sin\theta_1} \tag{6.13}$$

Davies *et al.* (1984) showed that eqn (6.13) will be too conservative for joints with $h_0 < b_0$ if f_{cr} is based on the buckling curve. On the other hand, a consistent set of formulae is obtained. (Other models using the frame analysis are also possible.)

6.5.3.6 Model for Shear of the Chord (Fig. 6.13)
Joints with a high β ratio and/or low h_0/b_0 ratio may fail by shear of the chord. This failure is determined by the strength of the chord cross-section

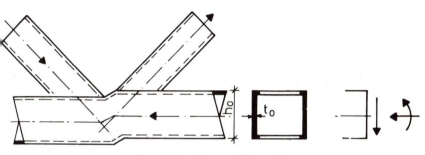

FIG. 6.13. Shear yield model.

between the bracings which can be analytically predicted using the basic interaction formulae for plastic design. The maximum shear load capacity is given by

$$N_{1y} = 0.58 f_{y0} (2h_0 t_0 + \alpha b_0 t_0) \frac{1}{\sin \theta_1} \qquad (6.14)$$

in which α depends on the relative gap size g/t_0 as shown by Wardenier (1982).

The axial load in this cross-section has to be transmitted by the remaining chord cross-sectional area or in general the Huber Hencky–von Mises criterion can be used.

6.5.4 Test Evidence
All types of joints discussed in this chapter have been extensively tested in many countries all over the world. Giddings & Wardenier (1986) give a more detailed description of the various research programmes carried out.

Initially, the research was concentrated on the static behaviour of small size joints. Stimulated by the offshore activities in the Gulf of Mexico and the North Sea, large size joints were also investigated and extensive programmes have been carried out to study the fatigue behaviour.

Although much research has been carried out, most of it relates to simple planar joints; especially with regard to multiplanar joints with multiplanar loading, more evidence is required.

6.5.5 Evaluation for Design Rules

Design rules may be of an analytical, experimental or semi-experimental nature. Purely experimental design rules should, in principle, be avoided unless no other information is available and the limitations are clearly defined. However, in most cases, pure analytical design rules are not applicable for tubular joints due to their complexity.

As a result, the best available design rules are of a semi-empirical nature. This means that the influencing parameters have been determined with simplified models whereas the final formulae have been modified using a statistical analysis of the test results. Care has to be taken that the available test evidence represents joints with the various possible parameters. In some codes formulae are given representing a lower bound to the test results.

International agreement for the evaluation for design rules has been obtained in the International Institute of Welding, Subcie XV-E (Welded Joints in Tubular Structures), and the working group (Welded Joints) of CIDECT (Comité International pour le Développement et l'Etude de la Construction Tubulaire). These committees have analysed the available evidence and have determined formulae for the ultimate static strength. From the ultimate strength formulae, characteristic strengths have been obtained using a semi-probabilistic approach. All variables have been taken into account, e.g. the scatter in test results but also the variation in mechanical properties and dimensions and the fabrication tolerances. The resulting formulae are sometimes simplified for practical use.

The characteristic joint strength N_k, representing the strength that 95% of the joints are expected to reach, is divided by a partial joint safety factor γ_m to obtain the design strength $\hat{N}$:

$$\hat{N} = \frac{N_k}{\gamma_m} \qquad (6.15)$$

In some countries the characteristic strength is multiplied by a resistance factor $\phi = 1/\gamma_m$.

The partial joint safety factor γ_m adopted in the International Institute of Welding (1982) and CIDECT recommendations (Giddings & Wardenier,

1986) varies between 1 and 1·25, depending on the joint deformation capacity and the reserve in strength. For example, the γ_m factors in Table 6.2 have been adopted for the joint strength formulae given later in this chapter.

TABLE 6.2
FACTORS γ_m ADOPTED FOR THE JOINT STRENGTH FORMULAE

Joint Brace	Joint Chord	Criterion		Adopted γ_m factor	Joint type
◯	◯	chord face failure	exp.	1·1[a]	all
		punching shear	th.	1·0	all
▢ ◯	▢	chord face failure	exp. th.	1·1 1·0	K, N T, Y, X
		punching shear	th.	1·0[b]	all
		side wall yielding		1·0[b]	T, Y, X
		side wall buckling	th.	1·25	X
		chord shear	th.	1·0[b]	K, N
		effective width (in b_e terms only)	exp.	1·25	all
▢ ◯	I	web yielding		1·0	all
		web shear	th.	1·0	K, N
		effective width	exp.	1·25	all

[a]For T-, Y- and X-joints loaded in tension the same formulae are used as for joints loaded in compression; this means actually that a $\gamma_m > 1·25$ is used.
[b]Not critical for square hollow section joints if within the range of validity given in Table 6.4.

In design, the effect of the factored loading, i.e. the loading S multiplied by the appropriate load factor γ_s, should not exceed the design strength $\hat{N}$:

$$\text{Effect } \gamma_s S \leqslant \hat{N} \tag{6.16}$$

In countries in which the 'permissible stress' method is used, the allowable load under working load conditions N_{wl} can be found by dividing the design strength $\hat{N}$ by the appropriate load factor γ_s:

$$\hat{N}_{wl} = \frac{\hat{N}}{\gamma_s} \qquad (6.17)$$

6.5.6 Restrictions

Joints in lattice girders can, in general, be considered as pin-ended in order to determine the axial load distribution in the members. Bending moments will, of course, result from the bending stiffness of the joints, eccentricities and the internal stiffness variation along the perimeter of the connection. These so-called secondary bending moments may be neglected for joint design if the joints have sufficient deformation/rotation capacity, and if the joints are within the validity range of the formulae. For hollow section joints it is further essential that the non-linear elastic stress distribution can be redistributed in the plastic range.

These requirements regarding deformation capacity make it necessary that the welds are not critical. This will always be satisfied if the welds are designed on the member strength (squash load) of the bracings. According to the IIW recommendations, this will be satisfied for all full penetration welds and for fillet welds if the throat thickness a satisfies the following conditions:

$$a \geqslant t \text{ for } f_y \leqslant 280 \text{ N/mm}^2$$

$$a \geqslant 1 \cdot 2t \text{ for } f_y = 360 \text{ N/mm}^2$$

If special welding procedures with deep penetration are used, the theoretical throat thickness may be decreased with the guaranteed penetration depth. This full strength requirement may be waived where justified with regard to strength and to deformation or rotational capacity.

The effect of eccentricities can be neglected for joint design if one of the

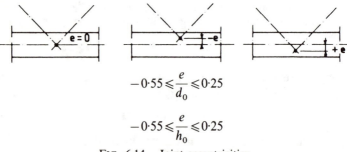

$$-0 \cdot 55 \leqslant \frac{e}{d_0} \leqslant 0 \cdot 25$$

$$-0 \cdot 55 \leqslant \frac{e}{h_0} \leqslant 0 \cdot 25$$

FIG. 6.14.   Joint eccentricities.

conditions of Fig. 6.14 is satisfied. For member design, these eccentricities have to be taken into account. Generally, the resulting bending moments are considered to be taken by the chord section.

6.6 JOINT DESIGN STRENGTH FORMULAE

Throughout the world, many sets of design rules exist for hollow section joints. Most of these have been prepared principally for either offshore or onshore structures. The IIW recommendations cover the whole field. This means there are no discontinuities. They have been drafted by an international group of experts and have been discussed in many international working groups.

Through this international coordination these recommendations have also been adopted by CIDECT and in the European recommendations (i.e. Eurocode 3), and they have been or are being implemented in various national codes or guidances. Since the publication of these recommendations in 1981 some modifications have been adopted which will be published in an updated version in 1989. These modifications have already been included in Eurocode 3 and the formulae presented in this chapter.

The following design formulae represent the currently approved IIW/CIDECT/Eurocode 3 recommendations.

6.6.1 Joints between Circular Hollow Sections

The joint strength formulae for joints between circular hollow sections given in Table 6.3 have in principle been based on the ring model analogy. However, modifications are introduced for the function of β whereas experimental functions have been introduced to account for the membrane action (γ), the influence of the gap (g') and the influence of the chord loading (n').

The function for the chord loading is based on the additional load in the chord, thus N_{op} in Fig. 6.15. Up to now it was not possible to modify this function in relation to the maximum chord stress, as used for joints between square sections.

6.6.2 Joints between Square Hollow Sections

For joints between square hollow sections, the formulae can be simplified if the range of validity is somewhat restricted, but still covering a practical range. The simplification $h_i = b_i$ and the limitation $\beta \leqslant 0.85$ for T-, Y- and X-joints ensures that various failure modes will not be critical. The joint

TABLE 6.3

DESIGN STRENGTH CAPACITY OF AXIALLY LOADED WELDED JOINTS BETWEEN CIRCULAR HOLLOW SECTIONS

Type of joint	Design strength ($i = 1$ or 2)

T, Y

$$\hat{N}_1 = \frac{f_{y0}\, t_0^2}{\sin \theta_1}(2\cdot8 + 14\cdot2\beta^2)\gamma^{0\cdot2}(f(n'))$$

X

$$\hat{N}_1 = \frac{f_{y0}\, t_0^2}{\sin \theta_1}\left(\frac{5\cdot2}{1 - 0\cdot81\beta}\right)f(n')$$

K, N gap or overlap

$$\hat{N}_i = \frac{f_{y0}\, t_0^2}{\sin \theta_1}\left(1\cdot8 + 10\cdot2\frac{d_1}{d_0}\right)f(\gamma g')f(n')$$

General

Punching shear check for T, Y, X and K, N, KT joints with gap

$$\hat{N}_i = \frac{f_{y0}}{\sqrt{3}}\, t_0 \pi d_i \frac{1 + \sin \theta_i}{2 \sin^2 \theta_i} \qquad (i = 1, 2 \text{ or } 3)$$

Functions

$$f(n') = 1\cdot0 \qquad \text{for } n' \geqslant 0$$
$$f(n') = 1 + 0\cdot3n' - 0\cdot3n'^2 \quad \text{for } n' < 0$$
$$\leqslant 1\cdot0'$$

Note: n' is negative for compression

$$f(\gamma, g') = (\gamma)^{0\cdot2}\left[1 + \frac{0\cdot024\gamma^{1\cdot2}}{\exp(0\cdot5g' - 1\cdot33) + 1}\right]$$

Validity range

$$0\cdot2 < \frac{d_i}{d_0} \leqslant 1\cdot0 \qquad \frac{d_i}{2t_i} \leqslant 25 \qquad \gamma \leqslant 25 \qquad -0\cdot55 \leqslant \frac{e}{d_0} \leqslant +0\cdot25$$

For X-joints: $\gamma \leqslant 20$ $\qquad g \geqslant t_1 + t_2$ or $O_v \geqslant 25\%$

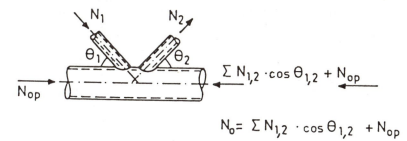

$$N_0 = \Sigma\, N_{1,2} \cdot \cos \theta_{1,2} + N_{op}$$

FIG. 6.15.   Chord loading in a K-joint.

strength formulae can now be restricted to those for chord face failure for T, Y, X and K, N gap joints and the brace effective width for overlap joints. The resulting formulae are shown in Table 6.4; the range of validity is given in Table 6.4A.

The chord face failure for T-, Y- and X-joints is based on the theoretical yield line criterion to limit deflections at service. For K- and N-joints with gap, the function for β and γ has been determined in an experimental analysis but has been checked with various theoretical approaches. Since the theoretical predictions were in good agreement with those calculated with this experimental function, the simpler experimental function has been adopted.

In the case of rectangular sections or outside the range of validity of Table 6.4A, other criteria such as chord side wall failure, chord shear failure, punching shear failure and brace effective width may also have to be checked. Detailed information is given by Wardenier (1982), Giddings & Wardenier (1986) and Packer *et al.* (1984).

6.6.3 Joints between Hollow Section Braces and I-Section Chords
The strength of joints with an I-section chord is governed by web failure, web shear or brace effective width. The resulting formulae are shown in Table 6.5, with the range of validity in Table 6.5A.

6.6.4 Special Types of Joints
The types of joints described before cover only a part of the practical applied joints. Joints loaded by bending moments have not been discussed. Information can be found in the references. It should be noted that the stiffness criteria are still a matter of discussion.

Detailed information on joints between plates or open sections and

TABLE 6.4
DESIGN STRENGTH CAPACITY OF AXIALLY LOADED WELDED JOINTS WITH SQUARE OR CIRCULAR BRACE MEMBERS AND A SQUARE HOLLOW SECTION CHORD

Type of joint	Design strength $(i=1$ or $2)$

T, Y, X

$$\hat{N}_1 = \frac{f_{y0} t_0^2}{(1-\beta)\sin\theta_1} \left(\frac{2\beta}{\sin\theta_1} + 4\sqrt{1-\beta} \right) f(n)$$

K, N, gap

$$\hat{N}_i = \frac{8\cdot9 f_{y0} t_0^2}{\sin\theta_i} \beta\gamma^{0\cdot5} f(n)$$

K, N, overlap

100% overlap		Only
$\hat{N}_i = f_{yi} t_i (3b_i - 4t_i + b_{e(ov)})$		overlapping brace
$50\% \leqslant O_v < 100\%$		to be
$\hat{N}_i = f_{yi} t_i (2b_i - 4t_i + b_e + b_{e(ov)})$		checked*

Joints with circular brace members	multiply the formulae by $\pi/4$ and replace b_i by d_i ($i=1$ or 2)

Functions	$f(n) = 1\cdot0$	for a tension force in the chord
	$f(n) = 1\cdot3 - \dfrac{0\cdot4}{\beta} |n|$	for a compression force in the chord
	$\leqslant 1\cdot0$	

$$b_e = \frac{10}{b_0/t_0} \frac{f_{y0} t_0}{f_{yi} t_i} b_i$$

$$b_{e(ov)} = \frac{10}{(b_i/t_i)_{ov}} \frac{(f_{yi} t_i)_{ov}}{f_{yi} t_i} b_i$$

Validity range	See Table 6.4A

*The overlapped member efficiency $\dfrac{N_i}{A_i \cdot f_{yi}}$ is not to be taken higher than that of the overlapping member.

TABLE 6.4A
RANGE OF VALIDITY OF TABLE 6.4A

Type of joint	Joint parameters (i=1 or 2)					
	$\dfrac{b_i}{b_0}$	$\dfrac{b_i}{t_i}$; $\dfrac{d_i}{t_i}$ Compression	Tension	$\dfrac{b_0}{t_0}$	$\dfrac{b_1+b_2}{2b_1}$, $\dfrac{b_i}{b_{1(ov)}}$	Gap/overlap
T, Y, X	$0.25 \leq \dfrac{b_i}{b_0} \leq 0.85^a$	$\dfrac{b_i}{t_i} \leq 1.25\sqrt{\dfrac{E}{f_{yi}}}$ ≤ 35	$\dfrac{b_i}{t_i} \leq 35$	$^a 10 \leq \dfrac{b_0}{t_0} \leq 35$	—	—
K and N with gap	$\geq 0.1 + 0.01\dfrac{b_0}{t_0}$			$^a 15 \leq \dfrac{b_0}{t_0} \leq 35$	$^a 0.6 \leq \dfrac{b_1+b_2}{2b_1} \leq 1.6^a$	$0.5(1-\beta) \leq \dfrac{g}{b_0} \leq 1.5(1-\beta)$ but $g \geq t_1 + t_2$
K and N with overlap and $t_{i(ov)} \geq t_i$	≥ 0.25	$\dfrac{b_i}{t_i} \leq 1.1\sqrt{\dfrac{E}{f_{yi}}}$		$\dfrac{b_0}{t_0} \leq 35$	$\dfrac{b_i}{b_{i(ov)}} \geq 0.75$	$50\% \leq O_v \leq 100\%$
Joints with circular braces	$0.4 \leq \dfrac{d_i}{b_0} \leq 0.8$	$\dfrac{d_i}{t_i} \leq 1.5\sqrt{\dfrac{E}{f_{yi}}}$	$\dfrac{d_i}{t_i} \leq 50$	Further limitations as above for $d_i = b_i$		

^{a}Outside this range of validity other failure criteria may be governing, i.e. punching shear, effective width, side wall failure, chord shear or local buckling.

TABLE 6.5
DESIGN STRENGTH CAPACITY OF AXIALLY LOADED WELDED JOINTS BETWEEN HOLLOW SECTION BRACES AND AN I-OR H-SECTION CHORD

Type of joint	*Design strength* $(i=1$ or $2)$	
	$\hat{N}_1 = \dfrac{f_{y0}\, t_w\, b_m}{\sin\theta_1}$ $\hat{N}_1 = 2f_{y1}\, t_1\, b_e$	
	$\hat{N}_i = \dfrac{f_{y0}\, t_w\, b_m}{\sin\theta_i}$ $\hat{N}_i = 2f_{yi}\, t_i\, b_e$ $\hat{N}_i = \dfrac{0.58 f_{y0}\, A_Q}{\sin\theta_i}$ $\hat{N}_{0(\text{gap})} \leqslant (A_0 - A_Q) f_{y0} + A_Q f_{y0}\sqrt{1 - \left(\dfrac{Q}{Q_p}\right)^2}$	Note*
	100% overlap $N_i = f_{yi}\, t_i (2h_i - 4t_i + b_i + b_{e(ov)})$ $50\% \leqslant O_v < 100\%$ $N_i = f_{yi}\, t_i (2h_i - 4t_i + b_e + b_{e(ov)})$	Only overlapping brace to be checked*

Functions	
RI-joints	$b_m = \dfrac{h_i}{\sin\theta_i} + 5(t_0 + r_0)$ $b_m \leqslant 2t_i + 10(t_0 + r_0)$
CI-joints	$b_m = \dfrac{d_i}{\sin\theta_i} + 5(t_0 + r_0)$

$$b_e = t_w + 2r_0 + 7\frac{f_{y0}}{f_{yi}} t_0 \qquad b_{e(ov)} = \frac{10}{(b_i/t_i)_{ov}}\,\frac{(f_{yi}t_i)_{ov}}{f_{yi}t_i}\, b_i$$

$$A_Q = A_0 - (2-\alpha)b_0\, t_0 + (t_w + 2r_0)t_0$$

RI-joints: $\alpha = \sqrt{\dfrac{1}{1 + \dfrac{4g^2}{3t_0^2}}}$ CI-joints: $\alpha = 0$

$$Q = (N_i \sin\theta_i)_{\max} \qquad Q_p = 0.58 f_{y0} A_Q$$

Note*	*Not to be checked if: $0.75 \leqslant \left(\dfrac{d_1}{d_2}\text{ or }\dfrac{b_1}{b_2}\right) \leqslant 1.33;\quad \beta \leqslant 1 - 0.03\gamma$ and $g' \leqslant 20 - 28\beta$
Validity range	See Table 6.5A

TABLE 6.5A
RANGE OF VALIDITY OF TABLE 6.5A

Type of joint	Joint parameters ($i = 1$ or 2)				
	$\dfrac{b_i}{b_{i(ov)}}$	$\dfrac{h_i}{b_i}$	$\dfrac{b_i/t_i;\ d_i/t_i}{\text{Compression}}$	Tension	$\dfrac{h_w}{t_w}$
T, Y, X	—	—	$\dfrac{b_i}{t_i} \leqslant 1\cdot1 \sqrt{\dfrac{E}{f_{yi}}}$	$\dfrac{b_i}{t_i} \leqslant 35$	$\dfrac{h_w}{t_w} < c \sqrt{\dfrac{E}{f_{y0}}}$
K and N with gap	—	1·0			$h_w \leqslant 400\text{ mm}$
K and N with overlap	$\geqslant 0\cdot75$		$\dfrac{d_i}{t_i} \leqslant 1\cdot5 \sqrt{\dfrac{E}{f_{yi}}}$	$\dfrac{d_i}{t_i} \leqslant 50$	with: $c = 1\cdot2$ for X joints $c = 1\cdot5$ for T, Y, K and N joints

circular hollow sections is given by Makino & Kurobane (1986). Hollow
sections are not only used in plane girders but often in space structures on
triangular girders. Tests have shown that for triangular girders the same
formulae can be used as for plane trusses but for particular loadings the
joint strength reduces by about 15%.

REFERENCES

DAVIES, G., PACKER, J. A. & COUTIE, M. G. (1984) The behaviour of full width RHS cross joints. In *Welding of Tubular Structures*. Pergamon Press, Oxford, pp. 411–18.

CEC (1988) Eurocode 3: Common Unified Rules for Steel Structures. Commission of the European Communities, Report EUR 8849, August 1988.

GIDDINGS, T. W. & WARDENIER, J. (1986) The Strength and Behaviour of Statically Loaded Welded Connections in Structural Hollow Sections. Monograph 6, CIDECT.

INTERNATIONAL INSTITUTE OF WELDING (1982). IIW-XV-E, Design Recommendations for Hollow Section Joints, Predominantly Statically Loaded. IIW Doc XV-491-81/XIII-1003-81 (a new version is to be published in 1989).

MAKINO, Y. & KUROBANE, Y. (1986) Strength and deformation capacity of circular tubular joints, *Safety Criteria in Design of Tubular Structures* (Proc. International Meeting, Tokyo, July). Maruzen Co., Tokyo.

218   J. WARDENIER

PACKER, J. A., BIRKEMOE, P. C. & TUCKER, W. J. (1984) Canadian Implementation of CIDECT Monograph 6. University of Toronto, Dept. of Civil Engineering, Publ. 84-04.
WARDENIER, J. (1982) *Hollow Section Joints.* Delft University Press, Delft.

Chapter 7

MOMENT-TRANSMITTING BOLTED ENDPLATE CONNECTIONS

W. M. JENKINS
School of Engineering, The Hatfield Polytechnic, Hatfield, UK

SUMMARY

Bolted endplates are the most frequently used method of connecting beams and columns in steel framed structures. In this chapter, attention is directed to the fundamental behaviour of these connections and a theoretical model is described. Attention is focussed on the properties affecting strength and stiffness. Proposals are included for standard details of flush and extended endplates. A proposed design basis is outlined and illustrated with respect to flush endplate connections for which design charts are provided.

NOTATION

EI	Flexural rigidity of beam
g	Grip length of bolt
K_T	Theoretical connection stiffness
L	Span of beam
M	Bending moment
M_L	Maximum moment for linear elastic behaviour
ϕ_L	Connection rotation corresponding to M_L
M_U	Ultimate bending moment
ϕ_U	Connection rotation corresponding to M_U

219

M_{UB}	Ultimate values of M_U and ϕ_U related to endplate (P), column
ϕ_{UB}	flange (C) and bolts (B)
M_{UC}	
ϕ_{UC}	
M_{UP}	
ϕ_{UP}	
M_{LB}	Linear elastic limit values related to endplate (P), column flange
ϕ_{LB}	(C) and bolts (B)
M_{LC}	
ϕ_{LC}	
M_{LP}	
ϕ_{LP}	
M_{CX}	Ultimate bending capacity of beam (BS 5950)
M_E	End (connection) moment
M_S	Maximum (design) span moment in beam
M_0	Maximum 'free' bending moment in beam
Q	Prying force
T	Bolt force
Y_C	Midspan deflection of beam
Y_{CO}	Midspan deflection of beam as simply supported
α	$2EI/K_T L$

7.1 INTRODUCTION

The behaviour of most structural steelwork connections is complex and the traditional approaches to design have involved considerable simplification. The classification of connection types has been based on the concepts of 'rigid' and 'pinned' connections; however, in reality few connections satisfy these extreme conditions and the majority of practical connections lie somewhere between the two. The fundamental structural characteristic is the moment–rotation relationship (Fig. 7.1). The 'rotation' is the *relative* angular rotation of the axes of the connected parts. A 'rigid' connection is one which exhibits no significant rotation whereas a 'pinned' connection transmits no significant bending moment. Some so-called 'rigid' connections exhibit a significant rotation the effect of which is to reduce the bending moment at the connection and increase the bending moment levels elsewhere in the structure. Some 'pinned' connections do in fact transmit significant levels of bending moment and, again, the design assumptions are

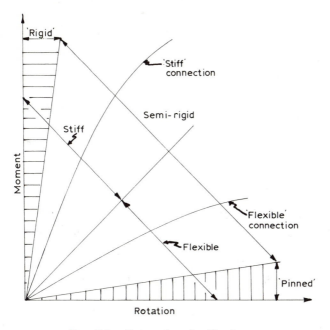

FIG. 7.1. Connection classifications.

not satisfied in the real structure. It is clearly important to obtain sufficient knowledge of the characteristics of connections and to base the approach to structural analysis and design on realistic predictions of behaviour. It is not possible to predict the behaviour of a structural frame reliably if unrealistic properties are assumed for the connections.

Until comparatively recently, structural steel research has been dominated by concern for the behaviour of structural elements and complete structures. Until the late 1970s, connection behaviour received scant attention but since that time a high level of international activity has developed. Considerable effort has been directed at the prediction of ultimate conditions in connections using a yield line approach leading to an upper bound on connection ultimate moment, M_U (Packer & Morris, 1977). These methods do not provide any information relating to the *actual* deformations occurring in a connection and so cannot lead to predictions of bending moments based on *stiffness*. A satisfactory approach to a comprehensive analysis of connection behaviour must include elastic and plastic behaviour (Jenkins *et al.*, 1986). The theoretical model must be

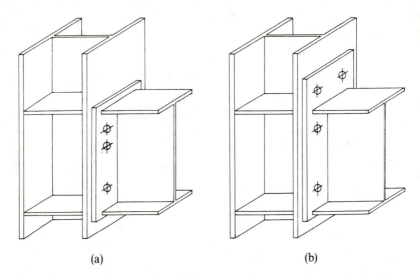

FIG. 7.2.   Bolted endplate connections: (a) flush endplate; (b) extended endplate.

capable of predicting the actual bolt forces occurring since these are crucial
in the connection design. It is important to establish that the bolt forces are
not greater than their maximum design loads at the design ultimate
moment of the connection.

It will be shown in subsequent sections that an elastic-plastic finite
element method can be used to model the complex behaviour of endplate
connections and that the model can include the bolt performance and
matters such as prying forces and the influence of stiffeners.

There are two principal types of moment-transmitting bolted endplate
connections; these are the 'flush' and 'extended' endplates shown in Fig. 7.2.
The extended endplate has a higher moment capacity than the flush
endplate and is frequently designed as a 'full-strength' connection, i.e. with
an ultimate moment of resistance at least equal to that of the beam. On the
other hand, the flush endplate is often designed as a 'pinned' connection in
spite of the fact that it can and does transmit significant levels of bending
moment.

The column web stiffeners shown in Fig. 7.2 increase the local moment
capacity of the column flange at the connection and, incidentally, simplify
the theoretical modelling. They are frequently omitted when using flush
endplates and sometimes omitted in extended endplate connections.

7.2 STANDARD DETAILS AND MATERIAL PROPERTIES

7.2.1 Standard Details

The adoption of standard details for structural connections offers several advantages in both design and fabrication. The behaviour of the bolted endplate is sensitive to the precise positions of the tension bolts. If these bolts are positioned close to the flange and web of the beam cross-section, this will produce a stiff connection which will in turn attract a higher bending moment. The connection will then, however, have a low rotation capacity since there will be little flexural deformation of the endplate at the bolt positions. It is generally true that bolt extensions generate little rotation capacity, and in these circumstances the rotation capacity available may be too low to permit the development of a plastic hinge at or near midspan of the beam, and hence plastic design may not be possible. If the bolts are positioned further away from the flange and web, the bending deformations of the endplate will be increased, resulting in a reduction in stiffness of the connection and an increased rotation capacity. Clearly a compromise is necessary. The standard details shown in Fig. 7.3 have been determined with such a compromise in mind.

In preparing the data in Fig. 7.3, each universal beam was examined and the dimensions Wp, G1, G2, S1 and S2 were determined. The universal beams are divided into two groups, A and B, with some overlap in the middle range. For group A, the standard details are based on the use of M24 bolts but either M24 or M20 may be used in design. For group B, the standard details are based on the use of M20 bolts but either M20 or M16 may be used in design.

It was decided that an approach based on a consideration of individual beams was preferable to one based on bolt diameter used. In order to simplify the theoretical modelling, some small adjustments were made to the standard details as shown in Fig. 7.4. Small departures from the standard details can be made but it should be borne in mind that substantial deviations will invalidate the theoretical results.

Apart from the advantages offered by standardisation in the design process, there is of course considerable advantage in fabrication, particularly when computer controlled cutting and drilling are used.

7.2.2 Material Properties

The maximum stress developed in bolted endplates is controlled, at the design ultimate load, by the design strengths (p_y) from BS 5950 clause 3.1.1. These are shown in Table 7.1; Young's modulus E is taken as $205 \, kN/mm^2$.

Group A
M20/M24 bolts

UB	Dp	Wp	H	S1	S2	S3	G1	G2
914x419	950	440	15	105	175	845	120	70
914x305	960	330	"	100	170	850	"	"
838x292	880	315	"	95	165	780	"	"
720x267	800	290	"	90	160	700	"	"
686x254	725	275	"	90	160	625	"	"
610x305	665	335	"	95	165	555	"	"
610x229	650	250	"	90	160	550	"	"
533x210	575	235	"	90	160	480	"	"
457x191	500	215	"	85	155	405	"	"
457x152	495	200	"	85	155	405	"	"
406x178	445	200	"	85	155	355	"	"
356x171	395	200	"	85	155	305	"	"
305x165	340	200	"	80	150	255	"	"

additional bolts if required

(a)

Group B
M16/M20 bolts

UB	Dp	Wp	H	S1	S2	S3	G1	G2
457x152	495	175	15	80	140	405	"	60
406x178	440	200	"	80	140	355	"	"
406x140	430	170	"	80	140	350	"	"
356x171	395	200	"	80	140	305	"	"
356x127	380	170	"	80	140	305	"	"
305x165	340	200	"	80	140	305	"	"
305x127	340	170	"	80	140	255	"	"
305x102	340	170	"	75	135	260	"	"
254x146	290	170	"	80	140	205	"	"
254x102	290	170	"	75	135	210	"	"
203x133	235	170	"	75	135	160	"	"

UB	Dp	Wp	H	S1	S2	S3	G1	G2
914x419	1050	440	115	60	205	945	120	70
914x305	1060	330	"	"	200	950	"	"
838x292	980	315	"	"	195	880	"	"
762x267	900	290	"	"	190	800	"	"
686x254	825	275	"	"	190	725	"	"
610x305	765	335	"	"	195	655	"	"
610x229	750	250	"	"	190	650	"	"
533x210	675	235	"	"	190	580	"	"
457x191	600	215	"	"	185	505	"	"
457x152	595	200	"	"	185	505	"	"
406x178	545	200	"	"	185	455	"	"
356x171	495	200	"	"	185	405	"	"
305x165	440	200	"	"	180	355	"	"

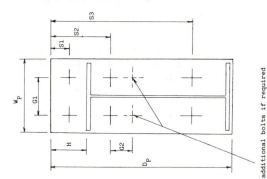

additional bolts if required

(b)

UB	Dp	Wp	H	S1	S2	S3	G1	G2
457x152	580	175	100	50	165	490	100	60
406x178	525	200	"	"	165	440	"	"
406x140	515	170	"	"	165	435	"	"
356x171	480	200	"	"	165	390	"	"
356x127	465	170	"	"	165	390	"	"
305x165	425	200	"	"	165	340	"	"
305x127	425	170	"	"	165	340	"	"
305x102	425	170	"	"	160	345	"	"
254x146	375	170	"	"	165	290	"	"
254x102	375	170	"	"	160	295	"	"
203x133	320	170	"	"	160	245	"	"

Fig. 7.3. Standard details for bolted endplate connections.

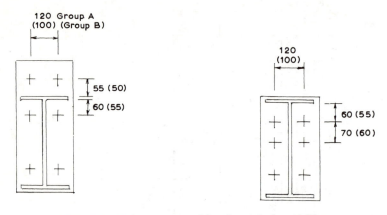

FIG. 7.4.   Bolt centres used for theoretical modelling.

TABLE 7.1
EXTRACT FROM TABLE 6, BS 5950, DESIGN STRENGTHS FOR STEEL TO
BS 4360. REPRODUCED BY PERMISSION OF THE BRITISH STANDARDS
INSTITUTION

Steel grade	Plate thickness, t	$p_y(N/mm^2)$
43 (A, B or C)	$t < 16$ mm	275
	$t < 40$ mm	265
50 (B and C)	$t < 16$ mm	355
	$t < 63$ mm	340

Bolt strengths to be used in design to BS 5950 depend on the bolt grades used. The popular grades are 4.6 and 8.8. It should be noted that the two digits used to identify the grade of material used in the bolt (M, N) are defined as follows:

$$M = \text{ultimate stress}/10$$

$$N = 10 \times \text{yield stress/ultimate stress}$$

Thus, if M and N are multiplied, the result is the material yield stress (units kgf/mm²), e.g.

$$4 \times 6 = 24 \, \text{kgf/mm}^2 \, (235 \, \text{N/mm}^2)$$

$$8 \times 8 = 64 \, \text{kgf/mm}^2 \, (630 \, \text{N/mm}^2)$$

The bolt strengths used in design (BS 5950 clause 6.3) are given in Table 7.2.

TABLE 7.2

Bolt diameter (mm)	Bolt strength (kN)		Effective area (mm²)
	Bolt grade 4.6	Bolt grade 8.8	
16	30·6	70·7	157
20	47·8	110	245
24	68·8	159	353

Bolt extensibilities $(g/AE)_{eff}$ tend to be greater than the theoretical values; however, it has been shown that the theoretical value of g/AE can be used conservatively to predict bolt extensions where g is taken as the 'grip' length.

7.3 FUNDAMENTAL STRUCTURAL ACTION AND CHARACTERISTICS

7.3.1 Introduction

When considering the structural action of a bolted endplate connection it is important to identify the fundamental parameters affecting the behaviour. Although the connection will generally transmit both bending moment and shear force, it is the transmission of bending which is the prime consideration in the majority of cases. If we assume that friction grip bolts are not used and that the endplate has 'slipped' to the extent that the bolts are in shear and bearing, we can concentrate our attention on the transmission of bending moment from the beam to the column through the endplate, bolts and column flange. The connection design will need to be checked for the transmission of shear but in most short to medium spans the two bolts on the compression side will be sufficient to carry the end shear from the beam. In longer spans it may be necessary to introduce additional bolts, as shown in Fig. 7.3 (a) and (b), to carry the shear. Beams will generally be deeper with longer spans so there is more space in which to accommodate additional row(s) of bolts.

7.3.2 Structural Action in a Bolted Endplate

The mechanism of transmission of bending moment is seen at its simplest form in the 'thick' endplate connections shown in Fig. 7.5 (a) and (b). If the endplate is thick enough to eliminate any significant distortion, the rotation

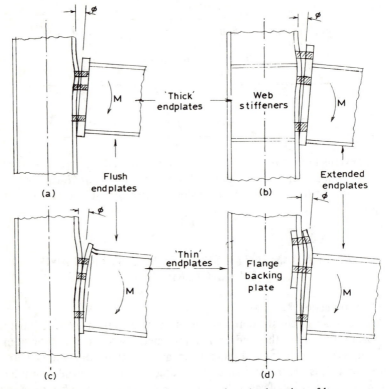

FIG. 7.5. 'Thick' and 'thin' endplate connections (end section of beam assumed undeformed).

(ϕ) of the connection is attributable to

  (i)   bolt extension,
  (ii) column flange bending, and
  (iii) column web stretching.

Furthermore, the axis of rotation of the endplate is at the bottom edge of the plate. The bolts on the tension side of the connection are principally in tension. Although there is evidence of bending in the bolts, it is reasonable to assume that tension predominates. There may be small tensions in the bolts on the compression side of the connection but these are negligible. The moment of resistance is then constituted by summing the bolt tensions multiplied by the lever arms taken from the bottom edge of the plate. The bolt extensions are usually small, but may be significant, so the principal contribution to the connection rotation ϕ is from the deformations taking place in the column flange and web. It is possible to strengthen and stiffen the column either by conventional stiffeners as shown in Fig. 7.5(b) or by the use of flange backing plates as shown in Fig. 7.5(d).

With 'thin' endplates (Fig. 7.5 (c) and (d)) an additional contribution to rotation comes from bending of the endplate but it is still reasonable to assume that rotation takes place about the compression edge of the plate. It is conventional in design to assume an axis of rotation corresponding to the centre of the compression flange of the beam. The difference is not great and is on the safe side.

From the points of view of strength and stiffness the 'extended' endplate (Fig. 7.5 (b) and (c)) is preferred to the flush endplate. In the extended endplate the tension bolts are much more favourably disposed relative to the tension flange of the beam and there is a natural tendency for all four tension bolts to be fully utilised. In the flush endplate (Fig. 7.5 (a) and (c)) the tension bolts are not equally loaded and thus the connection has a much reduced strength as compared with the extended endplate. The bolts nearest to the underside of the tension flange of the beam carry a much higher tension (two or three times) than the other tension bolts. Nevertheless it is possible to design a flush endplate connection to carry a significant level of bending moment, say 0·4–0·7 of the plastic moment of resistance of the beam. The extended endplate connection can usually be designed as 'full-strength' if desired.

The development of 'prying' forces can be a problem in endplate connections. These are contact forces developed between the endplate and the column flange caused by the bending curvature of the endplate (Fig. 7.6). The force P, which is the simplified action of the beam on the endplate, is resisted by the bolt tensions T. If the bolts have a severely limited extensibility, and there is significant bending of the endplate, the endplate is forced into double curvature by the contact force Q (the 'prying' force). The effect of Q is to increase the actual bolt forces since

$$T = \frac{P}{2} + Q \qquad (7.1)$$

Prying forces can be important especially in 'thin' extended endplates; they are usually of little consequence in flush endplates. Bolt strengths in BS 5950 include an allowance for prying action so that this aspect of behaviour can be ignored in design.

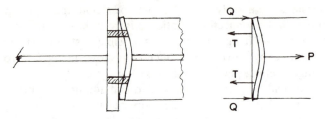

FIG. 7.6. Prying forces.

It has been seen that the behaviour of a bolted endplate connection is influenced by several factors:

(a) the type ('extended' endplate or 'flush' endplate);
(b) the bolts, bolt positions and whether the bolts are pretensioned;
(c) the endplate thickness;
(d) the column flange and web;
(e) whether conventional column web stiffeners or backing plates are used;

and also

(f) the welding of the endplate to the beam;
(g) any lack-of-fit existing between the endplate and the column.

Lack-of-fit does not tend to have an adverse affect on connection *strength* but can reduce stiffness if a gap exists on the compression side of the connection. It has been found necessary to allow for 'variability' in connection stiffness, whether caused by lack of fit or by other factors, by adopting a practical range of stiffness for a given connection such that the 'real' stiffness can be assumed to be *within* the range used.

The effect of pretensioning bolts is to increase the stiffness of a connection at levels of bending moment below the ultimate. Pretensioning has little effect, if any, on the strength of a connection and there is some doubt as to whether bolt pretensioning has any reliable long-term advantage.

7.3.3 Moment–Rotation Relationship

This relationship is of fundamental importance in studying the bolted endplate, or indeed any other connection type. The 'moment' is that applied to the connection, which will in part be determined by the characteristics of the connection itself. The 'rotation' is the *relative* angular rotation

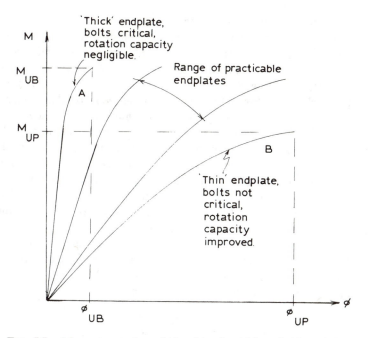

FIG. 7.7.   Moment–rotation relationships for thick and thin endplates.

developed between the axes of the beam and column (this angle is zero in a truly 'rigid' connection). The principal contributions to rotation are the deformations in the column (flange and web) and the endplate, followed by the bolt extensions. If a connection is made with a 'thick' endplate and a comparatively thick column flange, the rotation ϕ will be small and the moment–rotation relationship will be characterised by curve A in Fig. 7.7. In these circumstances the ultimate moment of the connection will be determined by the strength of the bolts (M_{UB}). In fact, for a given connection, M_{UB} will always represent an upper bound on the actual ultimate moment M_U.

If a very 'thin' endplate is used, and/or a thin column flange, the rotations will be larger and the moment–rotation curve will be more like B in Fig. 7.7. Now the ultimate moment (M_{UP}) will be determined by plastic bending of the plate and column flange, and M_{UP} may be less than M_{UB}. These are the extremes; the practical range of endplate connections will lie between A and B.

7.3.4 Moment–Stiffness Relationship

The stiffness of a connection is given by the slope of the tangent to the moment–rotation relationship. A detailed analysis of a moment–rotation relationship can be carried out using a cubic spline fit which closely represents the changing slope of the moment–rotation curve. A typical situation is shown in Fig. 7.13 where it will be seen that the connection stiffness reduces progressively as the bending moment is increased. Some connections exhibit a well defined plateau at low moment whereas others exhibit virtually no plateau. In general it is convenient to assume a constant value of stiffness up to a moment level M_L indicating the limit of linear behaviour of the connection. The assessment of M_L for any connection involves a study of all aspects of the connection behaviour. The value of stiffness corresponding to M_L is K_T, the theoretical connection stiffness. The implication of this approach is that, once M_L and K_T are determined, the behaviour (linear) of the connection is determined up to moment M_L.

At higher values of moment $(M > M_L)$ the stiffness of the connection is nonlinear and vanishes at the ultimate moment M_U. An approximate bilinear relationship can be used as shown in Fig. 7.13

$$K = K_T \frac{M_U - M}{M_U - M_L} \qquad (7.2)$$

7.4 THEORETICAL MODELLING

7.4.1 Basis of Theoretical Model

In view of the complexity of connection behaviour and the need to produce moment–rotation relationships in both elastic and plastic states, the elastic-plastic finite element approach offered the best prospect. The element adopted was the plate bending element described by Owen & Hinton (1980). A series of analyses were carried out on representative connections, producing continuous moment–rotation relationships using an incremental loading approach. These analyses were then followed by a parametric study producing generalised relationships for use in design. The detailed procedures have been described by Jenkins et al. (1986). The following is a brief synopsis of the method used.

7.4.2 Modelling of Endplate

The endplate was discretised using rectangular elements and omitting square elements at the bolt hole positions. In the endplate analysis the bolt extensions and column flange deformations are temporarily ignored. The endplate bending deformations at a particular level of applied moment are then obtained by finite element analysis assuming a value of the ratio of tension bolt forces T_1/T_2. In the case of flush endplates, this ratio is adjusted iteratively to satisfy compatibility conditions at the bolt positions, it being assumed that the end section of the beam is undeformed (Fig. 7.5). With extended endplates, a check is carried out for contact at prying force positions; if this exists, bolt forces are adjusted to satisfy compatibility, maintaining equilibrium. The transverse plate deformations at the bolt positions are then transformed into a rotation ϕ_p about the compression flange of the beam. In modelling the endplate at the weld positions, allowance was made for the increase in material yield stress caused by welding.

7.4.3 Modelling of Column Flange

The theoretical analysis of the column flange is simplified if web stiffeners are used in the column in line with the tension and compression flanges of the beam. In these circumstances the area of flange lying between the stiffeners acts in a similar way to the endplate and can be modelled in the same way. Without stiffeners, the problem becomes much more difficult in that the length of column flange contributing to rotation at the connection is unknown. Following a similar analysis to that for the endplate flexure, the connection rotation due to column flange bending can be obtained (ϕ_C).

7.4.4 Total Connection Rotation (ϕ)

The contribution to rotation caused by bolt stretching, ϕ_B, is generally small but is significant in assessing connection stiffness. This rotation is easily obtained once the bolt forces are known and an effective g/EA has been determined.

The total connection rotation, ϕ, at a particular value of applied moment, M, will then be

$$\phi = \phi_P + \phi_C + \phi_B \tag{7.3}$$

Thus a single point with coordinates (M, ϕ) has been located on the moment–rotation curve. The whole procedure is then repeated for a further increment in applied bending moment.

A degree of approximation is introduced by this procedure in that each contribution to the rotation ϕ is obtained on the assumption that each is independent of the others.

The theoretically predicted values of the main parameters are presented

234 W. M. JENKINS

in a set of figures in Section 7.6 and form the basis of an approximate design method. These curves were prepared from the results of the parametric study mentioned in Section 7.4.1.

7.5 CONNECTION STIFFNESS

The reliable estimation of connection stiffness is essential in the analysis and design of steel structures. The distribution of stress resultants throughout the structural frame will depend on the connection stiffnesses as well as the stiffnesses of the structural elements. The 'instantaneous' value of connection stiffness is given by the slope of the moment–rotation relationship (Fig. 7.7). These relationships are generally nonlinear and some approximation is needed to obtain a practicable representation. The bilinear relationship shown in Fig. 7.13 has been found reasonable and capable of incorporation in a practical design method.

Experimental investigation has shown a considerable variability in the actual stiffness exhibited by supposedly identical connections. If K_T is the theoretical value of stiffness, actual stiffnesses have been observed to lie in the range $K_T/3$ to $2K_T$. The higher value would appear to be significant when designing the connection, since this would lead to a higher bending moment at the connection, and the lower value would be significant when considering the strength and serviceability designs of the beam. In practice the upper limit is not crucial since the strength design of the connection should be directed at the ultimate moment M_U. However, the lower limit on connection stiffness is crucial in the design of the beam and it is recommended that this be used to check beam strength and deflection. The design method proposed in Section 7.7 uses $K_T/3$ for beam design in the range $0 < M_E \leqslant M_L$ and, in order to retain a simple pseudo 'elastic' approach at moments above M_L, $K_T/6$ for $M_L < M_E \leqslant \frac{1}{2}(M_L + M_U)$. Above $M_E = \frac{1}{2}(M_L + M_U)$, it is assumed that the connection has no elastic stiffness. These notional limits on connection stiffness are shown in Fig. 7.13.

The estimation of elastic connection stiffness (K_T) can be carried out as follows. For a particular connection, determine

$$K_{LP} = M_{LP}/\phi_{LP}$$
$$K_{LC} = M_{LC}/\phi_{LC} \qquad (7.4)$$
$$K_{LB} = M_{LB}/\phi_{LB}$$

Since the design bolt strengths will be within the linear elastic range, the third of eqns (7.4) may be replaced by

$$K_B = M_B/\phi_B \tag{7.5}$$

Thus, at any level of connection moment $M_E \leqslant M_L$, the connection rotation will be

$$\phi = M_E(\phi_{LP}/M_{LP} + \phi_{LC}/M_{LC} + \phi_B/M_B) \tag{7.6}$$

and

$$K_T = M_E/\phi$$
$$= 1/(\phi_{LP}/M_{LP} + \phi_{LC}/M_{LC} + \phi_B/M_B) \tag{7.7}$$

Equation (7.7) is valid at moment levels up to M_L, where M_L is the *lowest* of the values M_{LP}, M_{LC} and M_B.

Putting M_F as the fixed end moment from a symmetrical loading condition, with identical end connections in the beam, the end moment is given by

$$\frac{M_E}{M_F} = \frac{1}{1+\alpha} \tag{7.8}$$

where

$$\alpha = \frac{2EI}{K_T L} \tag{7.9}$$

Equations (7.7)–(7.9) can be used to assess the connection moments under actual, or assumed, linear elastic conditions. Moreover, the central deflection of the beam, Y_C, can then be determined from

$$Y_C = Y_{CO} - M_E L^2/8EI \tag{7.10}$$

where Y_{CO} is the central deflection at applied service load on a simply supported span.

In applying this theory in the design approach of Section 7.7, K_T would be factored according to the level of end moment obtaining.

7.6 CONNECTION STRENGTH

The most appropriate parameter in an assessment of connection strength is the ultimate moment M_U. This is assumed to be the maximum moment which can be accepted by the connection. M_U can be estimated by theoretical predictions, and comparisons between experiment and theory have been such as to justify a reasonable level of confidence in the predicted M_U.

It is suggested that the ultimate moment of a connection, M_U, is the smallest value of M_{UB}, M_{UP} and M_{UC}, the ultimate moment based on bolt tensions, endplate bending and column flange bending, respectively.

Whilst it is not good practice to allow the ultimate moment of a connection to be based on *ultimate* bolt tensions, since bolt fracture gives sudden failure, it is acceptable to use *design* ultimate bolt strengths (BS 5950) since these include provision for such effects as the increase in actual bolt forces due to prying action and are in general conservative.

In confining the M_U prediction to three values of ultimate moment, it is implied that failure will not take place from any other source. Design considerations need to include welds, web tension in the beam, shear capacity of the connection and shear and buckling in the column web.

The ultimate moment of a connection based on maximum (ultimate load) bolt tensions is shown in Fig. 7.8 for flush endplate connections with four tension bolts. The values are obtained using a linear relationship for the bolt tensions and assuming the use of grade 8.8 bolts. Values of M_B are plotted against overall depth of beam D and are given for M16, M20 and M24 bolts. Standard details as set out in Section 7.2 are assumed.

The ultimate moment of a connection may be determined by bending in the endplate (M_{UP}). Standardised connections have been analysed by elastic-plastic finite element analysis and the results subjected to a parametric study. The result of this study is shown in Fig. 7.9 where values of M_{UP} for flush endplate connections are shown plotted against endplate thickness t_p.

The third principal criterion for M_U is based on column flange bending (M_{UC}). A similar parametric study to that used for M_{UP} produced Fig. 7.10 in which M_{UC} is plotted against beam depth for a selection of universal columns. In producing the curves for Fig. 7.10, it was assumed that the column web was stiffened with conventional stiffeners in line with the flanges of the beam.

7.7 DESIGN OF FLUSH ENDPLATE CONNECTIONS

7.7.1 Principal Design Parameters

The principal parameters in the design of a bolted endplate connection are the moments M_U and M_L and the corresponding rotations ϕ_U and ϕ_L. It is

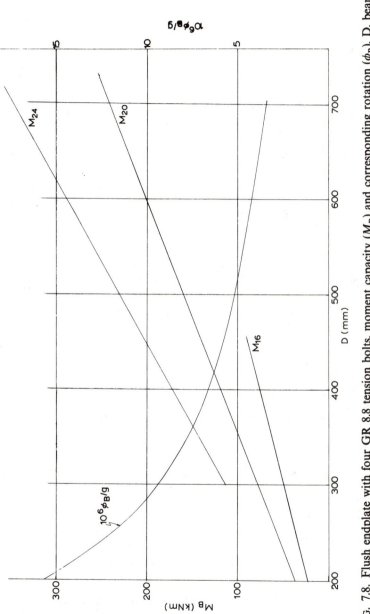

FIG. 7.8. Flush endplate with four GR 8.8 tension bolts, moment capacity (M_B) and corresponding rotation (ϕ_B). D, beam depth (mm); g, grip length (mm).

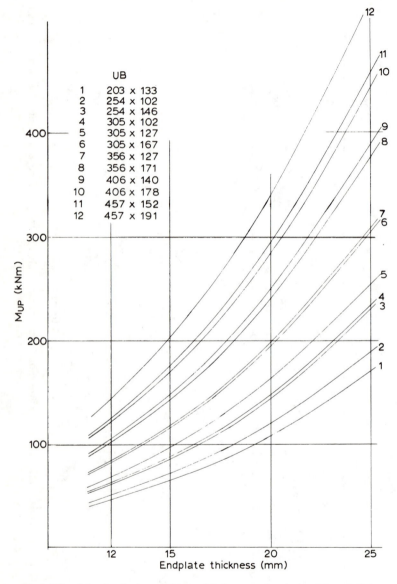

FIG. 7.9. M_{UP} for flush endplates with four tension bolts; $M_{LP} = 0.6M_{UP}$.

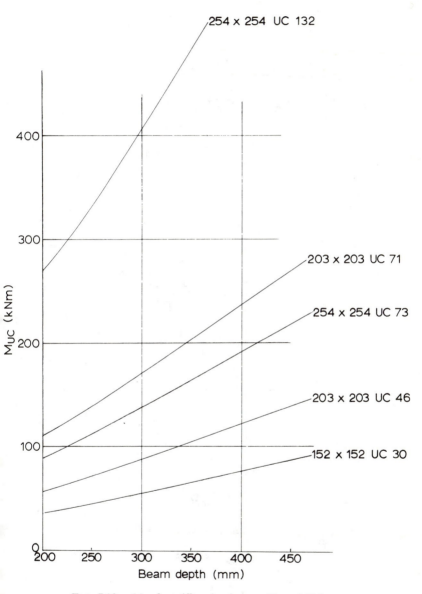

FIG. 7.10. M_{UC} for stiffened columns; $M_{LC} = 0 \cdot 6 M_{UC}$.

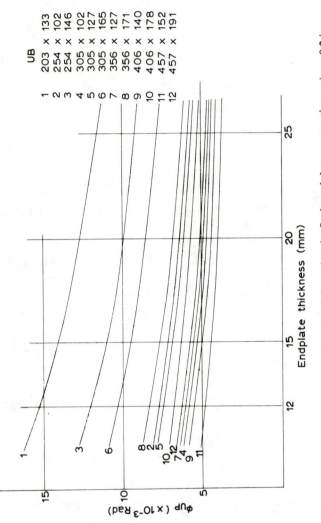

FIG. 7.11. Rotational capacity of endplate, ϕ_{UP} in flush endplate connections; $\phi_{LP} = 0 \cdot 2\phi_{UP}$.

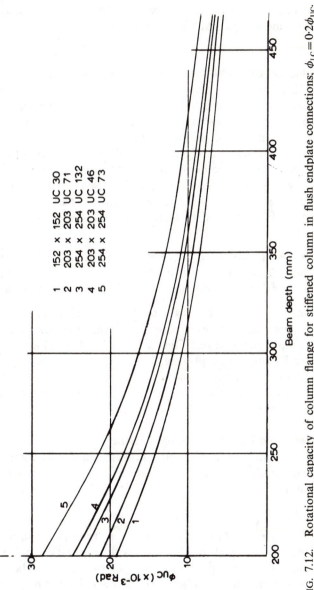

1	152 × 152	UC	30
2	203 × 203	UC	71
3	254 × 254	UC	132
4	203 × 203	UC	46
5	254 × 254	UC	73

Beam depth (mm)

ϕ_{UC} (× 10^{-3} Rad)

FIG. 7.12.   Rotational capacity of column flange for stiffened column in flush endplate connections; $\phi_{LC} = 0 \cdot 2\phi_{UC}$.

helpful to regard these as pairs of coordinate points on the moment–rotation diagram. From the first pair (M_L, ϕ_L) can be determined the theoretical (linear) elastic stiffness of the connection:

$$K_T = M_L/\phi_L \qquad (0 \leqslant M \leqslant M_L) \qquad (7.11)$$

This value of connection stiffness is important when assessing the serviceability limit state design of the beam, and also in assessing the strength capacity of the beam in conditions when the connection is elastic. In designing the connection, the critical value of moment is M_U, the ultimate moment of the connection. The corresponding value of rotation, ϕ_U, is also important since, if a plastic hinge is to develop in the beam at ultimate load, the connection must have sufficient rotation capacity.

The limit state design method proposed is based on the use of these four parameters; however, in assessing the design of a particular connection, attention needs to be paid to three separate aspects of the connection behaviour:

(i)   the bolt tensions and connection rotation due to bolt extension;
(ii) endplate bending and its contribution to connection rotation;
(iii) column flange bending and its contribution to connection rotation.

Using the theoretical elastic-plastic model described in Section 7.4, design data corresponding to these three aspects of behaviour have been prepared for flush endplate connections (Figs 7.8–7.12). In all cases four tension bolts and group B standard details (Fig. 7.3) are used.

The design of extended endplate connections can be carried out according to the same basic approach but as yet there are insufficient data for this purpose.

7.7.2 Connection Design at Ultimate Moment
The design method commences with consideration of 'trial' connection and beam design at ultimate load. A trial ratio of M_U/M_P is used to obtain M_U and M_P from

$$M_U + M_P \geqslant M_0 \qquad (7.12)$$

where M_0 is the maximum free moment on the beam at ultimate load. A value of M_U/M_P between 0·3 and 0·5 will be suitable at this stage, the lower value being appropriate for 'long' spans and the higher value for 'short' spans. Once the beam depth D is known, the bolt diameter can be chosen and M_B determined from Fig. 7.8. M_B should not be less than the required value of M_U from eqn (7.12). A choice of endplate thickness is then made using Fig. 7.9 such that M_{UP} is not less than the M_U required.

Assuming that a trial section has been chosen for the column, M_{UC} is determined from Fig. 7.10. The ultimate moment of the connection, M_U, is now the *smallest* of the three values M_B, M_{UP} and M_{UC}. This completes the 'trial' design of the connection at ultimate load. It may of course be necessary to revise this design in the light of subsequent considerations.

7.7.3 Beam Design at Ultimate Load

In order to simplify the treatment it is assumed here that the beam is restrained and that the design criterion takes the simple form

$$M_S \leqslant M_{CX} \tag{7.13}$$

where

$$M_S = M_0 - M_E \tag{7.14}$$

M_{CX} is the ultimate bending capacity of the beam according to BS 5950. M_E is the connection moment to be used in checking the beam design. This moment may be M_U or it may be less than M_U, depending on whether the connection is deemed to be elastic or plastic at ultimate load. Experimental studies on connections have shown that there is considerable variability in connection stiffness even from supposedly identical connections. Using the

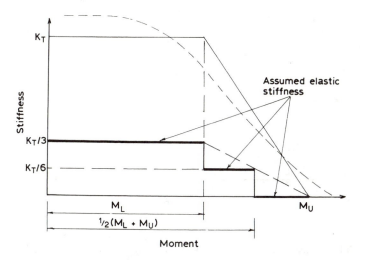

FIG. 7.13. Connection stiffness criterion for beam design—flush endplates.

theoretical elastic stiffness K_T as a reference, stiffnesses have been measured as low as $K_T/3$ and as high as $2K_T$. These wide differences are thought to be due to the considerable variability in 'fit-up' obtained with actual connections. Clearly it is important, in considering the beam design, to allow for the possibility of a connection exhibiting a stiffness at the bottom end of the range. Accordingly, the beam design should be checked for the moment consistent with elastic behaviour of the connection at $K = K_T/3$. This stiffness is valid up to a moment level M_L where M_L is the *smallest* of M_B, M_{LP} and M_{LC}. Above this level of moment, the connection stiffness reduces; a linear reduction to zero at M_U is shown in Fig. 7.13. At end moment (M_E) levels between M_L and $\frac{1}{2}(M_U + M_L)$ it is proposed that a further reduction be applied to the connection stiffness $(K_T/6)$ and that above $\frac{1}{2}(M_U + M_L)$ the connection be deemed to have no stiffness and the beam designed for constant end moment M_U. The effect of this on the maximum span moment (M_S) shown in Fig. 7.14. If the beam is plastic at ultimate load, connection rotation capacity needs to be checked using Fig. 7.15.

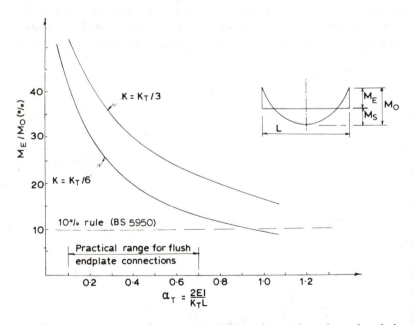

FIG. 7.14. Elastic connection moment (M_E) to be used to determine design ultimate moment for beam (M_S).

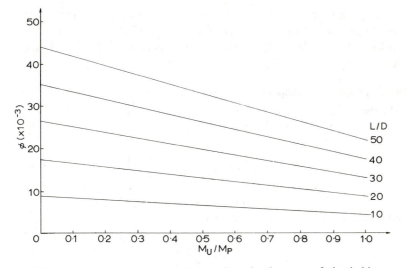

FIG. 7.15.   Connection moment needed to allow development of plastic hinge at midspan of beam.

Three cases need to be considered (Jenkins *et al.*, 1986):

(1) $M_U = M_{UP}$, then

$$\phi_U \simeq \phi_{UP} + \left[\phi_{LC} + (M_U - M_{LC}) \frac{\phi_{UC} - \phi_{LC}}{M_{UC} - M_{LC}} \right] \tag{7.15}$$

(2) $M_U = M_{UC}$, then

$$\phi_U \simeq \phi_{UC} + \left[\phi_{LP} + (M_U - M_{LP}) \frac{\phi_{UP} - \phi_{LP}}{M_{UP} - M_{LP}} \right] \tag{7.16}$$

(3) $M_U = M_B$, then

$$\phi_U \simeq \left[\phi_{LC} + (M_U - M_{LC}) \frac{\phi_{UC} - \phi_{LC}}{M_{UC} - M_{LC}} \right]$$
$$+ \left[\phi_{LP} + (M_U - M_{LP}) \frac{\phi_{UP} - \phi_{LP}}{M_{UP} - M_{LP}} \right] \tag{7.17}$$

Equations (7.15)–(7.17) are developed on the simplifying assumption that the moment–rotation relationships are bilinear between the origin,

(M_L, ϕ_L) and (M_U, ϕ_U). If the terms in parentheses become negative, these should be considered to be zero, and ϕ_{LC} in eqns (7.15) and (7.17) should be replaced by $\phi_{LC}(M_{UP}/M_{LC})$, and ϕ_{LP} in eqns (7.16) and (7.17) should be replaced by $\phi_{LP}(M_{UC}/M_{LP})$.

7.7.4 Elastic Behaviour of the Connection

The theoretical elastic stiffness of a connection can be obtained by summing the flexibilities of the bolts, the endplate and the column flange:

$$K_T = 1 \left/ \left(\frac{\phi_B}{M_B} + \frac{\phi_{LP}}{M_{LP}} + \frac{\phi_{LC}}{M_{LC}} \right) \right. \qquad (7.18)$$

This value of stiffness is valid for moments M_E not greater than M_L. Knowing K_T, M_E can be calculated from

$$M_E = \frac{M_F}{1 + \alpha} \qquad (7.19)$$

where M_F is the 'fixed-end' moment corresponding to a rigid connection, and

$$\alpha = \frac{2EI}{K_T L} \qquad (7.20)$$

EI is the flexural rigidity of the beam. In the design method, the theoretical stiffness K_T is factored as described in Section 7.7.3.

7.7.5 Serviceability Design of Beam

Beam deflection is checked for the unfactored imposed load. The end moment is calculated using $K_T/3$, then revised at $K_T/6$ if $M_E > M_L$, and the maximum beam deflection obtained from

$$Y_C = Y_{CO} - \frac{M_E L^2}{8EI} \qquad (7.21)$$

where Y_{CO} is the central deflection due to applied (service) load on the span as if simply supported.

7.7.6 Design Example

The design procedure is shown in the flow diagram in Fig. 7.16 and will now be illustrated with an example. A beam section and connections will be

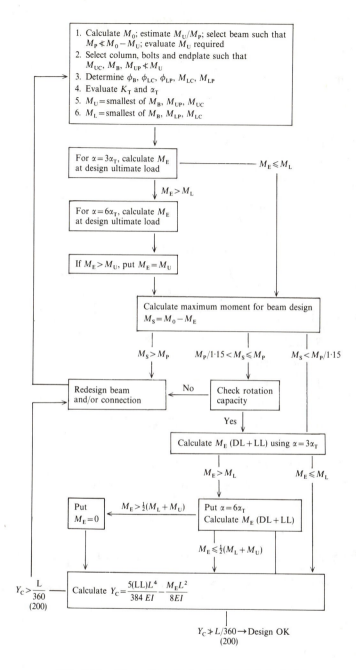

FIG. 7.16. Flow diagram for flush endplate design.

chosen for the following circumstances:

$L = 5$ m
Dead load $= 15$ kN/m
Live load $= 30$ kN/m
Load factors $= 1.4$ (DL); 1.6 (LL)
$P_Y = 275$ N/mm^2

The design ultimate load is

$$1.4 \times 15 + 1.6 \times 30 = 69 \text{ kN/m}$$
$$M_0 = 69 \times 5^2/8 = 215.6 \text{ kN m}$$

Try $M_U/M_P = 0.4$; $0.4M_P + M_P = 215.6$:

$$M_P = 154 = P_Y S$$
$$S = (154 \times 10^3)/275 = 560$$

Try 305×165 UB 40:

$$S = 624.5 \text{ cm}^3$$
$$Z = 561.2 \text{ cm}^3$$
$$I = 8523 \text{ cm}^4$$
$$D = 303.8 \text{ mm}$$
$$EI = 205 \times 8523 \times 10^{-2} = 17472 \text{ kN m}^2$$

Actual $M_P = 275 \times 624.5 \times 10^{-3} = 172$ kN m
Actual M_U required $= 215.6 - 172 = 43.6$ kN m

From Fig. 7.8, with $D = 303.8$ and using M20 8.8 bolts:

$M_B = 79$ kN m   (> 43.9 OK)
$\phi_B = 9.2 \times 10^{-6} \times g$

Assuming the column to be 254×254 UC 73, from Figs 7.10 and 7.12:

$M_{UC} = 130$ kN m   (> 43.6 OK)
$M_{LC} = 78$ kN m
$\phi_{UC} = 16 \times 10^{-3}$
$\phi_{LC} = 3.2 \times 10^{-3}$
$T = 14.2$ mm

From Fig. 7.9, choosing $t_p = 12$ mm:

$M_{UP} = 80$ kN m   ($> 43\cdot6$ OK)

$M_{LP} = 48$ kN m

and from Fig. 7.11:

$\phi_{UP} = 10\cdot5 \times 10^{-3}$

$\phi_{LP} = 2\cdot1 \times 10^{-3}$

Hence

$M_U = M_B = 79$ kN m (lowest of 79, 130 and 80)

and

$M_L = M_{LP} = 48$ kN m (lowest of 79, 78 and 48)

$g = 14\cdot2 + 12 = 26\cdot2$

$\phi_B = 9\cdot2 \times 26\cdot2 \times 10^{-6} = 0\cdot241 \times 10^{-3}$

Now,

$$K_T = 1 \Bigg/ \left(\frac{0\cdot241 \times 10^{-3}}{79} + \frac{2\cdot1 \times 10^{-3}}{48} + \frac{3\cdot2 \times 10^{-3}}{78} \right)$$

$$= 11386 \text{ kN m/rad}$$

Check beam design for $K = K_T/3$

$K = 11386/3 = 3795$

$$\alpha = \frac{2EI}{KL} \quad = \frac{2 \times 17472}{3795 \times 5} = 1\cdot84$$

$$M_E = \frac{M_F}{1+\alpha} \quad = \frac{69 \times 5^2/12}{2\cdot84} = 50\cdot6 \text{ kN m}$$

This is greater than M_L ($= 48$), hence re-calculate M_E using $K = K_T/6$:

$$M_E = 48 + 69 \times 5^2 \frac{(1 - 48/50\cdot6)}{12(1 + 2 \times 1\cdot84)}$$

$$= 49\cdot6$$

$$M_S = 215 \cdot 6 - 49 \cdot 6$$

$$= 166 \, \text{kN m}$$

This is acceptable compared with $M_P = 172 \, \text{kN m}$.

Check beam deflection

Unfactored imposed load $= 30 \, \text{kN/m}$

Corresponding $M_F = 30 \times 5^2/12 = 62 \cdot 5 \, \text{kN m}$

Using $K = K_T/3$, i.e. $\alpha = 1 \cdot 84$

$$M_E = \frac{62 \cdot 5}{2 \cdot 84} = 22 \; (\text{NB} < M_L)$$

$$Y_C = \frac{5}{384} \times \frac{30 \times 5^4 \times 10^3}{17472} - \frac{22 \times 5^2 \times 10^3}{8 \times 17472}$$

$$= 13 \cdot 97 - 3 \cdot 93 = 10 \, \text{mm}$$

$$Y_C/L = \frac{10}{5000} = \frac{1}{500} \left(\text{OK cf.} \; \frac{1}{360} \right)$$

Check rotation capacity

From Fig. 7.15 with $L/D = 5000/303 \cdot 8 = 16 \cdot 5$

$$\frac{M_U}{M_P} = \frac{79}{172} = 0 \cdot 46$$

$$\phi \, \text{reqd} \simeq 11 \times 10^{-3}$$

Since $M_U = M_B$, case (3) applies:

$$\phi_U \simeq 10^{-3} \left[3 \cdot 2 + \frac{79 - 78}{130 - 78} (16 \cdot 0 - 3 \cdot 2) \right] + 10^{-3} \left[2 \cdot 1 + \frac{79 - 48}{80 - 48} (10 \cdot 5 - 2 \cdot 1) \right]$$

$$= 10^{-3} (3 \cdot 2 + 0 + 2 \cdot 1 + 8 \cdot 14)$$

$$> 11 \times 10^{-3} \, \text{OK}$$

Experience has shown that some design situations occur where it is difficult to produce sufficient rotation capacity to allow a plastic hinge to develop within the span. In these circumstances the simplest solution is to increase the beam size and adopt elastic procedures in the beam design.

REFERENCES AND SELECT BIBLIOGRAPHY

BRITISH STANDARDS INSTITUTION (1985) BS 5950: Part 1: Structural Use of Steelwork in Building (2.1.2.4(a)), BSI, London.

HORNE, M. R. & MORRIS, L. J. (1981) Plastic Design of Low Rise Frames. Granada Publishing Limited, London.

HOWLETT, J. H., JENKINS, W. M. & STAINSBY, R. (Eds) (1983) Joints in structural steelwork. International Conference, Teesside Polytechnic, April 1981. Pentech Press, London.

JENKINS, W. M., TONG, C. S. & PRESCOTT, A. T. (1986) Moment-transmitting endplate connections in steel construction, and a proposed basis for flush endplate design, *Structural Engineer*, **64A** (5).

LOCAL FAILURES IN STEELWORK STRUCTURES (1983). BRE Contract F3/2/256. Interim Report No. 1, Building Research Establishment, Watford.

OWEN, D. P. J. & HINTON, E. (1980) *Finite Elements in Plasticity*. Pineridge Press.

PACKER, J. & MORRIS, L. J. (1977) A limit state design method for the tension region of bolted beam-column connections, *Structural Engineer*, **5** (10).

PRESCOTT, A. T. (1987) The Performance of Endplate Connections in Steel Structures and their Influence on Overall Structural Behaviour. PhD thesis, Hatfield Polytechnic.

TONG, C. S. (1985) The Elastic-Plastic Behaviour of Semi-Rigid Connections in Steel Structures. PhD thesis, Hatfield Polytechnic.

Chapter 8

ELASTIC BUCKLING OF SEMI-RIGID SWAY FRAMES

E. Cosenza,[a] A. De Luca[b] & C. Faella[a]

[a]Istituto di Ingegneria Civile, Università di Salerno, Italy
[b]Istituto di Scienza e Tecnica delle Costruzioni, Università della Basilicata, Italy

SUMMARY

The effect of semi-rigid connections on the elastic critical load of semi-rigid sway frames is analysed. Portal frames with fixed base and semi-rigid base are investigated first, and then the multi-storey one-bay frames. Analytical tools for deriving the critical load are provided together with simplified procedures. An approximate method ('linear method') is proposed for evaluating the critical load of the semi-rigid frame on the basis of the two extreme cases of pin-ended and fixed-ended frames. Illustrative examples are presented in order to show how the proposed approximate procedures may be applied.

NOTATION

A	Coefficient to be used in the 'linear method'
b_i	Factor for evaluating base connection effect on stiffness coefficients
c	Number of bays
E	Young's modulus of elasticity
f	Stability function
f'	Stability function modified for base connection effects
F	Lateral force
g	Stability function

h	Column height
h_0	Column effective length
H	Frame height
i	Storey index
I_c	Second moment of area of column
I_g	Second moment of area of girder
I_g^*	Modified second moment of area of girder; eqn (8.5)
K	Non-dimensional stiffness of beam-to-column connection
K_{ij}	Stiffness coefficient
K'	Non-dimensional stiffness of base connection
K_ϕ	Stiffness of beam-to-column connection
K'_ϕ	Stiffness of base connection
K^*	Equivalent spring stiffness; eqn (8.4)
l	Beam length
M	Bending force
n	Number of storeys
N	Reference axial load
N_c	Elastic critical load
N_c^*	Non-dimensional critical load; eqn (8.20)
$\bar{N}_c, \bar{\bar{N}}_c$	Approximate critical loads
$\bar{N}_{c0}, \bar{N}_{c\infty}$	Pin-end and rigid-end approximate critical loads
$T1$	Topological frame parameter; eqn (8.1)
$T1^*$	Modified topological frame parameter; eqn (8.8)
$T1_1^*, T1_c^*, T1_\infty^*$	One bay, c bays and infinite bays $T1^*$ parameters
$T2$	Topological frame parameter; eqn (8.42)
u	Factor depending upon axial load; eqn (8.19)
α_K	Elastic critical multiplier of semi-rigid frame
$\alpha_{K'}$	Elastic critical multiplier of semi-rigid frame with partial-restraint base connection
$\bar{\alpha}_K$	Approximate critical multiplier (flexibility method)
α'_K	Approximate critical multiplier ('linear method')
α_0, α_∞	Pin-end and fixed-end elastic critical multiplier
β	Effective length factor
δ	Sway displacement
δ^*	Non-dimensional sway; eqn (8.9)
ρ	Numerical constant; eqn (8.32)
ϕ	Joint rotation

ϕ^*	Non-dimensional joint rotation; eqn (8.9)
ϕ_i	Reduction factor of stiffness coefficient; eqns (8.17)
ϕ_i'	Reduction factor of stiffness coefficient modified for base connection effects; eqns (8.26)
[ ]	Square matrix
{ }	Vector
$[K]$	Stiffness matrix

8.1 INTRODUCTION

8.1.1 Introductory Remarks

In recent years several authors have studied the so-called semi-rigid connections. Some of these studies have been mainly oriented to investigating the local behaviour of the connection, thus resulting in experimental relations of different types together with approximate models for simulating this experimental behaviour (Frye & Morris, 1975; Ackroyd & Gerstle, 1977, 1982; Jones *et al.*, 1983; Nethercot, 1985). The behaviour of actual base connections has been analysed by, among others, Melchers (1987) and Picard & Beaulieu (1987).

Other studies have instead, been devoted to analysing the effect of connection flexibility on global frame behaviour (Cosenza *et al.*, 1984; Gerstle, 1985). All these experimental and theoretical studies are interconnected. In fact, by making use of the previous experimental studies, to define the specific mechanical properties (stiffness, strength etc.) of each connection type, it should be possible to establish if a given frame, with specified beam-to-column and base connections, can be analysed as pinned, fixed or semi-rigid frame. In this last case the analysis has to take into account the effective restraint conditions. In other words, all the experimental studies on semi-rigid connections provide, in a realistic manner, the bounds of elastic and inelastic properties of actual joints to be used in global frame analysis. Studies on the behaviour of semi-rigid frames enable the use of the previous studies to define how the frame behaviour is affected by the actual connections. With reference to this type of analysis it should be remembered that the constitutive relation of the connection is generally non-linear and both global elastic and inelastic behaviour of the structure would be affected.

In this chapter attention will be focussed on the elastic behaviour of semi-rigid sway frames and therefore only the elastic stiffness of the

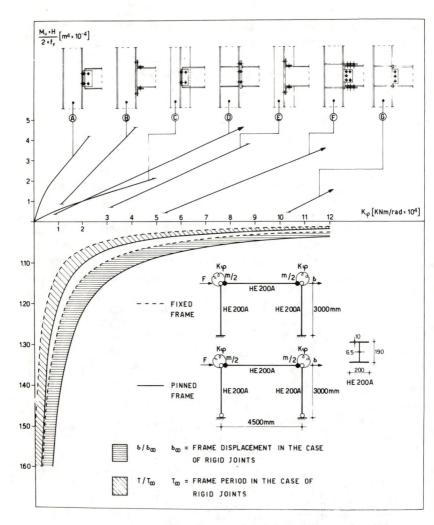

FIG. 8.1. Semi-rigid joint effect on global drift and natural period.

connections is of major concern. Inelastic frame behaviour, with particular reference to the inelastic buckling load, will be considered in the next chapter.

An example of how the elastic behaviour of the frame is affected by the connection topology is given in Fig. 8.1 in which the available experimental results reported by Ackroyd & Gerstle (1977) are provided in the upper part of the figure following the same representation used by them.

In the lower part of the figure it is shown how the global drift (sub-vertical dashed lines) and the natural period (horizontal dashed lines) of a portal frame are affected by connection flexibility. The use of this figure therefore allows one, for a given connection topology, to establish, from the upper part of the figure, the actual bounds of connection stiffness and, from the lower part of the figure, how the connection used affects the frame response.

The portal frame has been considered fixed (continuous line) and pinned (dashed line) at the base in order to define the complete range of behaviour. The response is non-dimensionalized with respect to the case of infinitely rigid connection. It may be pointed out that T-stub and fully welded connections practically approximate rigid restraint conditions. On the other hand, even web cleat connections do provide a certain degree of restraint.

8.1.2 Scope of This Chapter

As previously stated, the elastic behaviour of semi-rigid sway frames will be analysed in this chapter, with a view to providing analytical tools for deriving the critical load of semi-rigid sway frames; simplified procedures are presented which enable a designer to adopt reliable design procedures in the form of charts for immediate use. Studies on elastic stability of semi-rigid frames have been carried out previously by Ackroyd & Gerstle (1983), Simitses & Vlahinos (1985) and Cosenza *et al.* (1986a,b, 1987).

The evaluation of the critical load is of extreme importance since it provides a measure of the sensitivity of the structure to the second-order effects and therefore affects the global collapse load.

Section 8.2 will be devoted to the analysis of portal frames with fixed and semi-rigid base connections, while in Sections 8.3 multi-storey frames are analysed. Some illustrative examples are then provided in Section 8.4 in order to indicate the applicability of the approximate procedures proposed for evaluating the critical load of semi-rigid sway frames.

8.2 ANALYSIS OF PORTAL FRAMES

8.2.1 Definition of Main Parameters

Let us consider the portal frame in Fig. 8.2(a), in which the girders and columns are respectively characterized by flexural rigidities EI_g and EI_c and

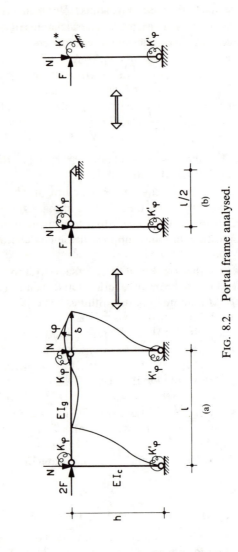

FIG. 8.2. Portal frame analysed.

lengths l and h. The axial and shear flexibility will be neglected in the analysis. In general, the beam will be connected to the columns by means of a semi-rigid connection characterized by the elastic constant K_ϕ, while the column will be connected to the base by a connection which has rigidity K'_ϕ. In order to approach the problem in a more general manner, it is convenient to introduce the following non-dimensional parameters:

$$T1 = \frac{EI_g/l}{EI_c/h} \tag{8.1}$$

$$K = \frac{K_\phi l}{EI_g}; \quad K' = \frac{K'_\phi h}{EI_c} \tag{8.2}$$

The first parameter characterizes the rigid portal frame while the other two parameters define the semi-rigid connections.

In the case of lateral forces acting on the structure, or where the elastic critical multiplier is to be evaluated, the structure in Fig. 8.2(a) is equivalent to the one in Fig. 8.2(b). Moreover, Fig. 8.2(b) is equivalent to the cantilever shown in Fig. 8.2(c), with rotational support at the end characterized by stiffness K^*.

In order to evaluate this rigidity it is necessary to apply a bending moment M at the end of the beam of length $l/2$ and then to compute the rotation ϕ (the ratio M/ϕ represents the stiffness K^*):

$$\phi = \frac{Ml/2}{3EI_g} + \frac{M}{K_\phi} = \frac{Ml}{6EI_g}\left(1 + 6\frac{EI_g}{K_\phi l}\right) \tag{8.3}$$

Hence, by making use of eqn (8.2), we obtain,

$$K^* = \frac{M}{\phi} = \frac{6EI_g}{l}\frac{K}{K+6} = \frac{6EI_g^*}{l} \tag{8.4}$$

in which

$$I_g^* = I_g\frac{K}{K+6} \tag{8.5}$$

The effect of the semi-rigid beam-to-column connection on the portal frame can therefore be expressed in terms of the fictitious value I_g^*.

If we indicate ϕ and δ respectively as the end rotation and displacement of the cantilever in Fig. 8.2(c), the flexural problem of the portal frame with a lateral force $2F$ can be written in matrix form:

$$\begin{bmatrix} K_{11} & K_{12} \\ K_{21} & K_{22} \end{bmatrix} \begin{Bmatrix} \phi \\ \delta \end{Bmatrix} = \begin{Bmatrix} 0 \\ F \end{Bmatrix} \tag{8.6}$$

where, assuming at first that $K'_\phi = \infty$, the terms of the stiffness matrix are given by

$$K_{11} = \frac{4EI_c}{h} + K^* \tag{8.7a}$$

$$K_{12} = K_{21} = \frac{6EI_c}{h^2} \tag{8.7b}$$

$$K_{22} = \frac{12EI_c}{h^3} \tag{8.7c}$$

It is convenient to set

$$T1^* = \frac{EI_g^*/l}{EI_c/h} = T1 \frac{K}{K+6} \tag{8.8}$$

$$\phi^* = \phi \frac{EI_c}{Fh^2}; \quad \delta^* = \delta \frac{EI_c}{Fh^3} \tag{8.9}$$

the first relation being the beam/column stiffness ratio modified in order to take into account the semi-rigid connection. The other two relations represent a convenient non-dimensionalization of displacement and rotation. We can therefore rearrange eqn (8.6) as follows:

$$\begin{bmatrix} 4 + 6T1^* & 6 \\ 6 & 12 \end{bmatrix} \begin{Bmatrix} \phi^* \\ \delta^* \end{Bmatrix} = \begin{Bmatrix} 0 \\ 1 \end{Bmatrix} \tag{8.10}$$

From the above we obtain the following generalization:

1. The behaviour of the portal frame with semi-rigid beam-to-column connection subjected to lateral force, having non-dimensional displacements ϕ^* and δ^*, is completely defined by the non-dimensional parameter $T1^*$.

In fact, if we write eqn (8.10) in an explicit form, we get

$$\phi^* = -\frac{6}{4 + 6T1^*} \delta^* \tag{8.11}$$

$$\delta^* = \frac{\delta}{F} \frac{EI_c}{h^3} = \frac{1}{12} \frac{4 + 6T1^*}{1 + 6T1^*} \tag{8.12}$$

If we now consider the effect of the base connection characterized by stiffness K'_ϕ, it will be seen that the stiffness matrix of the structure is affected by the following coefficients:

$$b_1 = \frac{3 + K'}{4 + K'} \tag{8.13a}$$

$$b_2 = \frac{2 + K'}{4 + K'} \tag{8.13b}$$

$$b_3 = \frac{1 + K'}{4 + K'} \tag{8.13c}$$

Hence

$$K_{11} = \frac{4EI_c}{h} b_1 + K^* \tag{8.14a}$$

$$K_{12} = K_{21} = \frac{6EI_c}{h^2} b_2 \tag{8.14b}$$

$$K_{22} = \frac{12EI_c}{h^3} b_3 \tag{8.14c}$$

It can easily be seen that the coefficients b_1, b_2 and b_3 tend to $1 \cdot 0$ when K' tends to infinity, thus reobtaining eqn (8.7) for a fixed base. When K' tends to 0, these coefficients respectively tend to $\frac{3}{4}, \frac{1}{2}$ and $\frac{1}{4}$, representing the case of a hinged frame. Statement 1 can therefore be generalized as follows:

2. The behaviour of the portal frame with semi-rigid beam-to-column and base connection, having non-dimensional displacements ϕ^* and δ^*, is defined by the stiffness parameters $T1^*$ and K'.

As in the case of a portal frame with a fixed base, the value of δ^* is given by

$$\delta^* = \frac{F}{\delta} \frac{h^3}{EI_c} = \frac{1}{12} \frac{4b_1 + 6T1^*}{4b_1 b_3 - 3b_2 + 6b_3 T1^*} = \frac{1}{12} \frac{4(3 + K') + 6(4 + K')T1^*}{K' + 6(1 + K')T1^*} \tag{8.15}$$

Obviously, for $b_1 = b_2 = b_3 = 1$ (or K' tending to infinity), we get relation (8.10).

8.2.2 Elastic Critical Load of Fixed Portal Frame

The elastic critical load, N_c, is the value of the axial load which is obtained by equating to zero the determinant of the stiffness matrix wherein the coefficients have to be modified in order to take into account axial load effects. If we then introduce Livesley & Chandler's (1956) functions ϕ_1, ϕ_2 and ϕ_3, the stiffness matrix of the portal frame will be

$$[K] = \begin{bmatrix} \dfrac{4EI_c}{h}\phi_1 + K^* & \dfrac{6EI_c}{h^2}\phi_2 \\[3mm] \dfrac{6EI_c}{h^2}\phi_2 & \dfrac{12EI_c}{h^3}\phi_3 \end{bmatrix} \tag{8.16}$$

In eqn (8.16), the coefficients, ϕ_1, ϕ_2 and ϕ_3 (less than 1 in the case of compressed bars because of the increased deformability due to geometric nonlinear effects) are given by

$$\phi_1 = 3f/(4f^2 - g^2) \tag{8.17a}$$

$$\phi_2 = 3g/(4f^2 - g^2) \tag{8.17b}$$

$$\phi_3 = (2f+g)/(4f^2 - g^2) - u^2/12 \tag{8.17c}$$

where

$$f = \frac{3}{u}\left(\frac{1}{u} - \frac{1}{tgu}\right) \tag{8.18a}$$

$$g = \frac{6}{u}\left(\frac{1}{\sin u} - \frac{1}{u}\right) \tag{8.18b}$$

When the axial load becomes N_c, the coefficient u is given by

$$u = \sqrt{\frac{N_c h^2}{EI_c}} = \pi\sqrt{N_c^*} \tag{8.19}$$

where

$$N_c^* = \frac{N_c h^2}{\pi^2 EI_c} \tag{8.20}$$

The coefficients ϕ_1, ϕ_2 and ϕ_3 are therefore dependent solely on the parameter N_c^*.

By equating to zero the determinant of the stiffness matrix

$$\det[K] = 0 \tag{8.21}$$

and simplifying, we get

$$\det \begin{bmatrix} 4\phi_1 + 6T1^* & 6\phi_2 \\ 6\phi_2 & 12\phi_3 \end{bmatrix} = 0 \qquad (8.22)$$

The transcendental equation in N_c^* is therefore

$$\phi_3(4\phi_1 + 6T1^*) - 3\phi_2^2 = F(N_c^*, T1^*) = 0 \qquad (8.23)$$

By solving this equation iteratively we get the value of N_c^* in terms of the parameter $T1^*$. Hence we reach the following conclusion:

3. The critical load expressed in a non-dimensional form (N_c^*) is completely defined by the non-dimensional parameter $T1^*$.

We can therefore say that, if the axial and shear deformability are neglected, two different symmetric portal frames, with the same $(EI_g^*/l)/(EI_c/h)$ ratio, are characterized by the same non-dimensional critical load $N_c h^2/\pi^2 EI_c$. If we express the effective length as $\beta h = h_0$ of the portal frame, we get

$$\beta = \sqrt{\frac{\pi^2 EI_c}{N_c h^2}} = \frac{1}{\sqrt{N_c^*}} \qquad (8.24)$$

hence the two portal frames with the same $T1^*$ are characterized by the same β value.

The effect of the semi-rigid connection can be studied by examining the variation of $N_c h^2/\pi^2 EI_c$ with K plotted in Fig. 8.3. The different curves are representative of some significant $T1$ values. The K parameter is plotted on a logarithmic scale in order to extend the study to low connection stiffness values. The non-dimensional critical load varies between 0.25 $(\beta = 2)$ in the case of connections with negligible stiffness $(K = 0)$ and 1.0 $(\beta = 1.0)$ in the case of an infinitely stiff beam $(K$ and $T1$ tending to $\infty)$. It is clear that, when the beam stiffness is negligible, the connection stiffness does not provide any effect since the structure is equivalent to a cantilever.

In order to evaluate the effect of connection stiffness on structural behaviour, it is interesting to evaluate the amount of decrease of the critical multiplier of the semi-rigid structure α_K with respect to the critical multiplier of the rigid structure α_∞. This effect is plotted in Fig. 8.4 for the range of parameters previously analysed. It has been shown by Cosenza et al. (1986a, b) that 80% of the α_∞ value is reached for K values greater than 10, while for small K values α_K is not negligible in comparison with α_∞.

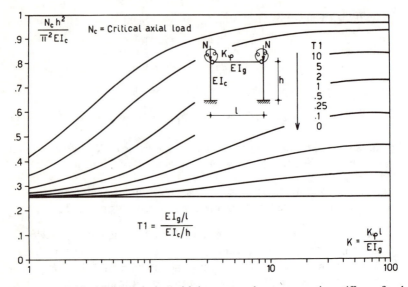

FIG. 8.3.   Critical load variation with beam-to-column connection stiffness; fixed base frame.

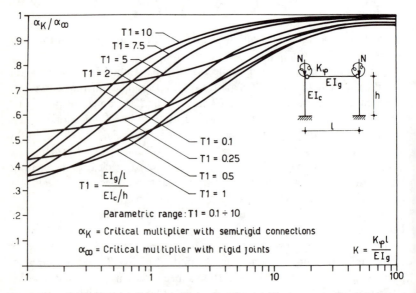

FIG. 8.4.   Critical multiplier non-dimensionalized with respect to fixed-end case; fixed base frame.

8.2.3 Elastic Critical Load of Portal Frame with Semi-Rigid Base Connection

The semi-rigid base connection further decreases column stiffness. Let us consider the column of height h with both ends simply supported and with a semi-rigid base connection K'_ϕ, subjected to axial load N. When a unit bending moment is applied to the end, the end rotation results:

$$\frac{h}{3EI_c}f(N_c^*)+\frac{1}{K'_\phi}=\frac{h}{3EI_c}\left[f(N_c^*)+\frac{3}{K'}\right]=\frac{h}{3EI_c}f'(N_c^*, K') \qquad (8.25)$$

where the function f is given by eqn (8.18a), and the non-dimensional coefficients N_c^* and K' are provided by eqns (8.20) and (8.1). The coefficients ϕ_1, ϕ_2 and ϕ_3 will therefore be substituted by the following coefficients, ϕ'_1, ϕ'_2 and ϕ'_3 in affecting the stiffness matrix of eqn (8.16):

$$\phi'_1 = 3f'/(4ff'-g^2) \qquad (8.26a)$$

$$\phi'_2 = 3g/(4ff'-g^2) \qquad (8.26b)$$

$$\phi'_3 = (f+f'+g)/(4ff'-g^2) \qquad (8.26c)$$

where the functions f and g are still given by eqns (8.18a) and (8.18b), while eqn (8.25) provides the following expression for f':

$$f' = f+\frac{3}{K'} \qquad (8.27)$$

It should be noted that, for K' tending to infinity (i.e. a fixed portal frame), the coefficient f' tends to f and therefore we obtain eqns (8.17a), (8.17b) and (8.17c). When axial loads are not present (i.e. u tending to 0), the functions f', f and g respectively tend to the following values:

$$f'\to 1+\frac{3}{K'}; \qquad f\to 1; \qquad g\to 1 \qquad (8.28)$$

If we introduce these values into eqns (8.26a), (8.26b) and (8.26c) we obtain the coefficients b_1, b_2 and b_3 given by eqns (8.13a), (8.13b) and (8.13c).

In analogy with eqn (8.22), the non-dimensional critical load is therefore given by

$$\det \begin{bmatrix} 4\phi'_1 +6T1^* & 6\phi'_2 \\ 6\phi'_2 & 12\phi'_3 \end{bmatrix} =0 \qquad (8.29)$$

This leads to the following relation to be solved iteratively:

$$\phi'_3(4\phi'_1 +6T1^*)-3\phi'^2_2 = F'(N_c^*, T1^*, K') \qquad (8.30)$$

The following result is then obtained:

4. The non-dimensional critical load of the semi-rigid portal frame with semi-rigid base connection is defined by the beam–column stiffness parameter $T1^*$ and by the base stiffness parameter K'.

In Fig. 8.5 the effect of K' on the non-dimensional critical load is shown. The different curves are representative of different $T1^*$ values. It will be recalled that this parameter takes into account the beam flexibility and the beam-to-column connection, as was seen in eqn (8.8).

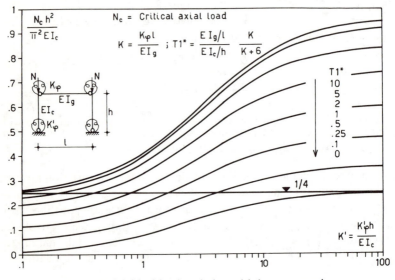

FIG. 8.5.   Critical load variation with base connection.

For a given portal frame, the critical load N_c can be obtained by using Fig. 8.5 and taking the effective length βh from eqn (8.24). The lowest curve of Fig. 8.5 refers to the pin-end scheme and N_c^* lies between 0 ($\beta = \infty$) for $K' = 0$ and $\frac{1}{4}$ ($\beta = 2$) for $K' \to \infty$. The upper curve refers to the case of an infinitely stiff beam and N_c^* lies between $\frac{1}{4}$ ($\beta = 2$) in the case of a hinged base and 1 ($\beta = 1$) in the case of a fixed base.

Figure 8.6 provides a synthetic representation of the structural behaviour of the semi-rigid base portal frame. In this figure K' is plotted against the ratio $\alpha_{K'}/\alpha_\infty$; $\alpha_{K'}$ represents the critical multiplier in the case of a semi-rigid base connection, and α_∞ represents the critical multiplier in the case of

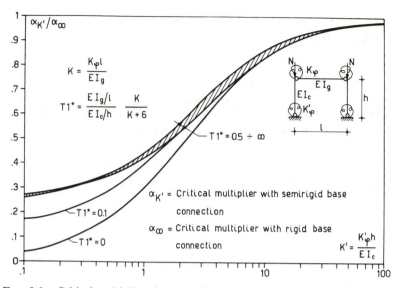

FIG. 8.6.   Critical multiplier of semi-rigid base frame non-dimensionalized with respect to fixed base frame.

a fixed base. The different curves provide the bounds of variation for $T1^*$ within a significant range. Excluding the cases characterized by very small $T1^*$ values (corresponding to the case having a hinge at the top), the range of the results is very restricted. It is therefore possible immediately to obtain the critical multiplier α'_K from the value of α_∞ as a function of the parameter K', regardless of the $T1^*$ value. If we adopt the approximate relation

$$\alpha_{K'} = \frac{K'+0\cdot7}{K'+3}\alpha_\infty \qquad (8.31)$$

we get an error in the estimate which is always within 6% on the conservative side for the whole parametric range analysed and for $T1^* > 0\cdot5$.

It may be pointed out that, for K' values higher than 10, 80% of the maximum critical load is obtained.

8.2.4 Approximate Evaluation of Elastic Critical Load by Means of Flexibility Check

It is well known that an indirect manner for estimating the critical load is represented by the evaluation of lateral drift. With reference to the portal frame shown in Fig. 8.2 analysed previously, an approximate evaluation of the critical load is given by

$$\bar{N}_c = \rho \frac{F}{\delta} h \qquad (8.32)$$

where ρ is an appropriate numerical coefficient. Stevens (1967) and Horne (1975) obtained eqn (8.32) by means of energy principles. The numerical coefficient ρ adopted by Stevens (1967) and Horne (1975) was set equal to 0·9. The method is also discussed by Anderson (1980) and Roberts (1985).

It is interesting to observe that, by using a numerical coefficient ρ equal to $\pi^2/12$, eqn (8.32) provides the exact value in the limiting cases of $T1^* = 0$ and $T1^* = \infty$:

$$T1^* = 0: \quad \frac{F}{\delta} = \frac{3EI_c}{h^3}; \quad N_c = \frac{\pi^2 EI_c}{4h^2} \qquad (8.33a)$$

$$T1^* = \infty: \quad \frac{F}{\delta} = \frac{12EI_c}{h^3}; \quad N_c = \frac{\pi^2 EI_c}{h^2} \qquad (8.33b)$$

For intermediate values of $T1^*$ an approximate value of N_c is obtained. This value is always on the conservative side and provides a maximum error equal to 6·5%. By adopting instead a numerical value of ρ equal to 0·9, the estimate is not always on the conservative side but is within 10%. The comparison of the two cases with the exact values is provided in Table 8.1 for different $T1^*$ values.

On the basis of the results given in Section 8.2.1 we can obtain the value of the approximate critical load. From eqns (8.32), (8.9) and (8.12) we get

$$\bar{N}_c = \rho \frac{F}{\delta} h = \rho \frac{EI_c}{h^2} \frac{1}{\delta^*} = 12\rho \frac{EI_c}{h^2} \frac{1 + 6T1^*}{4 + 6T1^*} \qquad (8.34)$$

More generally, if we consider the case of a semi-rigid base connection by making use of eqns (8.32), (8.9) and (8.15), we get

$$\bar{N}_c = \rho \frac{EI_c}{h^2} \frac{1}{\delta} = 12\rho \frac{EI_c}{h^2} \frac{K' + 6(1 + K')T1^*}{4(3 + K') + 6(4 + K')T1^*} \qquad (8.35)$$

In this case, by adopting $\rho = \pi^2/12$, eqn (8.35) provides a conservative estimate in the whole parametric range analysed ($T1^* = 0$ to ∞; $K' = 0·1$ to 100) with a maximum error of 18%.

TABLE 8.1

COMPARISON BETWEEN 'EXACT' AND APPROXIMATE VALUES OF CRITICAL LOAD COMPUTED BY MEANS OF FLEXIBILITY METHODS FOR THE PORTAL FRAME; N_c (approx.)/N_c ('exact')

$T1^*$	$\dfrac{N_c h^2}{\pi^2 EI_c}$	$\dfrac{\bar{N}_c}{N_c}$	$\dfrac{\bar{\bar{N}}_c}{N_c}$
0	0·250	1·000	1·094
0·1	0·358	0·972	1·063
0·25	0·479	0·949	1·038
0·5	0·611	0·935	1·023
0·75	0·693	0·934	1·022
1	0·748	0·936	1·025
2·5	0·855	0·957	1·047
5	0·937	0·973	1·065
7·5	0·957	0·981	1·073
10	0·968	0·985	1·078
∞	1·000	1·000	1·094

N_c = 'exact' critical load
$\bar{N}_c$ = approximate critical load, $\rho = \pi^2/12$
$\bar{\bar{N}}_c$ = approximate critical load, $\rho = 0·9$
$$T1^* = \frac{EI_g/l}{EI_c/h}\frac{K}{K+6}; \quad K = \frac{K_\phi l}{EI_g}$$

8.2.5 Approximate Evaluation of Elastic Critical Load by the 'Linear Method'

A more specific method for evaluating the critical load in the case of semi-rigid sway frames was introduced recently by Cosenza *et al.* (1986a, b). With reference to the fixed portal frame, if we indicate with $\bar{N}_c$, $\bar{N}_{c0}$ and $\bar{N}_{c\infty}$ the approximate values of the critical load in the cases of semi-rigid, pin-end and fixed joints respectively, eqn (8.34) provides

$$\frac{\bar{N}_c h^2}{EI_c} = 12\rho \frac{1 + 6T1^*}{4 + 6T1^*} \tag{8.36a}$$

$$\frac{\bar{N}_{c0} h^2}{EI_c} = 12\rho \frac{1}{4} \tag{8.36b}$$

$$\frac{\bar{N}_{c\infty} h^2}{EI_c} = 12\rho \frac{1 + 6T1}{4 + 6T1} \tag{8.36c}$$

If we then indicate with α_K, α_0 and α_∞ the critical multipliers, it can easily be shown that

$$\frac{\alpha_K - \alpha_0}{\alpha_\infty - \alpha_K} = AK \qquad (8.37)$$

where

$$A = \frac{2 + 3T1}{12} \qquad (8.38)$$

It is therefore clear that, by making use of the flexibility method, which leads to eqns (8.36), the approximate 'linear method' represented by eqns (8.37) and (8.38) can be derived. The $(\alpha_K - \alpha_0)/(\alpha_\infty - \alpha_K)$ ratio is homogeneous in K through the angular coefficient A which is linearly dependent upon $T1$. Figure 8.7 confirms that it is possible to express the ratio $(\alpha_K - \alpha_0)/(\alpha_\infty - \alpha_K)$ as a homogeneous function of K. In this figure are represented the 'exact' values of the critical multiplier for the portal frame. The curves are practically linear, all passing through the origin. In order to confirm these results for small K values, the same ratio is plotted in Fig. 8.8 on

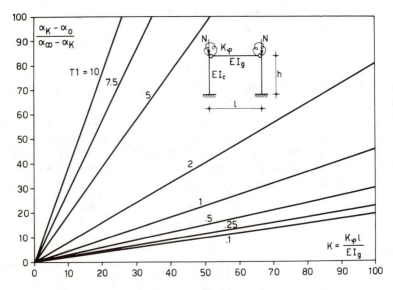

FIG. 8.7. Curves representing the critical multiplier α_K through the $(\alpha_K - \alpha_0)/(\alpha_\infty - \alpha_K)$ ratio.

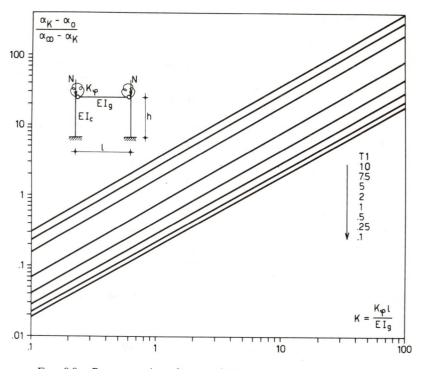

FIG. 8.8.   Representation of curve of Fig. 8.7 on bilogarithmic scale.

a bilogarithmic scale. Equation (8.37) yields

$$\log\left(\frac{\alpha_K - \alpha_0}{\alpha_\infty - \alpha_K}\right) = \log A + \log K \qquad (8.39)$$

and the curves in Fig. 8.8 are all approximately parallel in the whole parametric range analysed. Equation (8.37) therefore provides a solution for α_K:

$$\alpha_K = \frac{AK\alpha_\infty + \alpha_0}{AK + 1} \qquad (8.40)$$

Once the value of A is known, together with the critical multipliers of the limit cases (α_0, α_∞), the critical multiplier of the semi-rigid portal frame is immediately defined as a function of K. This is of particular interest since the evaluation of the connection stiffness is always provided within a given range.

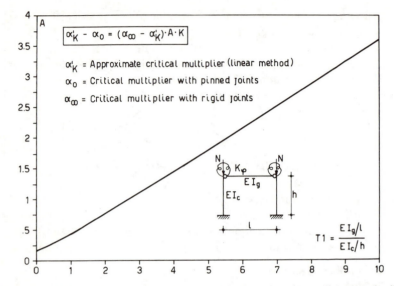

FIG. 8.9.   Value of the constant A to be used in the approximate 'linear method'.

In order to improve the approximation of eqn (8.40), the constant A is evaluated by means of the parametric analysis of the portal frame instead of by using eqn (8.38). For this purpose, Fig. 8.9 provides the value of the constant A, obtained by eqn (8.37) as an average within the range of K values for different $T1$ values. Hence, for any portal frame with semi-rigid beam-to-column connection, characterized by the stiffness ratio $T1$,

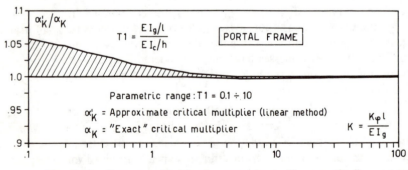

FIG. 8.10.   Error provided by the approximate 'linear method'.

Fig. 8.9 can be employed to obtain the A value. By using eqn (8.40), the α_K value is computed for a given K.

The estimate of error due to this approximate evaluation is plotted in Fig. 8.10, for the entire parametric range chosen for $T1$. The approximate critical multiplier α'_K evaluated by the 'linear method' and the 'exact' critical multiplier α_K are compared and it is shown that the error is always less than 6%.

8.3 ANALYSIS OF MULTI-STOREY FRAMES

8.3.1 Governing Parameters

A complete parametric analysis of the elastic critical load of multi-storey frames requires the introduction of several other parameters besides those for portals. A given frame is characterized by the following parameters:

(a) Number of storeys, n
(b) Number of bays, c
(c) Variation of stiffness of columns along the height
(d) Variation of stiffness of girders along the height
(e) Beam-to-column stiffness ratio
(f) Stiffness of semi-rigid connection

In the parametric analysis carried out by Cosenza *et al.* (1987), the number of storeys n has been varied between 1 and 10 for single-bay frames. The effects of girder and connection stiffness are included in the $T1^*$ value, analogous to the case of portals:

$$T1^* = \frac{EI_g^*/l}{EI_c/h} = T1 \frac{K}{K+6} \qquad (8.41)$$

The stiffnesses have to be considered as reference values since they can vary from one storey to another. In particular, conforming to common design procedure, beam stiffnesses have been considered constant at all storeys, while for the columns the following variation with the storey index i has been assumed:

$$\left(\frac{EI_c}{h}\right)_i = [1+(n-i)T2]\frac{EI_c}{h} \qquad (8.42)$$

EI_c/h in the second term of eqn (8.42) represents top-storey column stiffness.

Linear variations, characterized by the parameter $T2$, have therefore

274   E. COSENZA, A. DE LUCA & C. FAELLA

been considered. The case $T2=0$ corresponds to columns which do not vary with height, while $T2=1\cdot0$ corresponds to

$$\left(\frac{EI_c}{h}\right)_i = (n+1-i)\frac{EI_c}{h} \tag{8.43}$$

This means that bottom-storey column stiffness is equal to n times the stiffness of the top storey.

By generalizing what has been shown in the second section, it can be said that the antisymmetric deformed shapes and those connected to the critical load depend upon the number of storeys, n, and upon the parameters $T2$ and $T1^*$. It is convenient to separate this last parameter into $T1$ and K. The generic scheme analysed is provided in Fig. 8.11 where K_c and K_g represent

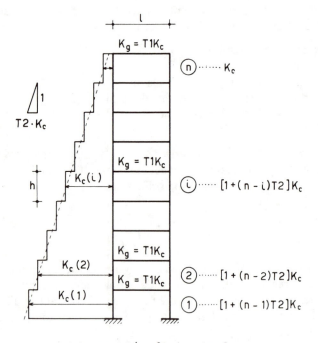

$$K_c(i) = EI_c(i)/h = [1+(n-i)T2]K_c$$

$$K_g(i) = EI_g(i)/l = T1\,K_c$$

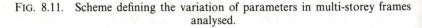

FIG. 8.11. Scheme defining the variation of parameters in multi-storey frames analysed.

column and girder stiffness. The parametric range analysed is the following:

$$n = 1 \text{ to } 10$$
$$T1 = 0 \cdot 1 \text{ to } 10$$
$$T2 = 0, \, 0 \cdot 5, \, 1 \tag{8.44}$$
$$K = 0 \cdot 1 \text{ to } 100$$

Even though the analysis has been restricted to the case of $c = 1$, it is obvious that the generic case with c bays is characterized by a $T1_c^*$ value which lies between those corresponding to the cases $c = 1$ and $c = \infty$:

$$T1_1^* \leqslant T1_c^* \leqslant T1_\infty^* \tag{8.45}$$

From Fig. 8.12 it is obvious that the upper bound of $T1_c^*$ can be determined by means of the present analysis by simply doubling the $T1_1^*$ value:

$$T1_\infty^* = 2T1_1^* \tag{8.46}$$

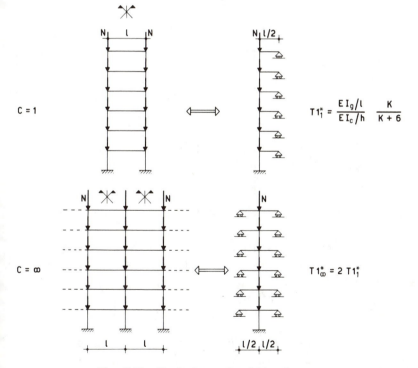

FIG. 8.12.   Equivalence of multi-bay frames.

8.3.2 Elastic Critical Load in Multi-Storey Frames

Hereafter the effects of the semi-rigid beam-to-column connection on the critical load will be examined. Vertical loads are assumed constant in each joint and their critical value is found. The analysis is performed by iteratively writing the stiffness matrix of the entire structure, obtained by the assemblage of the column matrices of the type presented in Section 8.2. Each matrix is affected by Livesley & Chandler (1956) coefficients which take into account the axial load effects. The critical load is represented by the smallest value which equates the determinant of the global stiffness matrix to zero.

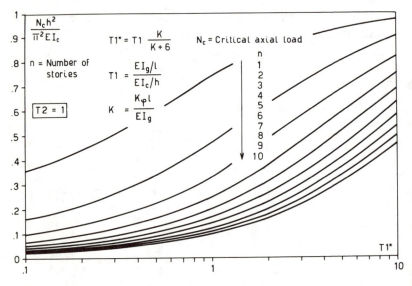

FIG. 8.13.   Critical multiplier of semi-rigid multi-storey frames; $T2 = 1$.

The values of the non-dimensional critical load N_c are given in Figs 8.13, 8.14 and 8.15 respectively for the cases characterized by $T2$ equal to 1, 0·5 and 0, for $T1^*$ varying from 1·0 to 10. These figures allow the evaluation of N_c for each value of the parameters examined which completely define the problem. The effective length can also be obtained analogously to what has been done for the portal frame. The non-dimensional critical load varies between 0 and 1, the smallest values being relative to the case of low stiffness of the beam and of the connection. It should also be noted that the critical load decreases with the number of storeys. Small values of $T1^*$ correspond

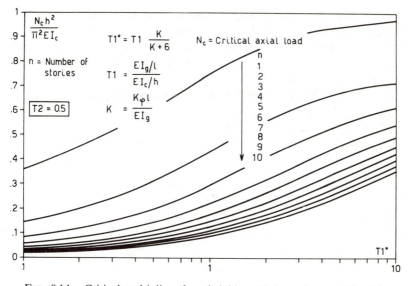

FIG. 8.14.   Critical multiplier of semi-rigid multi-storey frames; $T2 = 0.5$.

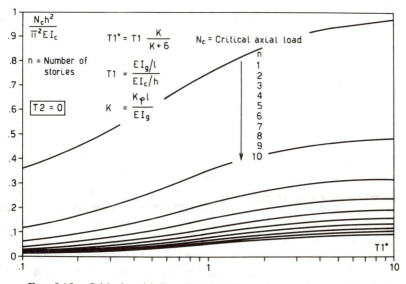

FIG. 8.15.   Critical multiplier of semi-rigid multi-storey frames; $T2 = 0$.

to a structure with pin-end beams, while for higher values of $T1^*$ a framed structure with infinitely rigid beams is indicated. Particularly, for $T2 = 1$, all the curves tend to the same asymptotic curve with increasing $T1^*$ since, with rigid beams and with variation of columns provided by eqn (8.43), each storey is characterized by the same ratio between axial load and stiffness EI_c/h; hence the global critical load coincides with that of the ith storey regardless of the number of storeys.

The effect of semi-rigid connection on the global critical load can be evaluated by examining Fig. 8.16. In this figure, the ratio α_K/α_∞ is plotted

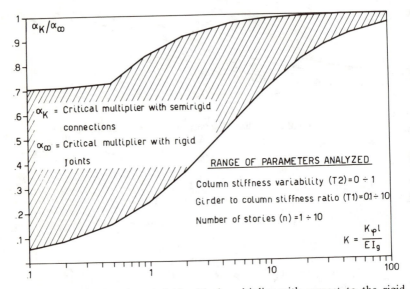

FIG. 8.16. Decrease of semi-rigid critical multiplier with respect to the rigid joint case in the entire parametric range analysed.

for the entire parametric range analysed. It will be noted that, for $K > 10$, 70% of α_∞ is reached. On the other hand, in the case of small K values, an appropriate analysis of the actual unstable behaviour can lead to considerable increase of the critical multiplier with respect to the case of hinged beams. The behaviour of the α_K/α_∞ ratio for a generic case ($T1 = 5$, $T2 = 1$) is given in Fig. 8.17 for n values between 1 and 10 and for varying K. It should be noted that the semi-rigid action is more effective with increasing number of storeys and that all the curves tend to the same value for increasing n. By comparing this figure with the one referred to the portal frame (Fig. 8.4), it

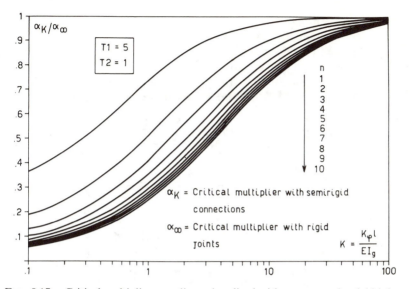

FIG. 8.17.   Critical multiplier non-dimensionalized with respect to the rigid joint
case; $T1 = 5$ and $T2 = 1$.

can be observed that

(a) the upper limit of the α_K/α_∞ values is provided by the portal frame curves, and

(b) the lower limit is represented by the cases with a large number of storeys.

These observations are independent of the law of variation of column stiffnesses, which means that the three ranges obtained for different $T2$ values are practically equal.

8.3.3 Approximate Evaluation of Elastic Critical Load by Means of Flexibility Check

It has been shown how the semi-rigid beam-to-column action can be treated by means of a decrease of the beam stiffness. The approximate methods for evaluating the critical multiplier provided by Stevens (1967) and Horne (1975), which suggest that an elastic analysis be performed, can still be adopted. For this purpose, the flexibility can be evaluated by considering the framed structure subjected to lateral forces proportional to the vertical load acting on the structure. In particular, if the vertical load is constant at each level, the lateral force will also be constant at each level.

TABLE 8.2

COMPARISON BETWEEN GLOBAL DISPLACEMENT AND HORNE METHOD FOR COMPUTING CRITICAL LOAD IN MULTI-STOREY FRAMES: N_c(approx.)/N_c('exact')

n	Method	$T2=0$			$T2=0.5$			$T2=1$		
		$T1*=0.1$	1	10	$T1*=0.1$	1	10	$T1*=0.1$	1	10
1	GD	0·972	0·936	0·985	0·972	0·936	0·985	0·972	0·936	0·985
	H	1·063	1·025	1·078	1·063	1·025	1·078	1·063	1·025	1·078
2	GD	0·886	0·948	1·238	0·896	0·895	1·053	0·908	0·889	0·954
	H	0·792	0·972	1·055	0·770	0·933	1·042	0·759	0·866	1·022
5	GD	0·928	1·124	1·490	0·898	1·007	1·074	0·893	0·972	0·979
	H	0·798	0·835	1·044	0·771	0·798	0·941	0·766	0·808	0·898
10	GD	1·074	1·283	1·612	0·956	1·112	1·111	0·926	1·073	1·060
	H	0·779	0·835	1·047	0·764	0·796	0·891	0·763	0·794	0·860

GD = Global displacement method; H = Horne method; n = number of storeys; N_c = critical load.

If δ represents the sway displacement at the top storey of the framed structure, and Δ_{max} represents the highest relative displacement, two different approximate evaluations of the critical load will be

$$\bar{\bar{N}}_c = \rho \frac{F}{\Delta_{max}} h \quad \text{(Horne's method)} \quad (8.47)$$

$$\bar{N}_c = \rho \frac{F}{\delta} H \quad \text{(Global displacement method)} \quad (8.48)$$

where h represents the storey height, H the global height and ρ a numerical coefficient introduced in Section 8.2.4. The first evaluation therefore refers to the flexibility index Δ_{max}/h, while the second one considers an average value δ/H. The first approximate value is therefore more conservative than the second one, and generally provides smaller values of the critical load. The comparison between the two evaluations is given in Table 8.2 which gives the ratio between the approximate and the exact critical load. In eqn (8.47) $\rho = 0.9$ has been used while in eqn (8.48) ρ has been set equal to $\pi^2/12$. The comparison has been carried out for four different numbers of storeys n: 1, 2, 5 and 10, $T1^*$ has been set equal to 0.1, 1 and 10, while the $T2$ values have been analysed for 0, 0.5 and 1. The $T2$ parameter plays a major role; in fact, for $T2$ different from 0, eqn (8.48) always provides a conservative result with an approximation which can reach 24%. Equation (8.47) provides an approximation within $\pm 12\%$. The results of a parametric analysis are shown in Fig. 8.18 for $T2=0.5$ and 1 for different K values.

In the case of constant stiffness columns, the global displacement method

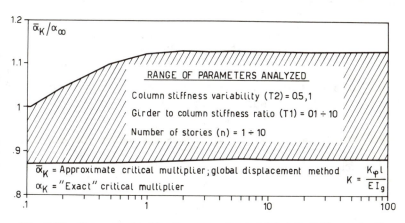

FIG. 8.18. Error provided by the approximate 'global flexibility method'.

provides unconservative results, especially with rigid beams, while the
Horne method provides good results even if not always conservative.

8.3.4 The 'Linear Method'

The 'linear method' proposed for the evaluation of the critical load in portal
frames can be easily extended to multi-storey frames. Figures 8.19 and 8.20
show the variation of the $(\alpha_K - \alpha_0)/(\alpha_\infty - \alpha_K)$ ratio in common and
bilogarithmic scales. In Fig. 8.19 the curves are practically straight lines

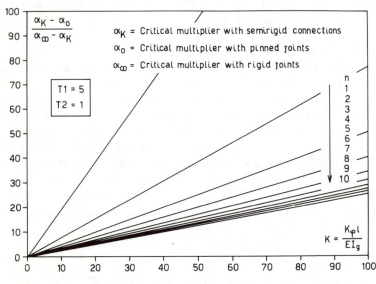

FIG. 8.19.   Curves representing the critical multiplier α_K through the $(\alpha_K - \alpha_0)/$
$(\alpha_\infty - \alpha_K)$ ratio; $T1 = 5$ and $T2 = 1$.

passing through the origin, while in Fig. 8.20 they correspond to parallel
lines. It is therefore possible to use the relation

$$\frac{\alpha_K - \alpha_0}{\alpha_\infty - \alpha_K} = AK \tag{8.49}$$

from which

$$\alpha_K = \frac{AK\alpha_\infty + \alpha_0}{AK + 1} \tag{8.50}$$

It is necessary to know the value of the constant A and of the critical
multipliers α_0 for pin-end joints and α_∞ for fixed-end joints in order to

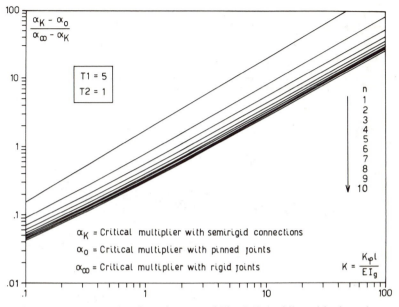

FIG. 8.20.   Representation of curves of Fig. 8.19 on bilogarithmic scale.

evaluate the critical multiplier α_K. The constant A is independent of the value of connection stiffness; it depends instead upon the topology of the frame. The value of the constant A can be determined as the average value of all the lines in Fig. 8.19 for the whole range of K. The result of this analysis for the entire parametric range analysed is given in Figs 8.21, 8.23 and 8.25 respectively for $T2 = 1$, 0·5 and 0. Figures 8.22, 8.24 and 8.26 represent the range of the α'_K/α_K ratio between the approximate and the 'exact' evaluation of the critical multiplier as a function of K.

For a given framed structure it is possible to evaluate the constant A from the corresponding curve. The maximum error is given by the corresponding α'_K/α_K curve and is always within 5% for all values of K higher than 2.

8.4 ILLUSTRATIVE EXAMPLES

In order to illustrate the applicability of the approximate methods suggested in this chapter for the evaluation of the elastic critical loads of semi-rigid sway frames, some numerical examples are presented for the portal fixed frame, portal semi-rigid base frame and multi-storey frame.

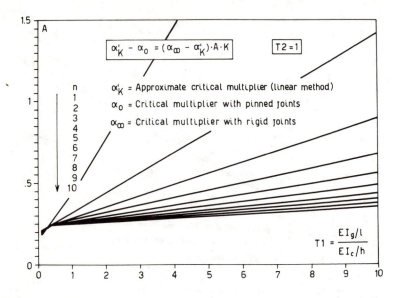

FIG. 8.21.   Value of the constant A to be used in the approximate 'linear method'; multi-storey frames with $T2 = 1$.

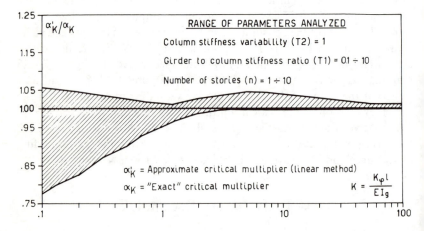

FIG. 8.22.   Error provided by the approximate 'linear method'; multi-storey frames with $T2 = 1$.

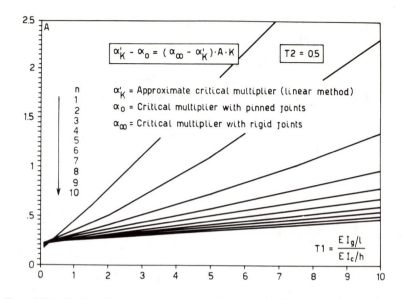

FIG. 8.23.   Value of the constant A to be used in the approximate 'linear method'; multi-storey frames with $T2 = 0\cdot5$.

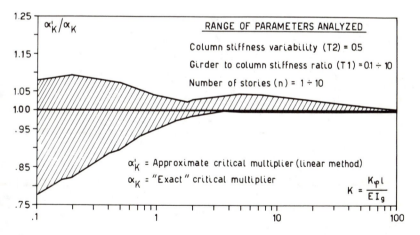

FIG. 8.24.   Error provided by the approximate 'linear method'; multi-storey frames with $T2 = 0\cdot5$.

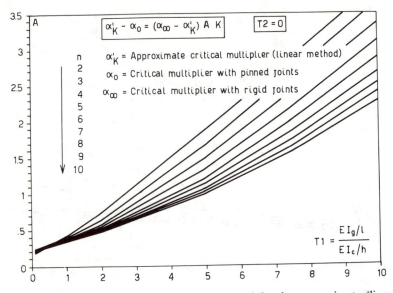

FIG. 8.25. Value of the constant A to be used in the approximate 'linear method'; multi-storey frames with $T2=0$.

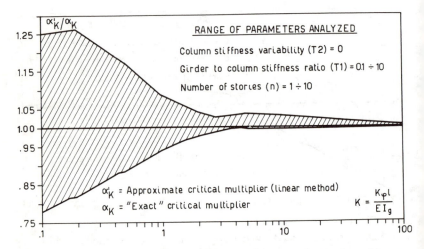

FIG. 8.26. Error provided by the approximate 'linear method'; multi-storey frames with $T2=0$.

8.4.1 Portal Fixed Frame

Let us consider a symmetric fixed base portal frame with equal vertical loads at the ends of the columns and characterized by the following parameters:

$$h = 3000 \text{ mm}$$
$$l = 6000 \text{ mm}$$
$$I_c = 1 \cdot 1259 \times 10^8 \text{ mm}^4$$
$$I_g = 3 \cdot 254 \times 10^8 \text{ mm}^4$$
$$E = 205\,000 \text{ N/mm}^2$$

The beam-to-column connection is assumed to be realized by means of end-plates. According to available experimental data (Fig. 8.1), a realistic value of connection stiffness can be set equal to

$$K_\phi = 6 \times 10^{10} \text{ N mm/rad}$$

The non-dimensional parameters which govern the problem are therefore

$$K = \frac{K_\phi l}{EI_g} = \frac{6 \times 10^{10} \times 6000}{205\,000 \times 3 \cdot 254 \times 10^8} = 5 \cdot 40$$

$$T1 = \frac{EI_g/l}{EI_c/h} = \frac{3 \cdot 254 \times 10^8/6000}{1 \cdot 1259 \times 10^8/3000} = 1 \cdot 445$$

$$T1^* = T1 \frac{K}{K+6} = 1 \cdot 445 \frac{5 \cdot 40}{5 \cdot 40 + 6} = 0 \cdot 6845$$

The evaluation of the 'exact' elastic critical load obtained by equating to zero the determinant of the stiffness matrix provides

$$N_c = 1 \cdot 708 \times 10^7 \text{ N}$$

while the critical loads of the fixed and hinged structure, $N_{c\infty}$ and N_{c0}, result:

$$N_{c\infty} = 2 \cdot 049 \times 10^7 \text{ N}$$
$$N_{c0} = 6 \cdot 328 \times 10^6 \text{ N}$$

The evaluation of the critical load N_c can be obtained by using the diagrams in Fig. 8.13, for $n = 1$:

$$\text{For } T1^* = 0 \cdot 6, \quad N_c^* = 0 \cdot 655$$
$$\text{For } T1^* = 0 \cdot 7, \quad N_c^* = 0 \cdot 687$$

Linear interpolation between these values provides

$$\text{For } T1^* = 0.6845: \quad N_c^* = 0.682$$

The following value of the critical load is therefore obtained:

$$N_c = \frac{\pi^2 EI_c}{h^2} N_c = \frac{\pi^2 \times 205\,000 \times 1.1259 \times 10^8}{3000^2} \times 0.682 = 1.73 \times 10^7 \text{ N}$$

This represents an error of about 1%.

An approximate value of the critical load can be derived by flexibility check (Section 8.2.4). From eqn (8.34) we get

$$N_c \simeq \rho \times 12 \frac{EI_c}{h^2} \frac{1 + 6T1^*}{4 + 6T1^*}$$

$$= \rho \times 12 \frac{205\,000 \times 1.1259 \times 10^8}{3000^2} \times \frac{1 + 6 \times 0.6845}{4 + 6 \times 0.6845}$$

$$= \rho \times 1.939 \times 10^7 \text{ N}$$

By setting $\rho = \pi^2/12$ we get

$$\bar{N}_c = \frac{\pi^2}{12} \times 1.939 \times 10^7 = 1.594 \times 10^7 \text{ N} = 0.934 N_c$$

while if we set $\rho = 0.9$ we get

$$\bar{\bar{N}}_c = 0.9 \times 1.939 \times 10^7 = 1.745 \times 10^7 \text{ N} = 1.022 N_c$$

The first evaluation yields a greater error but on the conservative side.

An approximate calculation of the critical load can also be made through the 'linear method' presented in Section 8.2.4. For this purpose it is necessary to obtain the coefficient A, as a function of $T1$, which provides the critical load by means of eqn (8.40). Figure 8.9 gives the following values of A:

$$\text{For} \quad T1 = 1, \quad A = 0.428$$
$$\text{For} \quad T1 = 2, \quad A = 0.772$$

and by linear interpolation:

$$\text{For} \quad T1 = 1.445, \quad A = 0.581$$

By adopting eqn (8.40) the critical load will be

$$N_c = \frac{AKN_{c\infty} + N_{c0}}{AK + 1}$$

$$= \frac{0 \cdot 581 \times 5 \cdot 40 \times 2 \cdot 049 \times 10^7 + 6 \cdot 328 \times 10^6}{0 \cdot 581 \times 5 \cdot 40 + 1}$$

$$= 1 \cdot 71 \times 10^7 \, \mathrm{N}$$

This value is practically the same as the exact result.

This last method has the advantage that the computation of the critical load can be made for different connection stiffnesses. For this purpose let us assume that there is an uncertainty in the value of K of $\pm 50\%$, hence the connection stiffness can vary between the following values:

$$K_{\min} = 0 \cdot 5 \times K = 0 \cdot 5 \times 5 \cdot 40 = 2 \cdot 70$$
$$K_{\max} = 1 \cdot 5 \times K = 1 \cdot 5 \times 5 \cdot 40 = 8 \cdot 10$$

Equation (8.40) leads to

$$N_{c \ \min} = \frac{0 \cdot 581 \times 2 \cdot 70 \times 2 \cdot 049 \times 10^7 + 6 \cdot 328 \times 10^6}{0 \cdot 581 \times 2 \cdot 70 + 1}$$

$$= 1 \cdot 50 \times 10^7 \, \mathrm{N} \quad (1 \cdot 491 \times 10^7 \, \mathrm{N})$$

$$N_{c \ \max} = \frac{0 \cdot 581 \times 8 \cdot 10 \times 2 \cdot 049 \times 10^7 + 6 \cdot 328 \times 10^6}{0 \cdot 581 \times 8 \cdot 10 + 1}$$

$$= 1 \cdot 80 \times 10^7 \, \mathrm{N} \quad (1 \cdot 804 \times 10^7 \, \mathrm{N})$$

The values in parentheses provide the 'exact' critical loads and therefore the 'linear method' provides practically the same results. It is interesting to note that even the 50% variation in the connection stiffness leads to only a small variation in the critical load. This result is very interesting from a practical point of view since it allows the elastic critical load of the semi-rigid sway frame to be estimated within acceptable approximation even though the connection stiffness is not accurately known.

8.4.2 Portal Frame with Semi-Rigid Base Connection

Let us consider the portal frame analysed in the previous section but defined by a base connection stiffness K'_ϕ:

$$K'_\phi = 6 \times 10^{10} \, \mathrm{N \, mm/rad}$$

This means the same value of the beam-to-column connection.

The non-dimensional parameter which governs the base behaviour is

$$K' = \frac{K'_\phi h}{EI_c} = \frac{6 \times 10^{10} \times 3000}{205\,000 \times 1 \cdot 1259 \times 10^8} = 7 \cdot 80$$

The 'exact' computation of the critical load gives

$$N_c = 1\cdot397 \times 10^7 \, \text{N}$$

Hence the critical load is 81·8% of that computed for the fixed-base connection.

The approximate evaluation can be performed by means of the curves presented in Fig. 8.5; with $K' = 7\cdot80$:

$$\text{For} \quad T1^* = 0\cdot5, \quad N_c^* = 0\cdot508$$
$$\text{For} \quad T1^* = 1, \quad N_c^* = 0\cdot615$$

By linear interpolation:

$$\text{For} \quad T1^* = 0\cdot6845, \quad N_c^* = 0\cdot547$$

The approximate elastic critical load is therefore

$$N_c = \frac{\pi^2 EI_c}{h^2} N_c^* = \frac{\pi^2 \times 205\,000 \times 1\cdot1259 \times 10^8}{3000^2} 0\cdot547$$

$$= 1\cdot385 \times 10^7 \, \text{N}$$

This value is practically the same as the exact one.

The approximate evaluation through a flexibility check is performed by employing eqn (8.35):

$$N_c \simeq \rho \times 12 \frac{EI_c}{h^2} \frac{K' + 6(1 + K')T1^*}{4(3 + K') + 6(4 + K')T1^*}$$

$$= \rho \times 12 \frac{205\,000 \times 1\cdot1259 \times 10^8}{3000^2} \times \frac{7\cdot80 + 6(1 + 7\cdot80) \times 0\cdot6845}{4(3 + 7\cdot80) + 6(4 + 7\cdot80) \times 0\cdot6845}$$

$$= \rho \times 1\cdot475 \times 10^7 \, \text{N}$$

If we set $\rho = \pi^2/12$ and $\rho = 0\cdot9$ we get

$$\bar{N}_c = \frac{\pi^2}{12} \times 1\cdot475 \times 10^7 = 1\cdot213 \times 10^7 \, \text{N} = 0\cdot869 N_c$$

$$\bar{N}_c = 0\cdot9 \times 1\cdot475 \times 10^7 = 1\cdot534 \times 10^7 \, \text{N} = 0\cdot950 N_c$$

Both computations provide conservative approximations.

A simple evaluation of the decrease of the critical load of the semi-rigid base frame with respect to the fixed-base frame can be performed through eqn (8.31) which leads to

$$N_c \simeq \frac{K' + 0\cdot7}{K' + 3} N_{c\infty}$$

in which $N_{c\infty}$ represents the critical load computed in the previous section. We therefore get

$$N_c \simeq \frac{7\cdot8+0\cdot7}{7\cdot8+3} \times 1\cdot708 \times 10^7 = 0\cdot787 \times 1\cdot708 \times 10^7 = 1\cdot344 \times 10^7\,\text{N}$$

This gives a conservative error of 4% compared with the 'exact' evaluation.

8.4.3 Multi-Storey Frame

As an example, a one-bay nine-storey frame will be analysed. The beam length is 6000 mm while the storey height is 3000 mm. The girders are all characterized by the same moment of inertia, $I_g = 3\cdot254 \times 10^8$ mm⁴, while the second moments of area columns vary as follows:

$$I_{c1} = I_{c2} = I_{c3} = 2\cdot5166 \times 10^8\,\text{mm}^4$$
$$I_{c4} = I_{c5} = I_{c6} = 1\cdot1259 \times 10^8\,\text{mm}^4$$
$$I_{c7} = I_{c8} = I_{c9} = 3\cdot831 \times 10^7\,\text{mm}^4$$

Stiffness values are worked out for girders and columns as follows:

Girders

$$\frac{EI_g}{l} = \frac{205\,000 \times 3\cdot254 \times 10^8}{6000} = 1\cdot111 \times 10^{10}\,\text{N mm}$$

Columns

$$i = 1, 2, 3: \left(\frac{EI_c}{h}\right)_i = \frac{205\,000 \times 2\cdot5166 \times 10^8}{3000} = 1\cdot720 \times 10^{10}\,\text{N mm}$$

$$i = 4, 5, 6: \left(\frac{EI_c}{h}\right)_i = \frac{205\,000 \times 1\cdot1259 \times 10^8}{3000} = 7\cdot694 \times 10^9\,\text{N mm}$$

$$i = 7, 8, 9: \left(\frac{EI_c}{h}\right)_i = \frac{205\,000 \times 3\cdot831 \times 10^7}{3000} = 2\cdot618 \times 10^9\,\text{N mm}$$

The beam-to-column connection is assumed to be the same as in the previous sections:

$$K_\phi = 6 \times 10^{10}\,\text{N mm/rad}$$
$$K = \frac{K_\phi l}{EI_g} = \frac{6 \times 10^{10}}{1\cdot111 \times 10^{10}} = 5\cdot40$$

The 'exact' computation of the elastic critical load for constant loads in each joint provides the following values:

$$N_c = 1{\cdot}443 \times 10^6 \, N$$
$$N_{c0} = 3{\cdot}757 \times 10^4 \, N$$
$$N_{c\infty} = 2{\cdot}336 \times 10^6 \, N$$

where N_c, N_{c0} and $N_{c\infty}$ respectively represent the cases of semi-rigid, hinged and fixed frames.

In order to compare this value with the approximate ones suggested in Section 8.3, it is necessary to obtain the parameters $T1$, $T1^*$ and $T2$. For this purpose, if we assume as reference the value of EI_c/h corresponding to the top storey, $T1$ can be computed as

$$T1 = \frac{EI_g/l}{EI_c/h} = \frac{1{\cdot}111 \times 10^{10}}{2{\cdot}618 \times 10^9} = 4{\cdot}244$$

from which

$$T1^* = T1 \frac{K}{K+6} = 4{\cdot}244 \frac{5{\cdot}40}{5{\cdot}40+6} = 2{\cdot}01$$

An approximate evaluation of $T2$ can be obtained by assuming a linear relation between the first and the last storey:

$$T2 \simeq \frac{(EI_c/h)_1 - (EI_c/h)_9}{9(EI_c/h)_9}$$
$$= \frac{1{\cdot}720 \times 10^{10} - 2{\cdot}618 \times 10^9}{9 \times 2{\cdot}618 \times 10^9} = 0{\cdot}62$$

These values of $T1^*$ and $T2$ can be applied to the diagrams of Figs 8.13 and 8.14 thus obtaining:

$$\text{For} \quad T2 = 0{\cdot}5, \quad N_c^* = 0{\cdot}162$$
$$\text{For} \quad T2 = 1, \quad N_c^* = 0{\cdot}183$$

By linear interpolation:

$$\text{For} \quad T2 = 0{\cdot}62, \quad N_c^* = 0{\cdot}167$$

Hence

$$N_c = \frac{\pi^2 \, EI_c}{h^2} N_c^* = \frac{\pi^2 \times 205\,000 \times 3{\cdot}831 \times 10^7}{3000^2} \times 0{\cdot}167 = 1{\cdot}44 \times 10^6 \, N$$

which is practically the same as the critical load obtained analytically.

The approximate computations of $\bar{N}_c$ and $\bar{\bar{N}}_c$ using eqn (8.48) and eqn (8.47) are as follows:

$$\bar{N}_c = 1.503 \times 10^6\,\text{N} = 1.042 N_c$$
$$\bar{\bar{N}}_c = 1.181 \times 10^6\,\text{N} = 0.818 N_c$$

Hence the global displacement method gives an unconservative estimate with an error of 4%, while the Horne (1975) method leads to a conservative one with an error of 18%.

Another approximate evaluation of the critical load can be made by means of the 'linear method' using the coefficient A given by eqn (8.50) and by linear interpolation of the curves of Figs 8.21 and 8.23 which for $T1 = 2$ and $n = 9$ yield:

$$\text{For} \quad T2 = 0.5, \quad A = 0.347$$
$$\text{For} \quad T2 = 1, \quad A = 0.297$$

By linear interpolation:

$$\text{For} \quad T2 = 0.62, \quad A = 0.335$$

This leads to

$$N_c = \frac{AKN_{c\infty} + N_{c0}}{AK + 1} = \frac{0.335 \times 5.40 \times 2.336 \times 10^6 + 3.757 \times 10^4}{0.335 \times 5.40 + 1}$$
$$= 1.52 \times 10^7\,\text{N}$$

with an error of 5%. If we also consider a 50% variation of the K_ϕ value, as previously:

$$K_{\min} = 0.5 \times 5.40 = 2.70$$
$$K_{\max} = 1.5 \times 5.40 = 8.10$$

The maximum and minimum N_c values are

$$N_{c\,\min} = \frac{0.335 \times 2.70 \times 2.336 \times 10^6 + 3.757 \times 10^4}{0.335 \times 2.70 + 1}$$
$$= 1.13 \times 10^6\,\text{N} \ (1.07 \times 10^6\,\text{N})$$
$$N_{c\,\max} = \frac{0.335 \times 8.10 \times 2.336 \times 10^6 + 3.757 \times 10^4}{0.335 \times 8.10 + 1}$$
$$= 1.72 \times 10^6\,\text{N} \ (1.65 \times 10^6\,\text{N})$$

Values in parentheses refer to the 'exact' case. The approximate method is thus shown to give acceptable results.

8.5 SUMMARY AND CONCLUSIONS

Semi-rigid connections have a significant influence on the critical load of semi-rigid sway frames. The semi-rigid effect can be introduced through the non-dimensional parameters K and K' defined in eqn (8.2). For K values greater than 10, 70% of the critical load computed under the hypothesis of rigid frames is reached while, for K values greater than 50, 90% is reached. Even within the range of low K values a good proportion of the critical load computed with fixed joints can be achieved, and therefore it is advisable to carry out an analysis which takes into account the effective restraint condition.

In those cases in which the critical load of the semi-rigid frame is to be evaluated, the approximate methods provided in this chapter can be conveniently employed.

If the maximum relative storey displacement method (Horne, 1975) is used, a generally conservative value is obtained with an approximation within 25%. If the global drift method is used, the approximation falls within $\pm 12\%$ even though it is not always on the conservative side.

The proposed 'linear method' provides very good approximations. Within the entire parametric range analysed, for K values greater than 2, the error is always less than 5%.

Charts have been provided which allow direct derivation of the critical load within the parametric range examined.

ACKNOWLEDGEMENT

The assistance of Mr. Guido Capria who drafted all the figures for this chapter is gratefully acknowledged.

REFERENCES

ACKROYD, M. H. & GERSTLE, K. H. (1977) Strength and stiffness of type 2 Steel Frames. Report to AISC, University of Colorado, USA.

ACKROYD, M. H. & GERSTLE, K. H. (1982) Strength and stiffness of type 2 steel frames. *Trans. ASCE, J. Struct. Div.*, **108** (ST7), 1541–56.

ACKROYD, M. H. & GERSTLE, K. H. (1983) Elastic stability of flexibly connected steel frames. *Trans. ASCE, J. Struct. Div.*, **109** (ST1), 241–5.

ANDERSON, D. (1980) Simple calculation of elastic critical loads for unbraced, multistorey steel frames. *Structural Engineer*, **61B**, 29.

COSENZA, E., DE LUCA, A. & FAELLA, C. (1984) Nonlinear behaviour of framed structures with semi-rigid joints. *Costruzioni Metalliche*, **4**, 199–211.

COSENZA, E., DE LUCA A. & FAELLA, C. (1986a) Elastic and inelastic stability of semi-rigid steel frames. *SSRC Annual Technical Session*, Washington, 57–72.

COSENZA, E., DE LUCA, A. & FAELLA, C. (1986b) Inelastic buckling and postcritical behaviour of steel structures with semi-rigid joints. Proc. Regional Colloquium 1986, Stability of Steel Structures, Budapest, Hungary.

COSENZA, E., DE LUCA, A. & FAELLA, C. (1987) A parametric analysis of semi-rigid joint effect on elastic stability of steel frames. Proc. 11th CTA Conf., Trieste, Italy (in Italian).

FRYE, M. J. & MORRIS, G. A. (1975) Analysis of flexibly connected steel frames. *Canad. J. Civil Engng*, **2**, 280–91.

GERSTLE, K. H. (1985) Flexibly connected steel frames. In *Steel Framed Structures: Stability and Strength* (ed. R. Narayanan). Elsevier Applied Science Publishers, London, pp. 205–39.

HORNE, M. R. (1975) An approximate method for calculating the elastic critical loads of multi-storey plane frames. *Structural Engineer*, **53**, 242.

JONES, S. W., KIRBY, P. A. & NETHERCOT, D. A. (1983) The analysis of frames with semi-rigid connection: a state-of-art report. *J. Construct. Steel Res.*, **2**, 2–13.

LIVESLEY, R. K. & CHANDLER, D. B. (1956) Stability Functions for Structural Frameworks. Manchester University Press, Manchester, UK.

MELCHERS, R. E. (1987) Modelling of column-base behaviour. Proc. Connections, State of Art Workshop, Cachan, France.

NETHERCOT, D. A. (1985) Steel beam to column connections: a review of tests data. CIRIA report, Project 338.

PICARD, A. & BEAULIEU, D. (1987) Column base plate connections. Proc. Connections, State of Art Workshop, Cachan, France.

ROBERTS, T. M. (1985) Matrix methods of analysis of multi-storeyed sway frames. In *Steel Framed Structures: Stability and Strength* (ed. R. Narayanan). Elsevier Applied Science Publishers, London, UK, pp. 31–54.

SIMITSES, G. J. & VLAHINOS, A. S. (1985) Elastic stability of rigidly and semi-rigidly connected unbraced frames. In *Steel Framed Structures: Stability and Strength* (ed. R. Narayanan). Elsevier Applied Science Publishers, London, UK, pp. 115–52.

STEVENS, L. K. (1967) Elastic stability of practical multi-storey frames. *Proc. Instn Civ. Engrs*, **36**, 99–117.

Chapter 9

INELASTIC BUCKLING OF SEMI-RIGID SWAY FRAMES

E. Cosenza,[a] A. De Luca[b] & C. Faella[a]

[a] *Istituto di Ingegneria Civile, Università di Salerno, Italy*
[b] *Istituto di Scienza e Tecnica delle Costruzioni,*
Università della Basilicata, Italy

SUMMARY

The effect of semi-rigid connections on the inelastic buckling load of sway frames is analysed. Using the analogy with the buckling of an axially compressed bar, the semi-rigid connection is considered as a global imperfection. The effects of the main parameters governing the inelastic buckling of portal and multi-storey frames are analysed. Methods of evaluation of the inelastic buckling load of imperfect sway frames are proposed.

NOTATION

d	Numerical constant; eqn (9.10)
d'	Numerical constant; eqn (9.13)
E	Young's modulus of elasticity
f	Stability function
f'_i, f'_j	Stability functions modified for connection effects; eqns (9.7)
f_y	Yield stress
F	Horizontal force
g	Stability function
h	Column height
H	Frame height

297

J	Second moment of area
J_c	Second moment of area of column
J_g	Second moment of area of girder
K	Non-dimensional stiffness of beam-to-column connection
K_i, K_j	Value of K at nodes i and j
K_ϕ	Stiffness of beam-to-column connection
$K_{\phi i}, K_{\phi j}$	Value of K_ϕ at nodes i and j
l, L	Beam length
M	Bending force
M_i, M_j	Value of bending moment at nodes i and j
$M_{u,c}$	Ultimate moment of column
$M_{u,g}$	Ultimate moment of girder
$M_{u,j}$	Ultimate moment of joint
N	Axial load
N_c	Critical axial load
N_y	Squash load
N_u	Ultimate axial load
T_i, T_j	Shear forces at nodes i and j
T_{0i}, T_{0j}	Fixed end shears
$T1$	Topological frame parameter
$T1^*$	Modified frame parameter; eqn (9.18)
$T2$	Topological frame parameter
$T3$	Plastic frame parameter
u	Factor depending upon axial load; eqn (9.5)
v	Sway displacement
v_0	Initial out-of-straightness
α	Multiplier
α_c	Elastic critical multiplier
α_u	Inelastic buckling multiplier
$\alpha_{u,\infty}$	Value of α_u for 'rigid framing' model
α_y	Squash multiplier
γ_h	Reduction factor of load vector modified for connection effects; eqns (9.15)
δ_i, δ_j	Nodal displacements at nodes i and j
$\bar{\lambda}$	Non-dimensional column slenderness; eqn (9.17)
λ_f	Non-dimensional frame slenderness; eqn (9.22)
ϕ	Joint rotation
ϕ_i, ϕ_j	Value of ϕ at nodes i and j
$\phi_i^1, \phi_j^1, \phi_{ij}^1$	Joint rotation with unit bending forces; Fig. (9.7)

ϕ'_{hk} Reduction factors of stiffness coefficients; eqns (9.9)
ψ Frame imperfection coefficient; eqn (9.16)

$[KSC]$ Secant stiffness matrix

9.1 INTRODUCTION

It is now well established that actual beam-to-column connections perform
in a semi-rigid manner since they are generally characterized by a nonlinear
moment–rotation relationship. Figure 9.1 shows the different behavioural

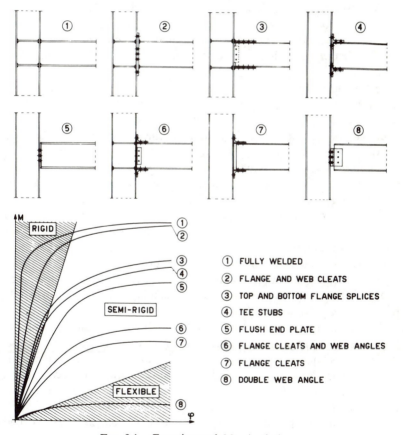

FIG. 9.1. Experimental $M-\phi$ relations.

curves which have been gathered by Nethercot (1985) on some of the most used connections ranging from the fully welded to the web angle types. It can be seen that the actual connections introduce a partial-restraint condition in the joint, thus modifying the frame behaviour from the ideal conditions of pinned or fixed frame.

The effects of the semi-rigid connection on elastic buckling of semi-rigid sway frames have been investigated in the previous chapter. The elastic critical load is very important in the definition of the collapse load, especially in the case of unbraced structures characterized by a high global slenderness; in fact, in this case the structure remains elastic and the collapse load is practically equivalent to the critical load.

The behaviour of 'slender frames' (governed by elastic critical load) can be extrapolated by considering the behaviour of slender columns, wherein the collapse loads are practically coincident with the critical loads. More generally a complete analogy between frame and column behaviour can be established in order to develop an insight into frame buckling behaviour.

The stability curve of a column identifies a region of high slenderness in which the critical load (Euler load) practically defines the column collapse; stocky columns are characterized by their plastic behaviour, and an intermediate region can be defined in which the two patterns of behaviour interact with each other.

In column buckling, the different imperfections contribute to modify the stability curve. Similarly, in the case of semi-rigid frames, the beam-to-column M–ϕ relation modifies the inelastic buckling load and can be therefore considered as an imperfection with respect to the ideal 'rigid framing' model. The analogy between the imperfect buckling load of the bar and that of the frame is shown in Fig. 9.2. It is clear that the imperfection which is contributed by the semi-rigid connection has to be analysed together with all the other imperfections. Clearly, the analysis has to be carried out on the entire structure, sub-assemblages not being sufficiently representative of the overall problem.

In this chapter an attempt is made to identify the parameters and the problems governing inelastic buckling of semi-rigid sway frames; the relationships between the global frame behaviour and the bar behaviour and their interaction are discussed. In this context, the semi-rigid connection is treated as an imperfection to be added to the others of the frame in order to evaluate the inelastic buckling load.

Useful indications for computing the inelastic buckling load of semi-rigid sway frames are provided.

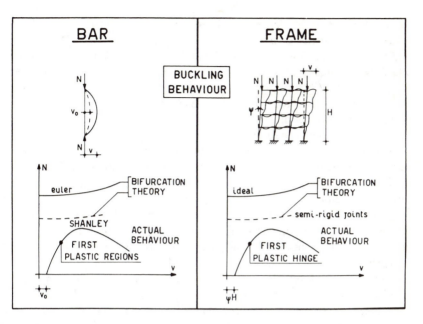

FIG. 9.2. Analogy between imperfect bar and imperfect frame buckling behaviour.

9.2 SEMI-RIGID JOINTS AND THEIR EFFECT ON NONLINEAR RESPONSE

9.2.1 Effects of Semi-Rigid Joints on Global Behaviour

The introduction of a localized deformability has to be taken into account in order to evaluate how the collapse load of the entire frame is affected by the semi-rigid connection. In particular, for the assessment of the inelastic buckling load of the frame, the elastic stiffness of the connection and its ultimate strength, together with the shape of the $M-\phi$ curve of the connection, are of interest to the designer.

The elastic deformability of the connection in fact increases the global deformability and therefore amplifies nonlinear effects thus leading possibly to plastifications in the structure. The strength of the connection together with the shape of the moment–rotation curve modifies the plastic properties of the whole structure thus affecting the collapse behaviour.

Some studies have been devoted to investigating the experimental behaviour of actual connections and have derived the elastic stiffness of different connection types. Ackroyd & Gerstle (1977) gathered much of the available experimental data.

Other experimental studies have been devoted to investigating both the elastic and inelastic behaviour of the connection. Among these is the one initiated by the CIRIA (Construction Industry Research and Information Association) (Nethercot, 1985) which has gathered more than 700 experimental data and has programmed new tests to be performed in order to cover the commonly used types.

The classification of the different connections is given in Fig. 9.1 in which are schematically shown the rigid, pinned region and the semi-rigid ones. From this figure it can be seen that practically all the connections should be considered semi-rigid.

Several studies have been developed in order to find the best way to fit the experimental curve. The methods for predicting moment–rotation curves are reviewed by Jones *et al.* (1983) and Nethercot (1985). These methods range from the simplest linear or bilinear methods to the more sophisticated ones: polynomial, cubic B-spline, Richard or Ramberg–Osgood formulae.

It is pointed out that the range of interest in the case of sway frames is the one represented in the upper part of Fig. 9.1. Connections characterized by small stiffness cannot be used when designing unbraced frames. For this reason, the semi-rigid effect will be considered an imperfection with respect to the ideal 'rigid framing' model. On the other hand, in the case of no-sway frames, the range of interest is the one represented in the lower part of Fig. 9.1. In fact, even small restraints provided by the connections which are commonly assumed as pinned can lead to savings in columns in designing braced frames.

9.2.2 Interaction between Girder and Connection Behaviour

In the previous section different experimental behavioural curves of connections have been shown regardless of the girders to which they are connected. However, the connection stiffness, strength and the shape of the M–ϕ curve have to be compared with the corresponding ones of the members to which the connections are made. Generally the ratio between the strength of the connection and that of the girder has to be analysed. In Fig. 9.3 are represented the three different cases found in practice:

$$M_{u,j}/M_{u,g} > 1\cdot0$$
$$M_{u,j}/M_{u,g} \simeq 1\cdot0 \qquad (9.1)$$
$$M_{u,j}/M_{u,g} < 1\cdot0$$

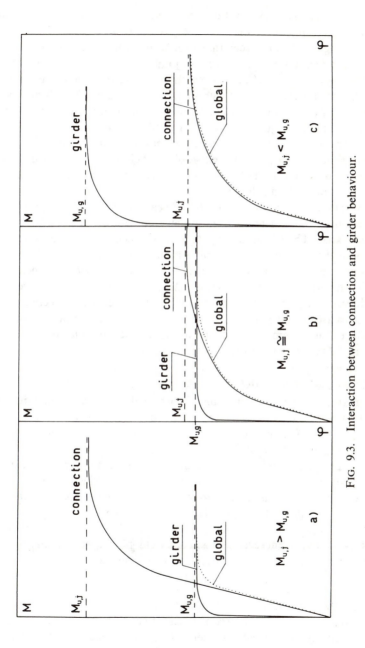

FIG. 9.3. Interaction between connection and girder behaviour.

These represent respectively the connection strengths $M_{u,j}$ higher than, practically equal to or lower than the girder strength $M_{u,g}$.

From Fig. 9.3 it can be seen that, even if the connection is characterized by a generally nonlinear behaviour, the joint relationship can be considered as elastoplastic when the connection to girder strength ratio exceeds 1·0. In the other cases, the joint behaviour is governed by the connection curve and therefore it would be necessary to introduce a more sophisticated model in order to simulate the joint behaviour. The models which can be used in the nonlinear analysis of semi-rigid sway frames are represented in Fig. 9.4.

In dealing with sway frames, elastoplastic behaviour is assumed for the connections since it is very likely that the design of the connection will lead to connections strength higher than that of the girder.

In any case partial-strength joints decrease the overall plastic properties of the structure and therefore usually affect the inelastic buckling load. This effect, described by Cosenza *et al.* (1986b), is shown in Fig. 9.5 in which are represented the effects of both connection deformability and connection strength on the load bearing capacity of a two-storey frame, with partial-strength joints characterized by $M_{u,j}/M_{u,c} = 0·5$, subjected to vertical and horizontal loads. It can be seen that partial-strength connections lead to a decrease, in this particular case, of about 30% in the capacity of the structure. This decrease has to be added to the one due to the elastic deformability introduced by the connection itself.

9.2.3 Methods of Analysis

The analysis of inelastic buckling of semi-rigid sway frames requires the study of a geometrical and mechanical nonlinear problem. A complete survey of the available methods of analysis of geometric nonlinearities can be found in Roberts (1985).

A simplified method for considering mechanical nonlinearities can be derived by the introduction of nodes at the points in which plasticizations are expected. The inelastic behaviour of these sections can be simulated by means of an appropriate M–ϕ relation which is of the semi-rigid type, i.e. elastoplastic (Fig. 9.4(b)) or generally nonlinear (Fig. 9.4(c)) at connection nodes, while at current sections it will be a rigid–plastic relation (Fig. 9.4(a)). In any case, the relation $M = M(\phi)$ can be expressed by

$$M = K_\phi \cdot \phi \tag{9.2}$$

From the numerical point of view, the problem can be reduced to the definition of the stiffness matrix of a beam element in which the geometric nonlinearity is introduced together with spring elements at the ends to

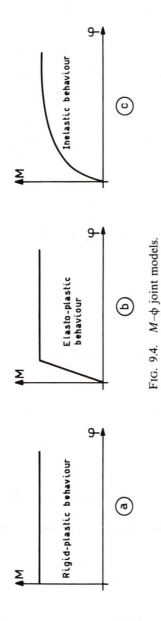

FIG. 9.4. M–ϕ joint models.

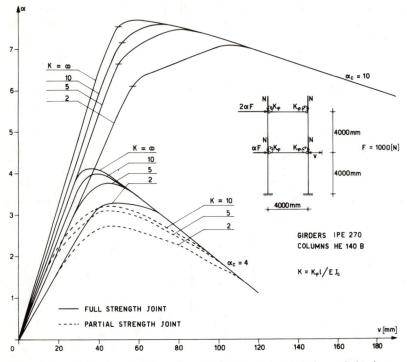

FIG. 9.5. Effect of partial strength connections on inelastic frame behaviour.

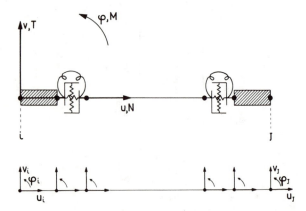

FIG. 9.6. Model for axial, shear and bending semi-rigid effect.

account for the bending connection stiffness. In this manner correction factors of the stiffness coefficients can be derived as shown by Gerstle (1985). This method, extended to the case of axial loads, is provided hereafter.

It is possible, by means of a matrix method, to take into account the axial and shear deformability of the connection together with the interactions, as shown by Cosenza *et al.* (1984) (Fig. 9.6). However, the available experimental data are not sufficient for extending such a method into design practice.

A method for analysing semi-rigid frames in the nonlinear range can be represented by the extrapolation of the concept of stability functions (Livesley & Chandler, 1956) to the case of semi-rigid bars.

For this purpose, with reference to the bar with nodes i and j with semi-rigid connections characterized by stiffness $K_{\phi i}, K_{\phi j}$ and an axial load

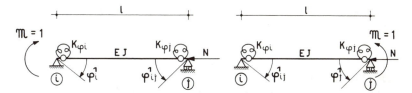

FIG. 9.7. Deformability coefficients of a bar with semi-rigid joints and axial load.

N (Fig. 9.7), the elastic coefficients ϕ_i^1, ϕ_j^1 and ϕ_{ij}^1 can be expressed as a function of the stability functions and, using the connection stiffnesses, as

$$\phi_i^1 = \frac{l}{3EJ} f + \frac{1}{K_{\phi i}} \tag{9.3a}$$

$$\phi_j^1 = \frac{l}{3EJ} f + \frac{1}{K_{\phi j}} \tag{9.3b}$$

$$\phi_{ij}^1 = \frac{l}{6EJ} g \tag{9.3c}$$

in which

$$f = \frac{3}{u}\left(\frac{1}{u} - \frac{1}{tgu}\right) \tag{9.4a}$$

$$g = \frac{6}{u}\left(\frac{1}{\sin u} - \frac{1}{u}\right) \tag{9.4b}$$

and

$$u = \sqrt{\frac{Nl^2}{EJ}} \tag{9.5}$$

If we set

$$K_i = \frac{K_{\phi i} l}{EJ}; \quad K_j = \frac{K_{\phi j} l}{EJ} \tag{9.6}$$

in order to define connections stiffnesses using the non-dimensional parameters K_i and K_j, eqns (9.3) yield

$$\phi_i^1 = \frac{l}{3EJ}\left(f + \frac{3}{K_i}\right) = \frac{l}{3EJ} f_i' \tag{9.7a}$$

$$\phi_j^1 = \frac{l}{3EJ}\left(f + \frac{3}{K_j}\right) = \frac{l}{3EJ} f_j' \tag{9.7b}$$

$$\phi_{ij}^1 = \frac{l}{6EJ} g \tag{9.7c}$$

where the reduction coefficients f_i' and f_j' are dependent upon N and K_i and K_j. It can be verified that, for K_i and K_j which tend to infinity, both coefficients tend to f.

In order to derive the expression for the secant stiffness matrix $[KSC]$, by extrapolating the expressions provided by Roberts (1985), it is sufficient to write equilibrium and compatibility equations which make use of the coefficients ϕ_i^1, ϕ_j^1 and ϕ_{ij}^1 provided by eqns (9.7). If we assume the conventions of Fig. 9.8, it can be shown that

$$[KSC] = \frac{EJ}{l^3}\begin{bmatrix} 12\phi_{11}' & 6l\phi_{12}' & -12\phi_{13}' & 6l\phi_{14}' \\ & 4l^2\phi_{22}' & -6l\phi_{23}' & 2l^2\phi_{24}' \\ \text{sym.} & & 12\phi_{33}' & -6l\phi_{34}' \\ & & & 4l^2\phi_{44}' \end{bmatrix} \tag{9.8}$$

The coefficients ϕ_{hk}' take into account the reduction of stiffness due to axial loads and to semi-rigid connections. They are provided by the expressions

$$\phi_{11}' = \phi_{33}' = \phi_{13}' = \frac{f_i' + f_j' + g}{d} - \frac{u^2}{12} \tag{9.9a}$$

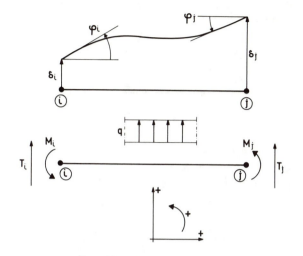

FIG. 9.8.   Sign conventions.

$$\phi'_{12} = \phi'_{23} = \frac{2f'_i + g}{d} \tag{9.9b}$$

$$\phi'_{14} = \phi'_{34} = \frac{2f'_j + g}{d} \tag{9.9c}$$

$$\phi'_{22} = \frac{3f'_j}{d} \tag{9.9d}$$

$$\phi'_{24} = \frac{3g}{d} \tag{9.9e}$$

$$\phi'_{44} = \frac{3f'_i}{d} \tag{9.9f}$$

in which

$$d = 4f'_i f'_j - g^2 \tag{9.10}$$

All the coefficients ϕ'_{hk} tend to the usual stability functions in the case of rigid connections. If the axial load is not present, we get

$$f'_i = 1 + \frac{3}{K_i}; \quad f'_j = 1 + \frac{3}{K_j}; \quad g = 1; \quad u = 0 \tag{9.11}$$

The coefficients ϕ'_{hk} in this case become

$$\phi'_{11} = \phi'_{13} = \phi'_{33} = \frac{K_i K_j + K_i + K_j}{d'} \tag{9.12a}$$

$$\phi'_{12} = \phi'_{23} = \frac{K_i K_j + 2K_j}{d'} \tag{9.12b}$$

$$\phi'_{14} = \phi'_{34} = \frac{K_i K_j + 2K_i}{d'} \tag{9.12c}$$

$$\phi'_{22} = \frac{K_i K_j + 3K_i}{d'} \tag{9.12d}$$

$$\phi'_{24} = \frac{K_i K_j}{d'} \tag{9.12e}$$

$$\phi'_{44} = \frac{K_i K_j + 3K_j}{d'} \tag{9.12f}$$

in which

$$d' = K_i K_j + 4(K_i + K_j) + 12 \tag{9.13}$$

The fixed-end force vector, with reference to the girders, characterized by uniformly distributed load q and in which the axial load effect is negligible, is obtained as follows:

$$T_{0i} = \frac{ql}{2}\gamma_1 \tag{9.14a}$$

$$M_{0i} = \frac{ql^2}{12}\gamma_2 \tag{9.14b}$$

$$T_{0j} = \frac{ql}{2}\gamma_3 \tag{9.14c}$$

$$M_{0j} = \frac{ql^2}{12}\gamma_4 \tag{9.14d}$$

where

$$\gamma_1 = 1 + \frac{K_j - K_i}{d'} \tag{9.15a}$$

$$\gamma_2 = \frac{K_i K_j + 6K_i}{d'} \tag{9.15b}$$

$$\gamma_3 = 1 - \frac{K_j - K_i}{d'} \tag{9.15c}$$

$$\gamma_4 = \frac{K_i K_j + 6K_j}{d'} \tag{9.15d}$$

Expressions (9.14) and (9.15) coincide with the ones provided by Gerstle (1985) and allow matrix analysis of semi-rigid frames without geometrical nonlinearities.

9.3 PROBLEM OF FRAME IMPERFECTIONS

9.3.1 Introduction

The semi-rigid connection, as has been pointed out in the introduction, can be considered as an imperfection to be added to the others which characterize the industrial frame. This 'industrial frame' concept has been developed by De Luca (1987) and by Cosenza et al. (1987c), and is analogous to the widely accepted concept of 'industrial bar' (Ballio & Mazzolani, 1983). In particular, the industrial frame is characterized by global geometrical and mechanical imperfections as shown in Fig. 9.9, to be added to the local imperfections of the bar. In Fig. 9.9(a) are provided the geometrical imperfections of the bar (initial out-of-straightness) together with the analogous out-of-plumb of the frame arising from erection tolerances. This global geometrical imperfection has been introduced in some provisions (ECCS, 1978; CEC, 1984) by means of an initial sway to be incorporated in the analysis or by means of allowable tolerances. The values of these imperfections have been based on a statistical evaluation of measured initial sway in actual multi-storey structures (Beaulieu, 1977; Lindner, 1984).

In the single bar under compression, the initial camber results in bending stresses in the cross section; in the case of a framed structure, out-of-plumb also results in bending stresses in the members, due to geometric nonlinearities. In both cases, unless approximate analyses are adopted, a second-order analysis is required to take this effect into account.

In the case of a bar, the residual stresses (which can be measured by means of a stub column test) have proved to be the most significant ones in differentiating the industrial bar behaviour from the ideal behaviour as far as buckling is concerned (Fig. 9.9(b)). If the bar is discretized into a finite number of longitudinal elements, each of these elements will be affected by

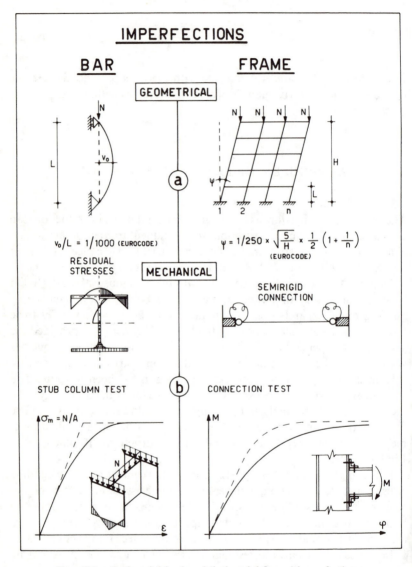

FIG. 9.9. 'Industrial bar' and 'industrial frame' imperfections.

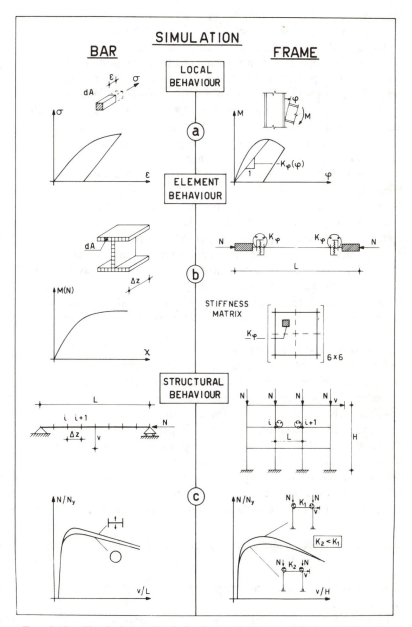

FIG. 9.10.   Simulation methods for 'industrial bar' and 'industrial frame'.

the residual stress distribution and therefore the moment–curvature relationship of the bar element itself will be modified.

Analogously, since a framed structure is formed by several bars, they can be assumed as representative elements of a discretization in which, at each joint, a new imperfection has to be introduced in order to simulate the actual beam-to-column joint. In analogy to the nonlinear moment–curvature relation introduced at the nodes of the discretized bar, a nonlinear moment–rotation relation will be introduced at the joints of the discretized frame (Fig. 9.9(b)). This nonlinear relation is obtained from the available experimental data on semi-rigid connections.

Figure 9.10 details the steps to be followed for evaluating the inelastic buckling load of a semi-rigid sway frame, by means of a nonlinear analysis. In particular, in this figure a procedure for simulating the nonlinear behaviour of an imperfect frame is summarized, and is analogous to the methods developed for deriving the stability curves of the industrial bar. This procedure consists of defining a curve representing the semi-rigid joint effect (Fig. 9.10(a)), which is then introduced into the stiffness matrix of the bar (Fig. 9.10(b)) as has been suggested in Section 9.2.3; the analysis of the frame characterized by all its imperfections is then performed. The definition of the imperfections to be used in the analysis is given hereafter.

9.3.2 Geometrical Imperfections

In Fig. 9.11 it is shown how local and global geometrical imperfections can be combined within a particular structure. Practically all the codes provide the value of local geometric imperfections to be assumed in the analysis for simulating the initial camber of the column.

With regard to the global geometrical imperfection (initial out-of-plumb), the subject is rather new and not enough experimental data exist on the measured out-of-plumb of entire structures. A statistical evaluation on actual structures has been performed by Beaulieu (1977) and Lindner (1984). The results of this evaluation have been introduced in the Eurocode (CEC, 1984), thus leading to the following values to be used in the analysis:

$$\psi = \frac{v_0}{H} = \frac{1}{250} r_1 r_2; \quad r_1 = \sqrt{\frac{5}{H}}; \quad r_2 = \frac{1}{2}\left(1 + \frac{1}{n}\right) \qquad (9.16)$$

where H is the overall frame height (m) and n is the number of stressed columns in a row.

Figure 9.11(c) shows one of the possible combinations of the local imperfections on the global structure. It is obvious that the possible

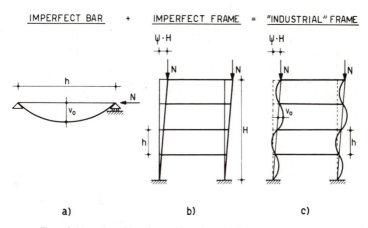

FIG. 9.11.   Combination of local and global imperfections.

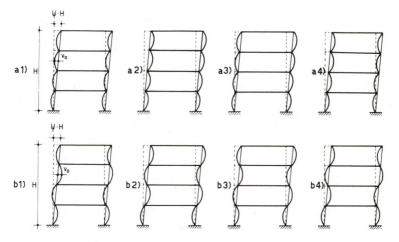

FIG. 9.12.   Possible distributions of local imperfections along the frame.

distributions of bar imperfections along the structure are many more than the one provided in that figure; Fig. 9.12 shows the most significant ones.

9.3.3 Mechanical Imperfections and Semi-Rigid Connections
As stated previously, local mechanical imperfections are mainly represented by the residual stress distribution. In order not to perform cumbersome

computations, the so-called 'equivalent geometrical imperfection' can be adopted. For all practical purposes, this equivalent imperfection results in the same column behaviour as that affected by residual stresses. An equivalent initial camber is assumed for this purpose. The camber assumed in this analysis is the same as that suggested by the Eurocode which ensures that the stability curve remains valid. The values suggested by the Eurocode are shown in Fig. 9.13.

EQUIVALENT BAR GEOMETRICAL IMPERFECTIONS

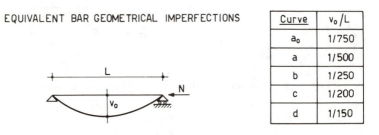

Curve	v_0/L
a_0	1/750
a	1/500
b	1/250
c	1/200
d	1/150

FIG. 9.13.   Equivalent imperfections suggested by the Eurocode.

With regard to the global mechanical imperfection (i.e. the semi-rigid connection), it has been assumed that the connections have strengths higher than those of the girders. Therefore, based on Section 9.2.2, the semi-rigid connections can be simulated by means of elastoplastic models (Fig. 9.3(b)) and hence are completely characterized by their elastic stiffness, the strength being immediately known for given girder properties.

9.3.4 Simplified Analysis of Columns with Semi-Rigid Connections
The model used for analysing inelastic buckling of columns with semi-rigid end restraints is shown in Fig. 9.14. This model is able to account for the bar geometrical and mechanical imperfections together with the semi-rigid connections at the ends. The column is divided into two deformable elements connected at mid-height by a rigid-plastic spring. The residual stress distribution is introduced by means of an equivalent geometrical imperfection which therefore includes the initial camber of the bar as well. Two nonlinear springs are then connected at the ends of the bar in order to introduce the semi-rigid joint effect.

This model is very effective in simulating the column buckling behaviour, as can be seen in Fig. 9.15 in which the stability curves as derived by this model are compared to those provided by the Eurocode. It can be seen that

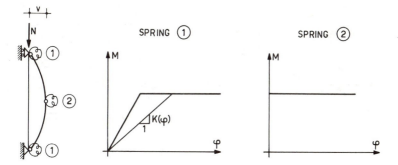

FIG. 9.14.   Simplified model for semi-rigid column.

in the whole range of non-dimensional slenderness $\bar{\lambda}$ where

$$2{\cdot}65 > \bar{\lambda} = \frac{1}{\pi} \frac{l}{r} \sqrt{\frac{f_y}{E}} > 0{\cdot}26 \tag{9.17}$$

the agreement between the simulated points and the Eurocode is very satisfactory, leading to errors which respectively reach peak values of 3%, 5% and 6% for the three stability curves, with an average error of about 2%. A part of the error is also attributable to the approximation of the equivalent imperfection concept.

9.4 ANALYSIS OF SEMI-RIGID SWAY FRAMES

9.4.1 Definition of Main Parameters
The parameters which govern the inelastic buckling behaviour of semi-rigid sway frames can be divided into elastic and plastic parameters.

The variables which affect the elastic behaviour have been defined in the previous chapter and can be identified in:

(1) the ratio between the flexural stiffness of the girder, modified in order to take into account the semi-rigid joint, and the column stiffness;
(2) the variation of stiffness parameters along the frame height;
(3) frame topology.

These parameters, as has been shown in the previous chapter, allow one completely to define the elastic critical multiplier.

The plastic parameters can be mainly grouped in:

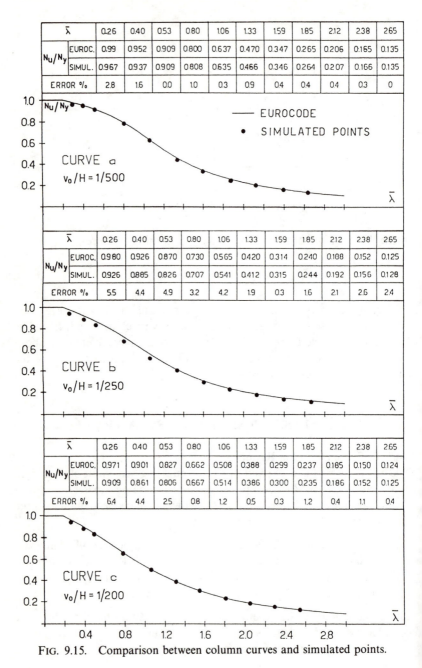

$\bar{\lambda}$		0.26	0.40	0.53	0.80	1.06	1.33	1.59	1.85	2.12	2.38	2.65
N_u/N_y	EUROC.	0.99	0.952	0.909	0.800	0.637	0.470	0.347	0.265	0.206	0.165	0.135
	SIMUL.	0.967	0.937	0.909	0.808	0.635	0.466	0.346	0.264	0.207	0.166	0.135
ERROR %		2.8	1.6	0.0	1.0	0.3	0.9	0.4	0.4	0.4	0.3	0

CURVE a

$v_0/H = 1/500$

— EUROCODE
• SIMULATED POINTS

$\bar{\lambda}$		0.26	0.40	0.53	0.80	1.06	1.33	1.59	1.85	2.12	2.38	2.65
N_u/N_y	EUROC.	0.980	0.926	0.870	0.730	0.565	0.420	0.314	0.240	0.188	0.152	0.125
	SIMUL.	0.926	0.885	0.826	0.707	0.541	0.412	0.315	0.244	0.192	0.156	0.128
ERROR %		5.5	4.4	4.9	3.2	4.2	1.9	0.3	1.6	2.1	2.6	2.4

CURVE b

$v_0/H = 1/250$

$\bar{\lambda}$		0.26	0.40	0.53	0.80	1.06	1.33	1.59	1.85	2.12	2.38	2.65
N_u/N_y	EUROC.	0.971	0.901	0.827	0.662	0.508	0.388	0.299	0.237	0.185	0.150	0.124
	SIMUL.	0.909	0.861	0.806	0.667	0.514	0.386	0.300	0.235	0.186	0.152	0.125
ERROR %		6.4	4.4	2.5	0.8	1.2	0.5	0.3	1.2	0.4	1.1	0.4

CURVE c

$v_0/H = 1/200$

FIG. 9.15. Comparison between column curves and simulated points.

(4) the ratio between ultimate strength of column and girder sections, provided that full-strength joints are adopted;
(5) the nonlinear curve characterizing the joint;
(6) the amount and distribution of local and global imperfections.

Furthermore, an important elastoplastic parameter is the non-dimensionalized slenderness $\bar{\lambda}$ of the highly stressed column defined by eqn (9.17).

Complete analyses which evaluate all the effects of the parameters previously mentioned are not yet available. In this chapter, some of the influences are shown with particular reference to the imperfection introduced by the semi-rigid connection.

9.4.2 Representation of Results

In the following sections, analysis of some multi-storey framed structures is carried out in which the imperfections are characterized by:

—an equivalent bar imperfection defined by its initial out-of-straightness equal to 1/200 of the bar length; this imperfection corresponds to the stability curve 'c' of the Eurocode;
—an initial out-of-plumb ψ defining an initial sway equal to 1/400 of the global height H of the frame;
—a mechanical imperfection defined by the semi-rigid joint assumed as elastoplastic and therefore characterized by a stiffness K_ϕ and by a strength $M_{u,j}$ equal to that of the girder $M_{u,g}$.

It is convenient to non-dimensionalize the connection stiffness and therefore adopt the parameter K defined as in eqn 6:

$$K = \frac{K_\phi l}{EJ_g}$$

This stiffness (as stated in the previous chapter) affects the global behaviour through the parameter $T1^*$:

$$T1^* = T1 \frac{K}{K+6} \tag{9.18}$$

where

$$T1 = \frac{EJ_g/l}{EJ_c/h} \tag{9.19}$$

All the examples are characterized by girders which are constant at each level. The variation in column stiffness can be taken into account through the parameter $T2$ defined in the previous chapter, and it has been assumed constant or stepwise varying along the height.

The strength of the elements, always in non-dimensional terms, is characterized by the parameter $T3$ which represents the ratio between girder strength $M_{u,g}$ (equal to that of the joint $M_{u,j}$) and column strength $M_{u,c}$:

$$T3 = \frac{M_{u,g}}{M_{u,c}} \tag{9.20}$$

Figures 9.16–9.19 show curves relating the vertical load to sway displacement. In particular it is assumed that vertical loads N are concentrated at joint locations and the inelastic buckling multiplier α_u is found. The vertical load multipliers are normalized with respect to the squash multiplier α_y, defined as the collapse multiplier of the perfect structure, which therefore leads to yield stress in the highly stressed columns. Horizontal displacements v are non-dimensionalized with respect to the initial global geometrical imperfection ψH.

A synthetic representation of the results, adopted in Figs 9.21–9.24, is provided in terms of frame stability curves, as has been proposed by Cosenza et al. (1987b). The non-dimensional column slenderness $\bar{\lambda}$ (eqn (9.17)) is plotted on the x-axis while the α_u/α_y ratio is given on the y-axis. This representation is one of the possible generalizations of the well known column stability curves.

9.4.3 Portal Frames

In Figs 9.16 and 9.17 are represented the behavioural curves of two semi-rigid portal frames, geometrical properties of which are given in the same figures. The values of the imperfections assumed are of the type suggested by the Eurocode. The two figures refer to the extreme cases of infinitely rigid connection ($K = 10\,000$) and deformable connection ($K = 0\cdot1$).

The different curves provided in each figure represent different column non-dimensional slenderness $\bar{\lambda}$ and are therefore representative of different global slendernesses of the frame. The different slendernesses have been obtained by changing the height of the portal frame and taking the ratio $l/h = 2\cdot0$ to be constant as shown in the figures. From a comparison between the two figures it can be deduced that the semi-rigid connection leads to a decrease of the inelastic buckling multiplier even though with a less steep post-buckling branch.

This aspect is more evident in Figs 9.18 and 9.19. These figures refer to the

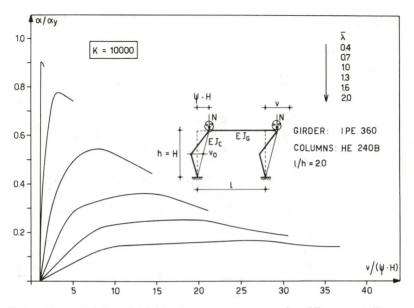

FIG. 9.16.   Multiplier of axial load versus sway curves for different non-dimensional column slendernesses; $K = 10\,000$.

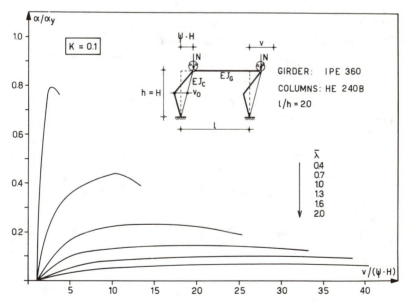

FIG. 9.17.   Multiplier of axial load versus sway curves for different non-dimensional column slendernesses; $K = 0 \cdot 1$.

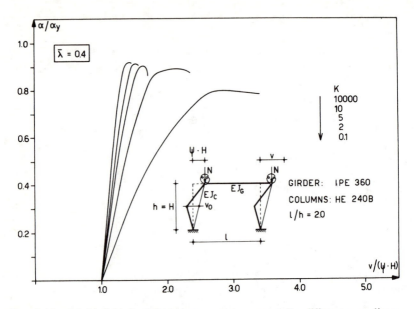

FIG. 9.18. Multiplier of axial load versus sway curves for different non-dimensional stiffness of connections; $\bar{\lambda} = 0.4$.

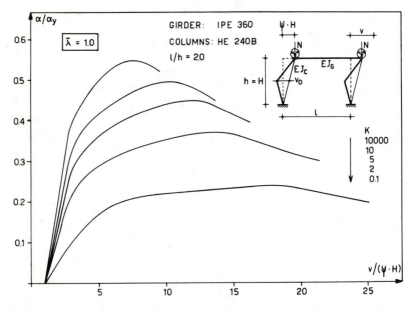

FIG. 9.19. Multiplier of axial load versus sway curves for different non-dimensional stiffness of connections; $\bar{\lambda} = 1.0$.

non-dimensional column slenderness of 0·4 and 1·0 respectively and represent different behavioural curves related to a particular value of connection stiffness as shown by Cosenza et al. (1986a). From Fig. 9.18 as well as from Fig. 9.19 it can be seen that the semi-rigid connection leads to an increase of deformability and to a decrease of collapse multiplier. From a comparison between the two figures it can be argued that these effects are more evident in the case of higher column slenderness. Over the entire parametric range of connection stiffness K, while for $\bar{\lambda} = 0·4$ the decrease of the inelastic buckling load is about 10%, in the case of $\bar{\lambda} = 1·0$ the decrease reaches about 50%. This effect can be easily explained if we observe that, for small values of non-dimensional column slenderness, plastic behaviour governs and therefore the deformability introduced by the semi-rigid connection is less effective than in the other cases.

The decrease of inelastic buckling load of the semi-rigid frame, with respect to the rigid framing model, is better evidenced in Fig. 9.20. In this figure is shown the decrease of inelastic buckling load with respect to the degree of fixity of the connection (as represented by the non-dimensional parameter K). This figure is divided into three regions: in the intermediate one the portal frame previously analysed, characterized by $T1 = 0·723$, is represented, while in the upper and lower parts of the figure the value of $T1$ has been changed to 0·257 and 1·498 by modifying the girder shapes. The inelastic buckling multiplier of the semi-rigid frame α_u, represented on the y-axis of the figure, has been normalized with respect to the value of the rigid connection multiplier $\alpha_{u,\infty}$. The different curves refer to values of $\bar{\lambda}$ varying from 0·4 to 2·0, as represented in the figure. In the same figure is also given, by a dashed line, the curve representing the elastic case.

It is clear that the elastic behaviour represents a lower bound for the decrease of the collapse multiplier α_u with respect to the reference value $\alpha_{u,\infty}$. As expected, the plastic behaviour attenuates the effect of the semi-rigid connection, especially in cases of lower column slenderness. It is pointed out that, for $K > 10$, at least 80% of $\alpha_{u,\infty}$ can be reached.

The same results are given in Fig. 9.21 in the form of stability curves. In these curves the x-axis represents the slenderness of the column, and the y-axis the inelastic buckling multiplier α_u normalized with respect to the squash multiplier α_y of the columns. The different curves are relative to the different values of connection stiffness and therefore show how this imperfection affects the inelastic buckling behaviour of the frame. In the regions of smaller slenderness, in which the plastic behaviour governs, the effect of the semi-rigid connection is less severe, leading to a smaller decrease of the collapse load.

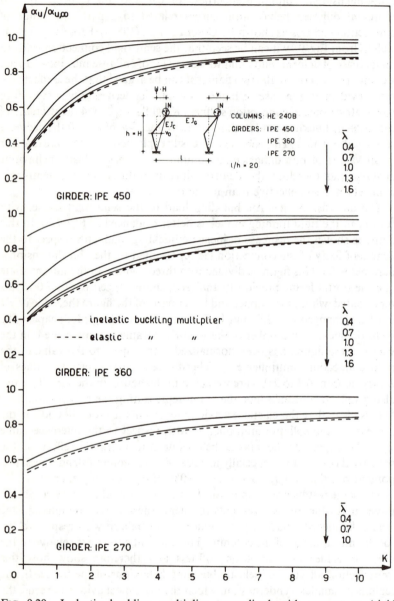

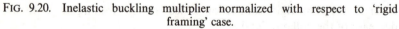

FIG. 9.20. Inelastic buckling multiplier normalized with respect to 'rigid framing' case.

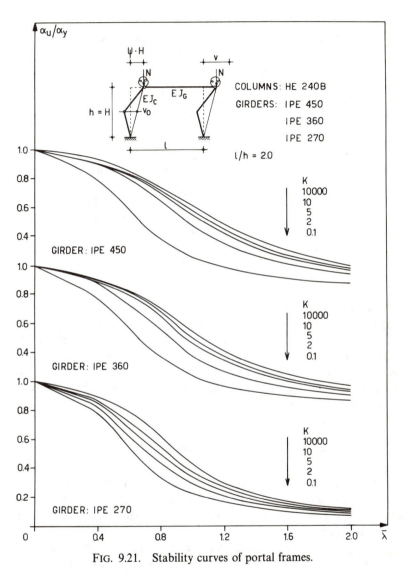

FIG. 9.21.   Stability curves of portal frames.

As has been outlined in the previous chapter, two different portal frames can be considered equivalent from the elastic point of view when they are characterized by the same $T1^*$ value. Table 9.1 shows that this parameter completely defines the inelastic buckling load as well, when the parameter

TABLE 9.1
EFFECT OF GIRDER TO COLUMN STRENGTH PARAMETER
ON INELASTIC BUCKLING MULTIPLIER

$$\text{Portal frame: } T1^* = \frac{EJ_g/l}{EJ_c/h} \frac{K}{K+6} = 0.20$$

$$T3 = M_{u,g}/M_{u,c}$$

$\bar{\lambda}$	α_u/α_y		
	IPE 450 (T3 = 1·62)	*IPE 360* (T3 = 0·97)	*IPE 270* (T3 = 0·35)
0·4	0·904	0·904	0·902
0·7	0·673	0·673	0·673
1·0	0·387	0·387	0·387
1·3	0·241	0·241	0·240
1·6	0·163	0·163	0·162
2·0	0·106	0·106	0·106

$T3$ does not come into the picture since plastic hinges form in the column. It may be concluded that the inelastic behaviour of portal frames is generally very well defined by the elastic parameter $T1^*$, which includes the effect of the semi-rigid connection, and by the column slenderness $\bar{\lambda}$. The stability curves provided in Fig. 9.21 enable the evaluation of the effect of the semi-rigid connection on the decrease of inelastic buckling load over the entire range of interest of column slendernesses.

9.4.4 Multi-Storey Frames

Semi-rigid joints have a significant effect on the multi-storey frame response. As it is not conceivable to carry out a complete parametric analysis devoted to investigate all the parameters outlined in Section 9.4.1, only a limited number of cases are presented; these refer to three-storey symmetric and non-symmetric frames and to six-storey symmetric frames (see also Cosenza *et al.*, 1987a).

Figure 9.22 gives the results pertaining to a three-storey frame, using the representation suggested in Section 9.4.2 and used for the evaluation of the results for portal frames. The frame is characterized by geometrical and mechanical properties which are constant along the height.

The curves in this figure are similar to the ones shown in Fig. 9.21, which refer to portal frames; the effect of semi-rigid joints, evaluated by means of the non-dimensional parameter K, is seen to be more important in this case.

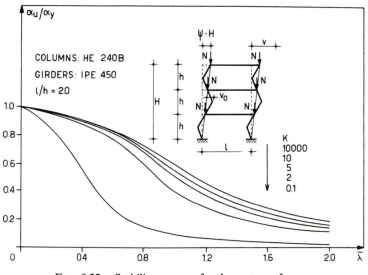

FIG. 9.22.   Stability curves of a three-storey frame.

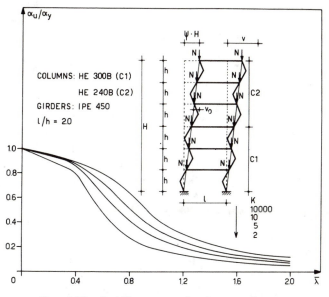

FIG. 9.23.   Stability curves of a six-storey frame.

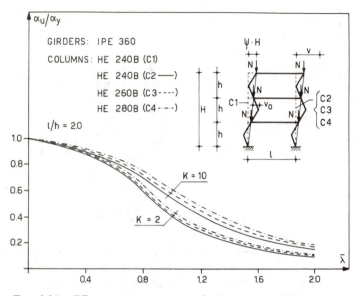

FIG. 9.24.   Effect on non-symmetry of columns on stability curves.

In fact, over the entire range of non-dimensional column slenderness, the variation of K results in a more consistent decrease of the inelastic buckling load. This effect is even more evident in the case of the six-storey frame represented in Fig. 9.23. The frame chosen is provided with a variation of column stiffness along the height.

A three-storey frame in which the two columns are characterized by different structural shapes (and therefore different stiffnesses) is examined in Fig. 9.24, in which the x-axis represents the non-dimensional slenderness of the weakest column. This example is representative of actual situations of multi-bay frames in which not all the columns are subjected to the same vertical load or are oriented in the major as well as in the minor axis planes. The figure demonstrates how the increase of stiffness of the right column leads to an increase of the inelastic buckling load due to the decreased global deformability of the frame.

9.4.5 On the Computation of the Inelastic Buckling Load of Semi-Rigid Sway Frames

In order to understand the inelastic behaviour of sway frames it is useful to represent the curve relating to the elastic critical multiplier (dashed line of

Fig. 9.25) along with the one pertaining to the collapse multiplier of the frame. Figure 9.25 shows the previously examined curve relating to the three-storey frame characterized by $K = 2.0$ and girder IPE 450. This figure demonstrates how well the frame behaviour is described by the elastic curve for higher values of column slenderness, analogous to what happens for single columns.

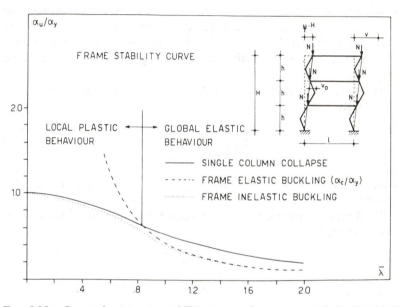

FIG. 9.25. Comparison among stability curve, column curve and elastic critical curve of a three-storey frame.

For smaller values of the non-dimensional slenderness (in this particular case $\bar{\lambda} < 0.8$) the actual behaviour differs from the elastic one and is closer to the curve representing the collapse multiplier of the single column (dashed line of Fig. 9.25), with effective length assumed to be coincident with the inter-storey height.

Figure 9.25 is very valuable for the comprehension of the problem, but does not provide any practical means for the evaluation of the inelastic buckling load since the distances of the collapse curve from the elastic one and from the local curve vary considerably with frame topology.

On the other hand, the curves represented in Figs 9.20, 9.22, 9.23 and 9.24, pertaining to one-, three- and six-storey frames, provide very useful quantitative indications on the effect of the semi-rigid joint on the inelastic buckling load even though they are strictly applicable to the particular cases analysed.

This is probably due to the particular choice of representing, on the x-axis, the parameter $\bar{\lambda}$ relating to the highly stressed column. This parameter, being a local one, cannot interpret the global frame behaviour. It may be pointed out that in the case of single columns the non-dimensional slenderness of the column represents accurately the column buckling behaviour, and the scatter of actual results, with respect to the stability curve, is very limited. On the other hand, in the case of multi-storey frames, the scatter (which can be obtained by comparing Figs 9.21, 9.22 and 9.23) is very wide.

The definition of non-dimensional slenderness of a single column of eqn (9.17) is given by

$$\bar{\lambda}=\frac{1}{\pi}\frac{l}{r}\sqrt{\frac{f_y}{E}}=\sqrt{\frac{N_y}{N_c}} \tag{9.21}$$

were N_c and N_y respectively are the critical load and the squash load of the column.

An immediate generalization of this concept to the case of multi-storey frames seems to be

$$\lambda_f=\sqrt{\frac{\alpha_y}{\alpha_c}} \tag{9.22}$$

where the elastic critical load of the bar is replaced by the elastic critical multiplier of the entire frame.

The application of this 'global slenderness' λ_f in the representation of the inelastic buckling multiplier of multi-storey frames is provided in Fig. 9.26. In this figure are represented all the results previously examined in Figs 9.20, 9.21 and 9.23. It should be noted that the scatter obtained in this representation is considerably smaller than the one previously obtained, thereby confirming the validity of the frame parameter λ_f in representing the frame behaviour.

It is interesting to draw on the same figure the curve relating to the elastic critical multiplier of the bar (dashed line) and the usual column curve (dotted line). It will be seen that the column curve, by adopting this new definition of frame slenderness λ_f, provides good approximations of the inelastic buckling load of semi-rigid sway frames.

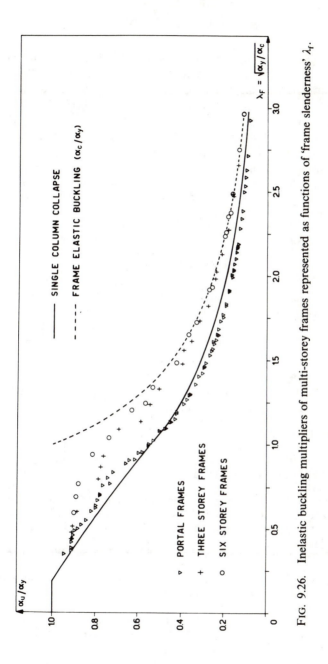

FIG. 9.26. Inelastic buckling multipliers of multi-storey frames represented as functions of 'frame slenderness' λ_f.

9.5 SUMMARY AND CONCLUSIONS

The inelastic buckling behaviour of semi-rigid sway frames has been analysed by considering the imperfections, as the most significant parameter.

In particular, geometrical and mechanical imperfection of the bar have been included by means of the equivalent imperfection. Global imperfections have also been considered, the geometrical ones by means of an initial out-of-plumb and the mechanical ones, mainly consisting in the joint behaviour, by means of connection deformabilities.

Following this procedure, several curves representative of different structural schemes have been represented. The effects of main parameters have been demonstrated and some indications for evaluating the inelastic buckling load have been provided.

ACKNOWLEDGEMENT

The assistance of Mr Guido Capria who drafted all the figures of this chapter is gratefully acknowledged.

REFERENCES

ACKROYD, M. H. & GERSTLE, K. H. (1977) Strength and Stiffness of Type 2 Steel Frames. AISC Report, Project No. 199.

BALLIO, G. & MAZZOLANI, F. M. (1983) *Theory and Design of Steel Structures.* Chapman & Hall, London, p. 377.

BEAULIEU, D. (1977) The Destabilizing Forces Caused by Gravity Loads Acting on Initially Out-of-plumb Members in Structures. PhD dissertation, Dept. of Civ. Eng., University of Alberta.

CEC (1984) Eurocode 3: Common Unified Code of Practice for Steel Structures. Commission of the European Communities, Rapport EUR 8849, Brussels.

COSENZA, E., DE LUCA, A. & FAELLA, C. (1984) Nonlinear behaviour of framed structures with semi-rigid joints. *Costruzioni Metalliche,* **4**, 199–211.

COSENZA, E., DE LUCA, A. & FAELLA, C. (1986a) Elastic and inelastic stability of semi-rigid frames. SSRC Annual Technical Session, Washington. SSRC, Bethlehem.

COSENZA, E., DE LUCA, A. & FAELLA, C. (1986b) Buckling and postcritical behaviour of steel structures with semi-rigid joints. Regional Colloquium 1986, Stability of Steel Structures, Budapest, Hungary.

COSENZA, E., DE LUCA, A. & FAELLA, C. (1987a) Inelastic Buckling of Semi-rigid Sway Frames. Technical Report, Istituto di Ingegneria Civile, Università di Salerno.

COSENZA, E., DE LUCA, A. & FAELLA, C. (1987b) Stability curves of frames: an introduction to the problem. 11th CTA Congress, Trieste (in Italian).

COSENZA, E., DE LUCA, A., FAELLA, C. & MAZZOLANI, F. M. (1987c) Imperfection sensitivity of 'industrial' steel frames. In *Steel Structures: Advances, Design and Construction* (ed. R. Narayanan). Elsevier Applied Science Publishers. London, pp. 326–36.

DE LUCA, A. (1987) Effects of imperfections on load bearing capacity of industrial steel frames. PhD Dissertation, Istituto di Tecnica delle Construzioni, Università di Napoli (in Italian).

ECCS (1978) European Recommendations for Steel Construction. European Convention for Constructional Steelwork, Brussels.

GERSTLE, K. H. (1985) Flexibly connected steel frames. In *Steel Framed Structures: Stability and Strength* (ed. R. Narayanan). Elsevier Applied Science Publishers London, pp. 205–40.

JONES, S. W., KIRBY, P. A. & NETHERCOT, D. A. (1983) The analysis of frames with semi-rigid connections: a state-of-art report, *J. Construct. Steel Res.*, 3(2), 2–13.

LINDNER, J. (1984) Ungewollte Schiefstellungen von Stahlstutzen. IABSE 12th Congress, Vancouver.

LIVESELEY, R. K. & CHANDLER, D. B. (1956) *Stability Functions for Structural Frameworks*. Manchester University Press, Manchester.

NETHERCOT, D. A. (1985) Steel Beam to Column Connections: Review of Tests Data. CIRIA, Project 338.

ROBERTS, T. M. (1985) Matrix methods of analysis of multi-storeyed sway frames. In *Steel Framed Structures: Stability and Strength* (ed. R. Narayanan). Elsevier Applied Science Publishers, London, pp. 31–54.

Chapter 10

ANALYSIS OF STEEL FRAMES WITH FLEXIBLE JOINTS

W. F. Chen

Department of Civil Engineering, Purdue University,
West Lafayette, Indiana, USA

SUMMARY

This chapter summarizes several practical computer-based numerical pro-
cedures for the analysis and design of flexibly-connected steel frames, and
presents highlights of some numerical results on the effect of connection
flexibility on the stability analysis and design of steel frames.

To this end, the first part of this chapter discusses the behavior and modeling
of semi-rigid steel beam-to-column connections, and presents a rigorous
second-order elastic method of analysis of flexibly-connected frames. In the
latter part of this chapter, a rigorous elastic–plastic second-order method of
analysis is described from which the true nonlinear behavior of in-plane frames
with flexible joints is studied using the refined computer model developed.
Finally, the effects of connection flexibility and panel zone deformation on the
behavior and strength of plane steel frames are summarized and discussed.
Directions of further research are also indicated.

10.1 INTRODUCTION

In the conventional analysis and design of steel frameworks, the frames are
analyzed and designed under the simplifications that the connections are
treated either as ideally pinned or fully rigid. The use of the ideally pinned
condition implies that no moment will be transmitted between the beam

and the column. Insofar as rotation is concerned, the beam and the column that are jointed together by a pin will behave independently. On the other extreme, the use of the fully rigid condition implies that no relative rotation will occur between the adjoining members. The angle between the beam and the column remains virtually unchanged as the frame deforms.

Although the use of these idealized joint behaviors simplifies the analysis and design procedures drastically, the predicted response of the frame may not be realistic as most connections used in actual practice transmit some moment and experience some deformation upon loading. Thus, the ideally pinned and fully rigid joint assumptions represent only extreme conditions which are rarely encountered in real structures. To assess the actual behavior of the frame, it is necessary to incorporate the effect of connection flexibility in the analysis. Although provisions for flexibly connected frames are contained in the present American Institute of Steel Construction's (AISC) Allowable Stress Design (ASD) (AISC, 1978) and Load and Resistance Factor Design (LRFD) (AISC, 1986) specification, specific guidelines for the analysis and design of such frames are not provided. This chapter focuses on the methods of analysis that enable designers to assess this behavior, and also attempts to provide some insight into the semi-rigid nature of the steel beam-to-column connections and their influence on frame response. Particular attention is given to our recent studies of the effects of connection flexibility and panel zone deformation on the strength, deflection and internal force distribution of steel framed structures.

The first part of the chapter discusses the behavior and modeling of steel beam-to-column connections (Sections 10.2 and 10.3) that are required for the subsequent developments. A method of analysis, based on a rigorous second-order elastic analysis, is then developed (Sections 10.5 and 10.6). A rigorous elastic-plastic second-order analysis is also developed in the latter part of this chapter (Section 10.8). Studies of the true nonlinear behavior of in-plane braced frames with flexible joints using the more refined method for inelastic analysis are presented (Section 10.9). Finally, the effects of connection flexibility and panel zone deformation on the behavior of plane steel frames are summarized and discussed (Sections 10.10 and 10.11).

10.2. BEHAVIOR OF CONNECTIONS

Before proceeding to the discussion of the analysis of flexibly connected frames, we shall first discuss in this section how a typical connection behaves under load. In the following section, we shall show how this behavior can be modeled mathematically for an analysis.

A connection is a medium through which forces and moments are transmitted from one member to another. For a beam-to-column connection, a general set of forces that may be transmitted includes axial force, shearing force, bending moment and torsion. For an in-plane study, the effect of torsion can be neglected. Furthermore, for most connections, the axial and shearing deformations are usually small compared to the rotational deformation. Consequently, for practical purposes, we need to consider only the rotational deformation of the connection. The rotational deformation is customarily expressed as a function of the moment in the connection. When a moment M is applied to a connection, it rotates by an amount θ_r. As depicted in Fig. 10.1, the rotation represents the change in angle between the beam and the column from its original configuration. The angle θ_r is a measure of the relative rotation of the beam to the column.

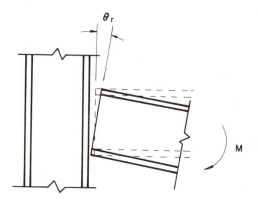

FIG. 10.1.   Relative rotation of beam to column.

Figure 10.2 shows schematically the moment–rotation $M-\theta_r$ behavior of a variety of commonly used semi-rigid connections. The single web angle connection represents a very flexible connection and the T-stub connection represents a rather rigid connection. Several observations can be made from this figure:

1. All types of connection exhibit a $M-\theta_r$ behavior that falls between the extreme cases of ideally pinned (the horizontal axis) and fully rigid (the vertical axis) conditions.

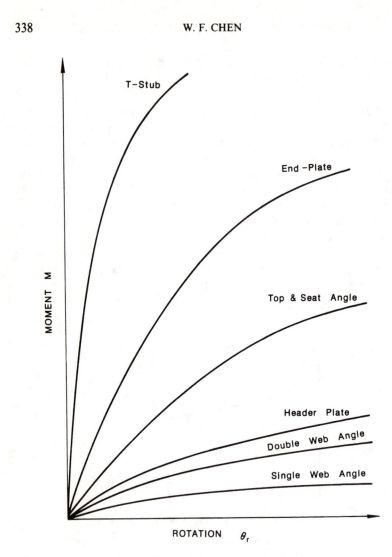

FIG. 10.2.   Connection moment–rotation curves.

2. For the same moment, the more flexible the connection is, the larger the value of θ_r. Conversely, for a specific value of θ_r, a more flexible connection will transmit less moment between the adjoining members.

3. The maximum moment that a connection can transmit (herein

referred to as the ultimate moment capacity) decreases with the more flexible connection.

4. The $M-\theta_r$ relationship for the semi-rigid connections is typically nonlinear over virtually the entire range of loadings.

As will be shown later, a linear approximation of the initial portion of the curve is acceptable for the frame under its serviceability limit state, but it becomes unacceptable for the frame under its ultimate limit state.

When a moment is applied to a connection, the connection rotates according to the curves shown in Fig. 10.2. However, if the direction of moment is reversed, the connection will unload and follow a different path which is almost linear with a slope equal to the initial slope of the $M-\theta_r$ curve. This phenomenon is depicted in Fig. 10.3. Because of this behavior,

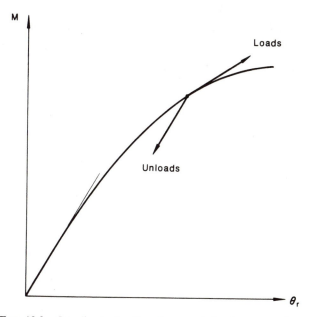

FIG. 10.3.   Loading/unloading characteristic of a connection.

identical connections at the ends of a beam may not always behave identically. This can best be illustrated by the simple portal frame shown in Fig. 10.4 that is subjected to gravity load only. Under the action of the gravity load, the connections at the ends of the beam will experience a moment of M_g on the $M-\theta_r$ curve (Fig. 10.4(a)). Now, if a lateral force is

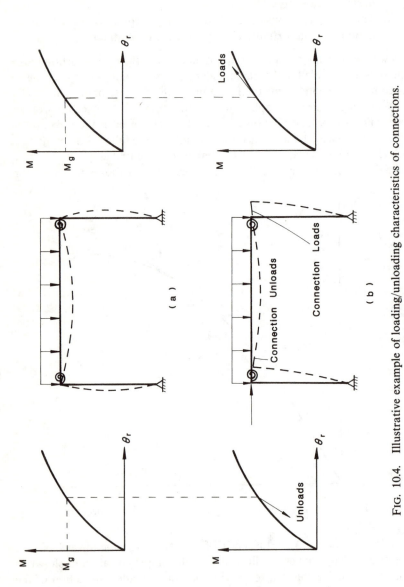

Fig. 10.4. Illustrative example of loading/unloading characteristics of connections.

applied to the frame, the leeward connection will continue to load but the windward connection will unload (Fig. 10.4(b)). As a result, the apparent stiffnesses of connections under the action of this lateral force will be different. Depending on the magnitude of M_g and the characteristic of the $M-\theta_r$ curve of a particular connection, the difference in stiffnesses of the two connections may be quite substantial. For the extreme case that the gravity load moment equals the ultimate moment capacity of the connections, the leeward connection will behave virtually like a pinned connection with the almost constant ultimate moment capacity, whereas the windward connection will respond like a linear elastic connection with a stiffness equal to its initial stiffness. This loading/unloading characteristic of the connection must be properly modeled in order to predict the response of the frame reliably.

10.3 MODELING OF CONNECTIONS

Curves such as those shown in Fig. 10.2 are obtained almost exclusively from experiments. Although analytical studies of connection behavior using the finite element techniques have been reported (Krishnamurthy *et al.*, 1979; Patel & Chen, 1984), the time and cost involved as well as the uncertainty inherent in the analysis render these analytical techniques unacceptable for practical use. At present, the most commonly used approach to describe the $M-\theta_r$ relationship is to curve-fit the experimental data with simple expressions. Numerous experiments on connections have been performed in the past resulting in a rather large body of $M-\theta_r$ data (Goverdham, 1984; Nethercot, 1985; Kishi & Chen, 1986a, b; Chen, 1988; Chen & Kishi, 1989). Using these available data, various nonlinear connection $M-\theta_r$ models have been curve-fitted (Kishi & Chen, 1986a, b). Some of the important ones are summarized below.

10.3.1 Frye–Morris Polynomial Model (1976)
In this model, the $M-\theta$ relationship is represented by an odd-power polynomial of the form

$$\theta_r = C_1(KM)^1 + C_2(KM)^3 + C_3(KM)^5 \qquad (10.1)$$

where K is a standardization parameter dependent upon the connection type and geometry and C_1, C_2, C_3 are curve-fitting constants. This model represents the $M-\theta_r$ behavior reasonably well. The main drawback is that the nature of a polynomial is to peak and trough within a certain range. The connection stiffness, which is represented by the slope of the $M-\theta_r$ curve, may become negative at some values of M. This is physically unacceptable. In addition, it may cause numerical difficulties in the analysis of frame structures using the tangent stiffness formulation.

10.3.2 Jones–Kirby–Nethercot B-Spline Model (1982)

In this model, the experimental $M-\theta_r$ data are divided into a number of subsets, each spanning a small range of moment. A cubic B-spline curve is then used to fit each and every subset of data with continuities of first and second derivatives enforced at their intersections. This model circumvents the problem of negative stiffness and represents the nonlinear $M-\theta_r$ behavior extremely well. However, a large number of data are required in this curve-fitting process.

10.3.3 Colson Power Model (1983)

This model uses a power function of the form

$$\theta_r = \frac{|M|}{R_{ki}} \frac{1}{(1 - |M/M_{cu}|^n)} \tag{10.2}$$

where (Fig. 10.5) R_{ki} is the initial connection stiffness, M_{cu} is the ultimate moment capacity of the connection and n is a parameter to account for the curvature of the $M-\theta_r$ relationship. Since the model has only three parameters (R_{ki}, M_{cu}, n), it is not as accurate as the B-spline model. However, the number of input data required for this model is drastically reduced.

10.3.4 Ang–Morris Power Model (1984)

The Ang–Morris power model has the form

$$\frac{\theta_r}{(\theta_r)_0} = \left| \frac{KM}{(KM)_0} \right| \left[1 + \left(\left| \frac{KM}{(KM)_0} \right| \right)^{n-1} \right] \tag{10.3}$$

where $(\theta_r)_0$, $(KM)_0$ and n are parameters defined in Fig. 10.6; K is the standardization constant dependent upon the connection type and geometry. The Ang–Morris power model is a four-parameter model. It can represent the nonlinear $M-\theta_r$ behavior of a variety of connections reasonably well.

10.3.5 Lui–Chen Exponential Model (1986)

An exponential function is used here to represent the nonlinear connection

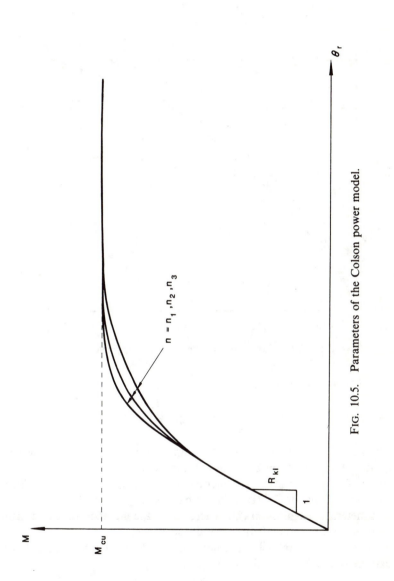

FIG. 10.5.   Parameters of the Colson power model.

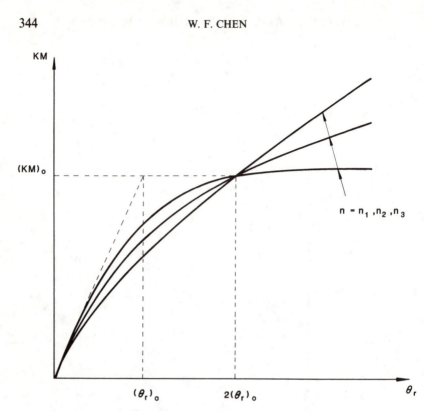

FIG. 10.6. Parameters of the Ang–Morris power model.

behavior. It has the form

$$M = \sum_{j=1}^{m} C_j[1 - \exp(-|\theta_r|/2j\alpha)] + M_0 + R_{kf}|\theta_r| \tag{10.4}$$

where M_0 is the starting value of the connection moment to which the curve
is fitted, R_{kf} is the strain-hardening stiffness of the connection, α is a scaling
factor (for the purpose of numerical stability) and C_j are curve-fitting
constants. This model is a multi-parameter model. The number of
parameters needed is $(m+3)$ where m is the number of curve-fitting
constants (C_j) in eqn (10.4). Generally speaking, $m=4$ to 6 is sufficient for
most cases. The model represents the nonlinear connection behavior
extremely well (Lui, 1985; Lui & Chen, 1985).

10.3.6 Other Nonlinear Connection Models
In addition to the connection models described in the preceding sections,

numerous researchers have developed their own special models that were used to describe the nonlinear behavior of their own connection tests. Examples are the double-web-angle connection model by Lewitt *et al.* (1969), the header plate connection model by Sommer (1969) and the end-plate connection model by Yee & Melchers (1986). Because of the specific nature in application of these models, they are not discussed here. Interested readers should refer to the references cited for a comprehensive discussion of these models.

10.4 METHODS OF ANALYSIS OF FLEXIBLY CONNECTED FRAMES

Having discussed the behavior and modeling of connections in the preceding sections, we now describe several analytical schemes which one can use to predict the response of a flexibly connected frame. Various schemes differ in the manner in which the types and degree of nonlinearity are considered in the analysis. The nonlinearities in a flexibly connected frame are of three types: (1) the nonlinear $M-\theta_r$ relationship of the connection; (2) the geometrical nonlinearity of the member ($P-\delta$ effect) and of the frame ($P-\Delta$ effect); (3) the material nonlinearity or yielding in the members of the frame. Thus, depending on the types of nonlinearity and the degree of accuracy required, three different analysis techniques can be used. These techniques are briefly discussed in the following sections, ranging from the second-order elastic analysis (Sections 10.5 and 10.6) to the second-order elastic-plastic hinge analysis (Section 10.7), and to the second-order elastic-plastic analysis (Sections 10.8 and 10.9) for the members in the frame structures with nonlinear flexible connections and/or with panel zone deformation (Sections 10.10 and 10.11).

10.5 ELASTIC FRAME ANALYSIS WITH NONLINEAR CONNECTIONS

In this analysis, the nonlinear $M-\theta_r$ behavior of the connections is considered. However, material yielding in the columns and beams is not considered. These members are assumed to behave elastically throughout the entire loading process. Although the material nonlinearity in the members is not considered, geometrical nonlinearities ($P-\delta$ and $P-\Delta$ effects) of the framed structure are accounted for in the analysis. This type of analysis is called the second-order elastic analysis with modifications to account for the connection flexibility.

10.5.1 Column Stiffness Relationship

Referring to Fig. 10.7, the force–displacement relationship of the column taking into account the geometrical nonlinear effects in the absence of

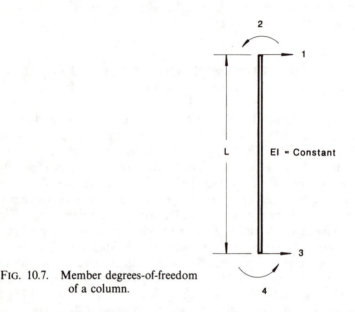

FIG. 10.7.   Member degrees-of-freedom of a column.

in-span loadings can be expressed symbolically as (Chen & Lui, 1987)

$$\mathbf{r} = \mathbf{kd} \tag{10.5}$$

where

$$\mathbf{r} = \{r_1, r_2, r_3, r_4\}^T \text{ is the member end force vector} \tag{10.6a}$$

$$\mathbf{d} = \{d_1, d_2, d_3, d_4\}^T \text{ is the member end displacement vector} \tag{10.6b}$$

$$\mathbf{k} = \frac{EI}{L} \begin{bmatrix} 12\phi_1/L^2 & 6\phi_2/L & -12\phi_1/L^2 & 6\phi_2/L \\ & 4\phi_3 & -6\phi_2/L & 2\phi_4 \\ \text{sym.} & & 12\phi_1/L^2 & -6\phi_2/L \\ & & & 4\phi_3 \end{bmatrix} \tag{10.6c}$$

$$= \text{secant stiffness matrix of the member}$$

where, for the compressive axial force

$$\phi_1 = \frac{(kL)^3 \sin kL}{12\phi_c} \tag{10.7a}$$

$$\phi_2 = \frac{(kL)^2 (1 - \cos kL)}{6\phi_c} \tag{10.7b}$$

$$\phi_3 = \frac{kL(\sin kL - kL \cos kL)}{4\phi_c} \tag{10.7c}$$

$$\phi_4 = \frac{kL (kL - \sin kL)}{2\phi_c} \tag{10.7d}$$

$$\phi_c = 2 - 2 \cos kL - kL \sin kL \tag{10.7e}$$

$$k = \sqrt{P/EI} \tag{10.7f}$$

and for the tensile axial force

$$\phi_1 = \frac{(kL)^3 \sinh kL}{12\phi_t} \tag{10.8a}$$

$$\phi_2 = \frac{(kL)^2 (\cosh kL - 1)}{6\phi_t} \tag{10.8b}$$

$$\phi_3 = \frac{kL (kL \cosh kL - \sinh kL)}{4\phi_t} \tag{10.8c}$$

$$\phi_4 = \frac{kL (\sinh kL - kL)}{2\phi_t} \tag{10.8d}$$

$$\phi_t = 2 - 2 \cosh kL + kL \sinh kL \tag{10.8e}$$

$$k = \sqrt{P/EI} \tag{10.8f}$$

If the axial force in the column is zero, it can be shown by applying the l'Hospital rule successively that $\phi_1 = \phi_2 = \phi_3 = \phi_4 = 1$. For a small axial force, eqns (10.7a–d) and (10.8a–d) may become numerically unstable. To circumvent this situation and also to avoid the use of different expressions for compressive and tensile forces, a power series expansion can be used to simplify the expressions:

$$\phi_1 = \left\{ 1 + \sum_{n=1}^{\infty} \frac{1}{(2n+1)!} [(kL)^2]^n \right\} / 12\phi \tag{10.9a}$$

$$\phi_2 = \left\{ \frac{1}{2} + \sum_{n=1}^{\infty} \frac{1}{(2n+2)!} [(kL)^2]^n \right\} / 6\phi \qquad (10.9\text{b})$$

$$\phi_3 = \left\{ \frac{1}{3} + \sum_{n=1}^{\infty} \frac{2(n+1)}{(2n+3)!} [(kL)^2]^n \right\} / 4\phi \qquad (10.9\text{c})$$

$$\phi_4 = \left\{ \frac{1}{6} + \sum_{n=1}^{\infty} \frac{1}{(2n+3)!} [(kL)^2]^n \right\} / 2\phi \qquad (10.9\text{d})$$

$$\phi = \frac{1}{12} + \sum_{n=1}^{\infty} \frac{2(n+1)}{(2n+4)!} [(kL)^2]^n \qquad (10.9\text{e})$$

where the quantity $(kL)^2 = PL^2/EI$ is positive for a tensile force and negative for a compressive force. It has been shown that the series will converge to a high degree of accuracy with just 10 terms (Goto & Chen, 1987b).

If the axial force in the member falls within the range $-2 \leqslant P/P_e \leqslant 2$ where P_e is the Euler load of the column, the following expressions can be used to closely approximate the ϕ_i values (Lui & Chen, 1986):

$$\phi_1 = 1 + \tfrac{1}{10}(kL)^2 - \left[\frac{1 \cdot 351 \times 10^{-4}(kL)^2 + 0 \cdot 095}{8 \cdot 183\pi^4 + \pi^2(kL)^2} \right] (kL)^4 \qquad (10.10\text{a})$$

$$\phi_2 = 1 + \tfrac{1}{60}(kL)^2 - \left[\frac{1 \cdot 351 \times 10^{-4}(kL)^2 + 0 \cdot 095}{8 \cdot 183\pi^4 + \pi^2(kL)^2} \right] (kL)^4 \qquad (10.10\text{b})$$

$$\phi_3 = 1 + \tfrac{1}{30}(kL)^2 - \left[\frac{2 \cdot 533 \times 10^{-4}(kL)^2 + 0 \cdot 136}{4\pi^4 + \pi^2(kL)^2} \right.$$

$$\left. + \frac{1 \cdot 013 \times 10^{-4}(kL)^2 + 0 \cdot 071}{8 \cdot 183\pi^4 + \pi^2(kL)^2} \right] (kL)^4 \qquad (10.10\text{c})$$

$$\phi_4 = 1 - \tfrac{1}{60}(kL)^2 + \left[\frac{5 \cdot 066 \times 10^{-4}(kL)^2 + 0 \cdot 272}{4\pi^4 + \pi^2(kL)^2} \right.$$

$$\left. - \frac{2 \cdot 026 \times 10^{-4}(kL)^2 + 0 \cdot 143}{8 \cdot 183\pi^4 + \pi^2(kL)^2} \right] (kL)^4 \qquad (10.10\text{d})$$

where, as in the previous case, $(kL)^2 = PL^2/EI$ is positive for a tensile force and negative for a compressive force. For most practical applications, eqns (10.10a–d) give an excellent correlation to the exact values of ϕ_i.

Notice that the stiffness matrix expressed in eqn (10.6c) depends on the axial force in the member, which in turn depends on the displaced configuration of the structure that is not known in advance. As a result, the solution can only be obtained through an iterative process. A brief description of the iterative process will be given in the latter part of this section.

10.5.2 Beam Stiffness Relationship

To incorporate the effect of connection flexibility into the beam slope–deflection relationship, it is a common practice to model the connection as springs with the moment–rotation relationship described by one of the models described in the preceding sections. These springs are then physically tied to the ends of the beam by enforcing equilibrium and compatibility at their junctions. The procedure will be demonstrated below.

Referring to Fig. 10.8(a) in which a beam and two connections (A and B)

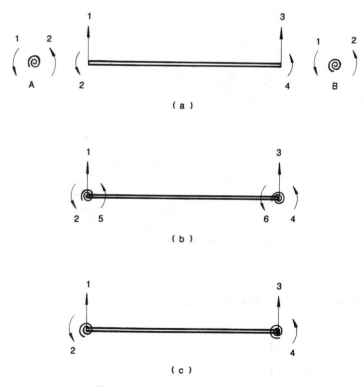

FIG. 10.8. Hybrid beam element.

are shown as three separate elements, the moment–rotation relationships for connections A and B can be expressed as

$$\begin{Bmatrix} r_{1cnA} \\ r_{2cnA} \end{Bmatrix} = \begin{bmatrix} R_{kA} & -R_{kA} \\ -R_{kA} & R_{kA} \end{bmatrix} \begin{Bmatrix} d_{1cnA} \\ d_{2cnA} \end{Bmatrix} \qquad (10.11)$$

$$\begin{Bmatrix} r_{1cnB} \\ r_{2cnB} \end{Bmatrix} = \begin{bmatrix} R_{kB} & -R_{kB} \\ -R_{kB} & R_{kB} \end{bmatrix} \begin{Bmatrix} d_{1cnB} \\ d_{2cnB} \end{Bmatrix} \qquad (10.12)$$

In the above equations, the r's are the moments in the connections and the d's are related to the rotations by $\theta_r = d_{1cn} - d_{2cn}$. R_k is the stiffness of the connection which can be obtained from the M–θ_r curve or the particular connection model used. The subscripts A and B designate the A and B connections, respectively.

On the other hand, the slope–deflection relationship of the beam with in-span loading is given symbolically as

$$\mathbf{r} = \mathbf{kd} + \mathbf{r}_F \qquad (10.13)$$

where $\mathbf{r}$, $\mathbf{d}$ and $\mathbf{k}$ are expressed in eqns (10.6a–c) respectively. $\mathbf{r}_F$ is the fixed-end force vector that depends on the types of in-span loading on the beam. For the simple case of a uniformly distributed loading of intensity w, for example, $\mathbf{r}_F$ can be expressed as

$$\mathbf{r}_F = \left\{ \frac{wL}{2}, \quad \frac{wL^2}{12}\left(\frac{3}{2\phi_3 + \phi_4}\right), \quad \frac{wL}{2}, \quad -\frac{wL^2}{12}\left(\frac{3}{2\phi_3 + \phi_4}\right) \right\}^T \qquad (10.14)$$

To attach the connections to the beam to form a hybrid beam element, it is convenient to consider an intermediate hybrid beam element as shown in Fig. 10.8(b). The slope–deflection relationship for this element can easily be obtained by the standard matrix technique. The process is accomplished by first writing moment–rotation and the slope–deflection relationships for the three elements shown in Fig. 10.8(a) in an augmented form as

$$\begin{Bmatrix} r_{1cnA} \\ r_{2cnA} \\ \mathbf{r} \\ r_{1cnB} \\ r_{2cnB} \\ 8 \times 1 \end{Bmatrix} = \begin{bmatrix} R_{kA} & -R_{kA} & & & & \\ -R_{kA} & R_{kA} & & & & \\ & & \mathbf{k} & & & \\ & & & R_{kB} & -R_{kB} \\ & & & -R_{kB} & R_{kB} \\ & & 8 \times 8 & & \end{bmatrix} \times$$

$$\times \begin{Bmatrix} d_{1\text{cnA}} \\ d_{2\text{cnA}} \\ \mathbf{d} \\ d_{1\text{cnB}} \\ d_{2\text{cnB}} \\ 8 \times 1 \end{Bmatrix} + \begin{Bmatrix} 0 \\ 0 \\ \mathbf{r}_F \\ 0 \\ 0 \\ 8 \times 1 \end{Bmatrix} \tag{10.15}$$

Symbolically, the above relationship can be written as

$$\begin{array}{cccc} \mathbf{r}_{\text{aug}} = & \mathbf{k}_{\text{aug}} & \mathbf{d}_{\text{aug}} + & \mathbf{r}_{F\text{aug}} \\ \{8 \times 1\} & [8 \times 8] & \{8 \times 1\} & \{8 \times 1\} \end{array} \tag{10.16}$$

Next, consider the kinematic relationships between the degrees of freedom of the three elements in Fig. 10.8(a) and those of Fig. 10.8(b). For a small displacement, we can write

$$\begin{Bmatrix} d_{1\text{cnA}} \\ d_{2\text{cnA}} \\ d_1 \\ d_2 \\ d_3 \\ d_4 \\ d_{1\text{cnB}} \\ d_{2\text{cnB}} \\ 8 \times 1 \end{Bmatrix} = \begin{bmatrix} 0 & 1 & 0 & 0 & 0 & 0 \\ 0 & 0 & 0 & 0 & 1 & 0 \\ 1 & 0 & 0 & 0 & 0 & 0 \\ 0 & 0 & 0 & 0 & 1 & 0 \\ 0 & 0 & 1 & 0 & 0 & 0 \\ 0 & 0 & 0 & 0 & 0 & 1 \\ 0 & 0 & 0 & 0 & 0 & 1 \\ 0 & 0 & 0 & 1 & 0 & 0 \\ & & 8 \times 6 & & & \end{bmatrix} \begin{Bmatrix} d_{1\text{int}} \\ d_{2\text{int}} \\ d_{3\text{int}} \\ d_{4\text{int}} \\ d_{5\text{int}} \\ d_{6\text{int}} \\ 6 \times 1 \end{Bmatrix} \tag{10.17}$$

Symbolically, the above kinematic relationship can be written as

$$\mathbf{d}_{\text{aug}} = \mathbf{T}\, \mathbf{d}_{\text{int}} \tag{10.18}$$

By the contragradient law, the equilibrium relationship is

$$\mathbf{r}_{\text{int}} = \mathbf{T}^{\text{T}} \mathbf{r}_{\text{aug}} \tag{10.19}$$

where $\mathbf{r}_{\text{int}}$ and $\mathbf{r}_{\text{aug}}$ are the corresponding force vectors acting on the degrees of freedom of Figs 10.8(b) and 10.8(a) respectively. Substitution of eqn

352   W. F. CHEN

(10.18) into eqn (10.16) and then into eqn (10.19) gives

$$\mathbf{r}_{int} = \mathbf{T}^T \mathbf{k}_{aug} \mathbf{T} \mathbf{d}_{int} + \mathbf{T}^T \mathbf{r}_{Faug} \tag{10.20}$$

or

$$\begin{matrix} \mathbf{r}_{int} & = & \mathbf{k}_{int} & \mathbf{d}_{int} & + & \mathbf{r}_{Fint} \\ \{6 \times 1\} & & [6 \times 6] & \{6 \times 1\} & & \{6 \times 1\} \end{matrix} \tag{10.21}$$

where

$$\mathbf{k}_{int} = \mathbf{T}^T \mathbf{k}_{aug} \mathbf{T} = \begin{bmatrix} k_{11} & 0 & k_{13} & 0 & | & k_{12} & k_{14} \\ 0 & R_{kA} & 0 & 0 & | & -R_{kA} & 0 \\ k_{13} & 0 & k_{33} & 0 & | & k_{23} & k_{34} \\ 0 & 0 & 0 & R_{kB} & | & 0 & -R_{kB} \\ - & - & - & - & | & - & - \\ k_{12} & -R_{kA} & k_{23} & 0 & | & R_{kA}+k_{22} & k_{24} \\ k_{14} & 0 & k_{34} & -R_{kB} & | & k_{24} & R_{kB}+k_{44} \end{bmatrix} \tag{10.22}$$

in which k_{ij} are the entries of the stiffness matrix expressed in eqn (10.6c)

$$\mathbf{r}_{Fint} = \begin{Bmatrix} r_{F1} \\ 0 \\ r_{F3} \\ 0 \\ - \\ r_{F2} \\ r_{F4} \end{Bmatrix} \tag{10.23}$$

in which r_{Fi} are the entries of the fixed-end force vector of the beam in Fig. 10.8(a).

Having developed the force–displacement or the stiffness relationship for the intermediate hybrid beam element of Fig. 10.8(b), this relationship for the hybrid beam element of Fig. 10.8(c) can then be obtained by statically condensing out the degrees of freedom 5 and 6. To accomplish this task, the stiffness relationship of eqn (10.21) is first partitioned as

$$
\left\{\begin{matrix} \mathbf{r}_{\text{inta}} \\ 4\times1 \\ \overline{} \\ \mathbf{r}_{\text{intb}} \\ 2\times1 \end{matrix}\right\} = \left\{\begin{matrix} \mathbf{k}_{\text{intaa}} & | & \mathbf{k}_{\text{intab}} \\ 4\times4 & | & 4\times2 \\ \overline{} & | & \overline{} \\ \mathbf{k}_{\text{intba}} & | & \mathbf{k}_{\text{intbb}} \\ 2\times4 & | & 2\times2 \end{matrix}\right\} \left\{\begin{matrix} \mathbf{d}_{\text{inta}} \\ 4\times1 \\ \overline{} \\ \mathbf{d}_{\text{intb}} \\ 2\times1 \end{matrix}\right\} + \left\{\begin{matrix} \mathbf{r}_{\text{Finta}} \\ 4\times1 \\ \overline{} \\ \mathbf{r}_{\text{Fintb}} \\ 2\times1 \end{matrix}\right\} \qquad (10.24)
$$

Knowing

$$
\mathbf{r}_{\text{intb}} = 0 = \mathbf{k}_{\text{intba}}\,\mathbf{d}_{\text{inta}} + \mathbf{k}_{\text{intbb}}\,\mathbf{d}_{\text{intb}} + \mathbf{r}_{\text{Fintb}} \qquad (10.25)
$$

we have

$$
\mathbf{d}_{\text{intb}} = -\mathbf{k}_{\text{intbb}}^{-1}(\mathbf{k}_{\text{intba}}\,\mathbf{d}_{\text{inta}} + \mathbf{r}_{\text{Fintb}}) \qquad (10.26)
$$

Back-substituting eqn (10.26) into the first set of equations (10.24), we obtain

$$
\mathbf{r}_{\text{inta}} = (\mathbf{k}_{\text{intaa}} - \mathbf{k}_{\text{intab}}\,\mathbf{k}_{\text{intbb}}^{-1}\,\mathbf{k}_{\text{intba}})\,\mathbf{d}_{\text{inta}} + (\mathbf{r}_{\text{Finta}} - \mathbf{k}_{\text{intab}}\,\mathbf{k}_{\text{intbb}}^{-1}\,\mathbf{r}_{\text{Fintb}}) \qquad (10.27)
$$

or

$$
\begin{array}{cccc} \mathbf{r}_{\text{hyb}} = & \mathbf{k}_{\text{hyb}} & \mathbf{d}_{\text{hyb}} + & \mathbf{r}_{\text{Fhyb}} \\ \{4\times1\} & [4\times4] & \{4\times1\} & \{4\times1\} \end{array} \qquad (10.28)
$$

where

$$
\mathbf{r}_{\text{hyb}} = \mathbf{r}_{\text{inta}} \qquad (10.29\text{a})
$$

$$
\mathbf{d}_{\text{hyb}} = \mathbf{d}_{\text{inta}} \qquad (10.29\text{b})
$$

$$
\mathbf{k}_{\text{hyb}} = \mathbf{k}_{\text{intaa}} - \mathbf{k}_{\text{intab}}\,\mathbf{k}_{\text{intbb}}^{-1}\,\mathbf{k}_{\text{intba}} \qquad (10.29\text{c})
$$

$$
\mathbf{r}_{\text{Fhyb}} = \mathbf{r}_{\text{Finta}} - \mathbf{k}_{\text{intab}}\,\mathbf{k}_{\text{intbb}}^{-1}\,\mathbf{r}_{\text{Fintb}} \qquad (10.29\text{d})
$$

It should be pointed out that the stiffness matrix expressed in eqn (10.29c) and the fixed-end force vector expressed in eqn (10.29d) for the hybrid beam element account for *both* the effect of axial force and the effect of connection flexibility of the member. In addition, the stiffness of the connections at the ends of the beam need not be equal. In other words, this formulation allows us to consider cases in which the axial force in the member is appreciable and the connections at the ends of the member are behaving differently. The latter condition may occur even if the connections are identical as a result of their loading/unloading characteristics discussed earlier in this chapter.

10.5.3 Numerical Analysis

In an actual analysis, it is a common practice to express the element stiffness matrix as a 6×6 rather than a 4×4 array in order to take into account the effect of axial deformation. If the effect of curvature shortening (bowing effect) is neglected, a 6×6 element stiffness matrix for the column (Fig. 10.9(a)) and for the beam (Fig. 10.9(b)) can be obtained readily by augmenting the stiffness matrices expressed in eqns (10.6c) and (10.29c), respectively. That is

$$
\mathbf{k}_{col} = \frac{EI}{L}
\begin{bmatrix}
k_{11} & 0 & k_{12} & k_{13} & 0 & k_{14} \\
 & A/I & 0 & 0 & -A/I & 0 \\
 & & k_{22} & k_{23} & 0 & k_{24} \\
 & & & k_{33} & 0 & k_{34} \\
 & & & & A/I & 0 \\
\text{sym.} & & & & & k_{44}
\end{bmatrix}
\tag{10.30}
$$

where k_{ij} are the entries of the matrix $\mathbf{k}$ expressed in eqn (10.6c)

$$
\mathbf{k}_{beam} = \frac{EI}{L}
\begin{bmatrix}
A/I & 0 & 0 & -A/I & 0 & 0 \\
 & k_{11} & k_{12} & 0 & k_{13} & k_{14} \\
 & & k_{22} & 0 & k_{23} & k_{24} \\
 & & & A/I & 0 & 0 \\
\text{sym.} & & & & k_{33} & k_{34} \\
 & & & & & k_{44}
\end{bmatrix}
\tag{10.31}
$$

where k_{ij} are the entries of the matrix $\mathbf{k}_{hyb}$ expressed in eqn (10.29c), and the fixed-end force vector becomes

$$
\mathbf{r}_{Fbeam} =
\begin{Bmatrix}
0 \\
r_{Fhyb1} \\
r_{Fhyb2} \\
0 \\
r_{Fhyb3} \\
r_{Fhyb4}
\end{Bmatrix}
\tag{10.32}
$$

where r_{Fhybi} refers to the entries of the vector $\mathbf{r}_{Fhyb}$ expressed in eqn (10.29d).

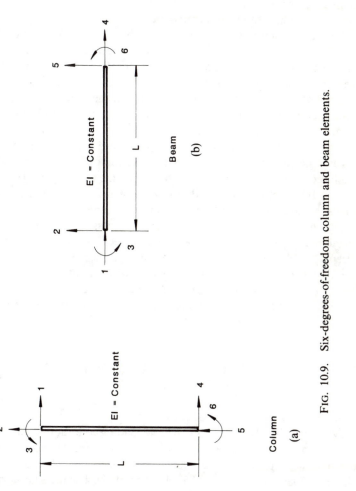

FIG. 10.9.   Six-degrees-of-freedom column and beam elements.

It should be noted that the arrays expressed in eqns (10.30)–(10.32) are functions of the member axial force (P) as well as the connection stiffness (R_{kA} and R_{kB}). All these quantities change continuously as the analysis progresses. As a result, the analysis must be carried out in an iterative manner. To enhance the convergence, the loads should also be applied to the structure in a series of increments.

After the structure stiffness matrix has been formed by assembling the member stiffness matrices, an increment of external force is applied to the structure. Using the structure stiffness relationship, the structure displacement increment can be solved and this increment is added to the cumulative displacement of the structure. Knowing the displacement characteristic of the structure, member internal forces can be calculated. The computed internal forces must be compared to the external applied forces; the discrepancy between the two sets of forces constitutes a set of unbalanced forces. The presence of unbalanced forces indicates that the calculated displaced configuration of the structure is not the true displaced configuration. To refine the geometry of the displaced structure, the set of unbalanced forces should be applied to the structure and a correction to the displacement vector is obtained. This process is repeated until the unbalanced forces or the displacement correction vector falls within an acceptable tolerance. To speed up the convergence, it is advisable to update the stiffness matrix and the fixed-end force vector as often as possible. The solution techniques for nonlinear problems are well documented (Oden, 1972; Zienkiewicz, 1977). Interested readers should refer to the literature for a more thorough discussion of the subject.

10.6 NUMERICAL EXAMPLES OF FLEXIBLY CONNECTED ELASTIC FRAMES

10.6.1 Study of an I-Shaped Subassemblage

Shown in Fig. 10.10 are the geometry and loading conditions of an I-shaped subassemblage. In load sequence 1, the column and beams of this subassemblage are preloaded with concentrated forces of 0·25 kips (1·11 kN). All beam loads are applied at mid-spans of the beams. The horizontal column loads are applied to simulate the out-of-straightness of the column. In load sequence 2, in addition to the column load of $5P$, mid-span beam loads of P are applied in the upper right beam and lower left beam so that single curvature bending of the column will result. The subassemblage was analyzed twice, one analysis being with rigid connections and the other

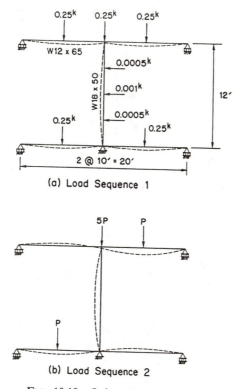

(a) Load Sequence 1

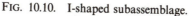

(b) Load Sequence 2

FIG. 10.10.   I-shaped subassemblage.

with flexible connections with the connection moment–rotation behavior shown in Fig. 10.11.

Figure 10.12 shows the distribution of joint moments for the upper joint of the rigidly connected and flexibly connected cases. In both cases, the moment of the left beam M_{BL} and the moment of the column M_C act opposite to the moment of the right beam M_{BR}. Nevertheless their relative magnitudes are quite different. In Fig. 10.13 the moment ratios M_{BL}/M_{BR} and M_C/M_{BR} for both cases are plotted. For the rigidly connected case, the percentages of M_{BR} shared by M_{BL} and M_C do not differ too much because the relative stiffness of the beam and column are quite comparable. For the flexibly connected case, the percentages of M_{BR} shared by M_{BL} and M_C differ significantly because of the presence of the connection; the apparent stiffness of the beam is reduced. For the entire stage of loadings, no

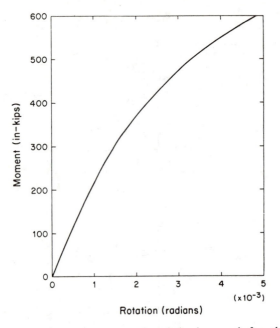

FIG. 10.11. Connection moment–rotation behavior used for the I-shaped
subassemblage.

unloading of the connection was detected in the analysis. As a result, the
tangent stiffness R_{kt} governed the behavior of all the connections for the
whole range of loadings.

If we examine the directions of the column end moments, it can be seen
that they would enhance and not restrain the buckling of the column (Fig.
10.14). For both cases, the analysis was terminated when a plastic hinge
formed at mid-height of the column.

Figure 10.15 shows a subassemblage which is geometrically identical to
the one in Fig. 10.10. The loadings in load sequence 1 are also identical.
However, the loadings in load sequence 2 are altered so that double
curvature bending of the column will result. The distribution of joint
moments of the upper joint for two cases (rigid connection and flexible
connection with moment–rotation behavior shown in Fig. 10.11) is shown
in Fig. 10.16. During the analysis, unloading occurred in the connection
which is attached to the right beam at the upper joint. Consequently, the
initial stiffness rather than the tangent stiffness was used for this connection.

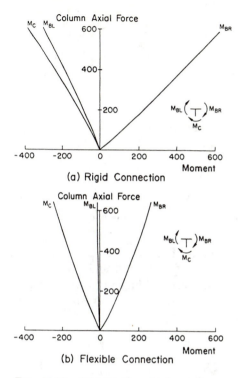

FIG. 10.12. Distribution of joint moments.

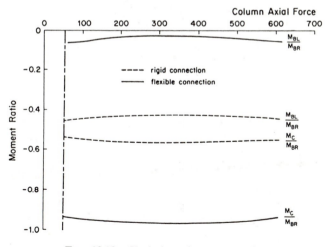

FIG. 10.13. Variation of moment ratio.

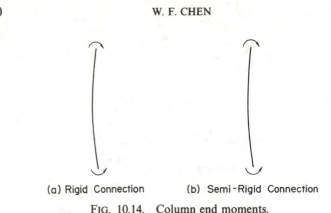

(a) Rigid Connection   (b) Semi-Rigid Connection

FIG. 10.14.   Column end moments.

Note that the directions of the column end moments are such that the column in both the rigidly connected and flexibly connected subassemblages are restrained against buckling (Fig. 10.17). Analysis was terminated when plastic hinges developed in the column at the lower and upper joints

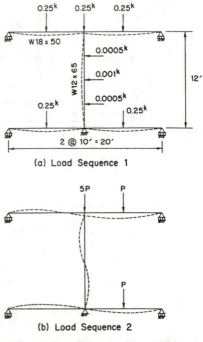

FIG. 10.15.   I-shaped subassemblage.

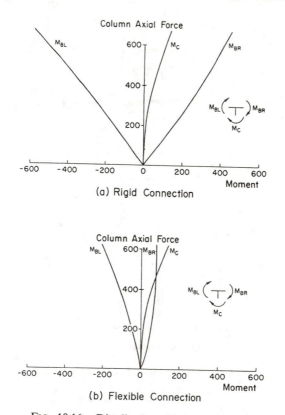

(a) Rigid Connection

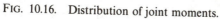

(b) Flexible Connection

FIG. 10.16.   Distribution of joint moments.

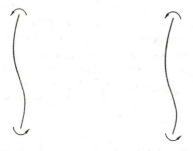

(a) Rigid Connection   (b) Semi-Rigid Connection

FIG. 10.17.   Column end moments.

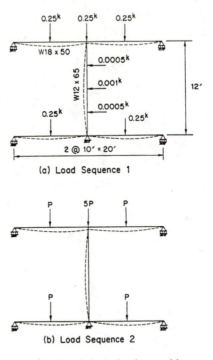

FIG. 10.18.   I-shaped subassemblage.

of the subassemblage for both the rigidly connected and flexibly connected cases.

The behavior of the I-shaped subassemblage if mid-span beam loads are present in all the beams in the second load sequence (Fig. 10.18(b)) can be studied by examining Fig. 10.19 in which the distribution of joint moments of the upper joints is plotted. As can be seen, although the magnitude of beam moments for the rigidly connected case is much larger than that for the flexibly connected case, the column end moments for both cases are almost zero, which means the beams neither induce moment to the column nor restrain it against buckling. Consequently, the column behaves as if it were a centrally loaded column.

10.6.2 Study of a Simple Portal Frame
Shown in Fig. 10.20 is a simple portal frame loaded by horizontal column forces in load sequence 1 to simulate column imperfections and acted on by

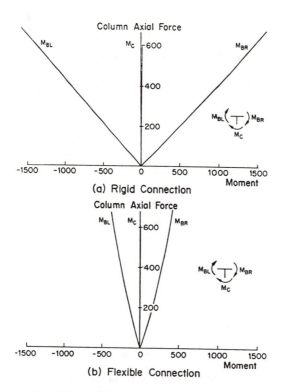

FIG. 10.19.   Distribution of joint moments.

two concentrated forces P, each on each column, in load sequence 2. Five different types of connections (Fig. 10.21) were used in the analyses.

Because of symmetry, only the right half of the structure is modeled. The joint moments before and after the application of load sequence 2 are shown in Figs 10.22 (a) and (b), respectively. The net result of these moments is shown in Fig. 10.22(c) as M_{RC}. Note that M_{RC} is a restraining moment because it restrains the column against buckling.

Figure 10.23 shows quantitatively the variation and magnitude of M_{RC} as P increases for the five different connections. A negative M_{RC} means it is acting clockwise on the column end. As can be seen, regardless of the types of connections used, the beam always provides restraint to the column. The stiffer the connection, the more restraint the beam can offer to the column. Depending on the characteristic of the connection moment–rotation behavior, the restraint that is offered to the column changes as P changes.

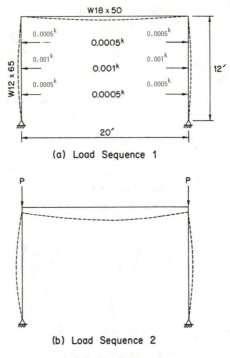

(a) Load Sequence 1

(b) Load Sequence 2

FIG. 10.20.   Simple portal frame.

Except for the very flexible single web connection, the restraint increases as P increases.

In the above example, the beam offers restraint to the column for the entire range of loading because there are no loads on the beam. The behavior of the portal frame will be different if beam loads are present. Figure 10.24 shows such a loading condition. Beam loads are present in load sequence 1 and as a result the direction of joint moment acting on the joint before application of the column load P will be as shown in Fig. 10.25(a). Although the direction of the joint moment induced as a result of application of P (Figs 10.25 (b) and (c)) is opposite to that due to the beam loads, the net result of these moments is being applied to the column (Fig. 10.25 (c)). Consequently, the column should be designed as a beam-column.

The magnitude of the moment M_{RC} that the beam is applying to the column changes as P changes. Except for the very flexible single web angle,

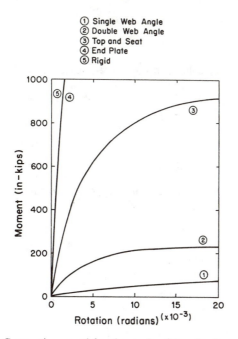

① Single Web Angle
② Double Web Angle
③ Top and Seat
④ End Plate
⑤ Rigid

FIG. 10.21.   Connections used for the study of the simple portal frame.

M_{RC} decreases as P increases as shown in Fig. 10.26. As a matter of fact, depending on the geometry of the frame, the beam and column sections used and the types of connection selected, the magnitude of the moment induced due to the application of P (Figs 10.25 (b) and (c)) may exceed the magnitude of the moment from the beam (Fig. 10.25(a)) with the result that the column will be restrained at a later stage of loading. Since the direction of joint moment changes as soon as P is applied, unloading occurs at the connection and so the initial stiffness R_{ki} of the connection will govern the behavior of the connection.

For the portal frames of Figs 10.20 and 10.24, sway does not occur because both the loading and structure are symmetrical. A more general case in which sway occurs is shown in Fig. 10.27. Sway is induced by the application of a horizontal force H in load sequence 2. The load–deflection curves of this frame using the various types of connections (Fig. 10.21) are shown in Fig. 10.28. Note the increase in load-carrying capacity of the frame as the rigidity of the connection increases. For connections (1), (2) and (3), failure of the frame was due to the formation of a plastic hinge in the

(a) Joint moment before application of P

Translation

Rotation

(b) Joint moment induced as a result of
application of P

(c) Net Result

FIG. 10.22.   Decomposition of joint moment.

connection, whereas for connections (4) and (5) failure was due to the formation of a plastic hinge in the column. Another observation that can be made from Fig. 10.28 is the appreciable increase in drift for the more flexible connections.

Figures 10.29 and 10.30 show the variation of the end moments M_{BA} and M_{BB} for the beam during the entire stage of loading. The dashed lines in these figures mark the demarcation of the two load sequences. If we examine the ratio of these end moments M_{BA}/M_{BB} (Fig. 10.31), an interesting phenomenon can be observed. The rate of increase of M_{BA}/M_{BB} is faster for the more flexible connection. The reason for this can be explained by reference to Fig. 10.32. At the end of load sequence 1, the moments in the connections are not zero, but equal to M_A (Figs 10.32 (a) and (b)) obtained by intersecting the connection moment–rotation curve by a beam line (Frye & Morris, 1976). As load sequence 2 commences, the left

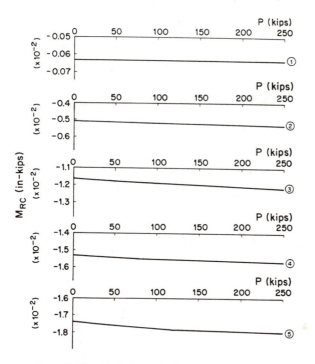

FIG. 10.23.   Variation of column end moment.

connection unloads whilst the right connection loads. As a result, the behavior of the left connection will be governed by its initial R_{ki} while the tangent stiffness R_{kt} will govern the behavior of the right connection (Figs 10.32 (c) and (d)). Since the magnitude of the initial stiffness is always equal to or greater than that of the tangent stiffness, the left end of the beam is comparatively stiffer than its right end with the result that more moment will be drawn to the left end. Usually, the rate of degradation of connection stiffness is higher for the more flexible connection. As a result, for such connections, the ratio of initial stiffness to tangent stiffness will be increased at a higher rate. Consequently, the rate of increase of M_{BA}/M_{BB} will be accelerated for the more flexible connection.

10.6.3 Study of a Four-Story Frame
In order to investigate the effect of connection flexibility on the moment distribution and drift of a multi-story frame, a four-story frame was analyzed in the present study. The geometry and loading conditions of the

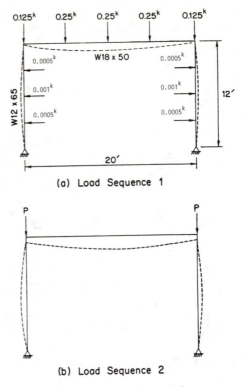

FIG. 10.24. Simple portal frame.

frame are shown in the inset of Fig. 10.33. All the beams are W16 × 40 sections, the columns for the bottom story are W12 × 79 sections and for the other stories are W10 × 60 sections. All sections have a yield stress of 36 ksi (248 MPa). For the purpose of comparison, the frame was analyzed twice, first with rigid connections and then with flexible connections. The flexible connections used were end-plate connections whose moment–rotation behavior is shown in Fig. 10.34.

Two phenomena can be observed from Fig. 10.33. Firstly, the sequence of plastic hinge formation is different for the two frames. Secondly, the flexibly connected frame drifts more than the rigidly connected frame. The percentage increase in drift for each story is shown in Fig. 10.35. As can be seen, although the rigidity of the end-plate connections is quite considerable (Fig. 10.34), a noticeable difference is observed in the moment distribution and drift in the frame.

(a) Joint moment before application of P

Translation   Rotation

(b) Joint moment induced as a result of
application of P

M_{RC}

(c) Net Result

FIG. 10.25.   Decomposition of column end moment.

10.7 ELASTIC-PLASTIC HINGE FRAME ANALYSIS WITH NONLINEAR CONNECTIONS

In this analysis, yielding in the members of the frame is considered. The yielding is assumed to occur ideally in the form of plastic hinges. For segments between plastic hinges or between a connection and a plastic hinge, the member is assumed to behave elastically. This type of analysis can be used to predict the ultimate load-carrying capacity of a steel frame with sufficient accuracy.

Consider Fig. 10.36 in which two hybrid beam elements 1 and 2 are joined together at B. Connections A and C are real connections. Therefore their M–θ_r relationships are given by the connection models described

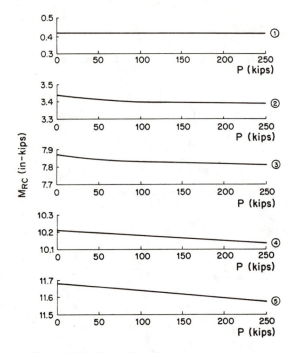

FIG. 10.26.   Variation of column end moment.

previously. Connection B is a pseudo-connection; it is used here to simulate the behavior of a plastic hinge. Therefore its moment–rotation behavior has the following characteristics (Fig. 10.37):

$$\text{For } M_B < M_{pc}, \quad R_{kB} = \infty \tag{10.33a}$$

$$\text{For } M_B \geqslant M_{pc}, \quad R_{kB} = 0 \tag{10.33b}$$

where M_B is the moment at B and M_{pc} is the plastic moment capacity of the section reduced for the presence of axial force. For wide-flange hot-rolled shapes bent about their strong axis, M_{pc} can be expressed approximately as

$$M_{pc} = 1 \cdot 18 \left(1 - \frac{P}{P_y} \right) \tag{10.34}$$

where P is the axial force in the member and P_y is the yield load of the member. Equation (10.33a) implies that, if the moment at B is less than M_{pc},

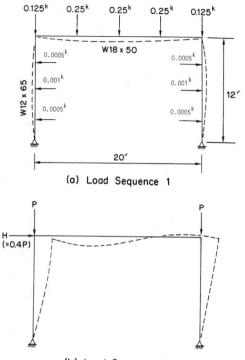

FIG. 10.27.   Simple portal frame with sway.

the right end of member 1 and the left end of member 2 are rigidly joined
together and the two members behave like one continuous beam. On the
other hand, if the moment at B has reached or exceeded M_{pc}, connection
B will behave like a pinned connection and so members 1 and 2 will behave
like a member with a plastic hinge at B. Thus, by using the appropriate
value of R_{kB}, the effect of the presence of a plastic hinge in a member can be
modeled. In numerical implementation, R_{kB} may be taken as $1 \times 10^{10}(EI/L)$
in eqn (10.33a).

It should be noted that the location of B is usually not known in advance.
This poses some difficulties in the preliminary modeling of the structure.
For frames loaded with concentrated forces only, all load points should be
modeled with pseudo-connections. For frames loaded with concentrated
forces and distributed forces, it is advisable to represent the distributed

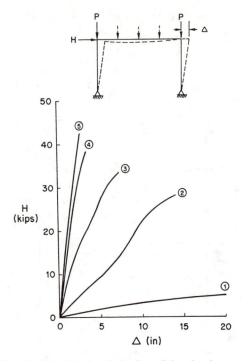

FIG. 10.28.   Load–deflection behavior of the simple portal frame.

force by a series of concentrated forces along the span of the member and
model the load points with pseudo-connections.

By using the above approach, the stiffness matrix expressed in eqn (10.31)
is directly applicable provided that proper values for R_k are used in forming
the matrix.

10.8 ELASTO-PLASTIC FRAME ANALYSIS WITH NONLINEAR CONNECTIONS

In this analysis, the yielding of the beam and column elements is considered
in a more elaborate manner than the elastic-plastic hinge approach. The
assumption of material yielding being concentrated at a point in the form of
a plastic hinge is obliterated. Yielding is a progressive process and so the
transition from elastic to plastic behavior in a cross section is a gradual

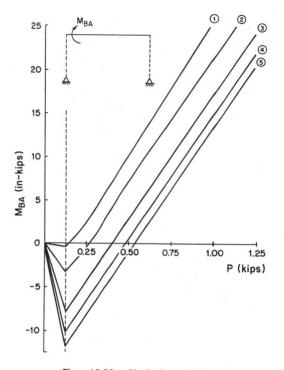

FIG. 10.29.   Variation of M_{BA}.

phenomenon. The gradual yielding process, known as plastification, is revealed in Fig. 10.38 in which a series of moment–curvature–thrust $(M–\Phi–P)$ curves are shown. As can be seen, the variation of moment M with curvature Φ under a constant axial thrust P consists of three regimes: an elastic regime in which the $M–\Phi$ relationship is linear; an elastic-plastic regime in which the $M–\Phi$ relationship is nonlinear; a fully plastic regime in which the curvature increases at an almost constant M. If the moment in the cross sections of the member falls within the first regime, the member will behave elastically whereas, if the moment at a particular cross section is equal to the moment of the third regime, a plastic hinge will form at that cross section. If the moment in the cross section falls in the second regime, the cross section is partially yielded and so the member will exhibit elastic-plastic behavior.

In the elastic-plastic hinge analysis presented in the previous section, we assumed that the second regime does not exist. In the elasto-plastic analysis

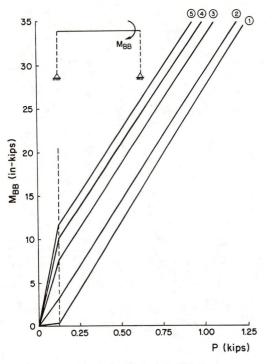

FIG. 10.30.   Variation of M_{BB}.

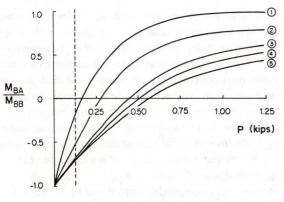

FIG. 10.31.   Variation of M_{BA}/M_{BB}.

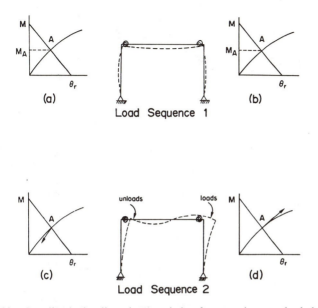

FIG. 10.32. Loading/unloading characteristic of connection on the behavior of the simple portal frame.

presented below, allowance is made to take into account the presence of this regime. The presence of the second regime represents an actual plastification process in the cross section. Thus, the inclusion of this regime in the analysis enables us to incorporate the effect of progressive yielding developed in a structure.

The discussion of the elasto-plastic analysis for a flexibly connected frame follows the work reported by Chen & Zhou (1987) which, in turn, is a modification and an extension of the method of Newmark (1943) for the determination of the maximum load-carrying capacity of a member. In the Newmark numerical procedure, a member is divided into several small segments; the nodes of the segments are referred to as stations. To proceed with the numerical scheme, a set of assumed displacements is assigned to the stations. With a set of known applied forces on the member, the external moments can be calculated at the stations using the assumed displacements. From the M–Φ–P relationship, one can obtain the curvatures at the stations using the calculated moments as input. The curvatures can then be integrated numerically to obtain a new set of displacements. Using this new set of displacements, a new set of external moments is calculated from which

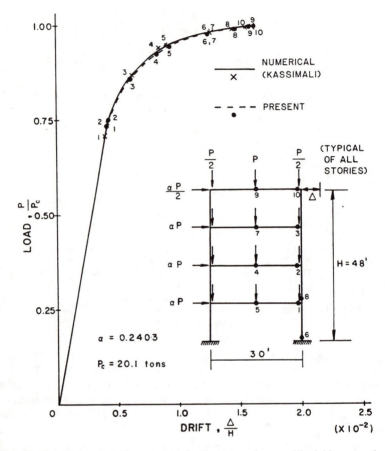

FIG. 10.33. (a)   Load–drift response of a four-story frame with rigid connections
(Kassimali, 1983).

a new set of curvatures can be evaluated. The integration of the new set of
curvatures results in an updated set of displacements. This process is
repeated until a convergence is achieved (i.e. the difference between the
displacements calculated in any two consecutive cycles is negligibly small).

To extend the numerical procedure for the analysis of a non-sway flexibly
connected frame, it is necessary to perform the following steps:

1. Analysis of the column
2. Analysis of the beam

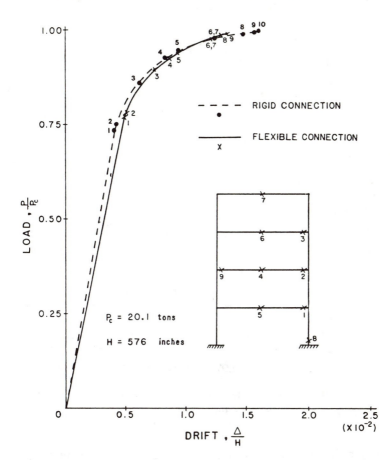

FIG. 10.33. (b) Comparison of the load–drift response of a four-story flexibly connected frame with its rigid counterpart (Kassimali, 1983).

3. Enforcement of equilibrium and compatibility at the beam–column junction.

Figure 10.39(a) shows schematically the result of a column analysis at a constant axial force P. The ordinate represents the column end moment M_{col} and the abscissa represent the column end rotation θ_{col}. Figure 10.39(b) shows schematically the result of a beam analysis under a uniformly distributed load αP. The ordinate represents the beam end moment M_{beam} and the abscissa represents the beam end rotation θ_{beam}. If a connection is

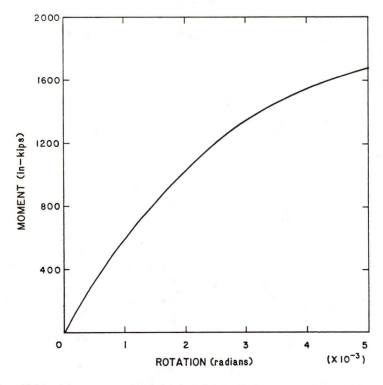

FIG. 10.34.   Moment–rotation behavior of the end-plate connection used for the study of the four-story frame.

present at the beam end (Fig. 10.40), compatibility requires that

$$\theta_{col} = \theta_{beam} - \theta_r \qquad (10.35)$$

where θ_r is the relative rotation of the beam to the column. On the other hand, joint equilibrium requires that

$$M_{col} = M_{beam} \qquad (10.36)$$

A solution satisfying both eqn (10.35) and eqn (10.36) can be obtained graphically as the intersection of the column end moment–end rotation curve of Fig. 10.39(a) with the modified beam end moment–end rotation curve. The modified beam end moment–end rotation curve is obtained by subtracting the $M–\theta_r$ curve of the connection from the beam end moment–end rotation curve of Fig. 10.39(b). This process is shown schematically in

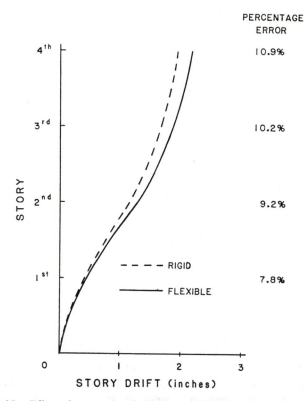

FIG. 10.35.   Effect of connection flexibility on the drift of the four-story frame.

Fig. 10.41(a). By repeating the process at various values of *P*, a moment–rotation curve for the frame can be constructed by connecting these solution points for several *P* values as shown by the dashed line in Fig. 10.41(b). Moreover, if a *P–θ* curve is desired, it can easily be constructed

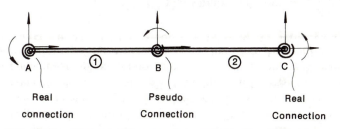

FIG. 10.36.   Element with a pseudo-connection for plastic hinge.

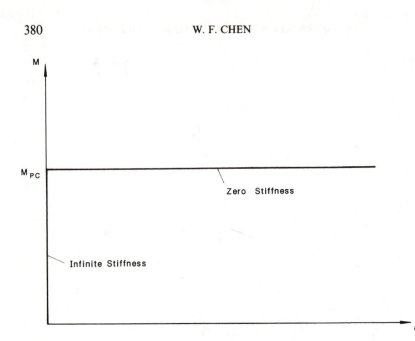

FIG. 10.37. $M–\theta_r$ relationship of the pseudo-connection of plastic hinge.

from the figure simply by reading the specific values of θ that correspond to the particular values of P. Thus, the solution scheme for an elasto-plastic frame analysis includes both an analytical phase and a graphical phase. It is therefore much more time-consuming to perform than the elastic or elastic-plastic hinge frame analysis discussed earlier. Nevertheless, the additional effort is rewarded by a more realistic model of the structure and hence a more reliable prediction of the frame response.

10.9 NUMERICAL EXAMPLES OF FLEXIBLY CONNECTED ELASTO-PLASTIC FRAMES

To gain a better insight into the response of flexibly connected frames, we shall consider the behavior of two simple frames subjected to three idealized loadings. In the forthcoming discussion, two examples will be presented to illustrate the effect of the connection flexibility on frame behavior. In the first example, an elasto-plastic frame analysis of a non-sway portal frame with pinned bases will be presented to demonstrate the effect of the connection stiffness on frame response and the interaction between the

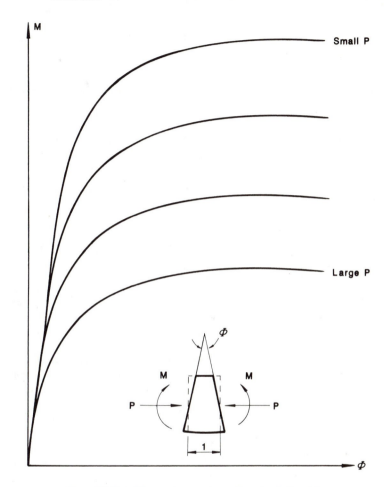

FIG. 10.38.   Moment–curvature–thrust relationship.

beam and column throughout the entire range of loading. In the second example, an elastic-plastic hinge analysis of a sway-permitted simple portal frame with pinned bases will be shown to illustrate the validity of using a linear elastic analysis to predict the frame response in the service load range and to discuss the effect of bracing on frame response.

10.9.1 Analysis of a Non-Sway Frame
Figure 10.42 shows a simple portal frame subjected to a uniformly

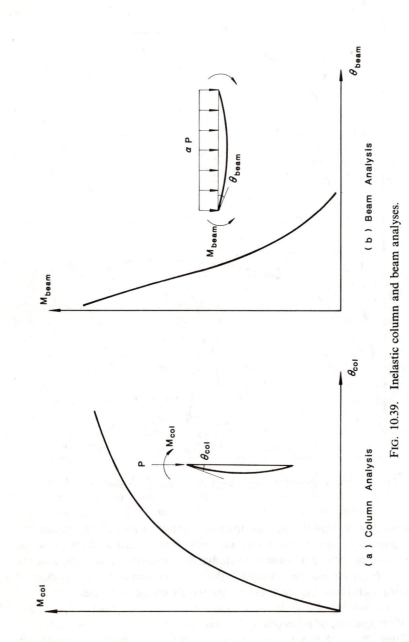

(b) Beam Analysis

(a) Column Analysis

FIG. 10.39.   Inelastic column and beam analyses.

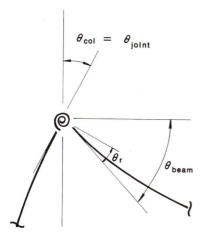

$$\theta_{col} = \theta_{joint}$$

$$\theta_r$$

$$\theta_{beam}$$

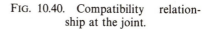

FIG. 10.40. Compatibility relationship at the joint.

distributed load of $2P/3L_b$ on the beam and an axial force of $2P/3$ on each column. The beam is a W16 × 50 section and the columns are W8 × 31 sections. Both residual stresses (for the beam and columns) and initial imperfection (for the columns only) are considered in the analysis. The assumed residual stress distribution and initial imperfection of the columns are shown in Fig. 10.43. An elasto-plastic analysis of the frame was carried out using three types of connections. The $M-\theta_r$ characteristics of the connections are shown in Fig. 10.44. Connection 1 is a rather flexible connection. The ultimate moment capacity of this connection is only 0·57 that of the column. Connection 2 is a rather stiff connection. Its ultimate moment capacity exceeds that of the column and the beam. Connection 3 is a rigid connection. Its behavior is therefore represented by the ordinate of the $M-\theta_r$ plot.

The results of the analysis are shown in Fig. 10.45. Figure 10.45(a) gives the non-dimensionalized load–joint rotation curves of the frame for the three connection types (P_y is the column yield load). An important observation is that the ultimate load-carrying capacities of the three frames are the same regardless of the connection types. The only difference is that the frame with the flexible connection deforms more. The failure of the frame (regardless of the connection types used) is due to column instability. During the final loading phase, progressive yielding in the columns causes them to weaken. Since the beam remains elastic, the apparent decrease in stiffness of the columns due to yielding causes the columns to shed their moments to the beam prior to failure. This phenomenon is depicted in

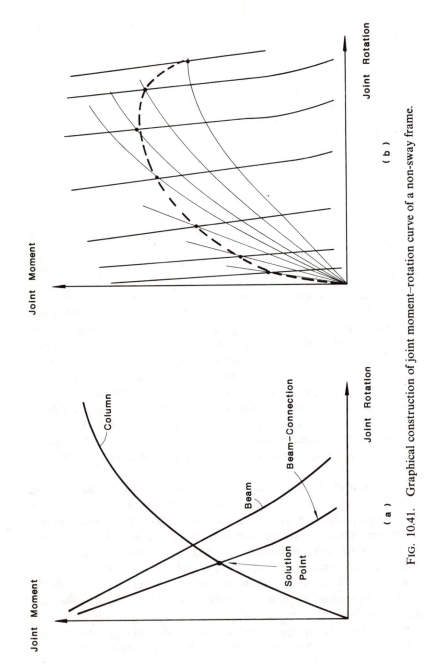

FIG. 10.41. Graphical construction of joint moment–rotation curve of a non-sway frame.

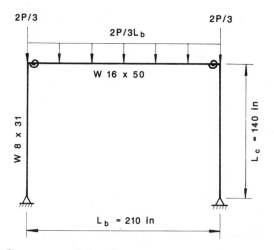

FIG. 10.42. Geometry and loading conditions of the non-sway frame 1
(1 in. = 25·4 mm).

Fig. 10.45(b) in which curves of non-dimensionalized column end moment versus applied force are plotted. Notice the decrease in column end moment prior to the attainment of the failure load of the frame. Also worth noting is that the columns of a frame with the more flexible connections shed their moments to the beam at a later stage than that with the stiffer or rigid connections. The maximum column end moments in three frames are $0.367M_{\text{pcol}}$, $0.396M_{\text{pcol}}$ and $0.404M_{\text{pcol}}$ (M_{pcol} is the plastic moment of the column) for frames with connections 1, 2 and 3, respectively.

From this example, it is clear that the ultimate load-carrying capacity of a simple portal frame is independent of the type of connection used provided that the maximum moment in the connection during the entire loading phase does not exceed its ultimate moment capacity. Furthermore, shedding of moment by the columns to the beam will result when yielding commences while the beam remains fully elastic. The column with the more flexible joint sheds its moment to the beam at a later stage; this can be explained by the fact that, the more flexible the connection is, the less moment it will transmit between the adjoining members for the same rotation. As a result, the yielding of the column with the more flexible joint will be delayed.

To support this argument, consider the simple portal frame shown in Fig. 10.46. The geometry and the loading pattern are the same as for the

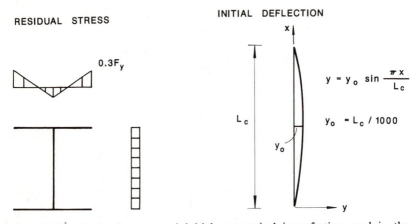

FIG. 10.43. Residual stress and initial geometrical imperfection used in the study.

previous frame, the only difference being that the uniform beam load is now increased to P/L_b and the column loads are decreased to $P/2$. The increase in beam load is such that the moment induced in the connection will exceed the ultimate moment capacity of connection 1 and that the beam will become inelastic prior to the failure of the frame. The non-dimensionalized load–joint rotation curves and the variation of column end moment with the applied force curves are shown in Figs 10.47 (a) and (b), respectively. Notice that the frame with the more flexible connection (connection 1) fails at a lower load level than the ones with the stiffer connection (connection 2) and the rigid connection (connection 3). The latter two frames fail virtually at the same load. From this observation, it is clear that, as long as the connection is strong enough to carry the moment from the adjoining members, the failure load of the frame can be obtained by simply assuming the connection to be rigid.

From the non-dimensionalized column end moment–applied force curves, it can be seen that no moment shedding by the columns to the beam occurs. This is attributed to the fact that the yielding in the columns is accompanied by the yielding in the beam as a result of the increased beam load. When both the beam and the column yield simultaneously, their relative stiffnesses will remain more or less unchanged and so the columns will not shed their moment to the beam. The failure mode for the frame with the rigid joint is due to the formation of a beam mechanism whereas the failure modes for the frames with flexible connections are due to both the

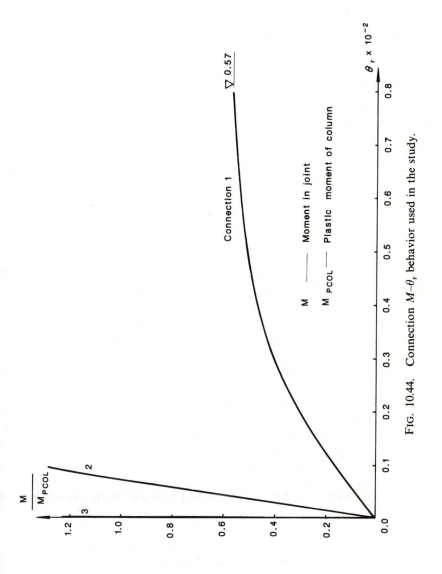

FIG. 10.44.   Connection M–θ_r behavior used in the study.

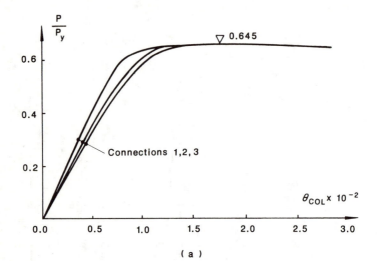

(a)

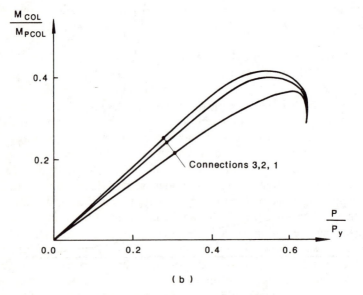

(b)

FIG. 10.45.   Response of non-sway frame 1.

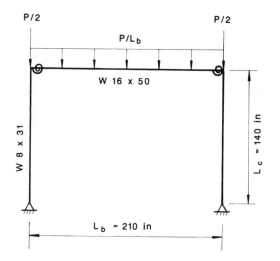

FIG. 10.46. Geometry and loading condition of the non-sway frame 2 (1 in. = 25·4 mm).

formation of a plastic hinge at the mid-span of the beam and the instability of the columns.

10.9.2 Analysis of a Sway Frame

Figure 10.48 shows the geometry of the unbraced frame to be analyzed. The beam is made of a W12 × 22 section and the columns are made of W8 × 31 sections. The loading is applied in two stages: the gravity load is first applied to the beam as a concentrated force at mid-span until it reaches 10 kips (45 kN), and the lateral load is then applied monotonically until failure occurs. The purposes of this analysis are: (1) to investigate the drift behavior of the frame with flexible joints and (2) to study the effect of bracing on the frame response under service load conditions. The elastic-plastic hinge method of frame analysis was used and again three types of connections (Fig. 10.44) were considered in the study.

The load–deflection behavior of the frame with the three types of connections is shown in Fig. 10.49. The discontinuities of the curves labelled 2 and 3 for connections 2 and 3 are due to the formation of plastic hinges in the columns. Again, notice that the two curves merge at the failure load when a sway mechanism is developed in the frame at around 14·3 kips (64 kN). As for the frame with the flexible connection (connection 1), the load–deflection behavior is quite different. It becomes nonlinear at the load

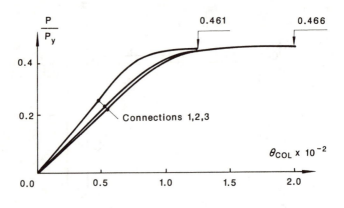

(a)

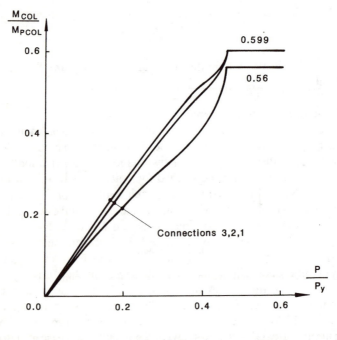

(b)

FIG. 10.47.   Response of non-sway frame 2.

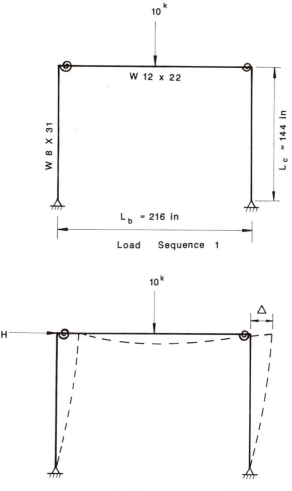

FIG. 10.48. Geometry and loading condition of a sway frame (1 in. = 25·4 mm; 1 kip = 4·45 kN).

level of about 4 kips (18 kN) and shows an appreciable increase in deflection compared to that of the other two frames. As the lateral force reaches about 11 kips (49 kN), the ultimate moment capacity of the leeward connection is reached. The analysis was terminated because the large deflection exper-

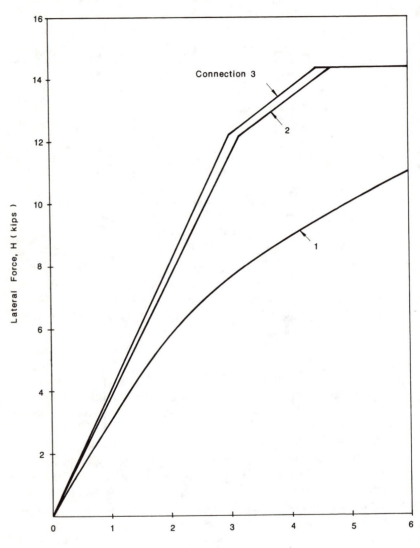

FIG. 10.49. Load–deflection behavior of the sway frame (1 kip = 4·45 kN;
1 in. = 25·4 mm).

ienced by the frame rendered it unstable under the combined action of the lateral and vertical forces. The nonlinear behavior of the flexible frame is attributed mainly to the nonlinear behavior of the connection. Because of the sequence by which the loads are applied, the leeward connection will continue to load whilst the windward connection will unload upon application of the lateral force. Therefore, in the analysis, the instantaneous stiffness was used for the leeward connection whilst the initial stiffness was used for the windward connection. In other words, although the connections are identical, their behaviors were modeled differently in the second stage of loading.

The loading/unloading characteristics of the connections are shown in Fig. 10.50 in which the variations of the left and right beam end moments, designated as M_{BL} and M_{BR} in the figure, are plotted during the second loading stage. The sign convention used for the moment is that a positive moment acts counter-clockwise. At a lateral load of about 8 kips (36 kN), the two curves cross each other with the result that the numerical value for M_{BL} will be larger than M_{BR}. The disproportional variation of moment at the two ends of the beam is due to the difference in stiffness of the two connections. Since the windward connection is relatively stiffer than the leeward connection, more moment will be drawn to the left end of the beam. Hence, the rate of increase of M_{BL} will be greater than that of M_{BR}. In other words, because of the loading/unloading behavior of the connections, the beam will behave as if it were non-uniform with a larger moment of inertia at the windward side of the frame.

So far, we have been dealing only with the strength aspect of the frame. A satisfactory design requires one to consider the serviceability aspects as well. Referring back to Fig. 10.49, if we take the service load to be $14·3/1·7 = 8·4$ kips (37 kN), it can be seen that the deflection of the frames far exceeds the allowable value of 0·48 in. (12 mm) for the most part of the service load range. The value of 0·48 in. was calculated assuming that the maximum drift of the frame may not exceed 1/300 of its height. To reduce the drift of the frame within the acceptable limit in the service load range, bracing must be provided.

The effect of bracing was then considered in this analysis. A diagonal brace made of 5×19 section was used in the model. Bracing elements were modeled as truss elements in the present analysis. The load–deflection response of the braced frame with the same three types of connections but in the service load range is shown in Fig. 10.51. Quite surprisingly, the three curves virtually coincide, indicating that, as far as serviceability is concerned, the response of the frame is independent of the types of

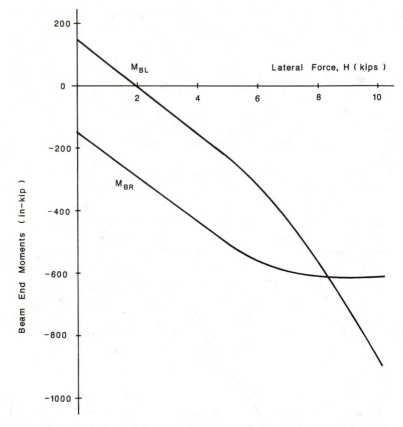

FIG. 10.50.   Variation of beam end moments (1 in.-kip = 0·113 kN-m; 1 kip = 4·45 kN).

connections used if bracing is provided. Furthermore, the response of this braced frame is virtually linear, indicating that a linear elastic analysis may be sufficient for predicting the frame response in the service load range. The response of flexibly connected frames with bracings certainly depends on the relative sizes of the braces and the beams and columns. Their influence on frame behavior should warrant further studies.

10.9.3 General Remarks
Experiments carried out on steel beam-to-column connections over the past decades have demonstrated clearly that the response of a connection is nonlinear when the connection is loaded but becomes linear when it is

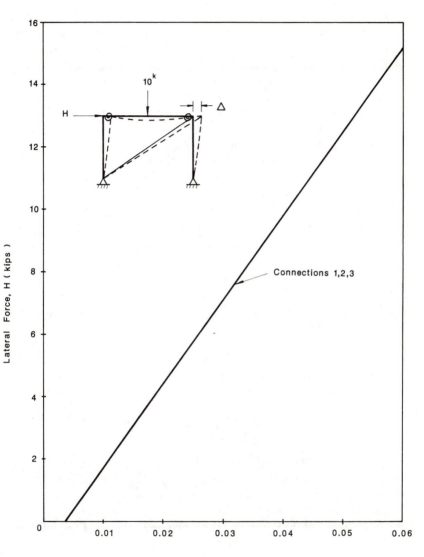

Lateral Displacement , Δ (inches)

FIG. 10.51.   Load–deflection behavior of a sway frame with diagonal brace
(1 kip = 4·45 kN; 1 in. = 25·4 mm).

unloaded. Various mathematical models to represent the connection $M-\theta_r$ behavior have been proposed in the past years by a number of researchers. Some of these models are summarized in this chapter. There are no ironclad rules as to which one is superior to the others; each has its advantages and disadvantages. Nonetheless, all these models can represent the $M-\theta_r$ behavior of the connection fairly well and they have all been successfully used in the analysis of framed structures with flexible joints.

Three different methods of analysis for flexibly connected frames are presented. They range from fairly simple to rather rigorous ones. All these approaches require the use of an iterative scheme because of the nonlinear nature of the problem. The choice of the method of analysis depends on the nature of the problem and the degree of accuracy required.

The analyses of a non-sway frame and a sway frame are presented. Based on these analyses, the following conclusions can be drawn:

1. If the ultimate moment capacity of a connection is larger than the maximum moment it experiences during the entire load history of the frame, the maximum load-carrying capacity of the frame is independent of the types of connection used.

2. Although the maximum load-carrying capacity of the frame may not be affected by the connection, the frame with flexible connections does deform more.

3. Inelasticity in the column may cause the column to shed its moment to the beam provided that the beam remains elastic. The more flexible the connection is, the later the column will shed its moment to the beam because less moment is transmitted to the column from the beam.

4. Connection flexibility may cause early nonlinear behavior for the frame and the loading/unloading characteristics of the connection will alter the moment distribution in the frame.

5. The use of bracing drastically reduces the drift of the frame and the presence of bracing seems to obscure the nonlinear behavior of the connections. Because of this, a linear elastic frame analysis may be sufficient for flexibly connected frames loaded in the service load range.

10.10 FRAME ANALYSIS WITH PANEL ZONE DEFORMATION

In a steel frame, if the beam is framed into the flange of the column, there exists a region called the panel zone which is composed of the web and flanges of the column (Fig. 10.52). The behavior of this panel zone has

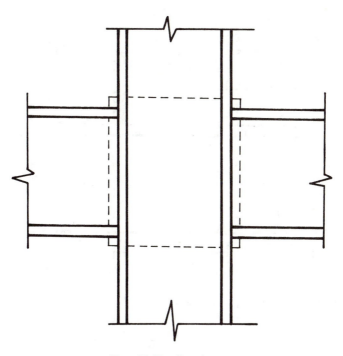

FIG. 10.52.   Panel zone.

a significant influence on the behavior of the frame. Figure 10.53 shows
a possible system of forces that act on the joint panel of an interior
beam-to-column connection. Under the action of these forces, the joint
panel will deform. The various deformation modes are shown in Fig. 10.54.
In addition to causing deformation, these forces may cause premature
yielding of the panel zone, resulting in a reduction in strength and stiffness
of the frame.

Numerous tests (Fielding & Huang, 1971; Bertero *et al.*, 1972; Becker,
1975) have been performed in the past decade to investigate the load–deformation behavior of the joint panel using connection subassemblages.
Particular attention was given to the shear capacity of the panel zone and the
effect of panel zone shear deformation on the strength and stiffness of the
subassemblages. The significant features observed in these tests are (Fielding
& Chen, 1973; Krawinkler, 1978; Kato, 1982):

1. There are two distinct stiffnesses in the joint shear force–deformation
    response of the panel: an elastic stiffness, followed by a smaller, almost

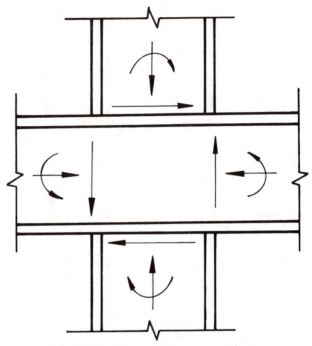

FIG. 10.53.   Forces acting on a panel zone.

constant stiffness for a long range of deformation (Fig. 10.55).
2. Large ductility of the joint panel is observed before failure.
3. Failure is usually caused by fracture of the welds or beam flange on the face of the column flange.

The existence of a second or post-yield stiffness in the shear force–deformation response is attributed to the following (Fielding & Chen, 1973):

1. The resistance of the boundary elements such as the column flanges and stiffeners of the joint panel
2. The onset of strain-hardening of the web of the joint panel before complete yielding of the boundary elements
3. The restraint from the adjoining beams and columns

Based on these observations, a finite element model of the panel zone is presented. This model is capable of representing the various modes of deformation depicted in Fig. 10.54. In addition, yielding and strain-hardening of the web panel are considered. The validity of this model will be demonstrated by comparison with experiments.

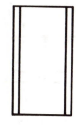
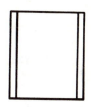

EXTENSION

SHEAR

BENDING

FIG. 10.54.   Deformation modes of a joint panel.

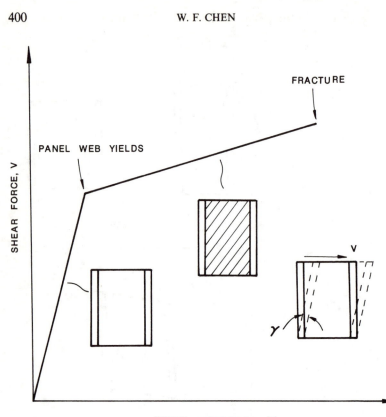

FIG. 10.55.   Typical shear force–distortion behavior of a joint panel.

10.10.1 Basic Assumptions
The assumptions used for the model are:

1. An elastic-perfectly plastic-strain hardening stress–strain behavior of the web panel is assumed (Fig. 10.56).
2. Although large rigid body rotation of the joint panel is allowed, the deformation or distortion of the joint panel remains small.
3. No local buckling or lateral torsional buckling of the panel is allowed. In other words, only strength limit state will be considered for the joint panel in the model.
4. Yielding of the web of the joint panel will occur as the state of stress reaches the yield surface described by the von Mises or J_2 theory.

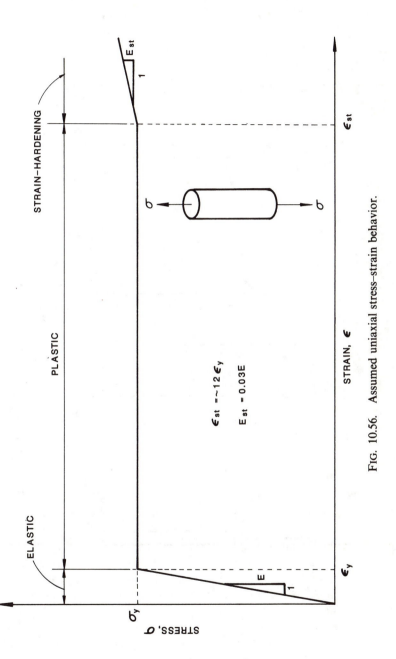

FIG. 10.56. Assumed uniaxial stress–strain behavior.

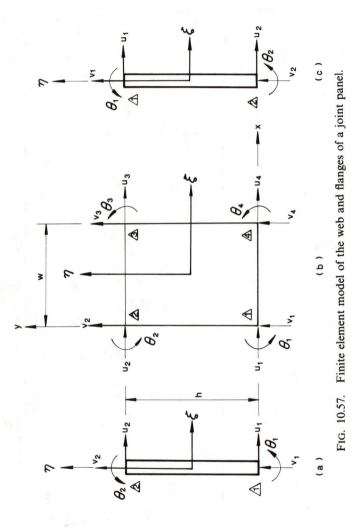

FIG. 10.57.   Finite element model of the web and flanges of a joint panel.

5. The isotropic hardening rule is used to describe the subsequent yield or loading surfaces.
6. Fracture of the material is not considered.

10.10.2 Finite Element Model of Panel Zone
The finite element model of the panel zone is shown in Fig. 10.57. It consists of three elements: one web element and two flange elements. The local (ξ, η) coordinate systems and degrees of freedom of these elements are shown in the figure.

10.10.2.1 Web Panel
Referring to Fig. 10.57(b), the assumed displacement field for this element is

$$
\begin{Bmatrix} u \\ v \\ \theta \end{Bmatrix} = \begin{Bmatrix} u(\xi,\eta) \\ v(\xi,\eta) \\ -\dfrac{\partial u(\xi,\eta)}{\partial y} \end{Bmatrix}
$$

$$
\begin{Bmatrix} u \\ v \\ \theta \end{Bmatrix} = \begin{bmatrix} 1 & \xi & \eta & \xi\eta & \eta^2 & \xi\eta^2 & \eta^3 & \xi\eta^3 & 0 & 0 & 0 & 0 \\ 0 & 0 & 0 & 0 & 0 & 0 & 0 & 0 & 1 & \xi & \eta & \xi\eta \\ 0 & 0 & -\dfrac{2}{h} & -\dfrac{2\xi}{h} & -\dfrac{4\eta}{h} & -\dfrac{4\xi\eta}{h} & -\dfrac{6\eta^2}{h} & -\dfrac{6\xi\eta^2}{h} & 0 & 0 & 0 & 0 \end{bmatrix} \begin{Bmatrix} \alpha_1 \\ \alpha_2 \\ \alpha_3 \\ \alpha_4 \\ \alpha_5 \\ \alpha_6 \\ \alpha_7 \\ \alpha_8 \\ \beta_1 \\ \beta_2 \\ \beta_3 \\ \beta_4 \end{Bmatrix}
$$

$$(10.37)$$

where h is the height of the panel zone.

Using the twelve boundary conditions at the four nodes of the element, the nodal degrees of freedom (u, v, θ) can be related to the generalized degrees of freedom (α, β) by

$$
\begin{Bmatrix} u_1 \\ u_2 \\ u_3 \\ u_4 \\ v_1 \\ v_2 \\ v_3 \\ v_4 \\ \theta_1 \\ \theta_2 \\ \theta_3 \\ \theta_4 \end{Bmatrix} = C_1 C_2 \begin{Bmatrix} \alpha_1 \\ \alpha_2 \\ \alpha_3 \\ \alpha_4 \\ \alpha_5 \\ \alpha_6 \\ \alpha_7 \\ \alpha_8 \\ \beta_1 \\ \beta_2 \\ \beta_3 \\ \beta_4 \end{Bmatrix} \tag{10.38}
$$

where

$$
C_1 = \begin{bmatrix}
1 & & & & & & & & & & & \\
& 1 & & & & & & & & & & \\
& & 1 & & & & & & & & & \\
& & & 1 & & & & & & & & \\
& & & & 1 & & & & & & & \\
& & & & & 1 & & & & & & \\
& & & & & & 1 & & & & & \\
& & & & & & & 1 & & & & \\
& & & & & & & & \dfrac{-2}{h} & & & \\
& & & & & & & & & \dfrac{-2}{h} & & \\
& & & & & & & & & & \dfrac{-2}{h} & \\
& & & & & & & & & & & \dfrac{-2}{h}
\end{bmatrix} \tag{10.39a}
$$

$$\mathbf{C}_2 = \begin{bmatrix} 1 & -1 & -1 & 1 & 1 & -1 & -1 & 1 & 0 & 0 & 0 & 0 \\ 1 & -1 & 1 & -1 & 1 & -1 & 1 & -1 & 0 & 0 & 0 & 0 \\ 1 & 1 & 1 & 1 & 1 & 1 & 1 & 1 & 0 & 0 & 0 & 0 \\ 1 & 1 & -1 & -1 & 1 & 1 & -1 & -1 & 0 & 0 & 0 & 0 \\ 0 & 0 & 0 & 0 & 0 & 0 & 0 & 0 & 1 & -1 & -1 & 1 \\ 0 & 0 & 0 & 0 & 0 & 0 & 0 & 0 & 1 & -1 & 1 & -1 \\ 0 & 0 & 0 & 0 & 0 & 0 & 0 & 0 & 1 & 1 & 1 & 1 \\ 0 & 0 & 0 & 0 & 0 & 0 & 0 & 0 & 1 & 1 & -1 & -1 \\ 0 & 0 & 1 & -1 & -2 & 2 & 3 & -3 & 0 & 0 & 0 & 0 \\ 0 & 0 & 1 & -1 & 2 & -2 & 3 & -3 & 0 & 0 & 0 & 0 \\ 0 & 0 & 1 & 1 & 2 & 2 & 3 & 3 & 0 & 0 & 0 & 0 \\ 0 & 0 & 1 & 1 & -2 & -2 & 3 & 3 & 0 & 0 & 0 & 0 \end{bmatrix}$$

$$(10.39b)$$

From, eqn (10.38), we can write

$$\begin{Bmatrix} \alpha_1 \\ \alpha_2 \\ \alpha_3 \\ \alpha_4 \\ \alpha_5 \\ \alpha_6 \\ \alpha_7 \\ \alpha_8 \\ \beta_1 \\ \beta_2 \\ \beta_3 \\ \beta_4 \end{Bmatrix} = \mathbf{C}_2^{-1} \mathbf{C}_1^{-1} \begin{Bmatrix} u_1 \\ u_2 \\ u_3 \\ u_4 \\ v_1 \\ v_2 \\ v_3 \\ v_4 \\ \theta_1 \\ \theta_2 \\ \theta_3 \\ \theta_4 \end{Bmatrix} \qquad (10.40)$$

Upon substitution of eqn (10.40) into eqn (10.37) and rearranging, we obtain

$$
\left\{\begin{matrix} u \\ v \\ \theta \end{matrix}\right\} = \begin{bmatrix} N_{u1} & 0 & N_{u2} & N_{u3} & 0 & N_{u4} & N_{u5} & 0 & N_{u6} & N_{u7} & 0 & N_{u8} \\ 0 & N_{v1} & 0 & 0 & N_{v2} & 0 & 0 & N_{v3} & 0 & 0 & N_{v4} & 0 \\ N_{\theta1} & 0 & N_{\theta2} & N_{\theta3} & 0 & N_{\theta4} & N_{\theta5} & 0 & N_{\theta6} & N_{\theta7} & 0 & N_{\theta8} \end{bmatrix} \left\{\begin{matrix} u_1 \\ v_1 \\ \theta_1 \\ u_2 \\ v_2 \\ \theta_2 \\ u_3 \\ v_3 \\ \theta_3 \\ u_4 \\ v_4 \\ \theta_4 \end{matrix}\right\}
$$

(10.41)

where

$$N_{u1} = \tfrac{1}{8}(2 - 3\eta + \eta^3)(1 - \xi)$$

$$N_{u2} = \frac{-h}{16}(1 - \eta - \eta^2 + \eta^3)(1 - \xi)$$

$$N_{u3} = \tfrac{1}{8}(2 + 3\eta - \eta^3)(1 - \xi)$$

$$N_{u4} = \frac{-h}{16}(-1 - \eta + \eta^2 + \eta^3)(1 - \xi)$$

$$N_{u5} = \tfrac{1}{8}(2 + 3\eta - \eta^3)(1 + \xi)$$

$$N_{u6} = \frac{-h}{16}(-1 - \eta + \eta^2 + \eta^3)(1 + \xi)$$

$$N_{u7} = \tfrac{1}{8}(2 - 3\eta + \eta^3)(1 + \xi)$$

$$N_{u8} = \frac{-h}{16}(1 - \eta - \eta^2 + \eta^3)(1 + \xi)$$

$$N_{v1} = \tfrac{1}{4}(1-\xi)(1-\eta)$$

$$N_{v2} = \tfrac{1}{4}(1-\xi)(1+\eta)$$

$$N_{v3} = \tfrac{1}{4}(1+\xi)(1+\eta)$$

$$N_{v4} = \tfrac{1}{4}(1+\xi)(1-\eta)$$

$$N_{\theta 1} = \frac{-1}{4h}(1-\xi)(-3+3\eta^2)$$

$$N_{\theta 2} = \tfrac{1}{8}(1-\xi)(-1-2\eta+3\eta^2)$$

$$N_{\theta 3} = \frac{-1}{4h}(1-\xi)(3-3\eta^2)$$

$$N_{\theta 4} = \tfrac{1}{8}(1-\xi)(-1+2\eta+3\eta^2)$$

$$N_{\theta 5} = \frac{-1}{4h}(1+\xi)(3-3\eta^2)$$

$$N_{\theta 6} = \tfrac{1}{8}(1+\xi)(-1+2\eta+3\eta^2)$$

$$N_{\theta 7} = \frac{-1}{4h}(1+\xi)(-3+3\eta^2)$$

$$N_{\theta 8} = \tfrac{1}{8}(1+\xi)(-1-2\eta+3\eta^2)$$

Symbolically, eqn (10.41) can be written as

$$\mathbf{u}_w = \mathbf{N}_w \mathbf{d}_w \tag{10.42}$$

The next step in evaluating the element stiffness matrix using the finite element method is to formulate the strain–displacement relationship. The strain–displacement relationship can be written as

$$\boldsymbol{\varepsilon}_w = \left\{ \begin{array}{c} \varepsilon_x \\ \varepsilon_y \\ \gamma_{xy} \end{array} \right\} = \begin{bmatrix} 1 & 0 & 0 & 0 \\ 0 & 0 & 0 & 1 \\ 0 & 1 & 1 & 0 \end{bmatrix} \begin{bmatrix} \mathbf{J}^{-1} & 0 \\ 0 & \mathbf{J}^{-1} \end{bmatrix} \begin{bmatrix} \dfrac{\partial}{\partial \xi} & 0 & 0 \\[2mm] \dfrac{\partial}{\partial \eta} & 0 & 0 \\[2mm] 0 & \dfrac{\partial}{\partial \xi} & 0 \\[2mm] 0 & \dfrac{\partial}{\partial \eta} & 0 \end{bmatrix} \mathbf{N}_w \mathbf{d}_w$$

$$\tag{10.43}$$

where J^{-1} is the inverse of the Jacobian matrix given by

$$\mathbf{J}^{-1} = \begin{bmatrix} \dfrac{\partial x}{\partial \xi} & \dfrac{\partial y}{\partial \xi} \\[2mm] \dfrac{\partial x}{\partial \eta} & \dfrac{\partial y}{\partial \eta} \end{bmatrix}^{-1} = \begin{bmatrix} \dfrac{w}{2} & 0 \\[2mm] 0 & \dfrac{2}{h} \end{bmatrix}^{-1} = \begin{bmatrix} \dfrac{2}{w} & 0 \\[2mm] 0 & \dfrac{2}{h} \end{bmatrix} \tag{10.44}$$

Carrying out the matrix manipulation, eqn (10.43) can be written as

$$\varepsilon_w = \mathbf{B}_w \mathbf{d}_w \tag{10.45}$$

where

$$\mathbf{B}_w = [\mathbf{B}_{w1}\, \mathbf{B}_{w2}\, \mathbf{B}_{w3}\, \mathbf{B}_{w4}] \tag{10.46}$$

$$\mathbf{B}_{w1} = \begin{bmatrix} \dfrac{-1}{4w}(2-3\eta+\eta^3) & 0 & \dfrac{h}{8w}(1-\eta-\eta^2+\eta^3) \\[3mm] 0 & \dfrac{-1}{2h}(1-\xi) & 0 \\[3mm] \dfrac{1}{4h}(1-\xi)(-3+3\eta^2) & \dfrac{-1}{2w}(1-\eta) & \dfrac{1}{8}(1-\xi)(-1-2\eta+3\eta^2) \end{bmatrix}$$

$$\mathbf{B}_{w2} = \begin{bmatrix} \dfrac{-1}{4w}(2+3\eta-\eta^3) & 0 & \dfrac{h}{8w}(-1-\eta+\eta^2+\eta^3) \\[3mm] 0 & \dfrac{1}{2h}(1-\xi) & 0 \\[3mm] \dfrac{1}{4h}(1-\xi)(3-3\eta^2) & \dfrac{-1}{2w}(1+\eta) & \dfrac{-1}{8}(1-\xi)(-1+2\eta+3\eta^2) \end{bmatrix}$$

$$\mathbf{B}_{w3} = \begin{bmatrix} \dfrac{1}{4w}(2+3\eta-\eta^3) & 0 & \dfrac{-h}{8w}(-1-\eta+\eta^2+\eta^3) \\[3mm] 0 & \dfrac{1}{2h}(1+\xi) & 0 \\[3mm] \dfrac{1}{4h}(1+\xi)(3-3\eta^2) & \dfrac{1}{2w}(1+\eta) & \dfrac{-1}{8}(1+\xi)(-1+2\eta+3\eta^2) \end{bmatrix}$$

$$\mathbf{B}_{w4} = \begin{bmatrix} \dfrac{1}{4w}(2-3\eta+\eta^3) & 0 & \dfrac{-h}{8w}(1-\eta-\eta^2+\eta^3) \\[3mm] 0 & \dfrac{-1}{2h}(1+\xi) & 0 \\[3mm] \dfrac{1}{4h}(1+\xi)(-3+3\eta^2) & \dfrac{1}{2w}(1-\eta) & \dfrac{-1}{8}(1+\xi)(-1-2\eta+3\eta^2) \end{bmatrix}$$

in which h is the height of the panel zone and w is the width of the panel web.

Having developed the strain–displacement relationship, the stiffness matrix of the web of the panel zone can be written as

$$\mathbf{k}_w = \int_V \mathbf{B}_w^T \mathbf{D} \mathbf{B}_w \, dV = t_w \int_{-1}^{1} \int_{-1}^{1} \mathbf{B}_w^T \mathbf{D} \mathbf{B}_w |J| \, d\xi \, d\eta \qquad (10.47)$$

where t_w is the thickness of the column web in the panel zone

$$|J| = \begin{bmatrix} \dfrac{w}{2} & 0 \\[2mm] 0 & \dfrac{h}{2} \end{bmatrix} = \dfrac{hw}{4}$$

$$\mathbf{D} = \begin{cases} \mathbf{D}^e & \text{if the panel web element is elastic} \\ \mathbf{D}^{ep} & \text{if the panel web element has yielded} \end{cases}$$

in which

$$\mathbf{D}^e = \dfrac{E}{1-v^2} \begin{bmatrix} 1 & v & 0 \\ v & 1 & 0 \\ 0 & 0 & \dfrac{1-v}{2} \end{bmatrix}$$

and $\mathbf{D}^{ep}$ is the elastic-plastic stress–strain relationship (see eqn (10.68)).

Equation (10.47) can be integrated numerically by using a 2×4 Gauss–Legendre quadrature (Fig. 10.58), i.e.

$$\mathbf{k}_w = \dfrac{hwt_w}{4} \sum_{i=1}^{2} \sum_{j=1}^{4} W_i W_j [\mathbf{B}_w^T \mathbf{D} \mathbf{B}_w]_{\xi=\xi_i,\ \eta=\eta_j} \qquad (10.48)$$

where W_i and W_j are weight coefficients (Table 10.1)

$\mathbf{k}_w$ expressed in eqn (10.48) is the stiffness matrix of the web element of the panel zone with reference to a local coordinate system. The incremental

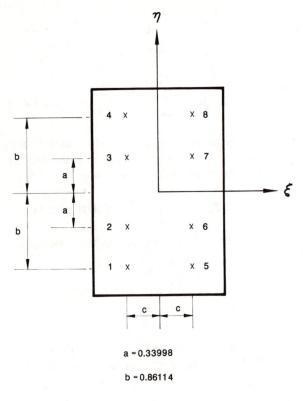

a = 0.33998

b = 0.86114

c = 0.57735

Fig. 10.58.　Gauss points of the panel web element.

TABLE 10.1
WEIGHT COEFFICIENTS

Gauss point	W_i	W_j
1	1·00 000	0·34 785
2	1·00 000	0·65 215
3	1·00 000	0·65 215
4	1·00 000	0·34 785
5	1·00 000	0·34 785
6	1·00 000	0·65 215
7	1·00 000	0·65 215
8	1·00 000	0·34 785

form of this stiffness matrix is the same as $\mathbf{k}_w$ since the entries of $\mathbf{k}_w$ are independent of the displacement, i.e.

$$\acute{\mathbf{k}}_w = \mathbf{k}_w \tag{10.49}$$

10.10.2.2 Flange Element

The local (ξ, η) coordinate system and the degrees of freedom of the two flange elements for the panel zone are shown in Figs 10.57(a) and 10.57(c), respectively.

For simplicity, the stiffness matrices used for these flange elements are those of the ordinary frame element, i.e. for the left flange

$$
\mathbf{k}_{lf} = \frac{EI_f}{h^3}
\begin{bmatrix}
12 & 0 & -6h & -12 & 0 & -6h \\
 & \dfrac{h^2 A_f}{I} & 0 & 0 & \dfrac{-h^2 A_f}{I} & 0 \\
 & & 4h^2 & 6h & 0 & 2h^2 \\
 & & & 12 & 0 & 6h \\
 & \text{sym.} & & & \dfrac{h^2 A_f}{I} & 0 \\
 & & & & & 4h^2
\end{bmatrix}
\tag{10.50}
$$

and for the right flange

$$
\mathbf{k}_{rf} = \frac{EI_f}{h^3}
\begin{bmatrix}
12 & 0 & 6h & -12 & 0 & 6h \\
 & \dfrac{h^2 A_f}{I} & 0 & 0 & \dfrac{-h^2 A_f}{I} & 0 \\
 & & 4h^2 & -6h & 0 & 2h^2 \\
 & & & 12 & 0 & -6h \\
 & \text{sym.} & & & \dfrac{h^2 A_f}{I} & 0 \\
 & & & & & 4h^2
\end{bmatrix}
\tag{10.51}
$$

where h is the height of the panel zone

$$I_f = \frac{1}{12} b_f t_f^3$$

$$A_f = b_f t_f$$

in which b_f is the width of the column flange and t_f is the thickness of the column flange.

The corresponding incremental forms of $\mathbf{k}_{lf}$ and $\mathbf{k}_{rf}$ are

$$\dot{\mathbf{k}}_{lf} = \mathbf{k}_{lf} \tag{10.52}$$

$$\dot{\mathbf{k}}_{rf} = \mathbf{k}_{rf} \tag{10.53}$$

Now, the incremental stiffness matrices for the three elements of the panel zone (Figs 10.57(a–c)) are developed, the incremental stiffness matrix $\dot{\mathbf{k}}_{lp}$ of the panel zone (Fig. 10.59) with respect to a local coordinate system can be obtained by assemblage

$$\dot{\mathbf{k}}_{lp} = \text{assembling} \begin{array}{c} \mathbf{T}_{olf}^T \dot{\mathbf{k}}_{lf} \mathbf{T}_{olf} \\ \mathbf{T}_{ow}^T \dot{\mathbf{k}}_w \mathbf{T}_{ow} \\ \mathbf{T}_{orf}^T \dot{\mathbf{k}}_{rf} \mathbf{T}_{orf} \end{array} \tag{10.54}$$

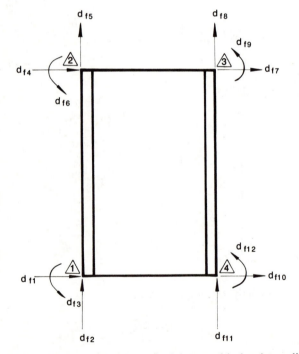

FIG. 10.59.   Degress of freedom of a joint panel in local coordinate.

where

$\mathbf{T}_{olf}$ = offset transformation matrix of the left flange element

$$= \begin{bmatrix} \mathbf{H}_{lf} & \mathbf{0} \\ \mathbf{0} & \mathbf{H}_{lf} \end{bmatrix} \qquad (10.55)$$

in which

$$\mathbf{H}_{lf} = \begin{bmatrix} 1 & 0 & 0 \\ 0 & 1 & t_f/2 \\ 0 & 0 & 1 \end{bmatrix} \qquad (10.56)$$

$\mathbf{T}_{ow}$ = offset transformation matrix of the web element

$$= \begin{bmatrix} \mathbf{H}_{lw} & 0 & 0 & 0 \\ 0 & \mathbf{H}_{lw} & 0 & 0 \\ 0 & 0 & \mathbf{H}_{rw} & 0 \\ 0 & 0 & 0 & \mathbf{H}_{rw} \end{bmatrix} \qquad (10.57)$$

in which

$$\mathbf{H}_{lw} = \begin{bmatrix} 1 & 0 & 0 \\ 0 & 1 & t_f \\ 0 & 0 & 1 \end{bmatrix} \qquad (10.58)$$

$$\mathbf{H}_{rw} = \begin{bmatrix} 1 & 0 & 0 \\ 0 & 1 & -t_f \\ 0 & 0 & 1 \end{bmatrix} \qquad (10.59)$$

$\mathbf{T}_{orf}$ = offset transformation matrix of the right flange element

$$= \begin{bmatrix} \mathbf{H}_{rf} & \mathbf{0} \\ \mathbf{0} & \mathbf{H}_{rf} \end{bmatrix} \qquad (10.60)$$

in which

$$\mathbf{H}_{rf} = \begin{bmatrix} 1 & 0 & 0 \\ 0 & 1 & -t_f/2 \\ 0 & 0 & 1 \end{bmatrix} \qquad (10.61)$$

In the above equations, t_f is the thickness of the column flange.

These offset transformation matrices are needed due to the fact that the degrees of freedom of the web and flange elements (Figs 10.57(a–c)) do not coincide with those of the panel element (Fig. 10.59). In writing these matrices, it is tacitly assumed that the through-thickness and shear strains of the flanges of the column are negligible. These assumptions are in conformity with experimental observations.

The incremental stiffness matrix expressed in eqn (10.54) was developed with respect to a local coordinate system which translates and rotates with the element. To incorporate the panel element in a general frame analysis, this stiffness matrix must be expressed with respect to a fixed or global coordinate system. The incremental stiffness matrix of the panel element expressed with respect to a fixed (X, Y) coordinate system is given by

$$\dot{\mathbf{k}}_{gp} = \mathbf{T}_{lg}^{\mathsf{T}} \dot{\mathbf{k}}_{lp} \mathbf{T}_{lg} \tag{10.62}$$

where

$$\mathbf{T}_{lg} = \begin{bmatrix} \mathbf{t}_{lg} & 0 & 0 & 0 \\ 0 & \mathbf{t}_{lg} & 0 & 0 \\ 0 & 0 & \mathbf{t}_{lg} & 0 \\ 0 & 0 & 0 & \mathbf{t}_{lg} \end{bmatrix} \tag{10.63}$$

in which

$$\mathbf{t}_{lg} = \begin{bmatrix} \cos \theta_{lg} & \sin \theta_{lg} & 0 \\ -\sin \theta_{lg} & \cos \theta_{lg} & 0 \\ 0 & 0 & 1 \end{bmatrix} \tag{10.64}$$

where (see Fig. 10.60)

$$\theta_{lg} = \frac{1}{4}\left(\tan^{-1} \frac{d_{g1} - d_{g4}}{h + d_{g5} - d_{g2}} + \tan^{-1} \frac{d_{g8} - d_{g5}}{w + d_{g7} - d_{g4}} \right.$$

$$\left. + \tan^{-1} \frac{d_{g10} - d_{g7}}{h + d_{g8} - d_{g11}} + \tan^{-1} \frac{d_{g11} - d_{g2}}{w + d_{g10} - d_{g1}} \right) \tag{10.65}$$

10.10.2.3 Panel Zone Plasticity

When the state of stress of the panel web reaches a limit defined by the von Mises (or J_2) theory (Chen, 1982; Chen & Han, 1988)

$$f = J_2 - \frac{\sigma_y^2}{3} = 0 \tag{10.66}$$

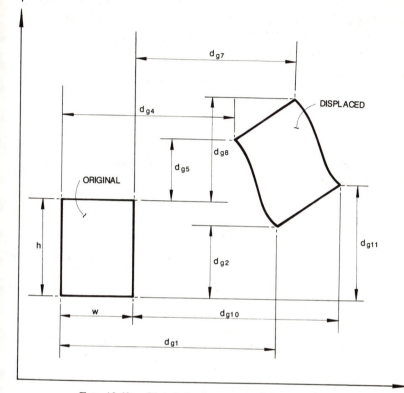

FIG. 10.60. Global displacements of the panel element.

where, for plane stress case

$$J_2 = \tfrac{1}{3}(\sigma_{xx}^2 - \sigma_{xx}\sigma_{yy} + \sigma_{yy}^2 + 3\tau_{xy}^2)$$

σ_y is the yield stress of the material under the uniaxial tension test (Fig. 10.56); the column web of the panel zone is assumed to be yielded.

If strain-hardening of the material is considered (Fig. 10.56) then, in addition to describing the initial yield surface (eqn (10.66)), we need to define a subsequent yield (or loading) surface. If isotropic hardening is assumed in which the loading surface is described by a uniform expansion of the initial yield surface, then eqn (10.66) can be generalized to

$$f = J_2 - k^2 = 0 \qquad (10.67)$$

where k is the hardening parameter.

Once eqn (10.66) or eqn (10.67) is satisfied, the elastic-plastic stress–strain matrix $\mathbf{D}^{ep}$ will be used in place of the elastic stress–strain matrix $\mathbf{D}^e$ in evaluating $\mathbf{k}_w$ in eqn (10.47) or eqn (10.48).

The elastic-plastic stress–strain matrix is given (Chen, 1982) by

$$\mathbf{D}^{ep} = \mathbf{D}^e - \frac{\mathbf{D}^e \left(\dfrac{\partial f}{\partial \boldsymbol{\sigma}}\right) \left(\dfrac{\partial f}{\partial \boldsymbol{\sigma}}\right)^T \mathbf{D}^e}{\left(\dfrac{\partial f}{\partial \boldsymbol{\sigma}}\right)^T \mathbf{D}^e \left(\dfrac{\partial f}{\partial \boldsymbol{\sigma}}\right) + A} \tag{10.68}$$

where, for the J_2 theory and the associate flow rule under the plane stress condition, we have

$$\mathbf{D}^e = \text{elastic stress–strain matrix}$$

$$\frac{\partial f}{\partial \boldsymbol{\sigma}} = \mathbf{S} = \text{deviatoric stress vector}$$

$$= \left\{ \begin{array}{c} \dfrac{2\sigma_{xx} - \sigma_{yy}}{3} \\[2mm] \dfrac{2\sigma_{yy} - \sigma_{xx}}{3} \\[2mm] 2\tau_{xy} \end{array} \right\} \tag{10.69}$$

$$A = \frac{4\sqrt{3}}{9} \sigma_e^2 H' \tag{10.70}$$

in which

$$\sigma_e = (\sigma_{xx}^2 - \sigma_{xx}\sigma_{yy} + \sigma_{yy}^2 + 3\tau_{xy}^2)^{1/2} \tag{10.71}$$

$$H' = \frac{dk}{d\varepsilon_p} = \left\{ \begin{array}{ll} 0 & \text{if } \varepsilon_p \leqslant 11\varepsilon_y \\[3mm] \dfrac{1}{\sqrt{3}} \dfrac{EE_{st}}{E - E_{st}} & \text{if } \varepsilon_p > 11\varepsilon_y \end{array} \right. \tag{10.72}$$

H' is the slope of the hardening parameter k versus the effective strain ε_p plot (Fig. 10.61). Note that $\mathbf{D}^{ep}$ is a function of the state of stress and the effective strain.

In the numerical analysis, once eqn (10.66) or eqn (10.67) is satisfied, this elastic-plastic stress–strain matrix is used in place of the elastic stress–strain

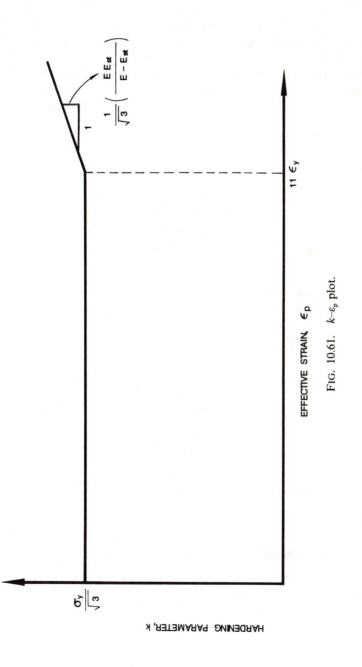

FIG. 10.61. k–ϵ_p plot.

matrix in evaluating the panel incremental stiffness matrix. It should be noted that, in many instances, the yield condition will be violated. A finite load increment may bring the state of stress of the element outside the yield surface (point Q in Fig. 10.62). If this is the case, the load increment is scaled down by a factor r defined as

$$r = \frac{-b + \sqrt{b^2 - 4ac}}{2a} \tag{10.73}$$

where

$$a = \dot{\sigma}_{xx}^2 + \dot{\sigma}_{yy}^2 - \dot{\sigma}_{xx}\dot{\sigma}_{yy} + 3\dot{\tau}_{xy}^2$$

$$b = 2\sigma_{xx}\dot{\sigma}_{xx} + 2\sigma_{yy}\dot{\sigma}_{yy} - \sigma_{xx}\dot{\sigma}_{yy} - \sigma_{yy}\dot{\sigma}_{xx} + 6\tau_{xy}\dot{\tau}_{xy}$$

$$c = \sigma_{xx}^2 + \sigma_{yy}^2 - \sigma_{xx}\sigma_{yy} + 3\tau_{xy}^2 - 3k^2$$

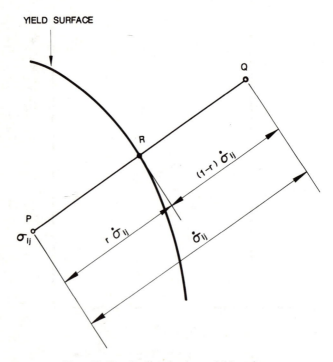

FIG. 10.62.   Scaling back to yield surface.

in which $\dot{\sigma}_{ij}$ is the increment of stress induced by the load increment (Fig. 10.62) assuming elastic behavior, σ_{ij} is the state of stress before the load increment (point P in Fig. 10.62), and k is the hardening parameter (Fig. 10.61). This scaling procedure is repeated until eqn (10.66) or eqn (10.67) is satisfied, i.e. until the state of stress of the element is at point R in Fig. 10.62.

In order to check the yield criterion of eqn (10.66) or eqn (10.67), the current state of stress of the element must be known. Since the strains and hence the stresses vary from point to point in the element, sample points must be chosen in such a way as to represent the state of the element in the best possible way in the numerical analysis. In the present study, the eight Gauss points (Fig. 10.58) and the centroid of the element are used as the sample points. Detailed calculations of stresses at these points are discussed by Lui (1985).

10.10.3 Modification of Incremental Beam–Column Stiffness Matrix for the Presence of Panel Zone

If a panel element is present at the end of a frame element, the three degrees of freedom at the end of the frame element must be related to the six degrees of freedom on the face of the panel element (Fig. 10.63). In order to relate the degrees of freedom of these two elements, the concept of equivalent nodal

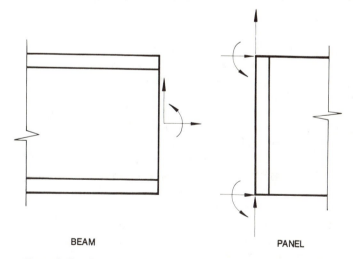

BEAM   PANEL

FIG. 10.63.   Junction of a beam–column and a panel element.

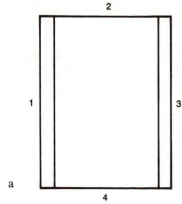

FIG. 10.64. Face numbering of a
panel element.

force used in the context of a finite element analysis is utilized. The forces
(axial, shear, moment) at the end of the frame element are regarded as the
applied forces and the energy equivalent forces developed at the nodes of
the panel element are evaluated using the energy balance concept. The
resulting matrix relating the two sets of forces is the equilibrium matrix.
Transposition of this matrix will give the kinematic matrix which relates the
degrees of freedom of the two elements.

Depending on the face of the panel element (Fig. 10.64) to which the
frame element is attached and the manner in which the frame forces are
assumed to be distributed (Fig. 10.65) on the panel face, several different
cases can be identified. It should be mentioned that faces 1 and 3 should be
treated differently from faces 2 and 4. This is because a frame element
attaches to face 1 or 3 of the panel element through a connection, whereas
for face 2 or 4 the junction of the frame and panel elements is physically
continuous. In this context, a connection element was inserted between the
frame and panel elements for face 1 or face 3 and a stiffener element with
high bending rigidity was inserted between the frame and panel elements for
face 2 or face 4. The assumed force distributions shown in Fig. 10.65 are for
face 1 or face 3 only. Category A is appropriate for such types of
connections in which continuity between the two elements exists along the
depth or at the two flanges of the frame element (Fig. 10.66(a)). Examples of
this category of connections are top and seat angles, header plate, end plate
and T-stub connections. Category B is appropriate for such connections in
which continuity exists more or less at the neutral axis of the frame element
(Fig. 10.66(b)). Examples of this category of connections are single web

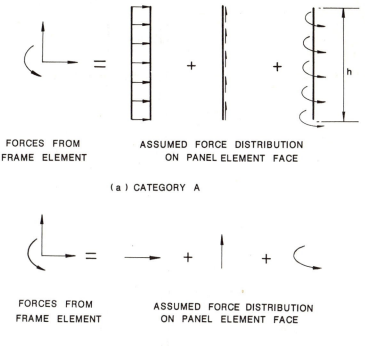

FORCES FROM
FRAME ELEMENT

ASSUMED FORCE DISTRIBUTION
ON PANEL ELEMENT FACE

(a) CATEGORY A

FORCES FROM
FRAME ELEMENT

ASSUMED FORCE DISTRIBUTION
ON PANEL ELEMENT FACE

(b) CATEGORY B

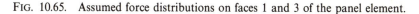

FIG. 10.65. Assumed force distributions on faces 1 and 3 of the panel element.

angle and double web angle connections. The kinematic matrices relating
the degrees of freedom of the two elements (frame and panel) for different
faces of the panel element and different categories of connections were
developed in detail by Lui (1985) and are summarized in Appendix 1.

Once the kinematic matrices have been developed, the 6×6 frame
element can be modified to a 9×9 frame element with panel attached to one
of its ends as follows.

If a panel is present at the A end of the frame element (Fig. 10.67)

$$\dot{\mathbf{k}}_{fm} = \begin{bmatrix} \mathbf{T}_{fP}^{T} & 0 \\ 0 & \mathbf{I}^{T} \end{bmatrix} \dot{\mathbf{k}}_{f} \begin{bmatrix} \mathbf{T}_{fP} & 0 \\ 0 & \mathbf{I} \end{bmatrix} \qquad (10.74)$$

If a panel is present at the B end of the frame element

$$\dot{\mathbf{k}}_{fm} = \begin{bmatrix} \mathbf{I}^{T} & 0 \\ 0 & \mathbf{T}_{fP}^{T} \end{bmatrix} \dot{\mathbf{k}}_{f} \begin{bmatrix} \mathbf{I} & 0 \\ 0 & \mathbf{T}_{fP} \end{bmatrix} \qquad (10.75)$$

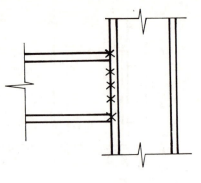

(a) CATEGORY A

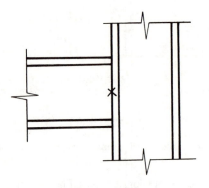

(b) CATEGORY B

X REGION OF ATTACHMENT OF A FRAME ELEMENT TO A PANEL

FIG. 10.66. Category A and category B connections.

where, in eqns (10.74) and (10.75)

$\dot{\mathbf{k}}_{fm} = 9 \times 9$ modified frame element tangent stiffness matrix

$\dot{\mathbf{k}}_f = 6 \times 6$ frame element tangent stiffness matrix (see Appendix 2)

$\mathbf{T}_{fp} = 3 \times 6$ kinematic matrix relating the three degrees of freedom at the end of the frame element to the six degrees of freedom on the face of the panel element.

$\mathbf{I} = 3 \times 3$ identity matrix

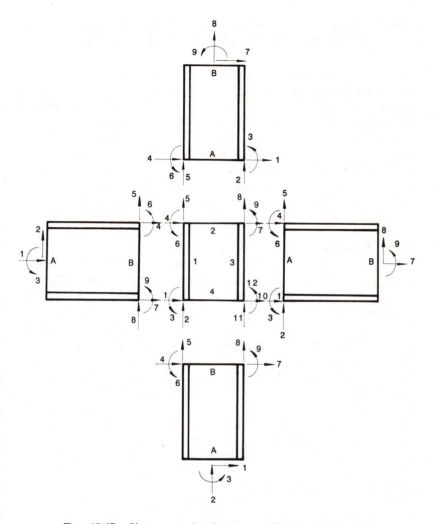

FIG. 10.67. Sign convention for the modified frame element.

Note that the modified incremental stiffness matrix of the frame element is 9×9, which means three additional degrees of freedom are introduced into the frame element (see Fig. 10.67).

If a plastic hinge or connection exists at the end of the frame element, modification to $\mathbf{k}_f$ is first performed and then used in place of the original $\mathbf{\dot{k}}_f$.

10.11 NUMERICAL EXAMPLES OF FLEXIBLY CONNECTED FRAMES WITH PANEL ZONE DEFORMATION

The panel element developed here is used in conjunction with the frame and connection elements developed previously to investigate the behavior of frames. A load-controlled incremental Newton–Raphson iterative solution technique is employed in the numerical analysis. Detailed discussion of the solution algorithm is given elsewhere (Lui, 1985). In this section, the validity of the panel zone model is first verified by comparison of the numerical results with experiments. A simple two-bar frame is then analyzed using different behavioral models regarding the deformational behavior of the connection and panel zone to demonstrate the effect of joint flexibility on the behavior of the frame.

10.11.1 Comparison with Experiments

Shown in the inset of Fig. 10.68 is a subassemblage used by Fielding & Huang (1971) to investigate the behavior of the joint panel. The joint details of the subassemblage are given in their paper. The column was first loaded with a compressive force of $0.5P_y$ where P_y is the yield load of the column. The load was then applied at the free end of the beam until failure. During the entire beam loading phase, the column load was maintained at $0.5P_y$. As a result, the panel zone is under a combined loading of axial force from the column load and shear and moment from the beam load. The experimental load–deflection behavior of this subassemblage is shown in Fig. 10.68. Yielding of the web of the panel zone occurs at a load of 86 kips (383 kN), after which a definite decrease in stiffness of the joint panel was observed. At 150 kips (667 kN), cracks were observed at the ends of the top horizontal stiffeners and the specimen was unloaded. Also shown in this figure as a dashed line is the numerically obtained load–deflection curve. It can be seen that good correlation exists between the results obtained numerically and experimentally in both the elastic and post-yield regimes. In the numerical solution, the actual measured (Fielding & Huang, 1971) material properties were used. The apparent larger stiffness and higher yield load obtained numerically as compared to test is attributed to the assumption of full fixity at both ends of the column in the numerical model, whereas in reality, noticeable column end rotations were observed (Fielding & Huang, 1971).

The insets of Figs 10.69 and 10.70 show two subassemblages (specimens A and B) of an experimental investigation of the behavior of the panel zone by Bertero et al. (1972). Specimen A is typical of an upper story and

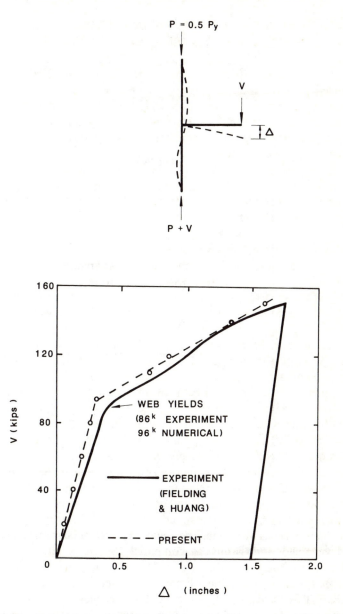

FIG. 10.68. Comparison of numerical and experimental connection subassemblage load–deflection behavior (Fielding & Huang) (1 kip = 4·45 kN; 1 in. = 25·4 mm).

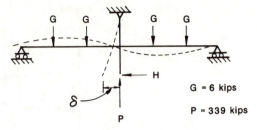

SPECIMEN A

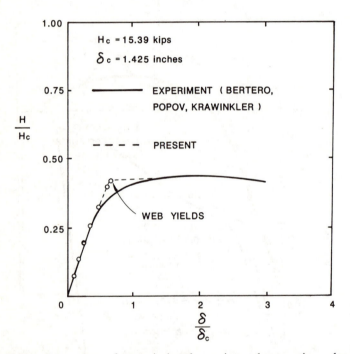

FIG. 10.69. Comparison of numerical and experimental connection subassemblage load–deflection behavior (specimen A; Bertero *et al.*, 1972) (1 kip = 4·45 kN; 1 in. = 25·4 mm).

specimen B is typical of a lower story. For specimen A, an axial force of $0.36P_y$, where P_y is the yield load of the column, was applied to the column and vertical beam forces of approximately 6 kips (27 kN) were applied at every third-point on the beams. For specimen B, an axial force of $0.48P_y$ was

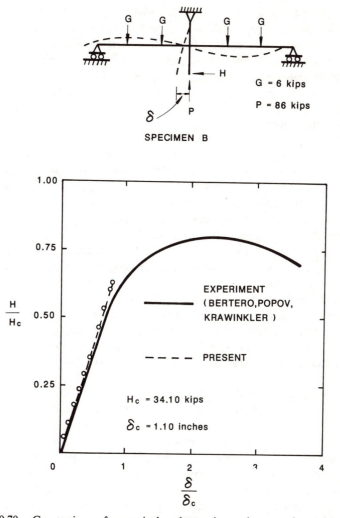

FIG. 10.70. Comparison of numerical and experimental connection subassemblage load–deflection behavior (specimen B; Bertero *et al.*, 1972) (1 kip = 4·45 kN; 1 in. = 25·4 mm).

applied to the column and vertical beam forces of approximately 6 kips (27 kN) were applied at every third-point on the beams. These subassemblages were then subjected to a horizontal force H applied cyclically at the free end of the column. Since the present analysis deals only with monotonic loadings, only the initial branch of the hysteresis load–deflection behavior of these subassemblages will be investigated. The experimental curves are shown as solid lines in Figs 10.69 and 10.70 for specimens A and B, respectively. For specimen A (Fig. 10.69), extensive yielding of the web of the joint panel was observed in the test. The numerically obtained load–deflection curve using the actual measured (Bertero *et al.*, 1972) material properties is shown as the dashed line in the figure. Good agreement between the two curves is observed. The numerically predicted yielding of the web occurs at $H = 6.4$ kips (28 kN) which agrees favorably with the experiment. Since no stiffeners are used in the panel zone, the structure becomes numerically unstable as soon as the panel yields (i.e. as soon as a panel hinge is formed). Consequently, the numerically generated load–deflection curve shows a plateau at $H = 6.4$ kips (28 kN).

The numerical and experimental load–deflection curves for specimen B (Fig. 10.70) also agree well with each other. Failure of this specimen was due to the formation of plastic hinges in the beams. In the numerical solution, convergence of the solution became impossible when a local collapse mechanism developed in the left beam at $H = 21.2$ kips (94.3 kN). However, in the experiment, additional load can be applied because, even after the formation of a local collapse mechanism in the left beam, the subassemblage is still statically determinate and so total collapse will not occur until a third hinge forms in the right beam. Consequently, the experimental load–deflection curve rises above $H = 21.2$ kips (94.3 kN) in Fig. 10.70.

Although the post-yield behavior of the specimen shown in Fig. 10.70 cannot be predicted by the model due to local failure of the beam, the model does give a good representation of the elastic behavior of the subassemblage.

In the practical design, it is customary to investigate the drift (i.e. lateral displacement) of a frame under service loading conditions to ensure that the frame will not deflect excessively so as to cause discomfort to the occupants or overstress in the connection elements. In the following section, a simple two-bar frame will be analyzed using a number of different behavioral models to demonstrate the importance of panel zone deformation on the drift of a structure.

10.11.2 Analysis of a Two-Bar Frame

Shown in Fig. 10.71 is a series of structural models for a two-bar frame. Model 1 (M1) is the conventional structural model commonly used by engineers and designers. The connection joining the beam and column is assumed to be rigid and center-to-center distances are used for the lengths

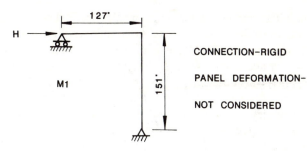

CONNECTION-RIGID

PANEL DEFORMATION-

NOT CONSIDERED

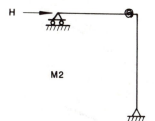

CONNECTION-FLEXIBLE

PANEL DEFORMATION-

NOT CONSIDERED

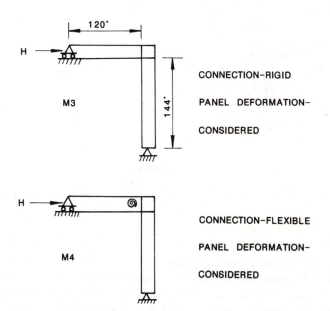

CONNECTION-RIGID

PANEL DEFORMATION-

CONSIDERED

CONNECTION-FLEXIBLE

PANEL DEFORMATION-

CONSIDERED

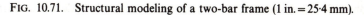

FIG. 10.71. Structural modeling of a two-bar frame (1 in. = 25·4 mm).

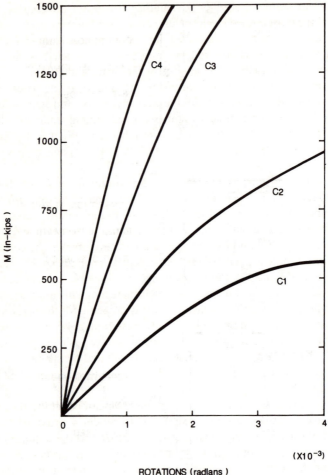

FIG. 10.72.   Connection moment–rotation behavior used for the two-bar frame
(1 in.-kip = 113 N-m).

of the beam and column. Model 2 (M2) is a more refined model. Although
center-to-center distances are still used for the lengths of the beam and
column, the connection is modeled by a spring having a rotational stiffness
as described by the nonlinear moment–rotation behavior of the connection.
Model 3 (M3) assumes that the connection is rigid but the finite size and
deformable capability of the panel zone are taken into account. In this

model, clear spans are used for the lengths of the beam and column. Model 4 (M4) is the most refined model of all. The connection is modeled as flexible with rotational stiffness described by the nonlinear moment–rotation behavior of the connection and the joint panel is modeled as deformable with clear spans used for the lengths of the beam and column.

For models 2 and 4, the moment–rotation characteristics of four commonly used connections (double web angles, top and seat angles, end plate and T-stub) compatible with the beam and column sections (W14 × 34) used are shown in Fig. 10.72. They are labeled as C1, C2, C3 and C4, respectively. C1 represents a very flexible and C4 represents a very stiff connection.

The two-bar frame is loaded by a horizontal force H as shown in Fig. 10.71; the load–deflection behavior of the frame using different models and connections is shown in Figs 10.73–10.76. Failure of the structure is due to the formation of a plastic hinge at the junction of the beam and column. For connections C1 and C2, the plastic hinge developed in the connection when the ultimate capacity of the connection was exhausted. However, for connections C3 and C4, the plastic hinge developed in the column at the beam and column junction because the ultimate moment capacities of these two connections exceed the plastic moment capacities of the sections. This explains why the ultimate loads of the subassemblages using connections C1 and C2 are less than those of the subassemblages using connections C3 and C4. For C1 and C2, the ultimate load is dictated by the strength of the connections, whereas for C3 and C4 the ultimate load is controlled by the strength of the sections.

If we examine Figs 10.73–10.76 carefully, we can conclude that model 2 will give a satisfactory approximation to model 4 provided that the connections are relatively flexible when compared to the adjoining beam and column (e.g. C1 and C2). This is because the contribution to additional drift from the flexible connection far outweighs the contribution from panel zone deformation. However, for relatively stiff connections (e.g. C3 and C4), model 2 and model 3 will give comparable results, which means that the contribution to additional drift from panel zone distortion will be as important as that from connection flexibility. As a rough estimate, if $(R_{ki}L/EI) \leqslant 5$, where R_{ki} is the initial stiffness of the connection and L, E and I are respectively the length, elastic modulus and moment of inertia of the member to which the connection is attached, then model 2 is justified for use in place of model 4.

To examine the effect of panel zone deformation on the drift of the frame, the load–deflection behavior of the two-bar frame assuming rigid connection

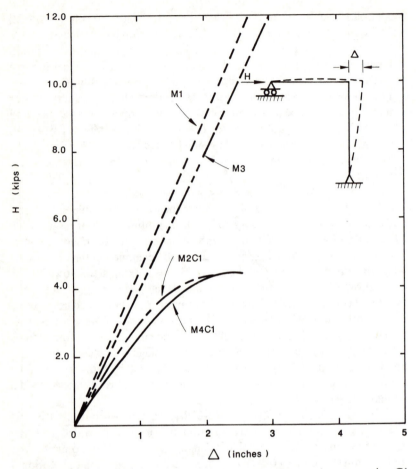

FIG. 10.73.   Load–deflection behavior of the two-bar frame using connection C1
(1 kip = 4·45 kN; 1 in. = 25·4 mm).

using model 1 and model 3 is shown in Fig. 10.77. It can be seen that, at
working load, 13% drift of the frame is due to panel zone deformation. This
indicates that panel zone deformation should be considered in the design of
moment-resisting frames.

10.11.3 General Remarks
The behavior of the panel zone is described and a model to represent the
panel deformational behavior (extensional, shear, bending) has been

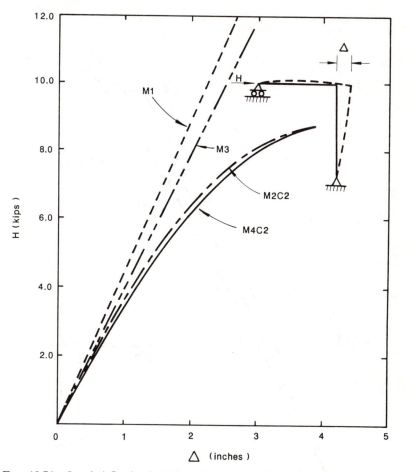

FIG. 10.74. Load–deflection behavior of the two-bar frame using connection C2
(1 kip = 4·45 kN; 1 in. = 25·4 mm).

presented in the preceding section. The validity of the model is shown here
by comparison with experiments, and the importance of the panel zone
deformation on the drift of a structure under service load is demonstrated
by the analysis of a two-bar frame.

Experiments on connection subassemblages conducted in the past
decade have shown that the panel zone plays an important role in affecting
the serviceability and ultimate behavior of moment-resisting frames.
Because of the deformational and inelastic behavior of the panel zone, the

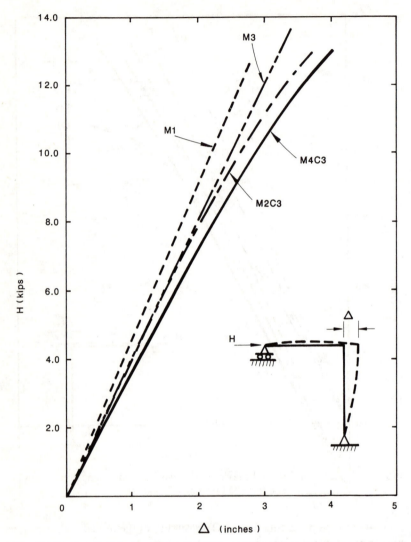

FIG. 10.75.   Load–deflection behavior of the two-bar frame using connection C3
(1 kip = 4·45 kN; 1 in. = 25·4 mm).

drift and strength of the frame will be affected. The effects of panel zone
deformation and inelasticity are usually undesirable since they will cause an
increase in frame drift and a decrease in frame strength. In this section,
a simple model to represent the behavior of the panel zone has been

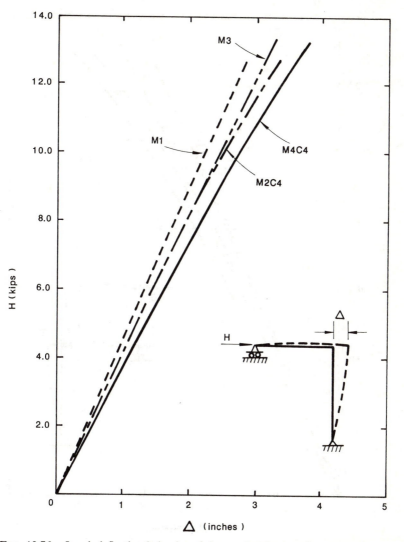

FIG. 10.76.   Load–deflection behavior of the two-bar frame using connection C4
(1 kip = 4·45 kN; 1 in. = 25·4 mm).

described and its implementation in structural analysis presented. The inclusion of panel zone deformation in frame analysis increases the number of degrees of freedom of the analytical model, yet better prediction of frame behavior can be achieved.

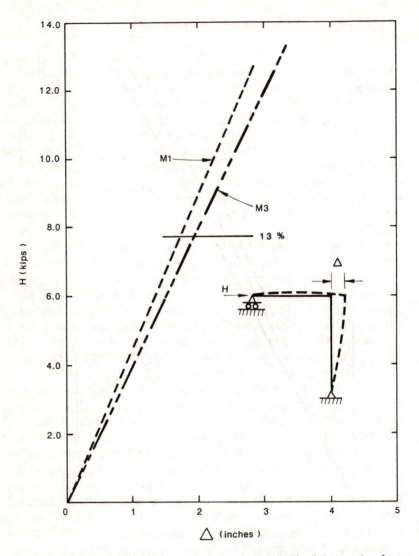

FIG. 10.77. Effect of panel zone deformation on the drift of the two-bar frame
(1 kip = 4·45 kN; 1 in. = 25·4 mm).

For moment-resisting frames in which connections of high rigidities are
used, panel zone deformation is an important factor to be considered in the
analysis and design of the frames.

10.12 CONCLUSIONS

It is well known that, in conventional analysis and design of steel frameworks, structures are often analyzed by assuming the connections or joints to be either fully rigid or perfectly pinned. These simplifications result in internal forces that may be quite different from the internal forces actually existing in a real structure. In many cases, these may lead to erroneous results. At present, the design of individual members is based on a more refined analysis but such a refinement is not generally consistent with the simplified analysis of the overall structure. The purpose of this chapter is therefore to present the more refined analysis methods for overall structural systems that are more consistent with the refined analysis methods used for individual members in the development of the present design specifications.

Experiments have shown that the so-called fully rigid connections do not exist in a practical construction, i.e. a fully rigid connection does possess some flexibility and a pinned connection does possess some rigidity. The actual joint behavior falls somewhere between the fully rigid and perfectly pinned behaviors. In addition, the moment–rotation behavior of these joints is always nonlinear. Since the behavior of a steel frame under loads is governed to a large extend by its joint deformations, the joint flexibility not only affects the behavior of the beams and the columns in a frame, it also strongly influences the overall strength and stability of the frame.

Recognizing the importance of the connection flexibility, the new AISC-LRFD specification (1986) recognizes explicitly two types of steel construction: type FR (fully restrained) construction and type PR (partially restrained) construction. The application of type PR construction implies that structural engineers should take into some reasonable consideration the effects of flexible connections in their structural analysis and design. However, at present there is no recommended analysis and design method available for the type PR construction in the new AISC-LRFD specification, even though a simplified second-order elastic analysis with B_1 and B_2 factors has been proposed for type FR construction.

Studies have been focussed in the past on the modeling of moment–rotation relationships for various types of flexible joints (Chen, 1985, 1987; Aggarwal & Coates, 1986). Several analytical expressions describing the actual moment–rotation curves have been reviewed in Section 10.3. It is of interest to note that the design of connections based on the semi-rigid method of analysis for steel frames was introduced into the code in the United Kingdom as long ago as 1936, and a semi-rigid construction has been identified in the present US steel specification (AISC, 1978) since 1946. However, this design consideration has been rarely utilized in practice because of the large amount of computational work involved in considering the connection flexibility.

Early frame analysis considering the flexibility of connections could solve only simple problems (Aggarwal & Coates, 1986). With the advent of computers, especially with the mini- and micro-computers, interest in semi-rigid construction has increased recently. In recent years, much attention has been paid in particular to the analysis and design of steel frames with flexibly jointed connections (Chen, 1985, 1986, 1987, 1988).

The development of modern numerical methods has made it possible for structural engineers to use computers to analyze these structures more accurately and to design them more realistically. At present, there are several methods of analysis available for the type PR construction. These computer-based analytical procedures can be utilized for investigations for a more realistic building system and for a more realistic engineering design using mini- and micro-computers. This chapter summarizes several practical procedures to analyze and design flexibly connected steel frames and also presents highlights of some numerical results on the effects of connection flexibility on the stability analysis and design of steel frames.

The first part of this chapter discusses various mathematical models that have been proposed to represent the nonlinear moment–rotation behavior of the semi-rigid steel beam-to-column connections (Sections 10.2 and 10.3). A brief description follows of rigorous elastic and elasto-plastic analyses capable of dealing with these models in flexibly connected steel frames (Section 10.4).

A second-order elastic method for analyzing the behavior of flexibly connected plane steel frames is first presented in some detail in Section 10.5. Two types of elements are used in the analysis procedure: the beam–column (frame) element and the connection element. The beam–column element formulation is based on an updated Lagrangian approach. Allowance for the coupling effect of axial force and bending moments, as well as for the formation of plastic hinges in the member (Section 10.7), is made for this beam–column. The nonlinear behavior of the connection is modeled by an exponential function and is used in the subsequent numerical studies (Section 10.6). Both loading and unloading responses of the connections are taken into consideration in the formulation. The monotonic load–deflection response of frames with flexible connections is traced using an incremental load control Newton–Raphson iterative technique. Based on subassemblage and frame analyses, it is concluded that connection flexibility has an important influence on frame behavior (Sections 10.6 and 10.7).

A second-order elasto-plastic method for analyzing the behavior of steel frames with flexible joints is then briefly presented in Section 10.8. A full description has been given in the paper by Chen & Zhou (1987). In this rigorous analysis, the assumption of material yielding being concentrated at a point in the form of a plastic hinge (Section 10.7) is obliterated. Yielding is now treated as a *progressive* process and the transition from elastic to plastic behavior considering the influence of residual stresses in a cross section is developed in a gradual manner, known as plastification. Joint flexibility, member imperfection, residual stress and load history can all be accounted for by the numerical procedure known as the Newmark method. The analysis as described in Section 10.8 is directly applicable to unbraced as well as braced frames. The validity of the analysis has been demonstrated by numerical examples in Section 10.9, where comparisons are made with the results of other methods of analysis. The method is found suitable for adoption in computer-based analysis and can serve as a bench-mark check for simplified procedures available for practical design use.

Finally, an analysis method for steel frameworks considering the effect of panel zone deformation on frame behavior is presented in Section 10.10. In the conventional analyses, center-to-center distances rather than clear spans are used for the lengths of the members. As is evident from experimental studies, the effect of panel zone deformation has a pronounced influence on frame behavior. In particular, the strength and drift of the frame will be affected if panel zone deformation is taken into consideration in the analysis. In this section, various deformation modes of the panel zone are first identified. A simple model which can be used to represent all these modes is then presented. The validity of this model is established by comparison with experiments on joint subassemblages (Section 10.11). A two-bar frame with different behavioral joint models is analyzed numerically to demonstrate the importance of using realistic models in frame analysis (Section 10.11).

REFERENCES

AGGARWAL, A. K. & COATES, R. C. (1986) Moment-rotation characteristics of bolted beam-column connections, *J. Construct. Steel Res.*, **4**, 303–19.

AMERICAN INSTITUTE OF STEEL CONSTRUCTION (1978) Specification for the Design, Fabrication and Erection of Structural Steel for Buildings. Chicago, Illinois.

AMERICAN INSTITUTE OF STEEL CONSTRUCTION (1986) Load and Resistance Factor Design Specification for Structural Steel Buildings. Chicago, Illinois.

ANG, K. M. & MORRIS, G. A. (1984) Analysis of three-dimensional frames with flexible beam-column connections, *Canad. J. Civil Engrs*, **11**, 245–54.

BECKER, R. (1975) Panel zone effect on the strength and stiffness of steel rigid frames, *Engng J.*, *AISC*, **12**(1), 19–29.

BERTERO, V. V., POPOV, E. P. & KRAWINKLER, H. (1972) Beam-column subassemblages under repeated loading, *J. Struct. Div.*, *Proc. ASCE*, **98**(ST5), 1137–59.

CHEN, W. F. (1982) *Plasticity in Reinforced Concrete*. McGraw-Hill, New York.

CHEN, W. F. (Ed.) (1985) Proceedings of a Session on Connection Flexibility and Steel Frames, 24 October. ASCE, New York.

CHEN, W. F. (1986) Semi-Rigid Connections in Steel Frames. High-Rise Building: Recent Progress. Council on Tall Building and Urban-Habitat, Bethlehem, Pennsylvania.

CHEN, W. F. (Ed.) (1987) Connection flexibility in steel frames (Special Issue), *J. Construct. Steel Res.*, **8**, 1–290.

CHEN, W. F. (Ed.) (1988) Steel beam-to-column building connections (Special Issue). *J. Construct. Steel Res.*, **10**, 1–482.

CHEN, W. F. & HAN, D. J. (1988) *Plasticity for Structural Engineers*. Springer-Verlag, New York.

CHEN, W. F. & KISHI, N. (1989) Semirigid Steel beam-to-column connections: Database and modeling. *J. Struct. Engng. ASCE*, **115**(1), 105–19.

CHEN, W. F. & LUI, E. M. (1987) *Structural Stability: Theory and Implementation*. Elsevier, New York.

CHEN, W. F. & ZHOU, S. P. (1987) Inelastic analysis of steel braced frames with flexible joints, *Int. J. Solids Struct.*, **23**, 631–49.

COLSON, A. & LOUVEAU, J. M. (1983) Connections Incidence on the Inelastic Behaviour of Steel Structures. Euromech Colloquium 174, October.

FIELDING, D. J. & CHEN, W. F. (1973) Steel frame analysis and connection shear deformation, *J. Struct. Div.*, *ASCE*, **99**(ST1), 1–18.

FIELDING, D. J. & HUANG, J. S. (1971) Shear on beam-to-column connections, *Welding J.*, **50**(7) (July), Research Supplement, 313s–26s.

FRYE, M. J. & MORRIS, G. A. (1976) Analysis of flexibly connected steel frames, *Canad. J. Civil Engrs*, **2**(3), 280–91.

GOTO, Y. & CHEN, W. F. (1987a) On the computer-based design analysis for flexibly jointed frames, *J. Construct. Steel Res.*, **8**(3), 203–31.

GOTO, Y. & CHEN, W. F. (1987b) On second order elastic analysis for frame design, *J. Struct. Engng. ASCE*, **113**, 1505–19.

GOVERDHAM, A. V. (1984) A Collection of Experimental Moment Rotation Curves and the Evaluation of Predicting Equations for Semi-Rigid Connections. Master's Thesis, Vanderbilt University, Nashville, Tennessee.

JONES, S. W., KIRBY, P. A. & NETHERCOT, D. A. (1982) Columns with semi-rigid joints, *J. Struct. Div.*, *ASCE*, **108**(ST2), 361–72.

KASSIMALI, A. (1983) Large deformation analysis of elastic-plastic frames, *J. Struct. Div.*, *ASCE*, **109**(8), 1869–86.

KATO, B. (1982) Beam-to-Column Connection Research in Japan, *J. Struct. Div.*, *ASCE*, **108** ST2, February, 343–60.

KISHI, N. & CHEN, W. F. (1986a) Data Base of Steel Beam-to-Column Connec-

tions. Structural Engineering Report CE-STR-86-26, School of Civil Engineering, Purdue University, West Lafayette, Indiana (two volumes).
KISHI, N. & CHEN, W. F. (1986b) Steel Connection Data Bank Program. Structural Engineering Report CE-STR-86-18, School of Civil Engineering, Purdue University, West Lafayette, Indiana.
KRAWINKLER, H. (1978) Shear in beam-column joints in seismic design of steel frames, *Engng J.*, *AISC*, **15**(3), 82–91.
KRISHNAMURTHY, N., HUANG, H. T., JEFFREY, P. K. & AVERY, L. K. (1979) Analytical M-θ curves for end-plate connections, *J. Struct. Div.*, *ASCE*, **105**(ST1), 133–45.
LEWITT, C. S., CHESSON, E. & MUNSE, W. H. (1969) Restraint Characteristics of Flexibly Riveted and Bolted Beam-to-Column Connections. Engineering Experimental Station Bulletin 500, University of Illinois at Urbana-Champaign.
LUI, E. M. (1985) Effects of Connection Flexibility and Panel Zone Deformation on the Behavior of Plane Steel Frames. PhD Dissertation, School of Civil Engineering, Purdue University, West Lafayette, Indiana.
LUI, E. M. & CHEN, W. F. (1985) Columns with end restraint and bending in load and resistance factor design, *Engng J.*, *AISC*, **22**(3), 105–32.
LUI, E. M. & CHEN, W. F. (1986) Analysis and behavior of flexibly-jointed frames, *Engng Structures*, **8**, 107–18.
NETHERCOT, D. A. (1985) Steel Beam-to-Column Connections: A Review of Test Data and Its Applicability to the Evaluation of Joint Behaviour in the Performance of Steel Frames. CIRIA Project Study.
NEWMARK, N. M. (1943) Numerical procedure for computing deflections, moments and buckling loads, *Trans. ASCE*, **108**, 1161.
ODEN, J. T. (1972) *Finite Elements of Nonlinear Continua*. McGraw-Hill, New York.
PATEL, K. V. & CHEN, W. F. (1984) Nonlinear analysis of steel moment connections, *J. Struct. Engng. ASCE*, **110**(8), 1861–74.
SOMMER, W. H. (1969) Behavior of Welded Header Plate Connections. Master's Thesis, University of Toronto.
YEE, Y. L. & MELCHERS, R. E. (1986) Moment-rotation curves for bolted connections, *J. Struct. Engng*, *ASCE*, **112**(3), 615–35.
ZIENKIEWICZ, O. C. (1977) *The Finite Element Method*. McGraw-Hill, London.

APPENDIX 1: KINEMATIC MATRICES

(1) Face 1; category A

$$\mathbf{T}_{fp}=\begin{bmatrix} 1/2 & 0 & h/12 & 1/2 & 0 & -h/12 \\ t_f/h & 1/2 & t_f/2 & -t_f/h & 1/2 & t_f/2 \\ -1/h & 0 & 0 & 1/h & 0 & 0 \end{bmatrix}$$

(2) Face 1; category B

$$\mathbf{T_{fp}} = \begin{bmatrix} 1/2 & 0 & h/8 & 1/2 & 0 & -h/8 \\ 3t_f/2h & 1/2 & 3t_f/4 & -3t_f/2h & 1/2 & 3t_f/4 \\ -3/2h & 0 & -1/4 & 3/2h & 0 & -1/4 \end{bmatrix}$$

(3) Face 2

$$\mathbf{T_{fp}} = \begin{bmatrix} 1/2 & 0 & 0 & 1/2 & 0 & 0 \\ 0 & 1/2 & 0 & 0 & 1/2 & 0 \\ 0 & 0 & 1/2 & 0 & 0 & 1/2 \end{bmatrix}$$

(4) Face 3; category A

$$\mathbf{T_{fp}} = \begin{bmatrix} 1/2 & 0 & -h/12 & 1/2 & 0 & h/12 \\ t_f/h & 1/2 & -t_f/2 & -t_f/h & 1/2 & -t_f/2 \\ 1/h & 0 & 0 & -1/h & 0 & 0 \end{bmatrix}$$

(5) Face 3; category B

$$\mathbf{T_{fp}} = \begin{bmatrix} 1/2 & 0 & -h/8 & 1/2 & 0 & h/8 \\ 3t_f/2h & 1/2 & -3t_f/4 & -3t_f/2h & 1/2 & -3t_f/4 \\ 3/2h & 0 & -1/4 & -3/2h & 0 & -1/4 \end{bmatrix}$$

(6) Face 4

$$\mathbf{T_{pf}} = \begin{bmatrix} 1/2 & 0 & 0 & 1/2 & 0 & 0 \\ 0 & 1/2 & 0 & 0 & 1/2 & 0 \\ 0 & 0 & 1/2 & 0 & 0 & 1/2 \end{bmatrix}$$

APPENDIX 2: FRAME ELEMENT TANGENT STIFFNESS MATRIX

The frame element tangent stiffness matrix is expressed (Lui, 1985) as

$$\mathbf{\dot{k}_f} = \mathbf{T_{cg}^T \dot{k}_c T_{cg}} + M_A \mathbf{T}_1 + M_B \mathbf{T}_2 + P \mathbf{T}_3$$

where

M_A = bending moment at the A end of the beam–column

M_B = bending moment at the B end of the beam–column

P = axial force

$$\mathbf{T_{cg}} = \begin{bmatrix} -s/L_f & c/L_f & 1 & s/L_f & -c/L_f & 0 \\ -s/L_f & c/L_f & 0 & s/L_f & -c/L_f & 1 \\ -c & -s & 0 & c & s & 0 \end{bmatrix}$$

$$\mathbf{T_1} = \mathbf{T_2} = \frac{1}{L_f^2} \begin{bmatrix} -2sc & c^2-s^2 & 0 & 2sc & -(c^2-s^2) & 0 \\ & 2cs & 0 & -(c^2-s^2) & -2sc & 0 \\ & & 0 & 0 & 0 & 0 \\ & \text{sym.} & & -2sc & c^2-s^2 & 0 \\ & & & & 2sc & 0 \\ & & & & & 0 \end{bmatrix}$$

$$\mathbf{T_3} = \frac{1}{L_f} \begin{bmatrix} s^2 & -sc & 0 & -sc & sc & 0 \\ & c^2 & 0 & sc & -c^2 & 0 \\ & & 0 & 0 & 0 & 0 \\ & \text{sym.} & & s^2 & -sc & 0 \\ & & & & c^2 & 0 \\ & & & & & 0 \end{bmatrix}$$

L_f = chord length of the deformed member

$s = \sin\theta$

$c = \cos\theta$

θ = inclination of the chord of the deformed member

$$\mathbf{\dot{k}_c} = \frac{EI}{L_f} \begin{bmatrix} s_1 & s_2 & 2AL_f(d_1\theta_A + d_2\theta_B)/I \\ & s_1 & 2AL_f(d_2\theta_A + d_1\theta_B)/I \\ \text{sym.} & & A/I \end{bmatrix}$$

$$s_1 = 4 + 2\pi^2\rho/15 - [(0{\cdot}010\rho + 0{\cdot}543)/(4+\rho) + (0{\cdot}004\rho + 0{\cdot}285)/(8{\cdot}183+\rho)]\rho^2$$

$$s_2 = 2 - \pi^2\rho/30 + [(0{\cdot}010\rho + 0{\cdot}543)/(4+\rho) - (0{\cdot}004\rho + 0{\cdot}285)/(8{\cdot}183+\rho)]\rho^2$$

$$d_1 = \frac{\pi^2 \rho s_2 - (s_1 + s_2)^2 (s_2 - 2)}{8\pi^2 \rho (s_1 + s_2)}$$

$$d_2 = \frac{-\pi^2 \rho s_2 - (s_1 + s_2)^2 (s_2 - 2)}{8\pi^2 \rho (s_1 + s_2)}$$

$$\rho = \frac{PL^2}{\pi^2 EI}$$

θ_A = rotation of the A end of the member with respect to its chord

θ_B = rotation of the B end of the member with respect to its chord

INDEX

445